P9-BHR-055

As the floodwaters rose in New Orleans, Jordan Flaherty began to write, rescuing precious truths about the reality of racism and solidarity in his city that risked being washed away in the tide of formulaic corporate journalism. I can think of no journalist that writes with deeper knowledge or more love about this highly contested part of the United States. With a new flood threatening life on the Gulf Coast—this time made of oil, not water, but powered, as always, by greed and neglect—these remarkable stories of injustice and resistance must be heard.

—**Naomi Klein, author,** *The Shock Doctrine*

Jordan Flaherty is one of the best and most courageous writers in America today. Beyond his obvious writing skills, what I admire most about Jordan is his dedication to truth-telling, to bringing the real and whole America to the American people. At a time in our nation when there is so much distortion of current events and history, Jordan Flaherty represents the core of who we truly are. And what we are capable of being as citizens of this ever-changing world.

—**Kevin Powell, author,** *Open Letters to America*

Jordan Flaherty is an independent journalist for the Hip-Hop generation. As a white anti-imperialist who is committed to social and racial justice, Jordan brings out the voices of the victims and survivors of Hurricane Katrina and the levee breach in New Orleans. This book not only speaks truth to power but is a rallying cry for all of us to take action. With this definitive work, the voices of the grassroots, the communities resisting displacement, finally have a voice.

—**Rosa Clemente, 2008 Green Party Vice Presidential candidate,**
Hip-Hop activist, and journalist

The usual Katrina narrative tracks government incompetence during the emergency phase and and corporate greed—or inertia—in its aftermath. Jordan Flaherty tells a less well known story, centered on the boisterous infrastructure of left-leaning community groups and nonprofits that were fired up by disaster and still struggle to shape New Orleans's recovery. Flaherty is part of that movement. His vantage brings hands-on intimacy to this chronicle and poignancy to his conclusions.

—**Jed Horne, author,** *Breach of Faith,*
Hurricane Katrina and the Near Death of a Great American City

Jordan describes reality from the ground up. You've heard of the eagle's eye view: this is the earthworm's. Jordan knows who actually turns over the earth, and he follows them, even when most look away. His book brings us the good news of who's working for change (and how) but also the reality about the price those people pay for our indifference.

—**Laura Flanders, host,** *Grit TV;* **author,** *Blue Grit:*
True Democrats Take Back Politics from the Politicians

Since Hurricane Katrina hit, Jordan Flaherty has—with spectacular dedication—chronicled New Orleans's political changes with care and passion. His stories are the ones we all want to read: the tireless work of organizers in the city, the obstacles they face and the triumphs they celebrate...which ultimately inspire all of us.

—Daisy Hernández, executive editor, *ColorLines*

Want to know what really happened to regular people during and after Katrina? Read this book and get the real stories. Read this book and get angry. Read this book and get busy making changes.

—Bill Quigley, legal director, Center for Constitutional Rights

Jordan Flaherty's work has been indispensable for social justice activists and organizations around the country who care about the inequities and social injustices that Hurricane Katrina revealed and exacerbated. He brings the sharp analysis and dedication of a seasoned organizer to his writing, and insightful observation to his reporting. Jordan unfailingly has his ear to the ground in a city that continues to reveal the floodlines of structural racism in America.

—Tram Nguyen, author, *We Are All Suspects Now:
Untold Stories from Immigrant Communities after 9/11*

After the flood, many of us turned to Jordan Flaherty's dispatches for real-time real talk about what was really going on in his beloved New Orleans. His from-the-low-ground accounts of how the politics of abandonment, the politics of containment, and racism combined to devastate this proud global city were brave and unsettling. His passionate, unsparing writing on the community organizers and the people struggling to make themselves and their city whole reminded us of the stakes. At this crucial point in American history, *Floodlines* captures the urgency of New Orleans and reveals why its recovery and renewal is one of the most important battles for justice in our time.

—Jeff Chang, author, *Can't Stop Won't Stop:
A History of the Hip-Hop Generation*

Floodlines

Community and Resistance
from Katrina to the Jena Six

JORDAN FLAHERTY

Haymarket Books
Chicago, Illinois

First published by Haymarket Books in 2010
© 2010 Jordan Flaherty

Haymarket Books
P.O. Box 180165
Chicago, IL 60618
773-583-7884
info@haymarketbooks.org
www.haymarketbooks.org

Trade distribution:
In the U.S., Consortium Book Sales and Distribution, www.cbsd.com
In Canada, Publishers Group Canada, www.pgcbooks.ca
In the UK, Turnaround Publisher Services, www.turnaround-uk.com
In Australia, Palgrave Macmillan, www.palgravemacmillan.com.au
All other countries, Publishers Group Worldwide, www.pgw.com

ISBN: 978-1-60846-065-6

Cover images by Abdul Aziz

Special discounts are available for bulk purchases by organizations and institutions. Please contact
Haymarket Books for more information at 773-583-7884 or info@haymarketbooks.org.

This book was published with the generous support of Lannan Foundation and
the Wallace Global Fund.

Printed in Canada on paper containing 100 percent post-consumer waste in accordance with
the guidelines of the Green Press Initiative, www.greenpressinitiative.org.

Library of Congress CIP Data is available

4 6 8 10 9 7 5 3

Contents

Acknowledgments   vii

Foreword by Amy Goodman   xi

Preface by Tracie Washington   xviii

Introduction: We Know This Place   1

1. We Won't Bow Down: Culture and Resistance in New Orleans   5

2. Lies on the News: The Flood and Its Aftermath   31

3. Still Got Me in Disbelief: New Orleans After the Storm   53

4. Wonder How We Doin': The Blank Slate   79

5. Dollar Day in New Orleans: Money and Relief   113

6. Behind Them Penitentiary Walls: Organizing in Prison   135

7. Serve and Protect: Criminalizing the Survivors   157

8. You Don't Want to Go to War: The Struggle for Housing   183

9. The Rest of the World Lives Here Too: Immigrant Struggles   213

10. Fight for What's Right: The Jena Generation   227

Conclusion: Desire   255

Appendix I—Organizations in the Struggle for Post-Katrina Justice   267

Appendix II—Letter from the People of New Orleans to Our Friends and Allies   274

Appendix III—Pledge in Support of a Just Rebuilding of St. Bernard Parish, Louisiana, and the U.S. Gulf Coast   277

Appendix IV—New Orleans Films   279

Notes   283

Index   295

Acknowledgments

This book is in many ways the result of a collective process. Several organizers, writers, and scholars who have deeply influenced my ideas read versions of this book and gave me direct feedback, including Kali Akuno, Clare Bayard, Rachel Breunlin, Nicole Daro, Mike Davis, Francesca Fiorentini, Rachel Herzing, Catherine Jones, Rachel Luft, Manju Rajendran, Emily Ratner, Katy Rose, and Charhonda Thomas. In addition, several other folks responded to individual sections and pieces. They all improved and deepened this work. Emily Ratner also helped me collect maps and graphs and assisted with other research, while Abdul Aziz, a brilliant photographer, allowed me to use his images, including the cover photos. This book would not be the same without their efforts.

Caroline Luft worked with me to edit this book for Haymarket and I'm extremely grateful for her crucial contribution.

Much of the reporting that formed the basis for this book was originally published elsewhere, primarily in *ColorLines Magazine*, which has frequently featured my writing over the past five years. Other print publications that ran early versions of the reporting in this book include New York's *Indypendent*, *Left Turn Magazine*, San Francisco's *BayView*, and New Orleans's *Data News*. I would like to thank all the editors of these publications, especially Daisy Hernandez from *ColorLines*, for asking me challenging questions and helping to shape my work. My work as an organizer and writer has also been developed in partnership with the wider collective of strategically engaged writers and activists that I work with to publish *Left Turn Magazine*.

For some of the material that makes up this book, I had direct collaborators. Jennifer Vitry interviewed families at the B. W. Cooper housing development and helped with my research on the Louisiana State Penitentiary at Angola. My interview with Pres Kabacoff was conducted for a news piece by Telesur reporter Reed Lindsey. I interviewed Robert "Kool Black"

Horton with filmmaker Jacqueline Soohen, who, along with her filmmaking partners Rick Rowley and Kouross Esmaeli, conducted many of the interviews with residents of Jena, Louisiana, that helped shape my reporting of events in that town.

Much of my recent social justice work and research has been supported immeasurably by my coworkers at the Louisiana Justice Institute: Tracie Washington, Jacques Morial, Saia Smith, and Shaena Johnson.

My analysis, the lens through which I've interpreted what I've seen in New Orleans over these past several years, has been developed through education, especially by community organizers, activists, and culture workers. Much of my schooling came from elders like John O'Neal and Curtis Muhammad, who were active in the grassroots civil rights movement of the '50s and '60s and joined with folks like Ella Baker and organizations such as the Student Nonviolent Coordinating Committee (SNCC) and the Congress of Racial Equality (CORE). I have also learned from New Orleanians like Althea Francois, Malik Rahim, and Robert Hillary King, who were Black Panthers in the '70s. Although they arose in different historical moments, both traditions were direct action–oriented and prioritized leadership by those most affected. This approach has profoundly shaped the way I view liberation struggles, and these elders have motivated and enlightened me. A younger generation of activists—many the children of New Orleans organizers of the '60s and '70s—have also informed my ideas, especially Shana griffin, whose radical feminist analysis has challenged and inspired me.

The Thirteenth Amendment to the U.S. Constitution outlawed slavery except for those convicted of a crime—and at that moment, the modern U.S. prison system was born. Perhaps nowhere is this link clearer than at the Louisiana State Penitentiary at Angola, a former slave plantation the size of Manhattan still known as "the Farm." Angola is populated with residents from around the state, but particularly with Black men from New Orleans. It is estimated that 97 percent of those incarcerated at Angola will die behind its walls.

This book was shaped by those who escaped that fate—the lucky 3 percent who have made it out of Angola and have gone on to lead and inspire, such as Norris Henderson, who served twenty-seven years before being exonerated; Mwalimu Johnson, a former political prisoner, released in 1992; and John Thompson, founder and director of Resurrection After Exoneration, an organization that works to help the exonerated adjust to life outside of prison. Men such as Albert Woodfox and Herman Wallace, still incarcerated but fighting for their freedom, also informed this effort.

The struggles for justice in New Orleans have not been fought by organizers and activists alone. There are also the defense lawyers and civil rights lawyers and other legal workers and researchers. Bill Quigley, Mary Howell, Emily Maw, Ron Wilson, Nick Trenticosta, Katie Schwartzmann, and Tracie Washington are just some of those who have served as collaborators as well as inspirations.

Several families in Jena, Louisiana, were incredibly generous in sharing their time and ideas with me, especially Tina Jones, Catrina Wallace, Caseptla Bailey, Marcus Jones, John Jenkins, and Theo Shaw. They have shaped my vision of the possibilities for movement victories and have redefined my understanding of strength and courage.

Antiracist activists in New Orleans, many of them involved with the organizations European Dissent and the People's Institute for Survival and Beyond (PISAB), have been crucial to supporting my development and thinking on strategies for fighting racism and white supremacy. I hope this book pays tribute to their work as well.

Several local journalists have stood out during this time by telling the stories that would otherwise have been ignored, and their reporting has enriched my analysis and this book. Standing far above all the others is New Orleans *Times-Picayune* reporter Katy Reckdahl, who has single-handedly written the most essential coverage of cultural, housing, and criminal justice issues. *Times-Picayune* columnist, reporter, screenwriter, and filmmaker Lolis Eric Elie has also influenced how I view this city. Reporters and scholars from outside New Orleans have contributed vital journalism, from Naomi Klein and Jeremy Scahill to A. C. Thompson, Avi Lewis at Al-Jazeera, and the producers and staff of *Democracy Now!*, especially Amy Goodman and Anjali Kamat.

Rachel Breunlin and Abram Himelstein, the founders of the Neighborhood Story Project, have helped New Orleanians tell their own stories, and the stunning books they have edited and published, as well as the principled way they undertake their work, has shaped my outlook profoundly, as well as my understanding of the city. Catherine Jones, a locally born doctor who founded the Latino Health Outreach Project, has inspired me with her writing and with hours of conversation. Catherine also wrote a blog in the months after the storm that helped generate the title of this book.

The people who create this city's culture have enriched my life. New Orleans would not be the same without the many musicians, performers, filmmakers, painters, and designers who have chosen to live here, despite the difficulty of making a living, because it's among the best places to create art. These folks both sustain and reinvent the city's unique way of life through their art and active involvement in their community. For most of these creators of culture, the twin missions of art and liberation are inseparable. I wish I could employ their beautiful art to tell the stories in this book—with the paintings and songs and dance that, together, evoke a history of time and place.

Finally, this book would not have happened without the support and inspiration of family. My mother raised me and taught me the values that shaped my view of the world. In addition, a large adopted family of New Orleans community activists and elders gave me the love, knowledge, and support that made this book possible. Among this family I would especially like to thank Charhonda Thomas, Sandra Berry, Joshua Walker, Jennifer Turner, Vera Warren-Williams, and Dr. Hana Safah.

Foreword

"Obama's Katrina" is one name that was quickly given to the environmental catastrophe that spewed from the BP offshore oil rig disaster in the Gulf of Mexico. In the cataract of disasters into which Barack Obama and his administration have been thrust, the BP-Transocean-Halliburton volcano of oil that still plumes uncontrollably (at the time of this writing) into an ever-widening cataclysm is among the worst, exceeding the *Exxon Valdez* many-fold. It is a modern day, hydrocarbon Chernobyl.

Yet "Obama's Katrina" is a misnomer, since Hurricane Katrina, simply put, is Obama's Katrina. Obama seamlessly received, from the Bush-Cheney junta, the ongoing saga of Hurricane Katrina and the rolling devastation of its aftermath, just as he inherited the wars and occupations of Iraq and Afghanistan. President Obama has continued the de facto policy of looking the other way as New Orleans and the Gulf Coast struggle to rebuild, virtually on their own, a half-decade after the Katrina storm surge destroyed the inadequate levees that protected the historic, vibrant city. A blog post on the website of the city planning magazine, *New American City*, lamented, on the fourth anniversary of Katrina,

> There are many differences between George Bush and Barack Obama, but they do share one thing in common: While the Gulf Coast reeled in need of recovery, both presidents were on vacation.... More than 50 Gulf Coast community leaders were asked in the survey to grade the president and Congress in eight key areas. Obama's grade? A D+, putting him only a hair above Bush, who scored the lowest possible score of D-.

When Katrina hit, Bush was in Crawford, Texas, and then visited Naval Base Coronado in San Diego where he received a guitar as a gift from country singer Mark Wills. He did take the time to fly over the Gulf region, and was pictured, infamously, peering out the window of Air Force One, inept, uncaring, removed. Some "lucky" survivors managed to get out of New Orleans for refuge in Houston's Astrodome. Touring the dome, with over eleven thousand desperate people camped out there, Bush's mother, Barbara Bush, said,

> What I'm hearing, which is sort of scary, is they all want to stay in Texas. Everyone is so overwhelmed by the hospitality. And so many of the people in the arena here, you know, were underprivileged anyway, so this is working very well for them.

First, consider the insult, suggesting that people whose lives had been turned upside down, many of whom had loved ones missing and presumed dead, people who had lost everything they owned, might find being crammed into an athletic arena "working very well for them." But the former first lady also admitted the prospect that these refugees might want to stay in Texas was "sort of scary." Barbara Bush had publicly voiced the concern that thousands of "underprivileged" African-Americans might permanently move to her home state. Scary, indeed. Her candor, and her son's apparent ambivalence, depicted the cruel landscape into which the people of New Orleans and the Gulf Coast were cast by the preventable disaster of Katrina.

A year before Katrina, Hurricane Ivan threatened the city as well. The same predictions were made, that the hurricane could cause a storm surge that would overwhelm New Orleans's levees, flood the city, drive thousands to overcrowded emergency shelter at the Superdome, and potentially kill thousands more. Walter Maestri, emergency manager for Jefferson Parish, reported that the city had ten thousand body bags on hand. Traffic leaving New Orleans backed up, making the sixty-mile trip to Baton Rouge a seven-hour drive. Earlier major hurricanes Betsy, Camille, and Georges, and the unnamed 1947 hurricane, all caused significant damage and some loss of life. But while the National Flood Insurance Program thoroughly succeeded in helping wealthy people restore their coastal vacation homes wrecked by hurricanes, the half-million residents of New Orleans had little to rely on but themselves.

This is where Jordan Flaherty's *Floodlines* makes a major contribution to any essential reading list for Katrina. The story of New Orleans, and more broadly, Louisiana, is a complex tapestry, with deep racial, economic, artistic, cultural, and political threads. Stretching from the region's early history and its connection to the slave rebellion in Haiti, the world's first black republic, through the Underground Railroad, the Jim Crow existence forced on the freed slaves and their descendants, to the civil rights crusades, to the racially charged subtext of the city's famous Mardi Gras celebrations and the white flight to the suburbs, Flaherty writes through the lens of struggle, of a long-oppressed peoples's indomitable spirit buttressed by solid community organizing. *Floodlines* tells the stories of survival and resistance, spanning the region, spanning generations.

It is increasingly difficult in the United States to gain a fair appreciation for the role of community organizing, or even to understand what "community organizing" means. There was a brief window during Barack Obama's presidential campaign when his early work as a community organizer in Chicago was highlighted as a credit to his character, since he could have easily parlayed his Harvard Law degree into a lucrative corporate position. His Republican opposition soon weighed in, with their vice presidential nominee Sarah Palin leading the charge, belittling the job of community organizer. But learning who community organizers are, what they do, and how they bring people, typically poor people, together to challenge powerful, entrenched institutions, is vital for a comprehensive, accurate understanding of the United States and its current and historical role in the world.

The media in the United States consistently fail to cover grassroots movements, and at best give people eight-second sound bites or two-minute "debates" on the cable networks, which often degenerate into shouting matches, favoring the loudest, not the most eloquent or accurate. Instead of learning from the media what is actually going on in the world, we get static—a veil of distortion, lies, omissions, and half-truths that obscure reality. We need a media that creates static of another kind: what the dictionary defines as "criticism, opposition, or unwanted interference." Instead of a media that covers for power, we need a media that covers the movements that create static and make history.

We at *Democracy Now!* had covered the threats to New Orleans the previous year, with Hurricane Ivan, and resumed as Katrina bore down on the coast. We were receiving frequent reports from Bill Quigley, a human rights attorney who was volunteering at Memorial Hospital, where his wife was an oncology nurse. He reported horrific conditions, with power and water outages, as the floodwaters rose day after day. They had to smash a hole in a wall to evacuate patients into a parking structure, in hopes of getting access to helicopter evacuations that were more readily available to the wealthier, private hospitals. We went down, got into the city, and connected with many of the people described in *Floodlines*—community activists and leaders such as Malik Rahim. Rahim is a veteran of the Black Panther Party in New Orleans. For decades he worked as an organizer of public housing tenants both there and in San Francisco, and once ran for New Orleans City Council on the Green Party ticket. He blasted New Orleans's mayor Ray Nagin and governor Kathleen Blanco for lack of leadership and preparedness.

Rather than wait around for help, Malik Rahim and others founded Common Ground Relief Collective, focusing on the scene of the greatest devastation, the Lower Ninth Ward. "Solidarity, not charity" was their slogan, and they began gutting houses, assembling tools and materials, and slowly, house by house, rebuilding. The nonprofit has grown, offering a community center with free Internet access, job training, a free legal clinic, programs on soil quality and wetlands preservation, and home rebuilding assistance, all with an overarching ethic of self-empowerment and grassroots solidarity. Common Ground, like the Black Panthers decades before, was infiltrated by an FBI informant, Brandon Darby, whose disruptive behavior drove away talented volunteers and hurt the group's efforts. Darby failed to cause serious damage, but served as a reminder that even legally operating grassroots groups successfully challenging entrenched power can become targets.

Radiating from the neighborhoods of New Orleans—including the Seventh Ward, the Ninth Ward, Central City, the French Quarter, and the Treme neighborhood (which now lends its name to an HBO series)—are communities connected through family, culture, history, and common purpose. Flaherty eloquently paints the picture of the city, its people, and their customs, and then goes beyond New Orleans, describing the vast state prison in Angola, Louisiana, where conditions for the mostly African American inmates are virtually identical to those endured by their enslaved forebears a century and a half earlier. Yet even within the prison, as Flaherty details, people organize for change.

Likewise, deeper into central Louisiana, Flaherty first broke the story of the Jena Six, the young African American high school students who were facing up to one hundred years in prison for a schoolyard fight prompted by a racist incident with a noose hung on a tree at their school. Flaherty was practicing principled, honest journalism, reporting a story of injustice and going to the sources. He talked to the young defendants, to their mothers, to both sides in this racially divided, rural Louisiana town. Through his work, along with a report he filed with the filmmakers from Big Noise Films, which got international exposure on *Democracy Now!*, Flaherty writes,

> In the week after this report aired, the Jena Six family's defense fund, which until then was virtually empty, suddenly had tens of thousands of dollars, almost all of it in small contributions mailed in by *Democracy Now* viewers and listeners. Suddenly the story of Jena exploded and it seemed that all the major national papers and networks were sending someone down to Louisiana.

A national movement grew, centered in Jena, and ultimately the young men beat the grossly disproportionate charges.

Katrina's floodwaters eventually receded, but not too long after, the tragedy of Katrina receded as well, from the headlines, from the television newscasts, and thus from the attention of many Americans. It is the responsibility of journalists, of news organizations, to follow up, to provide the drumbeat coverage. There have been several reporters doggedly following aspects of the post-Katrina story, from the vigilante and police violence against, and murder of, African Americans during the flood to the hellish conditions at Memorial Hospital and the investigation into whether doctors there euthanized patients during triage. *Democracy Now!* correspondent Jeremy Scahill first uncovered the presence of Blackwater mercenaries as we entered New Orleans days after the levees broke, and his subsequent work on private military contractors has changed the global debate on this issue. Excellent books on Katrina have been written. Documentaries have been made. But the drumbeat coverage on the television news (which is still how most Americans get their news) has essentially evaporated. *Democracy Now!*, incidentally, is deeply indebted to Jordan Flaherty for his consistent help with our ongoing coverage of Katrina.

We broadcast from the Lower Ninth Ward in 2007 when Malik Rahim took us on a tour of the area. He told us about the Mississippi River Gulf Outlet, commonly referred to as the "Mister GO" after its acronym, MRGO, the ill-conceived canal built by the U.S. Army Corps of Engineers, designed to expedite ship traffic between the Gulf of Mexico and the Mississippi River. The MRGO actually created a straight path for storm surges from hurricanes to race inland toward New Orleans, bypassing the wetlands and barrier islands that had protected the city for centuries. Rahim told us,

> The levees broke, I believe it was because of the fact of the Mississippi River Gulf Outlet, which is just about two miles away from here…it pushed that storm surge through that canal, it came through and it broke the levee here at Industrial Canal. And a barge came through, and that barge traveled about three-and-a-half blocks, just crushing houses.

The MRGO also introduced seawater into the fragile cypress swamps, destroying thousands of acres of crucial natural barrier and habitat. After Katrina, a movement solidified—"Mister GO Must Go"—and eventually the U.S. Congress forced the Corps of Engineers to block the waterway. The first stone barrier was finished in the summer of 2009. In late April 2010, the *New Orleans Times-Picayune*'s editorial board criticized the U.S. Army Corps of Engineers' dilatory progress, writing,

> The destructive Mississippi River-Gulf Outlet was closed to marine traffic last July amid great fanfare as the U.S. Army Corps of Engineers completed a rock barrier across Bayou La Loutre—ahead of schedule. A few months later, the corps completed the foundation for a 1.8 mile barrier to prevent storm surge from traveling up the shipping channel, a project that one corps official likened to driving "the last concrete stake" into the heart of the MR-GO. But even though the monster finally has been killed, the environmental destruction it left behind has yet to be addressed.

As people fight to undo the environmental damage left behind by the MRGO and the cascade of problems it helped spawn, a sea of oil from the BP eruption is making landfall at the same place. The executives from the guilty companies, BP, Transocean, and Halliburton, have begun their PR campaigns as they try to lay blame on each other. BP was told to cease its efforts to get coastal fishery workers to sign away their legal right to sue, in exchange for some promise of work in the cleanup. The city that suffered the worst devastation in U.S. history, New Orleans, now finds its coast threatened by what could turn out to be the worst environmental disaster in U.S. history. A call has come out from at least eight U.S. senators for the Department of Justice to consider criminal charges against corporate executives from the companies involved.

As this goes to press, the vital wetlands of Louisiana's coast are just now being severely hit by the oil. The massive plume is also reaching the "loop current," farther out in the Gulf of Mexico, which will likely carry the oil into the Florida Keys and up around onto the East Coast. BP, meanwhile, has finally admitted that the amount of oil being released far exceeds their initial public admissions.

The coastal people of southeast Alaska confronted not only by the devastation of the *Exxon Valdez* oil spill, but also the wealth and power of Exxon. Exxon spent whatever it took to avoid responsibility and tied up the victims with endless litigation. If BP and their cohorts behave as Exxon did, as is expected, the people of the Gulf Coast and New Orleans will be fighting BP for at least a generation.

Preface

How can five years seem like a lifetime? And how can it be that so much of what has happened to individuals and to our community has been lost—as though stripped from our collective memory?

These are the questions I struggled with when Jordan asked me to write the foreword to *Floodlines*. So much of my life—not just tangible items but memories as well—has been lost since the storm. It's mind-boggling how often someone has asked, "Remember when…?" and I've had no real recollection of the event. This "Katrina amnesia" is prevalent in New Orleans, mainly because we used all the energy we could muster just to survive: where to live, how to pay the bills, where to put the kids in school, not to mention dealing with the Road Home program. Who had time to document the atrocities that befell us—and the beauty of this community coming together in solidarity to face them?

That task has fallen to Jordan Flaherty, and for me and so many others who have returned to New Orleans, his gift is invaluable. Through the social justice lens of his writing the reader can see the struggle that has been missing from many of the reports about our lives both before and after Katrina.

Make no mistake—there was strong social justice advocacy in New Orleans prior to Katrina. What has been remarkable to me is how often these social justice warriors have moved adroitly from one issue to the next, all in an effort to support oppressed people of color. For example, prior to Katrina I met with Jennifer Lai, a young lawyer working in New Orleans on education equity issues with the Algebra Project (a national program founded by civil rights veteran Robert Moses). Jennifer and I met only once or twice, but I was incredibly impressed with her energy and tenacity. We exchanged phone numbers and committed to working together during the 2005–6 school year. I heard from Jen again one October afternoon while I was in Austin, Texas—my second "temporary" home after Katrina—when she called, frantic, to ask for my help with several Southeast Asian women who had been imprisoned by their employer, locked in their room each evening until their cleanup duties resumed the next morning: indentured servants in 2005. This case was amazing, certainly, but looking back what was even more remarkable was that, despite the fact neither Jen nor I had any experience in immigration or criminal law, we both recognized oppression, and we were able to mobilize a community of New Orleans advocates—regardless of where we were displaced—to help these women.

There are hundreds if not thousands of similar stories from that time period, but many of us have a difficult time remembering them. Maybe this Katrina amnesia acts as a protective shield to keep us from going completely mad; I'm not sure. What I am certain of, however, is the absolute need to have our stories and this history documented in the voices of those folks who witnessed, fought in, and continue the struggle to return to our city with dignity and respect.

News reports, textbooks, and histories are often written by those who have not experienced the subject matter at hand. This is not the case with *Floodlines*. This book is a firsthand account from someone who has marched with us, sacrificed with us, suffered with us, and who triumphs—yes TRIUMPHS—with us. Make no mistake, justice will prevail, and *Floodlines* will be the first installment of our chronicles of this victory.

TRACIE L. WASHINGTON, ESQ.
Managing Co-Director
Louisiana Justice Institute

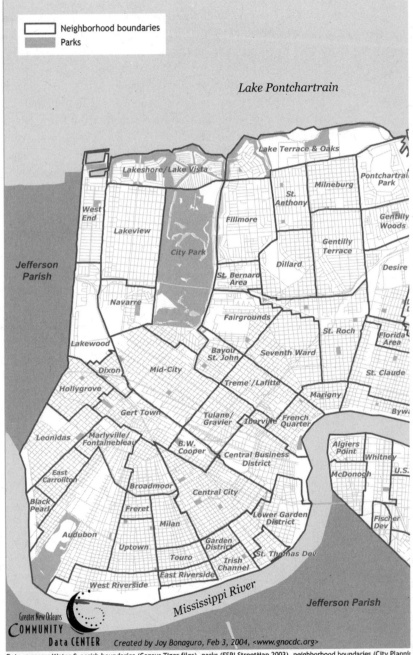

Neighborhood boundaries
Parks

Lake Pontchartrain

Lake Terrace & Oaks
Lakeshore/Lake Vista
Milneburg
Pontchartrain Park
St. Anthony
West End
Fillmore
Gentilly Woods
Lakeview
City Park
Gentilly Terrace
Jefferson Parish
Dillard
Desire
St. Bernard Area
Navarre
Fairgrounds
St. Roch
Florida Area
Lakewood
Bayou St. John
Seventh Ward
Dixon
Mid-City
St. Claude
Hollygrove
Treme'/Lafitte
Marigny
Gert Town
Tulane/Gravier
Iberville
French Quarter
Byw.
Leonidas
Marlyville/Fontainebleau
B.W. Cooper
Algiers Point
Whitney
East Carrollton
Broadmoor
Central Business District
McDonogh
U.S.
Black Pearl
Freret
Central City
Lower Garden District
Fischer Dev
Audubon
Milan
Garden District
St. Thomas Dev
Uptown
Touro
Irish Channel
West Riverside
East Riverside
Mississippi River
Jefferson Parish

Greater New Orleans
COMMUNITY
Data CENTER
Created by Joy Bonaguro, Feb 3, 2004, <www.gnocdc.org>

Data sources: Water & parish boundaries (Census Tiger files), parks (ESRI StreetMap 2003), neighborhood boundaries (City Plannir

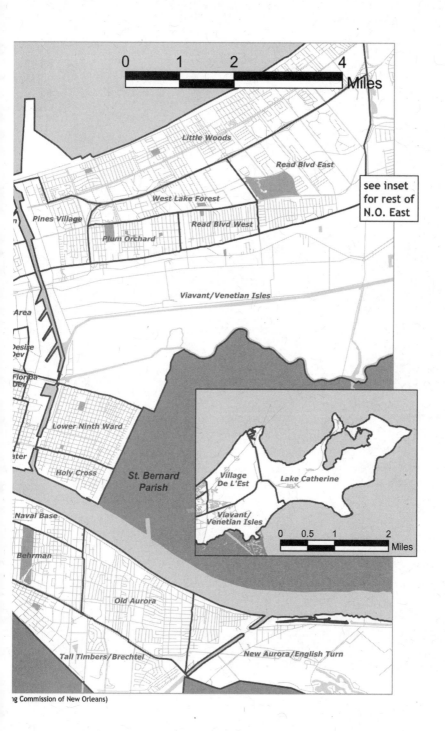

0   1   2   4
Miles

Little Woods

Read Blvd East

see inset
for rest of
N.O. East

West Lake Forest

Pines Village

Read Blvd West

Plum Orchard

Viavant/Venetian Isles

Area

Desire
Dev

Florida
Dev

Lower Ninth Ward

Holy Cross

St. Bernard
Parish

Village
De L'Est

Lake Catherine

Viavant/
Venetian Isles

0   0.5   1   2
Miles

ater

Naval Base

Behrman

Old Aurora

New Aurora/English Turn

Tall Timbers/Brechtel

ng Commission of New Orleans)

MARDI GRAS INDIAN, 2010. PHOTO BY ABDUL AZIZ.

We Know This Place

It happened in August, twenty-nine days in.
We are now five days out of the only place we knew
to call house and home.
Few things are certain.
One: we have no food.
Two: there are more bodies lying at the roadside than hot plates
being distributed
Or first aid being administered
Or recognition as a citizen
Fourteenth Amendment: X
Refugee: check.
And we know this place....

From "We Know This Place" by Sunni Patterson

This book is an attempt to document what I have learned from almost a decade of conversations and collaborations with hundreds of organizers, activists, artists, and community members in New Orleans in the years before and after Hurricane Katrina. This is an album of snapshots from the grassroots struggles for New Orleans during a heart-wrenching and extraordinary time. These are the stories left out of the official record.

What people here experienced in the years after Katrina was unique in countless ways—just as the storm and its aftereffects were a disaster unprecedented in U.S. history. But what we have seen are heightened struggles over the same concerns faced by folks everywhere: education, health care, housing, workers' rights, criminal justice, and the privatization of public services and resources.

The protagonists of this book are the people who have led the fight to save New Orleans. Because my own experience in this city—especially in the days and weeks after Katrina—has shaped my analysis, this narrative draws on some of my personal experiences. But telling my own story is not my objective. My hope is to describe an ethos of steadfast resistance, and to pay tribute to the people who have cultivated and shaped that way of life. I want the world to know that it's not too late to make a difference.

If this city is going to recover, the first step is getting out the truth that New Orleans is not "okay." Most of the country believes either that New Orleans has been rebuilt, or that, if not, it's because people here are lazy and/or corrupt and wasted the nation's generous assistance. But New Orleans is still a city in crisis. The oft-promised aid, whether from FEMA or various federal and private agencies, has not arrived. We don't need charity; we need the federal and corporate entities responsible for the devastation of New Orleans to be held accountable for supporting its rebuilding.

FRAMING THE DEBATE

Roots run deep here. Before the storm, New Orleans was the U.S. city with the largest percentage of its population living in the same town in which they were born. Acknowledging this fact is not to devalue the dedication and contribution of new arrivals who have made New Orleans their own. But I want to recognize what it means to have grown up somewhere, to have deep roots there—and then to be kept from returning. Or to try to stay in your community, to fight to hold on, while your family and neighbors are displaced.

As a white organizer who relocated to this city where so much African American culture has its origins, and where significant aspects of the city's history have been shaped by conflicts around race, I believe it is vital to lift up Black voices. It is not just that important stories of New Orleanians have not been told. It is that those who have spoken were generally not the people most affected by the disaster. Even in the progressive media, white voices such as mine have been overrepresented at the expense of the voices of people of color, and the voices of women of color are doubly missing.

This book aspires to address that imbalance, and its content amplifies the voices of Black New Orleanians. I recognize that, as a white writer, it is problematic for my book to serve as a filter for Black voices. I hope that readers will be motivated to seek out these voices directly. I am also concerned that by celebrating a long history of resistance of which I cannot claim to be a part, I am in some ways benefiting from others' struggles. I can't say that I've resolved this problem, but I've tried, in the process of writing this book, to find systems of accountability by engaging in dialogue and action with the people whose struggles are depicted in this book.

I also recognize that much of this book frames the discussion with a Black/white paradigm, and that this framing leaves out other racialized experiences, especially those of other people of color. I have tried to be honest about the reality of New Orleans, where dialogue about race often travels along a Black/white continuum, while trying to incorporate other experiences.

Katrina flooded eighty percent of the city. New Orleanians of all races and backgrounds lost everything they owned and more. Incredible pain and suffering crossed all boundaries of race, class, and gender. However, acknowledgment of the range and depth of loss doesn't alter the fact that this disaster both exposed and exacerbated the disparate treatment people received based on these factors.

On a national level, the destruction and abandonment of New Orleans led to promises from the media and politicians that our country would have a dialogue about race and poverty. Later, the mass mobilizations over the case of the Jena Six elicited similar promises from political leaders. That discussion has not yet happened, and the continuing silence diminishes us all.

I hope this book is a step in the direction of a national dialogue. More importantly, I hope that those of us concerned and angered by these issues can use this information as a tool not just for dialogue but also for action. The displacement and devastation of the Gulf Coast and the continued lack of recovery are not just local issues. These struggles are global, and should concern us all.

ZULU PARADE, MARDI GRAS 2010. PHOTO BY ABDUL AZIZ.

CHAPTER ONE

We Won't Bow Down: Culture and Resistance in New Orleans

We won't bow down
Not on that ground
You know I love to hear you call, my Indian Red

From "Indian Red,"
Traditional Mardi Gras Indian Song

I was fortunate. I had food and water and even a battery-powered radio. I stayed in the apartment of an acquaintance—a solid concrete building in the Midcity neighborhood. I had friends to house me in the immediate aftermath and a place in the city to return to not long after that. Thanks to a forged press pass, I was able to get back into the city a couple weeks after the disaster, while military checkpoints kept most people out.

In the days beforehand, Hurricane Katrina went very quickly from a vague weather warning to a major threat. The storm formed on August 23, 2005. On August 25, it hit Florida as a category one storm, the weakest hurricane rating, just above a tropical storm (the strongest hurricane rating is category five). By the morning of Friday, August 26, the storm had entered the Gulf of Mexico but had also been downgraded to a tropical storm and was not thought to be heading toward Mississippi or Louisiana. The situation changed very quickly after that. By the next morning, the storm had developed winds of well over one hundred miles per hour, moving it up to a category three storm. Trackers were also now predicting that the storm was heading to the Mississippi/Louisiana coast—possibly directly to New Orleans. Most people in the city had not heard anything about the storm prior to Saturday morning. Suddenly stores were closing, supermarkets and gas stations were packed, events were cancelled, and evacuations were underway.

By the time most people woke up on Sunday morning, Katrina had become a category five storm, with sustained winds of 175 miles per hour and gusts up to 215 miles per hour, and it was apparently pointed directly at New Orleans. Mayor C. Ray Nagin had ordered a mandatory evacuation, urging those who couldn't afford to leave the city to report to the Superdome as a "shelter of last resort." Television and radio reports were describing worst-case scenarios involving a city under twenty feet of chemically tainted water, with water snakes and alligators swimming through downtown New Orleans. It sounded impossible.

Friends and family asked if I would be leaving. Many people were looking for places to stay in the region—because of the massive amount of traffic, it can take ten hours to drive a hundred miles during an evacuation. Perhaps because I grew up in Miami and remembered hurricanes from my childhood as not a big deal, I chose not to leave. Even before the storm, I believed that natural disasters are not equal-opportunity threats. Dangerous weather is much more hazardous for people with less sturdy housing and in higher-risk areas (lower ground in New Orleans, for instance). If a home is flooded or hit by a tree, the elderly, children, and those with illnesses are at higher risk of death, injury, or other complications. At the time, staying in the city felt like a safe and certainly more affordable choice for me. I didn't believe the worst-case scenarios. We had heard similar predictions about Hurricane Ivan just the year before, and Ivan had bypassed New Orleans entirely.

As the warnings on television grew shrill, I decided to relocate from my apartment to a sturdier location: a complex developed from an old can factory in the Midcity neighborhood. There I stayed in an apartment leased by a friend of a friend of a friend who had left town but put out an open invitation for folks to stay at her place. The American Can Company Building, a project of developer Pres Kabacoff, was five stories high and made of concrete and brick. It stood about twenty-five blocks from the apartment in the Treme neighborhood I lived in at the time. There were seven of us in the apartment, and four cats. Some of us were friends and some had never met. What we and everyone else in the building had in common is that we were among the tens of thousands of New Orleanians who stayed behind. Many of those remaining in the city wanted to leave but couldn't afford to.

Residents still in the city sought out the sturdiest structures they could find. Thousands found refuge in the bricks and mortar of the city's public housing developments, which had long been known as some of the safest places in the city during a storm.

The Can Company felt very safe. There was even a rumor going around that it had generators, so we wouldn't lose power. In the hallways, I met some other friends of mine who didn't live in the building but were also staying there because it was so sturdy—Greta Gladney, a community activist from the Lower Ninth Ward, Jim Randels, an educator and director of the youth education program Students at the Center, and Jonathan Traviesa, a photographer with unruly white hair who lived in a shotgun apartment across the street.

On Sunday, August 28, Governor Kathleen Blanco appeared on television and urged us to "pray" the hurricane down to a category two. That was disconcerting, to say the least, but we still felt cautiously optimistic about the coming storm. Nervous, but safe. We had faith in the system of levees surrounding the city, which in retrospect seems naïve. At the time, President Bush was on vacation in Texas, his absence setting the stage for a federal response that was at best negligent.

The worst of the storm passed in the middle of the night and early morning. From within our solid housing, it didn't sound that bad, and I slept through most of it.

To this day, it is commonly thought that New Orleans was hit by a category five storm. However, although it registered as a category five in the Gulf, Katrina slowed quite a bit when it hit land, and also turned east in the last moments, largely missing the city. The winds that did strike us went no higher than category two.[1] Since the levees were supposed to be strong enough to withstand at least a category three storm, the city should have been safe. Had the Army Corps of Engineers done their job, and had funding for levee maintenance not been cut by Congress during both the Bush and Clinton administrations, the ensuing disaster would not have happened.

SECONDLINES

Those who have not lived in New Orleans have missed an incredible, glorious, vital city—a place with an energy unlike anywhere else in the world, a majority–African American city where resistance to white supremacy has cultivated and supported a generous, subversive, and unique culture of vivid beauty. From jazz, blues, and hip-hop to secondlines, Mardi Gras Indians, jazz funerals, and the citywide tradition of red beans and rice on Monday nights, New Orleans is a place of art and music and food and traditions and sexuality and liberation.

I love secondlines and jazz funerals—every jazz funeral is also a secondline, that is, a parade with a brass band, but not every secondline is a funeral. The name "secondline" comes from the formation for a funeral procession: the family and other mourners, as well as the musicians, form the first line (or "main line"), and everyone else is the second line. Hundreds of secondlines are held in New Orleans every year. Sometimes there are just a couple dozen people, crossing a few blocks in about an hour; sometimes there are thousands of people and three or more brass bands, traversing several miles over the course of four or five hours. The Social Aid and Pleasure Clubs, Black community institutions that originated during the Reconstruction era, put on secondlines nearly every weekend, but anyone can throw a secondline—all you need is a brass band. If you travel more than two blocks, people will come out and join you.

The city has more than forty Social Aid and Pleasure Clubs, and each club designates one Sunday out of the year to throw a parade. The Sunday secondlines start at noon or one p.m. and each takes a different route, but most travel through the African American neighborhoods of either Central City uptown or the Sixth and Seventh Wards downtown. The members of the sponsoring Social Aid and Pleasure Club are at the center of the parade, wearing matching outfits—sometimes changing uniforms once or twice along the way—and dancing the entire time. If you are walking down the street and you see a secondline coming, it looks like a flood of people that will sweep you away, washing over every part of the street, sidewalk, and even the front porches of houses with an ecstatic energy.

At every secondline, a few folks will pull coolers filled with beer, soda, and water for sale, and along the route people barbeque food—sometimes to sell, sometimes just for themselves and friends. Although police officers clear traffic in front of the parade and follow behind it, the area within the parade feels like a lawless but communal utopia where people can smoke pot and drink and act foolish and no one will bother them.

Historian Ned Sublette observed, "A second line is in effect a civil rights demonstration. Literally, demonstrating the civil right of the community to assemble in the street for peaceful purposes. Or, more simply, demonstrating the civil right of the community to exist."[2] The Social Aid and Pleasure Clubs are exactly what their name implies—societies dedicated to supporting their community and facilitating good times. Through those good times they help perpetuate a very specific culture and pass it down from generation to generation. Most of these organizations arose as mutual aid societies in the late 1800s, and much of their purpose lay in providing basic needs such as burial insurance for their members. By upholding this mission of supporting and uniting their communities, the clubs are a large component of what makes New Orleans unique, and new "S&P" Clubs continue to be formed. Through the parades that each club throws, they transform a revolutionary act—taking control of the streets—into something everyday.

One of my favorite holidays of the year doesn't show up on calendars outside of New Orleans. It's the last Sunday in November, when the Lady Buck Jumpers, the wildest and fiercest Social Aid and Pleasure Club, takes to the streets. (Some S&P Clubs are all men, some are all women, and some are mixed. Some clubs are all young, some are all older, and some have members ranging from eight to eighty.) Based in the Gert Town neighborhood, the Lady Buck Jumpers are a strong, powerful group of women of all ages who dance harder and better than any other secondline crew. Everyone that loves secondlines knows that the Buck Jumpers bring a great time, and their annual parade is always one of the biggest of the year, with thousands of people crowding the streets, dressed in their most fabulous outfits, and dancing like it's their last day on earth.

In 2006, the club wore matching camouflage suits in honor of Soulja Slim, a legendary local rapper who was shot and killed on Thanksgiving Day of 2003. As Buck Jumpers president (and Soulja Slim's mother) Linda Porter described it, "The ones here are jumping for the ones gone and the ones to come."[3]

At global justice protests and other demonstrations, people frequently chant, "Whose streets? Our streets!" And at those gatherings it can feel like a new world is being created simply through the reclaiming of public space as a liberated zone. In New Orleans, we get that feeling every Sunday. And it's beautiful.

More than anywhere else in the United States, New Orleans is a city where people often live in one neighborhood their whole lives and multiple generations can live on the same block. All of this is to say that New Orleans is not just a tourist stop. New Orleans has a unique and resilient set of cultures, with a history of place and a legacy of resistance. This city is defined by its difference, its cultural separation from the rest of the United States. Shortly after the city was flooded, Cornel West wrote,

> New Orleans has always been a city that lived on the edge...with Elysian Fields and cemeteries and the quest for paradise. When you live so close to death, behind the levees, you live more intensely, sexually, gastronomically, psychologically. Louis Armstrong came out of that unbelievable cultural breakthrough unprecedented in the history of American civilization. The rural blues, the urban jazz. It is the tragicomic lyricism that gives you the courage to get through the darkest storm. Charlie Parker would have killed somebody if he had not blown his horn. The history of Black people in America is one of unbelievable resilience in the face of crushing white supremacist powers.[4]

Often called North America's African city, New Orleans is steeped in traditions both African and Caribbean. This rich background can be attributed in part to the legacy of French colonialism, which—while still brutal and racist—allowed enslaved Black people to buy their freedom. These legal differences, as well as a strong "maroon" culture of escaped slaves, enabled African cultural traditions to be maintained in New Orleans in a way that they weren't elsewhere in the United States. For instance, the existence in New Orleans of a neighborhood of free Black people as early as 1725—Faubourg Treme, generally just called Treme—makes it unique among U.S. cities.

MORE THAN JUST THE FRENCH QUARTER

New Orleans is a small city shoehorned between the Mississippi River and Lake Ponchartrain. Aside from New Orleans East and the Lower Ninth Ward, which are separated from the rest of the city by the Industrial Canal, and Algiers and English Turn, which lie on the other side of the Mississippi, most parts of town can be easily reached by bicycle. This geography helps create a sense of closeness, as if we're all neighbors and together in our trials. The same families have frequently lived next door to each other for several decades. Imagine this and you begin to understand the special kind of familiarity experienced here. "Before the interstate highways were put in, it wasn't on the way to anywhere, so people were very isolated," explained Tulane University professor Felipe Smith. "[Our] whole family and acquaintance universe was centered around New Orleans. It just became like an echo chamber."[5]

With food, music, cultural traditions, and holidays that are distinct from the rest of the United States, New Orleans sometimes seems like a country unto itself. People around the United States have heard of Mardi Gras, but unless they've lived in a city that celebrates Carnival, they don't really know what it's like. For starters, there are several different incarnations of Mardi Gras. Some are public spectacles, others are shrouded in secrecy. New Orleans Mardi Gras celebrations are a marathon, not a sprint—they take up about a month out of the year, with planning and preparations often taking much longer.

The actual day of Mardi Gras is the last day before Lent (the "Fat Tuesday" of excess before the fasting or other self-denial that begins on Ash Wednesday). Ash Wednesday comes forty days before Easter, not counting Sundays. Easter falls on the first Sunday after the first full moon after the first day of spring (what that has to do with Jesus's rebirth I'll leave to the Biblical scholars). In effect, this means the date of Mardi Gras can range anywhere from February 3 to March 9.

In New Orleans, Mardi Gras season can be said to begin after Twelfth Night (also known as Epiphany) on January 6. Although the parades don't begin until a couple weeks before Mardi Gras, the whole city is on a relaxed schedule for all of January and sometimes (depending on the date of Mardi Gras) February as well. That relaxed schedule continues into the spring with various festivals—the largest and most famous of which is Jazz Fest—and then into the summer, which is so hot everything slows down. Actually, compared to the rest of the United States, New Orleans is on a relaxed schedule all year long.

New Orleans has other holidays that are all its own. For example, the cultural tradition of Mardi Gras Indians has four holidays: Mardi Gras, St. Joseph's Night—a traditional Italian Catholic holiday that has been claimed by New Orleans's Black community—and Indian Sunday, which actually falls on two separate days, one uptown and one downtown. Both occur in late spring.

On these holidays, the Mardi Gras Indians, as they are called—Black men, predominantly, and some women—dress in elaborate costumes that

they have spent all year designing and constructing. The costuming originated as a tribute to Native American communities, to acknowledge the
support they provided to Black people during the times of slavery. Native
communities served as stops on the Underground Railroad, offering
refuge for those escaping from slavery, and there is a long history of inter-
marriage between the communities. Like secondlines, this is a neighborhood tradition—put together by community members for the benefit of
others in that community. People spend thousands of dollars and hundreds of hours, all to engage in a tradition with their neighbors and whoever else might come by.

Most historians date the Mardi Gras Indian tradition to the Reconstruction era, while others trace its roots back as far as the mid-1700s. It is
a beautiful and hypnotic collection of complicated, intricate, and mysterious rituals. Two tribes, or "gangs," meet in the street, in full costume, and
challenge each other. Different members pose threateningly, issue challenges through song, words, and movement, and engage in a performed
battle that feels dangerous, even though it mainly involves singing and
dancing. It is intense, breathtaking, and utterly unique. Within the Mardi
Gras Indian tradition there is a familiar roster of songs, and most people
from New Orleans know them. Many contain titles or lyrics that sound
meaningless to outside observers ("Two Way Pocka Way"), but the words
often have historical meaning—for example, as references to routes to the
Underground Railroad—or serve as signals to what is happening in the
confrontation between the two gangs.

The meetings of these Indian gangs used to involve actual physical
violence, but legend has it that the violence was brought to an end
through the efforts of Allison "Tootie" Montana, a community elder and
"chief" of one of the tribes, who became known as the "Chief of Chiefs"
in recognition not only of his skills at costuming and performing, but
also of his transformative and unifying effect on the entire community
and tradition.

On Sunday evenings, in small neighborhood bars and other gathering spots in the city's Black neighborhoods (especially Central City and
the Seventh Ward), New Orleanians gather for a tradition called Indian
practice. These gatherings are in preparation for the music, dancing, and
rituals involved on the days that the Indians parade. A crowd of people

from the community, which can easily reach a hundred or more, packs close and sweaty into a small bar, all singing and chanting and drumming and dancing together to the classic songs of Black Mardi Gras, like "Indian Red": "Here comes the Big Chief / Big Chief of the Nation / The whole wild creation / He won't bow down / Not on that ground / You know I love to hear you call, my Indian Red." Indian practice happens throughout almost the entire year, getting more intense—and crowded— as Mardi Gras approaches.

Perhaps the most famous of the Indian songs is "Iko Iko," which was a hit song in the '60s, has been covered many times, and occasionally turns up in films and other pop culture. But the local version feels different, both ancient and new. When you hear Mardi Gras Indians sing "My flag boy told your flag boy / I'm gonna set your flag on fire," it feels like a real, albeit theatrical threat. The lyrics often vary, as Indian chiefs improvise new words, sometimes going on for what seems like hours, telling stories, boasting, relating history, all within the context of a song.

As with many New Orleans traditions, some conventional gender roles are subverted. The highest praise you can give to a male Mardi Gras Indian is to call him the "prettiest."

The big Mardi Gras parades are thrown by associations called krewes, the earliest of which were founded in the pre–Civil War era. Comus, one of the original krewes, was made up of the elite white leadership of the city. One early Comus parade, in 1873, was dedicated to mocking both Darwin's theory of evolution and Oscar J. Dunn, Louisiana's first Black lieutenant governor.[6] The Krewe of Zulu, which parades on Mardi Gras day, is one of three Black parades and the only one to roll down St. Charles, the main street of uptown New Orleans. According to legend, Zulu was started in 1909 to mock the white Mardi Gras traditions. Among the most shocking aspects of the Zulu parade, at least for out-of-towners, is that krewe members wear blackface, afro wigs, and grass skirts.

Each krewe appoints a new king every year. This is a ceremonial position—the king presides over the krewe's ball and rides on a special float in the parade. For krewes like Comus, the king is generally a krewe member and therefore part of the local elite. Other krewes, like Zulu, often reach outside their membership—past kings of Zulu have included Louis Armstrong and Spike Lee.

Most white krewes remained segregated until 1992, when the city council held hearings on the issue and ruled that, in order to use municipal resources and parade on Mardi Gras, they had to desegregate. Comus was one of three white krewes that chose to stop parading rather than integrate. The Comus krewe still exists, although without parading, and throws an exclusive Mardi Gras ball every year.

For a certain sector of New Orleans society, the king of Mardi Gras is King Rex, of the mostly white krewe of Rex, which parades on Mardi Gras day, just after Zulu. "People say we're one New Orleans," said political advisor Vincent Sylvain, "but we have two kings of Carnival. Take away King Zulu or King Rex and see what happens."

There is a lot more to Mardi Gras than the French Quarter. Mardi Gras can be found all over the city in private, invitation-only balls and informal neighborhood parades and parties. There are Mardi Gras traditions specific to nearly every neighborhood and community, a series of cultural customs ranging from King Cake, an extremely sweet confection usually made with cream cheese filling and eaten from Twelfth Night through Mardi Gras day, to the lewd displays of Krewe Du Vieux, an artist-organized parade through the Marigny and French Quarter neighborhoods that marks the beginning of parade season, a few weeks before Mardi Gras. Dogs walk in the "Barkus" parade, a spoof of the giant Bacchus parade and a huge annual event in its own right. Punks and artists parade in Krewe Du Eris, the anarchist parade, a winding, costumed spectacle replete with giant marching band and no police permit. Drag performers and fabulous costumes define the St. Ann parade, which travels from the Bywater to the Quarter early on Mardi Gras morning, is all-participants/no-spectator, and features the best costumes of the year.

The cultural traditions of Black Mardi Gras play a defining role in the holiday for many New Orleanians. They encompass everything from the Krewe of Zulu and Mardi Gras Indians to the Skeletons, who parade in the early morning and were allegedly devised in the 1800s as a way to scare children away from bad behavior, and the Baby Dolls—grown women dressed like sexualized Victorian-era dolls, a tradition rumored to have been started by sex workers during the era when prostitution was decriminalized in New Orleans.

The Black traditions of New Orleans have thrived despite opposition from the police and the power structure of the city. In fact, in some cases Black folks have carried on these traditions precisely as acts of defiance. You might think the people who create the art that has defined this city, who invented jazz and made billions of dollars for New Orleans's tourist industry, would be honored and supported. You'd be wrong.

As one example, in the months after Katrina, the city raised the permit fees for secondlines to several thousand dollars, which threatened to severely limit the tradition, until the local ACLU affiliate sued on behalf of the Social Aid and Pleasure Clubs. During most secondlines, block parties, and other neighborhood events in the Black community, the police generally come through at some point, sirens blaring, to disperse the crowds. Usually the disruption occurs when the event is about to end, but it can come at any time. This kind of official harassment never seems to happen at cultural events with mostly white crowds. For example, White Linen Night, an annual outdoor arts event in the city's arts district on Julia Street, would never be subject to this kind of police behavior.

Mardi Gras Indians have faced some of the worst police repression. In the spring of 2005, as the Indians were parading on St. Joseph's Night, scores of officers descended on the scene and disrupted the event, frightening the children present and arresting several of the performers. "Take off your fucking feathers or go to jail," officers reportedly told the Indians.[7]

Soon after, at a city council hearing on the incident, Allison "Tootie" Montana, the Chief of Chiefs, addressed the room. At eighty-two years of age, Montana had been a Mardi Gras Indian chief for five decades. He captivated the assembled crowd with details of a long history of police repression tied to racial discrimination, beginning with a police crackdown at his very first Mardi Gras many decades ago. Tootie ended his speech: "This has to stop." And those were his final words. He stepped back from the microphone and collapsed to the floor. Tootie was pronounced dead of a heart attack shortly afterward.

His funeral was a moving combination of cultural celebration and political demonstration. Thousands of people came out, dressed in all manner of costume, to commemorate the life of this brave fighter for freedom. As a longtime community leader, organizer of Downtown Indian Sunday, and friend of Montana's, former Congress of Racial Equality (CORE) organizer Jerome Smith inflamed the crowd, saying, "This is about a life that has passed, but it is also about the struggle against institutionalized racism in our city." The link between culture, especially that of Black New Orleans, and the movement for liberation was clear to everyone in attendance.

LEGACY OF RESISTANCE

New Orleans is a city of slave revolts and uprisings. In 1811, the largest slave uprising in U.S. history was launched just upriver, as more than five hundred armed and formerly enslaved fighters marched toward New Orleans. As one historian described, "The leaders [of the revolt] were intent on creating an [enslaved persons] army, capturing the city of New Orleans, and seizing state power throughout the area. Following the example of the Haitian revolution [1791–1804], they sought to liberate the tens of thousands of [enslaved people] held in bondage in the territory of Louisiana."[8] Although this uprising was defeated, it inspired more over the following years.

In 1862, New Orleans was the first major Southern city lost by the Confederacy. In battles and confrontations during the Reconstruction era, that war continued. In 1866, at least forty Black folks struggling for voting rights were killed in a downtown race riot that later became known as the Mechanics Institute Massacre.[9]

After the Civil War, Louisiana elected the first African American governor in U.S. history, Pinckney Benton Stewart Pinchback. Pinchback, who had also been Louisiana's second African American lieutenant governor, was subsequently elected to Congress and the U.S. Senate, but was prevented from being seated by his fellow legislators. The United States did not elect another African American governor until 1990.

One of New Orleans's most famous early residents, the voudou priestess Marie Laveau, was not just a religious figure. She also reportedly operated an Underground Railroad, buying enslaved Black people and helping them go north.[10] Many free Black women in the early 1800s in New Orleans, like Laveau, were business owners and community leaders. The first coffee vendor in the city, Rose Nicaud, was a free woman of color, and soon after she began her operation, several other free women of color opened coffee stands.[11]

In 1892, Homer Plessy and the Citizens' Committee planned the direct action that brought the first (unsuccessful) legal challenge to the doctrine of "separate but equal"—the challenge that became the Supreme Court case of *Plessy v. Ferguson*. Plessy, part of a community of Creole Black intellectuals and community leaders, boarded an all-white railcar after notifying the railroad company and law enforcement in advance. While the action was ultimately unsuccessful, it was an important turning point in this long history of locally led resistance to racist laws.

New Orleans activists were on the front lines of civil rights organizing. "Wherever you went across the South," CORE veteran Mattheo "Flukie" Suarez told journalist Katy Reckdahl, "there were always New Orleans people working in the Civil Rights Movement."[12] In 1961, 292 students (most from Southern University at New Orleans, a historically Black college near the lakefront) were arrested as they marched down Canal Street in New Orleans to protest the arrest of 73 students who had marched for civil rights in Baton Rouge[13]

In 1970, the Black Panthers formed an extremely popular branch in the city, based in the Desire housing projects, and also founded one of the nation's first Black Panther chapters in prison, at Louisiana State Penitentiary at Angola. "Panthers were doing what the city should have been doing," said Robert Tucker, a community activist who worked with the administration of then-Mayor Moon Landrieu. "You had people living in terrible conditions in Desire, half of them were under eighteen. The water was waist-high when it rained. The Panthers were feeding people, performing community services." When hundreds of New Orleans police came to evict the Black Panthers from the Desire projects, five hundred people—seemingly the entire neighborhood—stood between the police and the Panthers, and the police were forced to retreat.

You could say the spirit of the Panthers was born in Louisiana. The Deacons for Defense, an armed self-defense group formed in rural central Louisiana in 1964, inspired the Panthers and other radical groups. The Deacons went on to form twenty-one chapters in rural Louisiana, Mississippi, and Alabama, continuing a legacy of defiance that inspired future generations. Several civil rights workers and future revolutionaries were born in this state, including Black Panther leader Geronimo Ji-Jaga, born in Morgan City, and founder Huey P. Newton, born in Monroe. Jamil Abdullah Al-Amin, also known as H. Rap Brown, former chairman of the Student Nonviolent Coordinating Committee (SNCC) and later the justice minister of the Black Panther Party, was from Baton Rouge. Chicago Black Panther Fred Hampton's parents were also from Louisiana.

DEFINED BY RACE

Visitors from other parts of the United States, especially the East and West Coasts, often assume that New Orleans is an especially segregated place. I do believe that racism is intense in New Orleans, that many of our social spaces are segregated, and that many conflicts here are defined by race. However, I do not mean to give the rest of the United States a free pass. Race is a defining aspect of this country. Our nation was built by slave labor, lynchings were still common well into the last century, and Black people were systematically denied the right to vote—as well as to ride in the front of a bus or sit at a lunch counter—throughout much of this country until the 1960s.

The effects of this legacy continue today. Recent studies have shown that schools are as segregated today as they were before *Brown v. Board of Education* ordered desegregation—the New Orleans public schools, most of which are 98 to 100 percent Black, are a prime example of this. But so, sadly, are schools in many other U.S. cities, from Connecticut to California. In fact, a 2009 report from the Civil Rights Project of the University of California, Los Angeles found that in most of the country, school segregation was actually increasing, and overall was at greater levels nationwide than it was during the 1950s.[14]

I've experienced social segregation—even among progressive communities, people committed to racial justice—in other U.S. cities. In New Orleans I find that people are more honest about race and racism, and there is an ongoing conversation about the ways in which racism shapes our lives. Living here, I've learned about myself and the ways in which white supremacy informed my upbringing. I don't claim to have defeated my own racism—it's an ongoing process. Being raised in a racist society is a bit like being an alcoholic; you're always in recovery. "When we get around to talking about race, it's usually because someone is upset," noted civil rights attorney Tracie Washington. "White folks can go down to a Black neighborhood to watch a secondline and watch the Black people dance, and they don't feel a need to talk about race," she said. "But if they get robbed coming home, then that's when we talk about race."

The current racial divisions in New Orleans can be traced in part to white resistance to integration. The white-flight suburbs surrounding New Orleans—St. Bernard, Jefferson, and St. Tammany Parishes—all experienced a population explosion as soon as the civil rights movement hit New Orleans. This intensified especially after November 14, 1960, when a young girl in New Orleans named Ruby Bridges became the first Black child in the South to attend an all-white elementary school, and school integration became a reality in Orleans Parish.

Through the 1950s, both Black and white populations rose in New Orleans, but between 1960 and 1970 the white population declined sharply. In the 1960 census, New Orleans had 627,525 people and was 62.6 percent white. By 1970, nearly 70,000 white New Orleanians had moved out, and the white population was down to 54.5 percent.[15]

In 1970, Mayor Moon Landrieu (New Orleans's last white mayor until his son Mitch Landrieu was elected mayor in 2010) integrated city hall by hiring Black staffers for the first time to work in the leadership of city government. Many whites in New Orleans howled in protest. In 1978, local civil rights icon Ernest "Dutch" Morial became the city's first Black mayor, receiving 95 percent of the Black vote and 20 percent of the white vote. In 1982 Morial won re-election with only 14 percent of the white vote.

By 1980, another 90,000 white New Orleanians had left, while the Black population had risen by almost 40,000, and the city was now majority African American. By the 2000 census, another 100,000 white people had moved out of Orleans Parish.

MODELS OF ORGANIZING

I didn't really understand community until I moved to New Orleans. It is a city of kindness and hospitality, where walking down the block can take two hours because you stop and talk to people on every porch. Extended families and social networks fill the gaps left by city, state, and federal governments that have abdicated their responsibility for the public welfare. Folks you walk past on the street not only ask how you are, they also wait for an answer. New Orleans is a place where someone always wants to feed you.

Organizing in New Orleans looks different than it does in other places. It is more about building community and family, about sharing stories and meals. For people from New York or California, it can often be frustrating—the pace is different, as people often try to build a broad consensus and really get to know each other before moving forward. Many times here, I have gone to a three-hour meeting, and at the end of those three hours the only agenda item we've accomplished has been introductions.

New Orleans's cultural spaces are also sites of resistance. Ashé Cultural Arts Center, founded by Carol Bebelle and Douglas Redd, is an Afrocentric cultural venue in the Central City neighborhood that hosts a wide range of progressive artistic events from art shows to theatre, music, spoken word, and dance, as well as classes, workshops, and meetings. Ashé was one of the main partners that collaborated to support Eve Ensler's tenth-anniversary commemoration of the *Vagina Monologues* in 2007. "V to the 10th," as it was called, was a spectacular effort that brought two days of performances, speakers, and workshops—as well as free massages and other healing rituals—to the Superdome and New Orleans Arena. The relationship between Ensler and local cultural workers helped keep this national event rooted in a specific local context, and lent the gathering weight and power.

Throughout 2004 and 2005, I was part of a group called the Anti-Violence Coordinating Committee. This was a small group (usually fewer than ten of us) that met once a week. The group's core members were community elders who had grown up in New Orleans and had decades of experience: Malik Rahim, who had been among the founding New Orleans Black Panthers; Robert King, a recently freed member of the political prisoners known as the Angola Three; Ted Quant, the director of the Twomey Center for Peace Through Justice; and longtime community organizer Robert Tucker. The group was initiated by Orissa Arend, a writer and community mediator active in antiracism work. Most weeks, I just sat and listened to these community elders talk about their experiences and share their opinions. Although the group may not have been very active by some standards—we organized a handful of public events over the course of a couple years—to me it was an unparalleled opportunity to learn from folks with an incredible amount of knowledge and experience, and the process shaped me as an organizer and activist. These sorts of intergenerational exchanges are also, I have found, less common outside the South, and our movements lose a lot by not having more of these kinds of gatherings.

Organizers here are enmeshed in this city's traditions—we all share in them. The people I see at secondlines are many of the same people I see at demonstrations. We have celebrated and mourned together, often at the same time. We have eaten together and have met each other's families.

I came to New Orleans in fall 2000 inspired by the city's history and way of life, but what I found exceeded any of my expectations. The organizing landscape runs deep and wide, and there are a range of ways in which people come together. One of the key features of New Orleans organizing is the story circle—a process whereby people communicate and come together by telling personal stories on a theme. Story circles were developed by the Free Southern Theatre (FST), which formed out of SNCC and Freedom Summer in the mid-'60s as the theatrical branch of the civil rights movement. John O'Neal, another movement elder in New Orleans, is legendary for his work as a co-founder of the FST and for his lifetime at the intersection of social justice and performance. O'Neal helped develop the story circle in his work with the FST and described it this way: "When we tell stories we are sharing with each other how we put things together. When we share stories we share whole parts of ourselves. Stories come charged with the spirit of the teller and have lives of their own."[16]

SNCC veteran Curtis Muhammad was instrumental in making story circles a feature of New Orleans organizing. Coming together around our stories, and through that commonality finding a mutual path for moving forward, is a central aspect of New Orleans organizing that I haven't encountered elsewhere.

Kalamu Ya Salaam, a brilliant and world-renowned poet and educator, co-founded a project called Students at the Center, which utilizes the story circle in its work. Students at the Center places the needs and situations of students at the center of its approach in order to give students what they need to create powerful writing. As described by Jim Randels, a teacher and co-director of Students at the Center, "FST developed the Story Circle because it was dissatisfied with audience feedback sessions after their performances. They wanted a more democratic process that included all voices. They also wanted to emphasize story rather than argument, understanding that stories tend to bring people together, to help them find common ground or at least to understand each other."[17]

Freedom Schools are another tactic from the civil rights movement that continues as an integral part of New Orleans organizing. The schools were set up in the South by movement activists to help educate the community outside of the state-run schools, which were not aimed toward liberation but toward maintaining the status quo. The Freedom Schools' curriculum was designed to further mass participation in the movement for equality. Classes, often taught by college student volunteers, focused on voter registration campaigns as well as on encouraging independent thinking.

Movement veteran Jerome Smith educates children through a cultural organization he founded in 1968 called Tambourine and Fan. Dedicated to preserving and continuing Black New Orleans traditions, Smith describes Tambourine and Fan as a continuation of the Mississippi Freedom Schools, that is, an education project aimed at empowering young people to take an active role in struggles for justice, as well as educating them about Black cultural traditions. Programs designed on the Freedom School model exist across the United States, but the tradition is especially strong in New Orleans. The New Orleans chapter of the Children's Defense Fund (CDF) hosts Freedom Schools inspired by this model (as do CDF chapters across the country), and the People's Institute for Survival and Beyond (PISAB), an antiracist training collective, has long incorporated Freedom Schools into their work.

Comedian Dave Chappelle's parents had a hand in starting PISAB in 1980, along with Jim and Diana Dunn, Ron Chisom, and other community organizers and scholars. Kool Black (aka Robert Horton), a core trainer with the organization, was one of many young men who joined the organization as a result of their community work in neighborhoods like the St. Thomas public housing development. He joined in the '90s and soon became a leader of PISAB's Freedom Schools. "We believe that skills alone are not enough to become an organizer," he told me, describing the organization's philosophy. "You have to understand the culture and time we live in. Just because you develop skills, that doesn't make you a better organizer. If you don't address the issue of racism, then you just become a skillful racist."

For Kool, the Freedom Schools help pass on the revolutionary spirit and knowledge to a younger generation. "We developed Freedom Schools, modeled on the freedom schools that came out of the '60s, to take a message of antiracism to a younger audience. Kids as young as nine years old would participate. We would help kids get clarity on institutional power as it relates to racism. That experience helped shape my political perspective."

New Orleanians affiliated with INCITE! Women of Color Against Violence, a national coalition of radical feminist activists of color, have been active on issues of law enforcement violence through collaborations with organizations like Critical Resistance, a national prison-abolition organization with a New Orleans chapter, and the National Coalition to Free the Angola Three, which worked to free three imprisoned New Orleans members of the Black Panther Party. INCITE also held a national conference here in the spring of 2005, an historic gathering of radical feminists from around the United States who came to New Orleans to connect and strategize on issues of state violence and violence within our communities.

When I first arrived in the city, I attended a forum planned by Community Labor United (CLU). Curtis Muhammad was among the initiators of this coalition, and I knew as soon as I met him that he was someone I wanted to learn from. CLU met up about once a month and generally the meetings were on a certain theme: often education or criminal justice. With story circles and long group introductions, the process seemed very slow in relation to my East Coast background, but exciting collaborations came out of this group, including a student activist group called Teens with Attitude, supported by CLU members, who were committed to bringing community control to Frederick Douglass High School. As an alliance of grassroots community organizations and union locals, CLU put forth an important analysis: that the labor movement has money, but often lacks the deep roots that many community organizations have, while community organizations have roots but rarely have much money. Curtis believed that by combining forces both could be strengthened—a lesson I wish the labor movement would learn on a national scale.

Grassroots resistance runs deep in New Orleans, but it isn't always immediately visible to outsiders. It is often based deeply in community, involving elders passing on knowledge to a new generation, or people who have known each other all their lives coming together to take action. "People who want to come in solidarity should be respectful with when and how they enter a community," said Kool Black. "There was a lot of organizing in St. Thomas; we developed a lot of leaders. The people who were nine to twelve years old when we started, in seven years, led that program, and were the staff. That was the intention, to pass it on to that next generation of leaders."

ARTISTS IN ACTION

New Orleans is also the number one African American tourist destination in the United States. Every fall, seventy thousand people, most of them Black, attend the Bayou Classic, a college football game between two historically Black colleges, Grambling State and Southern University. During Fourth of July weekend, tens of thousands of people, mostly Black women in their twenties and up, come for the Essence Music Festival, which has featured musical guests from Beyoncé to Janet Jackson to Gil Scott Heron and presents dozens of seminars with authors, motivational speakers, and politicians that have included Al Sharpton and Congresswoman Barbara Lee. Although these gatherings might be categorized as tourist events, they contribute strongly to New Orleans's identity as a center of this country's African American life.

Every year, tens of thousands of people descend on the city for Jazz Fest, a commemoration of the sound New Orleans helped create. In celebrating the local heritage, there is sometimes an assumption that these cultural contributions exist only in the past, that the city is now a giant museum. The truth is that New Orleans continues to innovate and break new ground in the arts.

Bounce is the name given to a style of local hip-hop with a call-and-response style that owes a debt to Mardi Gras Indian songs, with lyrics filled with local references, and a distinctive, fast-paced beat. Although not widely heard outside the South, bounce is dominant in New Orleans clubs and originated in the poorer neighborhoods of the city, where it is sometimes called "project music."

"When you hear bounce," explained Lucky Johnson, a hip-hop promoter with a strong social conscience, "people in a club go wild. They just forget about it. They throw their hands up in the air, they catch the wall."

With the phrase "catch the wall," Johnson is referring to another characteristic element of bounce—the way people dance to it. When a bounce song comes on, people throughout the club (particularly women, but often a few men as well) grab something—a wall, the floor, or themselves—and rapidly "bounce" their butts in time to the beat.

In 2009 Johnson combined bounce with drama and produced a play called *Catch Dat Beat*. A celebration of New Orleans music and culture billed as the "first bounce musical," *Catch Dat Beat* sold out its several hundred seats every night. The show featured local hip-hop performers including Lucky (in two roles, as well as directing) and multi-talented trendsetter Tenth Ward Buck. A rising star named Big Freedia stole the show in the lead role.

Freedia is best known as part of a clique of gay rappers self-identified as "sissies," who are among the most popular performers in New Orleans clubs. They are often known as "sissy bounce" artists, but Freedia rejects that label, saying, "I'm a gay rapper, don't get me wrong. But there's no such thing as separating it into straight bounce and sissy bounce. It's all bounce music."

Although identifying as a man, Freedia, like many of the so-called sissy bounce artists, plays loose with gender pronouns. Freedia is one of several gay rappers who have broken down barrier after barrier to become some of New Orleans's most popular musicians. Like most bounce, the songs are frankly sexual, with titles like "Ass Everywhere," by Freedia, and "Crazy Bout My Boyfriend," by Sissy Nobby. Openly gay rappers Freedia and Nobby often play on the same bill with straight-identified performers like Tenth Ward Buck. In fact, the sissy bounce scene that was birthed a decade ago by gay rapper Katey Red with her 1999 album *Melpomene Block Party* has rejuvenated the bounce form, and performers like Freedia have gone from a novelty to a central part of bounce culture.

One of the main ways that bounce is transmitted to the community is through block parties. These celebrations, explained Johnson, are also about building community and supporting your neighbors. "Growing up in less fortunate neighborhoods, your parents would have card games, or suppers," described Johnson. "Say Miss Carol across the street's light bill was due. Miss Carol would have a supper. Everyone in the neighborhood would buy a plate to help her pay the light bill." In other words, continued Lucky, the block party comes from this tradition, and is ultimately about "how a people are able to come together in a time of need."

Johnson has produced many bounce hits, and sees producing as a way to support positive messages. "I can't sign a hip-hop gangster rapper," he said. "I don't advocate killing and drugs or slap that bitch. I'm not into that. I'm not gonna put my money behind it. If you come to me with something that says 'Get on the dance floor and have a good time,' then I can support it."

Bounce music faces a few obstacles on the way to national popularity. It is an art form so distinctly local that it's hard to imagine a bounce party in any other city. Most bounce songs feature neighborhood-specific references. It is sample-heavy, which makes getting the publishing rights difficult. The songs are musically spare in a way that sounds amazing in a New Orleans club, but doesn't quite work alone in your house. Overall, it just doesn't *sound* like anywhere but New Orleans.

Freedia believes bounce will keep growing, and isn't worried about any potential obstacles. Bounce artists like her bring lines around the corner when they perform here. She has labored in a homophobic music scene to become a star. "We been working really hard all these years of getting people to accept us," she said. "Maybe get throwed at and screamed at, but over time all that has changed. All the hard work has finally paid off."

With performances by Big Freedia, Katey Red, and Sissy Nobby at the 2009 and 2010 Jazz Fests in town and the 2010 South By Southwest music conference in Austin, as well as photo spreads and features in national music magazines, the music form is reaching new audiences. Elements of bounce have appeared in songs by national acts such as David Banner, Mike Jones, and Beyoncé. "For me it was the determination to change the people and make them love what we do," said Freedia. "And that's what my job was. When I became a gay bounce rapper I said that I was going to change it and make people love me, and make them love gay people."

Although there is certainly still homophobia in the hip-hop community, many straight producers like Johnson have no problem collaborating with gay rappers. Johnson explained that he wants to work with the performers with talent, whoever they may be. "Freedia is outstanding," said Johnson. "Every time he'd get the mic, he'd just light up the room." Tenth Ward Buck is also quick to praise Freedia. "As Freedia was coming up, a lot of people tried to drag him down," Buck said. "And he didn't care about what they said, he kept moving forward. I don't care if you straight or what, everyone is bouncing to Freedia's music."

As a small and community-oriented city, New Orleans artists are in constant dialogue and communication with each other. The hip-hop artists grew up with secondlines and Mardi Gras Indians, poets grew up with New Orleans jazz, brass bands grew up with bounce music, and this cross-pollination influences everyone's style.

Sunni Patterson can't remember a time when she wasn't a poet. The words flow naturally and seemingly effortlessly from her. When she performs, it is like a divine presence speaking though her body. Her frame is small but she fills the room. Her voice conveys passion and love and pain and loss. Her words illuminate current events and history lessons.

Patterson, who has performed around the United States and appeared on the HBO show *Def Poetry Jam*, is the best-known of a generation of spoken word artists from New Orleans. She is part of a large and vibrant community that follows in a tradition of poets, musicians, and artists. Since the late '90s, you could find spoken word poetry being performed somewhere in the city almost any night of the week.

These poets see their work as a continuation of New Orleans's musical culture of jazz, secondlines, and the call-and-response songs of the Mardi Gras Indians. "You have to understand," Patterson explains. "There's been jazz here, so of course there's been poetry. This is just something that's been passed down to us."

Patterson comes from New Orleans's Ninth Ward. "In that same house that I grew up, my great grandmother and grandfather lived," she said. "Everybody that lived around there, you knew. It was just that, it was family." The poetry community is also a family. Everyone knows each other and works to support each other. The host and organizers of one poetry night are part of the supportive audience another night. Most spoken word nights feature a headliner—either an accomplished local performer or a touring poet from elsewhere—and an open mic segment, in which anywhere from a handful to twenty poets perform. The content ranges from the personal to the revolutionary. Charlie Vaughn, known to most as Charlie V, is an accomplished artist—he designed album covers for local rappers including Soulja Slim—and the organizer and host, pre-Katrina, of one of the most successful weekly poetry gatherings, a Saturday night event called Pozazz. For seven years, Pozazz mixed poetry with live music and a local DJ named Dynamite Dave Soul. "I wanted to hear from the average person," said Vaughn. "A woman who was beaten on, a guy who just came out of jail. They turned into a neighborhood celebrity just from saying how they felt."

You can hear Sunni Patterson's influence in the performances of many young poets in New Orleans. And in the work of Patterson and other poets, you can hear the history of community elders passed along, the chants of Mardi Gras Indians, filtered through their voices, and the knowledge and embraces of neighbors and family and friends. "The community here is such a big family, it truly fosters the art and the love of the art here, because it fosters the person," Patterson said.

Most of these poets are also involved in community work. Patterson has taught with Kalamu Ya Salaam at Students at the Center. Others are employed as teachers or instruct at cultural spaces like Ashé Cultural Arts Center, and many mentor young poets on New Orleans's youth poetry slam team.

For Patterson, a responsibility to justice is the central part of any artist's work, especially if they are from New Orleans. "At some point all of our efforts just can't be a barbeque," she said. "The people that were left here to die, they won't forgive us. We need to heal the world, to make this a better place."

As with much of New Orleans culture, the poetry community here has a unique feel. "I think it was based on the kindness," said Vaughn. "The New Orleans spin we put on it. Everybody came in, and we made it feel like you were part of the family. We may not have the same last name, but you come in, I call you cousin."

Like New Orleans hip-hop, much of the poetry heard here is neighborhood-specific, with references that out-of-towners might be hard-pressed to understand. Like New Orleans food, this fiercely local work may not translate directly to other cities, but for New Orleanians, it is the best there is. "I see stuff in Atlanta," said Vaughn. "We would smash them like a giant to a grape."

To be a New Orleanian is to be part of a specific culture—a culture that has birthed incredible art, music, food, and tradition. New Orleans is, as many will tell you, almost a country unto itself. And it felt, in those first days after the storm, as if this nation might disappear forever. Even people who hadn't lived here felt the urgency. In 2007, Toni Morrison said, in a speech at Tulane University, "It would be so sad if New Orleans never became what it was before. But you have to hope that it can. It is more important than you could ever know."

PERCENT AFRICAN
AMERICAN BY
CENSUS BLOCK
GROUP IN
ORLEANS PARISH,
2000.

Neighborhoods

Major parks

- 0%
- 0.1% - 19.8%
- 19.9% - 46.6%
- 46.7% - 71%
- 71.1% - 88.7%
- 88.8% - 100%

New Orleans East

0   6 Miles

0   1   2   4 Miles

Source: U.S. Census Bureau. Census 2000 Full-count Characteristics (SF1). From a compilation by the GNO Community Data Center. <http://www.gnocdc.org>
Note: Percent *African American* is based on the number of people who checked *African American*, excluding those who checked the ethnicity *Hispanic*, on their 2000 Census form.

VIEW FROM ROOF OF AMERICAN CAN COMPANY BUILDING,
SEPTEMBER 2005. PHOTO BY JONATHAN TRAVIESA.

CHAPTER TWO

Lies on the News:
The Flood and Its Aftermath

Hurricane Katrina, we should've called it Hurricane Bush
Then they telling y'all lies on the news
The white people smiling like everything cool
But I know people that died in that pool
I know people that died in them schools
Now what is the survivor to do?
Got no trailer, you gotta move
Now it's on to Texas and to Georgia
They tell you what they want, show you what they want you to see
But they don't let you know what's really going on
Make it look like a lot of stealing going on
Boy them cops is killers in my home...
Man fuck the police and President Bush
So what happened to the levees, why wasn't they steady
Why wasn't they able to control this?
I know some folk that live by the levee
that keep on telling me they heard the explosions
Same shit happened back in Hurricane Betsy
1965, I ain't too young to know this...

From "Georgia...Bush" by Lil' Wayne

In the morning, after the storm had passed, we explored the streets. Power was out throughout the city, including in our building, but this was a common occurrence in New Orleans, even after minor storms. There was some flooding, but not much more than the city regularly experienced in a hard rainstorm—felled trees, some torn roofs. The area in front of the Can Company building was under less than a foot of water, though the floodwater was deeper on some side streets.

It seemed as if the worst-case scenarios predicted by the media had not come to pass. More than once that day, someone said, "We dodged the bullet again." New Orleanians know that the city is always at risk, and part of living here means becoming accustomed to that risk.

A few hours later, we heard some radio reports of more extensive flooding and destruction in the Ninth Ward, but no further details were given, and none of us could have guessed at the devastation already faced by some parts of the city. We decided to stay one more night in the Can Company building, assuming that by the next day the water outside would have drained to the point we could walk home. We anticipated that electricity would be restored to our neighborhood in a few days.

On the roof of the Can Company building, we talked to our temporary neighbors and watched the stars.

TUESDAY, AUGUST 30

We woke up to discover that the water level outside had risen about two feet. Rising water was not what any of us had expected, and no one was sure what it indicated or what we should do. An inventory of our food revealed that with tight rationing we would have enough to eat for about five days. While discussing our plans we repeatedly reassured ourselves, "Not that we'll be here that long, but if we had to…." Soon we discovered that running water in the building (and, as we learned, throughout the city) had been turned off.

The Can Company building stands near a bayou that runs through the Midcity neighborhood. In better times, the bayou is one of the nicest parts of the city, a lovely place to spend time watching fish jump and snapping turtles poke their heads out over the surface of the water. Now the area was barely recognizable, its geography transformed by the flood. Looking out from the roof, we saw water everywhere.

Many people in the neighborhood had boats, and out on the flooded bayou several folks were rowing around. Photographer Jonathan Traviesa, who was staying in an apartment upstairs from us, lived less than a block away and owned a small boat. Traviesa retrieved his boat from his house and went to work navigating the area, giving people rides and delivering supplies. In three separate trips, he brought over an entire family—who were panicked as water came rushing into their home—to the Can Company building.

In the courtyard of the Can Company, which was raised a few feet above the ground outside, a young man named Christopher invited everyone to a barbeque. Someone brought a grill, and people from all over the building collected food that was in danger of spoiling and cooked and ate it together. Christopher stood in front of the grill with water up to his calves. A similar ritual was repeated all over the city—New Orleans is a city where people love to come together over shared food and conversation.

With 268 apartments in total, about two-thirds of them empty, and many of those remaining occupied by multiple individuals, I estimated at the time that more than 200 people stayed through the storm at the Can Company, roughly half Black and half white. John Keller, a tall and imposing former marine staying in the building, went door to door in an attempt to get an accurate count, and put the number at 244 people, about 100 of them white.[1] Keller was later interviewed by the *Times-Picayune* about his role coordinating relief for elderly, sick, and frightened residents of the building, and his remarkable tale was reportedly optioned by Will Smith. I remember Keller, but only from brief glimpses—the large building was the site of hundreds of individual stories.

The Can Company apartments are newly renovated and fairly luxurious, but there is some class diversity in the building, as a number of units are rented to Section 8 and other low-income residents. Many people who stayed in the building during the storm were elderly and/or infirm. Another category included people in a situation like ours: they didn't live in the building but sought refuge there because the Can Company building was one of the most solid structures in the city (Keller estimated this group numbered about seventy-five). Several apartments were, like ours, crowded with seven or more people. Overall, people had supplies of food and water, but in most cases not enough to last several days.

In our apartment we had a small battery-powered TV/radio, but each time we switched it on, we soon turned it off in disgust. The newscasters offered no helpful information, just rumors and fear-mongering. New Orleans's media horizon is bleak in general—even with no storm, television and radio options were limited to corporate-owned, cookie-cutter news outlets. But with most of the city evacuated, only one station was broadcasting. It didn't tell us much, mostly just repeating a message for people who had left the city: "Don't come back yet." Throughout this time, we couldn't find a reliable source of information, which heightened the tension.

We finally heard on the radio that the levees had broken in several places, but still didn't comprehend how serious the situation was. We thought it was a breach that could be fixed. The broadcast described helicopters delivering sandbags, and we assumed a solution was underway. However, as reporters announced later in the day, the water level in the city would continue to rise, perhaps twelve to fifteen feet. Governor Kathleen Blanco was on the radio calling for a day of prayer. We later found out that the levees had breached in at least fifty-three places in the Greater New Orleans area, and water from Lake Ponchartrain and the Mississippi River Gulf Outlet was flowing into the city.

WEDNESDAY, AUGUST 31

Tensions in the building started to rise. With no power, brutally hot apartments, and an uninviting swamp of sewage engulfing the building, most people spent time on the roof and in other public spaces. There were also people living in the hallways and common areas, such as the large family Jonathan had ferried over, who had fled nearby homes that hadn't stayed as dry and safe as the Can Company building.

I heard white people whispering about their fears of "them." One woman complained of people in the building "from the projects," who she said were hoarding food. Others talked of gangs in the streets downtown, shooting, robbing—lawless chaos. There seemed to be a push and pull in people's minds between compassion and panic, between empathy and fear.

The national media added to the problem by reinforcing a view of New Orleanians as criminals. Days after the storm, CNN reporter Chris Lawrence commented that there were no "normal" people left in New Orleans, only armed ones. As he said this, the screen showed Black people at the Superdome.[2] City officials helped fuel the panic with exaggerated reports. Police Superintendent Eddie Compass told Oprah Winfrey, "We had little babies in there [the Superdome], some of the little babies getting raped."[3] Compass resigned in disgrace in late September 2005, but proved to be another example of law enforcement career longevity even in the face of gross incompetence when, in 2007, he was put in charge of the security guards in the city's public schools.

To me, the stories I was hearing—of gangs and mass murdering and looting around the city—seemed insane. These were rumors that arose from fear of the other and as a demonization of the poor, then were repeated without question by the media, and then recirculated and multiplied, as people grew panicked over an incompetent government response. But seeing our city underwater, with no help anywhere, also seemed insane, even to someone like me with a critical view of the U.S. government. It was as if all rules had fallen away—not just the rule of law, but rules of logic, of what I thought possible in this country.

Despite the rumors and fear, I witnessed samaritans traveling in boats, bringing food, giving lifts, sharing information. The general sense in the area was that people were pulling together and looking for ways to help others. This was the New Orleans I knew. In the months afterward, I heard more of these stories from neighborhoods around the city—and especially poorer communities. One such example involved the community leader and civil rights veteran Dyan French Cole, known to everyone as Mama Dee, who led a group called the "Soul Patrol" in the Seventh Ward. The Soul Patrol consisted mostly of working-class Black men who patrolled their neighborhood by boat and on foot, rescuing their neighbors and providing relief in the first days after the storm. Ricky Matthieu, a Soul Patrol volunteer, worked for days doing rescue and relief. The whole time, Matthieu said, he was harassed and threatened by the New Orleans Police Department (NOPD) and other police agencies, who accused Soul Patrol members of being looters. "These are my neighbors. I couldn't leave them behind," Matthieu explained. "Leave them for what? A rescue that came seven or eight days later?"[4] The so-called "first responders" did very little, according to Matthieu: they were more interested "in joyriding and trying out equipment. We [the Soul Patrol] rescued almost everyone in this area."

From each neighborhood with a housing development, I heard stories of young Black men—the same young Black men criminalized in the media—helping people. Years after the storm, photographers Keith Calhoun and Chandra McCormick created a photo show of what they called the "real first responders," dedicated to profiling the young men from their Lower Ninth Ward neighborhood who had rescued people when the government failed.

This story was never widely told. If the truth about how New Orleanians—especially young Black men—pitched in tirelessly to help one another had been publicized, a very different picture would have been painted of what was happening in New Orleans, and the nation's response would likely have been reshaped. Instead of tales of criminal gangs wreaking havoc while police and soldiers fought to maintain order, there were stories of collective action, of people looking out for each other and developing communal responses to the crisis. In most of these stories, the police and military were part of the problem, not the solution. The so-called gangs—the young Black men from housing developments like the St. Bernard and Lafitte—were actually the ones who stepped in to help.

Denise Moore was one of an estimated twenty thousand people at the Convention Center. Although the center—a large complex by the Mississippi River, a few blocks from the Superdome and just upriver from the French Quarter—had not been named as an official hurricane shelter, thousands of people gathered there anyway. "Yes, there were young men with guns there," Moore told family members. "But they organized the crowd. They went to Canal Street and 'looted,' and brought back food and water for the old people and the babies, because nobody had eaten in days. When the police rolled down windows and yelled out 'The buses are coming,' the young men with guns organized the crowd in order: old people in front, women and children next, men in the back, just so that when the buses came, there would be priorities of who got out first."

But the buses never came. "Lots of people being dropped off," said Moore. "Nobody being picked up. Cops passing by, speeding off. We thought we were being left to die."[5] "It was supposed to be a bus stop where they dropped people off for transportation," one officer told the *Washington Post*, explaining why a huge crowd had gathered at the Convention Center. "The problem was, the transportation never came."[6]

Larry Bradshaw and Lorrie Beth Slonsky, paramedics from Service Employees International Union Local 790, who were in the city for a convention, reported on their experience downtown after they and several thousand other guests had been kicked out of the hotel where they were staying:

> We walked to the police command center at Harrah's on Canal Street and were told...that we were on our own. And, no, they did not have water to give us. We now numbered several hundred. We held a mass meeting to decide a course of action. We agreed to camp outside the police command post. We would be plainly visible to the media and would constitute a highly visible embarrassment to the City officials.

The police told us that we could not stay. Regardless, we began to settle in and set up camp. In short order, the police commander came
across the street to address our group. He told us he had a solution: we
should walk to the Pontchartrain Expressway and cross the greater
New Orleans Bridge where the police had buses lined up to take us out
of the City....

We organized ourselves and the 200 of us set off for the bridge with
great excitement and hope.... As we approached the bridge, armed
Gretna sheriffs formed a line across the foot of the bridge. Before we
were close enough to speak, they began firing their weapons over our
heads. This sent the crowd fleeing in various directions....

All day long, we saw other families, individuals, and groups make
the same trip up the incline in an attempt to cross the bridge, only to
be turned away. Some chased away with gunfire, others simply told no,
others to be verbally berated and humiliated. Thousands of New Orleanians were prevented and prohibited from self-evacuating the city
on foot. Meanwhile, the only two city shelters [the Superdome and
Convention Center] sank further into squalor and disrepair. The only
way across the bridge was by vehicle. We saw workers stealing trucks,
buses, moving vans, semi-trucks, and any car that could be hot-wired.
All were packed with people trying to escape the misery New Orleans
had become.[7]

Mardi Gras Indian chief Kevin Goodman told a similar story:

Some guys in the neighborhood had boats the next day and took us to
the foot of the bridge. People were sitting all along the bridge with
everything they could carry. We walked from there to the Convention
Center. It felt like 120 degrees in the heat. We cut a piece of carpet for
the babies and laid down. Five minutes later, a stampede of people
started toward us 'cause they heard the buses were coming. People
started to pile up, hundreds. They kept saying, "The buses gonna
come," but they didn't. Day after day. We never saw no officials or city
leaders. We might have been satisfied to see someone in a suit and tie.[8]

Back at the Can Company building, by this time, fear was a palpable
presence. Rumors and half-truths were flying everywhere. There was a story
of a soldier shot in the head by looters (not true), stories of bodies floating in
the Ninth Ward (true), flooding in Charity Hospital (largely not true—only
in the basement), and huge masses, including police, emptying Wal-Mart

and the electronics stores on Canal Street (true—police looting was even caught on video). From the roof of the building, fires were visible in the distance, and someone told us the Lafitte housing projects were burning (not true).

Everyone in the building kept asking, Why has no one come? Helicopters occasionally flew by, but none would stop. Using foam from a fire extinguisher, Keller wrote out on the roof the number of people in the building and the need for food. Anyone in the helicopters could have clearly seen the writing, as well as the scores of people on the roof, but still no help arrived.

After we had gone several days without help, with people's illnesses worsening and no signs of rescue on the horizon, Keller had an idea: he told all the Black people to leave the roof, and had only elderly white residents standing there. Within minutes, the first helicopter arrived, hovering a few feet above the roof, and dropped off food and water. Soon after, a Coast Guard helicopter started picking people up. I would later discover that similar stories were unfolding all over the city, as racism affected every aspect of the rescue efforts.

Lance Hill, the executive director of the Southern Institute for Education and Research at Tulane University, has documented the story of a downtown hotel—the Ritz-Carlton—that put white guests and staff on a bus headed out of town, while Black staff and guests were transported to the Superdome. In congressional testimony, activist and attorney Ishmael Muhammad quoted Shelly, a thirty-one-year-old woman who was trapped in the Superdome: "When buses came to take us from the Superdome, they were taking tourists first. White people, they were just picking them out of the crowd. I don't know why we were treated the way we were. But it was like they didn't care."

When the helicopter first dropped food on the Can Company roof, there was a rush to grab it. But soon people in the building came together and started coordinating distribution, and collective action won out over competition.

Not far from our building, visible from the roof, was a small spot of dry land. Around this time, helicopters began landing there to pick people up. The aircrafts were large military transporters, and could fit perhaps ten or more adults at a time. Hundreds of inpatients from a nearby hospital made their way to the patch of land, wearing only flimsy institutional gowns. Most ended up waiting for hours in the sun. As more helicopters came, people started arriving from every direction, coming by boat or slogging slowly and deliberately through the sludge-filled water.

As evening approached, a helicopter hovered over our roof, and a soldier descended to announce that the following day everyone remaining in the building would be evacuated. Across the way, at least two hundred people spent the night huddled on that tiny patch of land, waiting to be rescued.

THURSDAY, SEPTEMBER 1

At dawn, people from our building lined up on the roof, waiting to be picked up by helicopters. The group set up a system to give priority to those most in need. Three helicopters came early in the morning and took a total of nine people. About seventy-five people spent the next several hours waiting on the roof, but no more help arrived. Everyone in our apartment was young and healthy, so we all resolved that we wouldn't even try to leave until most of the others had been evacuated. We didn't want to take resources from those with greater need.

Down in the parking garage, flooded with sewage and oil, a steady stream of boats ferried people, a few at a time, to various locations, mostly to the nearby helicopter pickup point. A self-organized, volunteer-run, local transportation system had developed, with boats taking people to drop points where they could disembark safely. The water under the boats was filled with chemicals and dead animals and who knows what else. You couldn't tell what was under you, or the level of the water. A boat might suddenly bump into a submerged car or some other obstacle and tip over.

Our group fractured, and people left at various times. Tensions were high. Most smokers had run out of cigarettes at this point, and nicotine withdrawal heightened the existing anxiety. Brett Evans, a nervous but friendly man from Lakeview who was staying in Jonathan's apartment, had begun smoking what Jonathan dubbed "Ponchartrain-soaked" cigarettes, from a pack salvaged from the floodwaters.

Two of us—myself and Planned Parenthood organizer Christina Kucera—got a ride from a boat, which took us to the nearby helicopter landing spot. Soon a helicopter flew us to an evacuee camp. What I witnessed there changed my life.

CAUSEWAY CAMP

The evacuee camp was along the I-10 freeway just outside of New Orleans, at the Causeway exit. In the camp, thousands of people—95 percent of them African American—were forced to stand, or else to sit in mud and trash, behind metal barricades under an unforgiving sun with heavily armed National Guard soldiers standing sentry. The camp was small—just a few hundred feet—and packed with people. It was also chaotic, with no hint as to who was in charge or where information could be received.

Whenever a bus came through, it stopped at a different spot from the time before. State police would open a gap in one of the barricades, and people would rush for the bus, with no information given about where it was headed. Once aboard the bus, evacuees would find out where they were being taken: Baton Rouge, Houston, Arkansas, Dallas, or other locations.

I was told that, for example, if you boarded a bus bound for Little Rock, even if you had family and a place to stay in Baton Rouge, you would not be allowed to get off the bus as it passed through Baton Rouge en route. You had no choice but to go to the shelter in Little Rock. If someone was willing and able to come pick you up, they could not come within seventeen miles of the camp barricades, as the I-10 was blocked off from civilian traffic all the way to LaPlace.

In this atmosphere of chaos, family members were separated from one another, and fear and misinformation dominated. Given the choice between being shipped off somewhere unknown or staying behind, hundreds of people opted to stand to the side, not even trying to get on a bus. Everyone, including small children and people in wheelchairs, waited in the sun. I was reminded of a description from the book *Rising Tide*, about the Mississippi River flood of 1927. Following the evacuation, Black folks were imprisoned in camps, under the guard of soldiers, and forced to work rebuilding the levees. "Canned peaches were sent in. None went to Blacks for fear it would 'spoil' them....The Blacks were no longer free. The National Guard patrolled the perimeter of the levee camp with rifles and fixed bayonets. To enter or leave, one needed a pass. They were imprisoned."[9] I watched a bus arrive and a mass swarm forward while state police and soldiers stood guard rather than helping, and felt that I was witnessing a repeat of this dehumanizing spectacle, almost eighty years later.

I walked throughout the camp and spoke to Red Cross supervisors, Salvation Army workers, National Guard soldiers, and state police. Although I was mostly greeted with smiles, no one could give me any details as to when buses would arrive, how many would come, where they would go, or any other information. I spoke to the teams of journalists parked just outside the camp, and asked if any of them had been able to get answers from federal or state officials to any of these questions. All of them, from German photographers to producers with a local Fox affiliate, complained of an unorganized, noncommunicative mess. One cameraman with a local TV station told me, "As someone who's been here in this camp for two days, the only information I can give you is this: Get out by nightfall. You don't want to be here at night." Although that seemed to be yet another instance of a member of the media demonizing the victims, it was undeniably true that this would be a bleak place to spend any amount of time, especially at night.

It was impossible to tell who was running the camp and no visible effort had been made to set up any sort of functional system for communication or transparency. As terrible as the situation was, a few adjustments might have helped alleviate some of the misery: a line for boarding buses, a way to register contact information or find family members, special needs services for children and the infirm, phone services, remedial medical treatment for possible disease exposure—to name just an obvious few. There was not even a single trash can, and waste was piling up quickly.

Individual soldiers and police officers were polite—at least to me. Yet in response to my questions nobody seemed to know what was going on. Instead, wave upon wave of evacuees kept arriving and were ushered behind the barricades onto mud and garbage, while heavily armed soldiers kept watch.

My memories of that place still haunt me. Every evacuee I spoke to had a horrible story to tell, of a home destroyed, of swimming across town, of corpses and fights, gunshots, vigilantes, and terror. The phrase "left to die" echoed again and again. People who had just come from the Superdome described shocking experiences, the horror still fresh. A young man told me a dramatic story of escaping and swimming up to Midcity to find his family. I just kept thinking, I can't believe this is the United States. I felt that if I were Black, I would not have been able to walk around as freely as I did. I didn't look like a "refugee," so I wasn't treated as one.

In this country, I am frequently reminded of my skin privilege. I have often run through red lights on my bike, right in front of a police car, and the officers never seem to notice or care. In contrast, young Black men in New Orleans have been arrested for riding a bike with one hand, or biking the wrong way down a one-way street. Never had this apartheid treatment felt more real and immediate than on that day in the Causeway camp. My whiteness felt like a uniform I was wearing, one that gave me access to a citizenship denied to the people all around me.

Michael Homan, a white blogger from New Orleans who also spent time in the Causeway camp, tells a similar story.

> On September 2nd-3rd, the night after I evacuated my house in New Orleans, I spent several hours inside this massive encampment of suffering people at the intersection of Causeway and Interstate 10. There I saw the most horrific scenes that I have ever witnessed. I estimated that I saw 20,000 people. A few were corpses, many were elderly, and in bad physical condition. I saw many people with Down syndrome, and casts, catheters, wheel chairs, all sorts of stuff. They were almost all people of color, except for the National Guard and police, who were almost all white. The National Guard and police were not letting people out of his area. Total disorder reigned on the ground inside the camp.... People inside the camp told me that they had been there three days. They were sitting outside without food and water in near 100-degree heat just waiting for buses. Every once in a while a bus will show up and there would be a mad rush of people to get a few seats out of that hell.... I still get very angry at this country when I think about those suffering people in that camp. I think about what if my mother or children had to see such sights, and I get furious....
>
> I still believe that race played a major role. I saw it personally. These National Guard troops were scared to death because of race. They were mostly from rural areas and for them their knowledge of African Americans comes from TV shows like Cops. They pointed guns at many people, and there were plenty of racial slurs.[10]

In congressional testimony, Leah Hodges, a Black woman who had been at Causeway, told a harrowing story, indicting the government that allowed this to happen.

> Those [aircrafts] could have taken us to any dry, safe city in America. Instead, they dumped us at a dumping ground, sealed us in there, and

they backed up all their authority with military M-16s. And there were thousands and thousands of people. On the last day we were in there…they handpicked the white people to ride out first. Every day, the crowd got darker and darker and darker until finally there were only—there were 95 percent people of color in that place…they broke up families and dispersed us…and they stood over us with guns and enforced their authority.[11]

I had been aware of crimes committed globally and domestically by the U.S. government, but I was still completely unprepared for what I saw in the evacuee camp. This neglect and abuse went beyond the systemic problems I knew existed. This looked like ethnic cleansing, here, in a U.S. city, in the twenty-first century.

Hours went by, and more people were arriving than were able to leave. Christina and I ran into Brett from our building, and the three of us walked out of the camp, planning to try to hitch a ride with departing relief workers or press. Almost immediately, we got a ride from Robert Penfold, an Australian TV anchor, who let us use his cell phone to call family and took us to Baton Rouge. Once there, we sat on the street and waited for Christina's mom, who was making the eight-hour round-trip drive from Houston to pick us up and then take us to her home. In the middle of the night in Baton Rouge, everyone we met had evacuated from somewhere—Bay St. Louis, Gulfport, Slidell, Covington. It was very late on a weeknight in a small city, but the roads were crowded. All those people were going somewhere. Many didn't know where they would end up.

Most people in the evacuee camp had no choice but to wait for whatever was dealt to them. My intersecting layers of privilege as a journalist and as a white male allowed me to escape and get a comfortable ride. While National Guard soldiers kept watch over others in the camp, they had barely noticed as the three of us walked out. We had resources and connections that many New Orleanians didn't, which meant that for us, a stay in a shelter was never a fear. We had friends and family to stay with in Houston and other nearby cities, and offers of places to stay from around the country.

Weeks later, I was back in New Orleans. The majority of those who had been in the camp with me may well remain exiled to this day, perhaps in Houston or Atlanta or Jackson, or maybe they lived in a FEMA trailer camp in Baton Rouge until they were evicted and ended up homeless. Some are certainly in prison, some are dead.

Later, when I learned how New Orleanians had been portrayed in the media during those initial days, I felt anger and dismay. The rampant mistreatment I had seen was unmentioned. Instead, the city was demonized and the people criminalized, while their homes were either destroyed or about to be demolished, and tens of thousands of New Orleans residents were being shipped by plane and bus to nearly all the fifty states.

FRIDAY, SEPTEMBER 2

Christina's mother drove us to Houston. It felt terrible leaving Louisiana. We wondered if we'd be able to come back. Everything seemed to be up in the air. Although we'd been traveling all night, I couldn't sleep. Instead, I wrote these words:

> I just evacuated from New Orleans. If you ever wondered if the U.S. government would treat the internally displaced the same way they treat Haitian refugees or Somali refugees, the answer is yes, if those who are displaced are poor, Black, and from the South.
>
> While the rich escaped New Orleans, those with nowhere to go and no way to get there were left behind. Adding salt to the wound, the local and national media have spent the last week demonizing those left behind. As someone that loves New Orleans and the people in it, this is the part of this tragedy that hurts the most....
>
> New Orleans's hurricane-ravaged population was transformed by the media into criminals. As if taking a stereo from a store is a greater crime than the governmental neglect and incompetence that did billions of dollars of damage and destroyed a city. This media focus is a deliberate tactic. It works in the same way as a focus during the 1980s on "welfare queens" and "super-predators" obscured the simultaneous and larger crimes of the Savings and Loan scams and mass layoffs. The hyper-exploited people of New Orleans are being used as a scapegoat.
>
> City, state and national politicians are the real criminals here. Since at least the mid-1800s, the danger faced by flooding to New Orleans has been widely known. The flood of 1927, which, like this week's events, was more about politics and racism than any kind of natural disaster, illustrated exactly the danger faced. Yet government

officials have consistently refused to spend the money to protect this poor, majority-Black city.

While the army corps of engineers and others warned of the urgent impending danger to New Orleans and put forward proposals for funding to reinforce and protect the city, the Bush administration, in every year since 2001, has cut or refused to fund New Orleans flood control, and ignored scientists' warnings of increased hurricanes as a result of global warming. Congress, since at least the 1990s, also refused to stand up for funding for levees or for badly needed coastal restoration. As the dangers rose with the floodlines, the lack of a rescue from the federal government dramatized vividly the callous disregard by our elected leaders.

In the coming months, billions of dollars will likely flood into New Orleans. This money can either be spent to usher in a "New Deal" for the city, with public investment, creation of stable union jobs, new schools, cultural programs and housing restoration, or the city can be "rebuilt and revitalized" to a shell of its former self, with newer hotels, more casinos, and with chain stores and theme parks replacing the former neighborhoods, cultural centers and corner jazz clubs.

Long before Katrina, New Orleans was hit by a hurricane of poverty, racism, disinvestment, deindustrialization and corruption. Simply the damage from this pre-Katrina hurricane will take billions to repair.

Now that the money will be flowing in, and the world's eyes are focused on Katrina, it's vital that progressive-minded people take this opportunity to fight for a rebuilding with justice. New Orleans is a special place, and we need to fight for its rebirth.

I emailed these words to friends and acquaintances, and they were widely forwarded. Soon I heard from friends dispersed by Katrina and from allies around the world. Everyone wanted to do something, but no one knew what to do. Those from New Orleans were traumatized. Even now, several years later, many still are.

ORGANIZING BEGINS

New Orleans is a word-of-mouth town. The way to find out about parties, secondlines, jazz funerals, and other events is from friends. In an increasingly disconnected world, New Orleans had always felt different—more concrete, more real. But after the levees broke, our communication network broke down, too. There were dozens of people I usually saw at least once a week around town whom I suddenly had no way of contacting. Even cell phones from the New Orleans area code were nonfunctioning for most of the first couple of weeks after the flood.

During those first weeks, many people forwarded emails with lists of friends and acquaintances from whom they'd had news, trying to track who was okay. Websites and blogs attempted to compile these lists. Despite these efforts, the sheer scale of the event and its aftermath was almost crushing. Thoughts of people for whom there was no information were overwhelming. When people from elsewhere asked, I just said, yes, as far as I know, everyone is all right. I couldn't really bring myself to think about it further than that.

Seeking some way to help, I went to the River Road shelter in Baton Rouge as part of a project initiated by Families and Friends of Louisiana's Incarcerated Children (FFLIC), an advocacy group for incarcerated youth and their families. FFLIC had originated in 2001 as a parents' support group within the Juvenile Justice Project of Louisiana (JJPL), which was founded in part through a grant from the Southern Poverty Law Center in 1997. FFLIC's mission of supporting the family members of young people caught up in Louisiana's prison pipeline complemented JJPL's legal work on behalf of incarcerated youth.

After the storm, FFLIC devoted their efforts to helping displaced New Orleans residents reconnect with loved ones who had gotten lost in the labyrinth of Louisiana's corrections system. At the time, FFLIC estimated that for the approximately 240 kids in state custody, only 6 or 7 parents had been able to track down their children.

In the River Road shelter, I met people who were desperately trying to find a sister, brother, child, or other family member. Those who had been picked up for minor infractions in the days before the hurricane ended up being shipped to prisons upstate, and were subsequently lost in the system. Most of the people I spoke with in the shelter just wanted to get a message to a loved one—"Tell him that we've been looking for him, that we made it out of New Orleans, and that we love him," said Angela, an evacuated New Orleans East resident.

Shortly after the evacuation, Barbara Bush, walking through the Houston Astrodome, which served as a shelter for thousands of displaced

New Orleanians, famously declared how fortunate the shelter residents were. "Almost everyone I've talked to says, 'We're going to move to Houston. What I'm hearing, which is sort of scary, is they all want to stay in Texas…so many of the people in the arena here, you know, were underprivileged anyway, so this, this is working very well for them.'"[12]

In the world outside of the former first lady's imagination, evacuees were feeling anything but sheltered. One woman in the River Road shelter told me she'd barely slept since she arrived in the shelter system. "I sleep with one eye open," she said. "It's not safe in there."

A week after the storm, the Department of Homeland Security estimated that 235,000 evacuees had been placed in 750 temporary shelters in 17 states. There were widespread reports of racism and discrimination in Red Cross shelters, especially in Lafayette, Lake Charles, and Baton Rouge. According to Jodie Escobedo, a physician from California who volunteered in the Baton Rouge shelters, "Local officials, including politicians, select Red Cross personnel, and an especially well-placed but small segment of the Louisiana medical community have managed to get themselves into positions of power, where their prejudices result in the hoarding of supplies, vilification of the needy, and substandard treatment of volunteers and refugees alike."

As a medical volunteer with a close-up view, Escobedo continued to paint a devastating portrait:

> I witnessed Red Cross staff treated abusively by shelter administration who also expressed contempt for the sheltered population. Dental abscesses abounded and when several cases of small, individual cases of Scope were donated, Red Cross staff was told not to distribute it because "They will drink it and get drunk." At the River Center the Red Cross hoarded hygiene supplies and basic necessities on a giant loading dock while kids could not go to school because they had no pants or shoes, babies drank from dirty baby bottles, people slept on the floor and donated clothes sat inaccessible. I tried for four days to get access to the Red Cross storehouse of hand sanitizer which was unfortunately off-site.[13]

Whitney Fry, an employee with the relief organization Save the Children, expressed shame at her profiting from the disaster: "We're getting a big per diem, on top of our salaries," she confessed to me. Frustrated with her experience with the organization, she continued, "Things take forever to be approved—sometimes so long that by the time we have the support we need, the effort has passed. There's so much money behind us—we can do whatever we want and don't have to worry about funding, but it feeds lifestyles that are much more demanding than I'd hope relief workers' would be."

Brooklyn-based journalist and community organizer Rosa Clemente (who ran for vice president on the Green Party ticket in 2008) visited shelters from Baton Rouge to Houston, attempting to provide support for evacuees and help get their stories out. Clemente described harrowing sights, including a National Guard soldier pointing a gun at a five-year-old. When she complained, Clemente herself was briefly placed under arrest. She described stores in the vicinity of shelters with signs stating that shelter residents were not welcome, and reported that people in the shelters were completely cut off from news about the outside world. "There are three TVs for three thousand people. We asked everyone we spoke with in the shelter what they thought about Kanye West's remarks [when he said on national television 'George Bush doesn't care about Black people'], and none of them had heard of it!"

In the River Road shelter, I recognized Chui Clark, an activist who worked on racial justice and anti-police brutality issues. "This is a lily-white operation," he told me. "You have white FEMA and Red Cross workers watching us like we're some kind of amusement." Despite repeated assurances from Red Cross and government officials that housing placements were being made, the population of the Baton Rouge shelters did not appear to be decreasing, according to Clark. "You have new arrivals all the time. Folks who were staying with families for a week or two are getting kicked out and they got nowhere else to go."

On September 3, while the city was still flooded, the Community Labor United coalition released a powerful declaration: "The people of New Orleans will not go quietly into the night, scattering across this country to become homeless in countless other cities while federal relief funds are funneled into rebuilding casinos, hotels, chemical plants and the wealthy white districts of New Orleans...."

The document announced the founding of the People's Hurricane Relief Fund and Organizing Committee (PHRF). PHRF united individuals

from New Orleans and around the United States in a Black-led coalition
to engage in a principled, radical struggle for the reconstruction of the
city. PHRF's work shaped much of the organizing in the coming months,
although over time, their work was disrupted by both internal and exter-
nal conflicts.

Criminal justice organizing also gathered momentum during those
first months, some of it linked with PHRF. "Our first priority was to help
those individuals who had been in Orleans Parish Prison prior to Katrina,
many of whom were being held illegally for minor, non-violent offenses,"
explained Norris Henderson, one of the key conveners of activists from different organizations that came together via PHRF to form a coalition called
Safe Streets/Strong Communities. A former inmate of the Louisiana State
Prison at Angola and Orleans Parish Prison (OPP), Henderson spent
twenty-seven years behind bars for a murder he didn't commit, until evidence proved his innocence and he was released in 2001. He was an organizer while behind bars, and continues to lead and inspire now that he
is free. Shortly after his release, Henderson founded VOTE: Voice of the
Ex-offender, an organization dedicated to building civic engagement and
political power for formerly incarcerated persons.

In the mainstream discourse on criminal justice, it is often said there
are two sides—those who advocate for prisoners and those who advocate
for victims. But, of course, the reality is that many people who have faced
prison time also know what it is like to face street crime and other violence. By calling themselves Safe Streets/Strong Communities, this new
organization made the point that mass incarceration doesn't make our
streets safer; it breaks up community, and real safety and security come
from strong communities.

Henderson lost his son to violence. The young man was killed three
years before Henderson's release. Despite whatever desire for vengeance
he may feel, Henderson knows that the solutions to our society's problems
are always more complicated than a desire for revenge. "In a fair and just
society," he said, "you can't create laws based on how you feel at the worst
moment of your life."

Another main organizer of Safe Streets was lawyer, organizer, and
criminal justice activist Xochitl Bervera, who articulated the coalition's
core focus: "Rising from the devastation of Katrina, we have an amazing

opportunity to rebuild a truly new and genuine system of public safety for New Orleans." Bervera, an inspiring leader with a brilliant strategic mind, had moved to New Orleans after graduating law school in New York City. She started as a legal worker with the Juvenile Justice Project of Louisiana, but soon moved on to organizing work with FFLIC, working directly with family members of incarcerated young people. After Katrina, she helped bring together the criminal justice coalition that founded Safe Streets.

In the transition from the immediate crisis of Katrina to the long-term catastrophe that persists in the city, Safe Streets focused its energy on ensuring that the people in communities most affected were shaping the organization's priorities and making the decisions. They did this through diligent outreach. Before Safe Streets was founded, many of its eventual members were organizing in the shelters, locating family members of incarcerated people, and offering assistance. Others went to the prisons to try to track down folks who had been lost in the system. After the initial crisis of the storm had subsided, they went door to door in communities like Central City, the site of the most violence in those early months, and spoke to people in the community about police issues. They combined this grassroots organizing strategy—working directly with the incarcerated, formerly incarcerated, and their family members—with political pressure and legal support.

Safe Streets has been a vital leader in the work for a just recovery for New Orleans. In direct response to pressure from Safe Streets, the city's entire public defender system was overhauled, and the private contracting of public defense—with some of the most deplorable lawyers in the city—was brought to an end. The New Orleans Indigent Defense Board was converted into an independent office with full-time, on-staff, dedicated attourneys. After Safe Streets turned its focus to policing issues, the city approved and funded the office of an independent monitor to oversee the New Orleans Police Department. The city council also began to consider downsizing OPP, as well as reducing the sheriff's budget, and tying funding to reform and greater accountability.

The main staffers of Safe Streets in those first years after the storm, in addition to Henderson and Bervera, were Ursula Price, Althea Francois, Seung Hong, and Evelyn Lynn. They were soon joined by Yvette Thierry, Robert Goodman, and Rosana Cruz. Collectively and individually, this group of organizers has been a source of knowledge and inspiration for me, and they have had a lasting influence on the city.

When Bervera moved to Atlanta in 2007, Cruz, a U.S.-born Cuban originally from Miami, joined Henderson as co-director of Safe Streets. Cruz was also among the founders of the New Orleans Workers' Center for Racial Justice (another organization that began as a PHRF working group) and had worked for the National Immigration Law Center (NILC) and Amnesty International. In 2009, she continued her work with Henderson as an associate director of VOTE.

As with many post-Katrina organizations, Safe Streets has by now transitioned into a new era with different staff. Most of those who started Safe Streets have moved on to other organizations, but their work has left a tangible and inspiring legacy.

SECONDLINE PARADE. PHOTO BY ABDUL AZIZ.

CHAPTER THREE

Still Got Me in Disbelief: New Orleans After the Storm

I've got New Orleans on my mind, I know that one day we gon' rise…
Sit on my porch on Congress and Villere
Seeing half of the block boarded up be killing me
My pants sagging so authorities grilling me
But I ain't here to hustle man, I'm here to rebuild these streets
I understand cause the murderers here with me
So now I gotta watch out for the criminals and police
Some neighborhoods still got me in disbelief
Cause ain't a fucking thing being done to give people relief
A lot of my people trying to make it back to New Orleans
But the roadblock home ain't what it seems
Our government dropped the ball on us
But when election time come they quick to call on us

From "New Orleans on My Mind" by T.L.

It took weeks for the city to dry out. Just when the water had finally drained from the Lower Ninth Ward, another hurricane reached category five status in the Gulf. Hurricane Rita, the tenth hurricane of the 2005 season, made landfall near the Louisiana-Texas border, causing massive damage to coastal communities. Although most of the storm's damage was felt far west of the city, the still-damaged levees could not handle the surge of water from Rita's outer bands of rain, and the Lower Ninth Ward and parts of Gentilly flooded again.

New Orleans itself was a health hazard. For months after Katrina, the ground in many neighborhoods was covered with a layer of black soot, the residue of the toxic water that had submerged the city. The National Guard and other military and police teams had broken into almost every house in the city's flood zones to search for bodies. Most homes had broken doors and spray-painted marks on the front that indicated the date the soldiers had come, the unit they were part of, and whether any bodies had been found.

There were practically no conversations that didn't reference Katrina. The storm defined every aspect of life in the city, not just the large-scale damage done but also in the small details. Traffic lights hadn't been fixed. Street signs were gone. Packs of abandoned dogs roamed the streets. Boats sat at random intersections around the city. Cars destroyed by flooding were everywhere, with hundreds parked under the highway overpass at Claiborne Avenue. Walking in your own neighborhood in those initial few months, you couldn't believe you were in New Orleans. You couldn't believe you were in the United States.

After the storm, there was a new sense of closeness among many New Orleanians. It seemed briefly as though everyone living here had experienced the same loss, at the same time. For those back in the city, at times it felt like differences of race and class had washed away.

However, the losses were not equal. Certain neighborhoods—those near the lake or the drainage canals, especially if they were on lower ground—were devastated, while others remained mostly untouched. Most of the areas that took water were at least 60 percent African American. With the exception of the Lakeview neighborhood—a white, middle-to-upper-class part of town that was devastated by fifteen feet of water—the neighborhoods that flooded the most, like New Orleans East, the Lower Ninth Ward, and Gentilly, were 80 to 95 percent African American. In the Seventh, Eighth, and Ninth Wards, a street called St. Claude functioned as a dividing line. On one side, the mostly African American neighborhoods flooded. On the other side, closer to the river, the mostly white neighborhoods stayed dry.

The French Quarter, which lies along the natural high ground of the Mississippi River (the "sliver by the river" or "isle of denial" as it's also sometimes called) was unaffected by flooding, and in fact, some bars and restaurants (running on a generator) reopened the day after the storm, while other parts of the city were still under fifteen feet of water.

FREE-MARKET TRIAGE

In the days after the storm, doctors in New Orleans's Memorial Medical Center performed a grotesque distortion of triage. Originally a battlefield term, triage, as applied to an emergency situation with limited medical resources, refers to the prioritizing of patients for treatment based on urgency of need. No one on the Memorial Medical Center team had any experience providing health care under such extreme circumstances, and their actions ran counter to all standards and protocols of triage. Instead of devoting resources to those with critical need and delaying care for those able to survive without it, as is standard practice, they assigned patients a status such that those who needed the most urgent care were last in line for medical attention. Several patients died under circumstances that are still hotly debated today, but eyewitness testimony indicates that doctors deliberately killed several patients by administering lethal doses of drugs, including to at least one patient who did not have a life-threatening illness.[1]

This perversion of triage reflects, on a larger scale, how the U.S. government treated New Orleans. The mostly undamaged French Quarter was the first neighborhood to be cleaned up and have its electricity and water services restored, while public housing was shuttered and slated for demolition. Federal dollars were assigned to homeowners but not to renters. People who had been convicted of minor offenses were left for months in maximum-security prisons, with no access to legal representation, while evidence of murder by police and white vigilantes was ignored. Public schools were closed and teachers were fired, while hundreds of millions of dollars were made available for rebuilding contracts to multinational corporations.

Immediately after Katrina, everything happened in hyperspeed, as those with political and financial power saw an opportunity to remake the city according to their vision. The post-Katrina period stands as a prime study in what Naomi Klein called "disaster capitalism"—the practice by elites of exploiting a time of collective trauma (war, natural disaster) to implement neoliberal free-market policies such as the privatization of public resources.

For observers, especially in the United States, the post-Katrina profiteering stood as a warning. Although more egregious and damaging policies have been carried out around the world from Argentina to Iraq, New Orleans is the starkest example of this type of greed and rapaciousness in the United States, and has come to stand for the waning of U.S. dominance and the fundamental shakiness of free-market economics. As housing advocate James Perry and scholar Melissa Harris Lacewell wrote:

> In 2008, the sub-prime lending market crashed, national housing values plummeted, unemployment rose sharply, and the stock market

crashed. When federal levees failed, New Orleans flooded with lake water. When federal oversight of banking failed, the nation flooded with bad debts and entered into an economic recession. Like New Orleanians after Katrina, Americans in communities throughout the United States faced disasters of home loss, job loss, and displacement. We are all living in Katrina Nation now. And it is time to confront the lessons of New Orleans or risk that our national recovery will be similarly delayed and incomplete...[2]

Disaster response has far-reaching political repercussions. In Nicaragua, corruption and theft of post-earthquake disaster aid in 1972 contributed to the eventual fall of the Somoza dictatorship. Faulty federal response to the 1985 earthquake that hit Mexico City ignited a grassroots movement in Mexico that helped end almost ninety years of one-party rule. The 1927 flooding of the Mississippi River helped elect Huey P. Long governor of Louisiana.

Two weeks after Katrina, as Bush administration approval numbers began to fall in the polls, FEMA director Michael Brown resigned. New Orleans police superintendent Eddie Compass soon followed suit. In January 2006, Marsha Evans, the president of Red Cross, was forced out. Governor Kathleen Blanco was so unpopular she didn't run for election in 2007. The severity of this disaster was created by politics, the "recovery" has been guided by politics, and the consequences have been felt in politics. But as politicians came and went, the policies stayed the same.

When I saw the floodwaters rising in New Orleans, I anticipated that poor folks would be cut out of the reconstruction money. What has surprised me is the extent to which the entire city has been left out. While some local elites have profited individually, on a deeper, structural level—from levees to housing aid to business loans—the money necessary to rebuild New Orleans simply never came.

Part of the justification for the federal abandonment of the city is local corruption. "The money will just be embezzled or squandered," was a widely repeated refrain. This assertion was also leveled against the people of New Orleans, who were accused of "wasting" their aid from FEMA and the Red Cross at liquor stores and strip clubs.

However, blaming corruption is a convenient tactic for diverting attention from the corporate agenda that drove New Orleans's recovery efforts.

The politicians and think tanks that pushed this agenda never planned to help and support poor people. Their agenda was to cut funding for cities, and they were, and continue to be, especially wary of supporting a Democrat-voting, culturally liberated, majority–African American city. In devastated New Orleans, free-market strategists saw a blank slate, and took advantage of the situation to make their vision into reality, with little concern for whoever stood in their way.

We have more than our share of corrupt politicians in New Orleans, but our problem is not politicians wasting recovery aid. Nor do our problems come from disaster victims who misspent FEMA checks. Our problems were entrenched long before the levees broke.

The truth about the devastation of New Orleans is akin to a murder mystery in which the real killer is never brought in for questioning by the police. New Orleans was a victim of a hurricane of greed and profit, not a natural disaster. The greed of the oil companies put us at risk. Louisiana's off-coast drilling caused coastal erosion, which left the Gulf Coast with less natural protection against tropical storms, and the byproducts of oil have contributed to global warming, which, in turn, increased the size and frequency of hurricanes. Since 1932 the Louisiana coast has lost an area the size of Delaware—mostly due to the effects of oil exploration—and it's still hemorrhaging about twenty-four square miles a year.[3] And this litany of damage doesn't include the unquantified catastrophe caused by a blowout at a BP oil platform off the coast of Louisiana in April 2010.

Twenty-five percent of domestic oil production and half of U.S. refining capacity come from the Gulf coast. Louisiana also provides 30 percent of all seafood for the continental United States. Louisiana fishermen brought in 90.4 million pounds of shrimp in 2008, or 44 percent of U.S. production, and 207 million pounds of oysters, more than a third of the U.S. total. The Port of South Louisiana is the nation's busiest. Combined with the Port of New Orleans, the two handle about 300 million tons of cargo a year.[4]

New Orleans and the Gulf Coast have brought tremendous value to the U.S. economy, but the people who live here not only haven't received the economic benefit, they have also been branded as freeloaders when they've asked the federal government to build safe levees. They have been placed in danger from the environmental effects of oil exploration, and then blamed for being so irresponsible as to live in a dangerous—yet valuable—place.

Multinational corporations made millions in the so-called reconstruction after Katrina, while they sub-contracted to companies that paid employees below minimum wage. Contractors, sub-contractors, and sub-sub-contractors victimized immigrant workers with low pay and hazardous working conditions. The federal government refused to allocate the money for sturdier levees and coastal restoration to protect our city—so we still don't feel safe behind the levees. The whole United States has been enriched by the art and culture of New Orleans, while the people who have created and sustained it have either been demonized or treated as though they did not exist.

SLOW REBUILDING AND RECOVERY

Contractors were everywhere in the months after the storm. But years later, rebuilding has still not come to some neighborhoods.

Eighty percent of housing in the city took in water. The city needed massive support to rebuild on the scale necessary for repairing such overwhelming devastation. In terms of garbage hauling alone, post-storm New Orleans needed to dispose of 22 million tons of debris, about fifteen times the volume removed after the Twin Towers fell in New York City.[5] With adequate funding, this work could have stimulated the city's economy and provided well-paid jobs in the reconstruction sector. But that was not on the Bush administration's agenda. Instead, immediately after the storm, President George W. Bush suspended the Davis-Bacon Act, which provides legal protections for employees. Rather than helping rebuild the local economy, he gave most of the rebuilding contracts to his out-of-state political allies, which opened the door to low wages, corporate profiteering, and exploitative working conditions.

The so-called recovery was the true disaster—man-made rather than natural, with more damaging aftereffects than the hurricane itself—and it is important to heed the lessons from this. Cornel West has called it "Hurricane Povertina."[6] Poet Suheir Hammad has referred to the "survivors of the rescue."

Mississippi faced the brunt of the storm, not Louisiana. We were hit by something worse, a confluence of forces that barraged New Orleans and its diaspora: a "disaster-industrial complex." This coinage describes the perfect storm created by the greed, opportunism, and short-sightedness of the disaster profiteers. The list of those who gained from our loss is large, and it includes everyone from the heavily armed employees of Wackenhut Security and Blackwater (now Xe) to the often well-meaning but ineffectual bureaucrats of Red Cross and FEMA, and from the multinational companies such as Halliburton that saw an opportunity for unfettered profit to the privatization "missionaries" who saw an opportunity to conduct experiments in free-market extremism.

There's no doubt that corporations were first in line for the profits. Days after the storm, Halliburton's Kellogg Brown & Root subsidiary (KBR) received a $500 million U.S. Navy contract for emergency repairs at Gulf Coast naval and marine facilities damaged by Hurricane Katrina.[7] Years later, many New Orleans homeowners are still waiting for even a few thousand dollars of rebuilding assistance. In most cases, renters were cut out of housing aid entirely.

The largest program for distributing federal rebuilding money, Louisiana Road Home, was initiated by the state in 2006 to give federal funding to those with homes damaged by Katrina and Rita, and it was a catastrophe. Although by 2010 more than one hundred twenty thousand homeowners had received more than eight billion dollars in aid,[8] the program was plagued with controversy and problems. The money was slow to come, with most not awarded until 2008 or later; it also went disproportionately to white and privileged applicants, and excluded renters.

According to a 2008 study by PolicyLink, 81 percent of those who received Road Home grants had insufficient resources to cover their damages. Statewide, the average Road Home recipient fell about $35,000 short of the money they needed to rebuild their home. In New Orleans, that gap rose to $55,000; in the Lower Ninth Ward, to more than $75,000. In addition, African American households on average had a shortfall almost 35 percent greater than white households.[9]

One New Orleanian, discussing the Road Home program, explained the process:

> This Road Home program, when you go in, you are guilty until proven innocent. You are guilty of lying that you own a home. You're fingerprinted, you're mug-shot, they spend—there's 67 something steps that a person goes through before they get to a closing. It was 78 steps. They whittled it down, because of complaints…then you have the auditing

agencies....They were afraid that people who didn't actually own homes would be getting Road Home money. And so people who were without any of their possessions, or their bank notes or anything, can't really prove that they owned things...you'd have a 90-year-old World War Two veteran go in, who's lived in his house for 70 years, and come out with nothing....The Road to Hell, is what we call it.[10]

A CHOICE BETWEEN RECONSTRUCTION AND EXPLOITATION

Although the issues highlighted by Katrina were not new, the storm did serve to open a crucial debate. The Bush administration's abdication of responsibility, the images broadcast internationally of a people abandoned, and the escalating chaos all set the stage for a debate over the characteristics of relief and reconstruction. One side pushed an agenda encompassing the corporatization, militarization, and privatization of aid, and the criminalization of those on the receiving end. On the other side were activists and community organizations committed to a fair and just recovery, one that also attempted to redress the "disaster before the disaster" of structural problems caused by systemic racism. People historically exploited and underserved by our government were fighting for local control of both the decisions and the finances behind the reconstruction of their city.

Unfortunately, many aid groups actually ended up contributing to these systemic problems. Although Red Cross, FEMA, religious charities, and others have helped Gulf Coast residents and are, to a great extent, filled with well-meaning and hard-working individuals, any effort at aid that does not address the deeper structural problems actually contributes to reinforcing those structures. In other words, despite best efforts, they become part of the problem.

In line with the Bush administration's goal of privatizing social services and increasing the role of religious institutions, churches and other religious charities—from the Salvation Army to the Scientologists—coordinated many relief efforts. Some groups provided vital aid, but their overall effort contributed to the repositioning of relief as a nongovernmental and apolitical function.

Before the storm, New Orleans was already one of the many U.S. cities abandoned by the industry and manufacturing jobs that had made up its economic base, leaving it with mostly low-paying, transient, and in-secure jobs in the service economy. Las Vegas also has a tourism-based economy, but through strong unions, workers in that city have managed to make its service-industry jobs among the best in the United States. New Orleans, in the middle of the nonunion South, is riddled with minimum-wage jobs, with no benefits and no job security.

After the storm, the labor movement pledged hundreds of thousands of dollars toward relief. Individual union locals, such as SEIU-1199 Ohio, pledged money to grassroots projects such as the People's Hurricane Relief Fund (PHRF). Union organizers and activists came down to volunteer with community groups.

Despite these efforts at relief, the labor movement as a whole seemed oblivious to the political potential of this moment in time. The financial and political support of the labor movement could have helped create a union city deep in the traditionally nonunion South. Instead, labor (both local and national) remained on the sidelines.

As labor activist, author, and scholar Bill Fletcher noted,

> In the aftermath of the Hurricane Katrina disaster on the Gulf Coast, organized labor restricted its role to providing relief (which it did so generously), yet it did nothing to build broad awareness, let alone a fightback, to address the deeper socio-economic roots of the Katrina disaster, specifically the racial and class oppression on the Gulf Coast and the economic policies followed by the Bush administration.

Fletcher also noted that labor repeated this misstep a few years later.

> In the fall of 2008, in the midst of the financial collapse and the tsunami of foreclosures and layoffs, organized labor was anemic in its response. Instead of mass demonstrations…labor's response took the form of press statements, emails, and web postings. This lack of an ac-tivist response ceded the ground to right-wing populists who have tapped into the intense anger felt by many white workers and profes-sional-managerial employees.[11]

Meanwhile, the administration's recovery agenda received behind-the-scenes support from old-money New Orleans families, a small, mostly white group that lives in Uptown (several of them on Audubon Place, a small, private street near Tulane University and Audubon Park).

Tulane University historian Lance Hill, author of *The Deacons for Defense*, a definitive book about civil rights movement icons, stayed in his Uptown home during the storm and in the weeks after. Hill looks the part of an Uptown professor, with his full beard and dark suit, and his Uptown residence and university connections allow him access to the worlds of New Orleans's white elites. But unlike many white men in the city, Hill is dedicated to speaking out against racial injustice in his community. Outraged by what he saw developing, Hill wrote these words in October 2005:

> Shocking as it may sound, the idea of purging New Orleans of its African American majority is appealing to some people. After all, proposals to forcibly exclude African Americans from the city in the 1950s in order to make New Orleans an all-white enclave enjoyed legitimacy and support in the same respected social circles that later went on to lead the Citizens' Council movement and other forms of resistance to integration. And today on the streets of New Orleans I am hearing many members of the same old moneyed "carnival royalty" families openly arguing that Katrina provides an opening to depose Black majority rule. These sentiments are deeply rooted in the psyche of those Southern whites who still bemoan the post–Civil War federal occupation of the South, and recall with pride the day that their Confederate forbearers overthrew bi-racial Reconstruction with the Southern Compromise of 1877. Today that situation is turned on its head as federal authorities prepare to "occupy" the city with a different form of reconstruction—only this time it will likely have the unintended consequence of restoring white majority rule. Even now, during the process of recovery, many of the city's leading businesses and institutions have brought in thousands of unskilled workers from outside Louisiana, while unemployed Black New Orleanians sit idle in relocation centers.[12]

Just days after the storm, James Reiss, scion of an old-money New Orleans family, told a journalist, "Those who want to see this city rebuilt want to see it done in a completely different way: demographically, geographically, and politically. I'm not just speaking for myself here. The way we've been living is not going to happen again, or we're out."[13] Reiss—who made a fortune as a supplier of electronics systems to shipbuilders—was one of a small group of local businessmen that met with Mayor C. Ray Nagin in Dallas only days after the flooding of New Orleans.

Reiss was also among those who took early steps to militarize the disaster, hiring former Israeli soldiers from a company called Instinctive Shooting International to guard his block on the exclusive Uptown street of Audubon Place in the days after the storm. Journalist Jeremy Scahill reported that the soldiers told him "they had served as professional soldiers in the Israeli military, and one boasted of having participated in the invasion of Lebanon. 'We have been fighting the Palestinians all day, every day, our whole lives,' one of them tells me. 'Here in New Orleans, we are not guarding from terrorists.' Then, tapping on his machine gun, he says, 'Most Americans, when they see these things, that's enough to scare them.'"[14]

The large-scale militarization of the disaster happened almost immediately. Notorious for their role in the occupation and "reconstruction" of Iraq, the private security firm Blackwater was among the first disaster profiteers to be ushered into New Orleans. Deputized by the governor, Blackwater guards were free to shoot to kill with no consequences. Along with Wackenhut and other such firms, these organizations represented the new approach to relief and reconstruction: security first, relief later. "This is a trend. You're going to see a lot more guys like us in these situations," a Blackwater employee told Scahill.

In one day, a couple of weeks just after the storm, I saw Chicago police camped out on a bar on Bourbon Street, Wackenhut security convoys riding down the highway, the Israeli security company guarding an Uptown street, and vehicles with National Guard soldiers patrolling in between. During this same time period, the city also had Blackwater guarding FEMA sites, and police forces from the DEA, INS, Louisiana state police, New Orleans police, and other agencies, including visiting cops from as far away as New York state. And, unreported by the corporate media, armed white vigilante gangs were patrolling the West Bank.

The storm and the recovery process changed the demographics of New Orleans in gender as well as race. The thousands of contractors and laborers that arrived from across the country—in addition to National Guard soldiers, police agencies, security guards, and others—were overwhelmingly male. Because most public schools remained closed for at least the fall semester, the city saw very few families with kids under the age of seventeen. Women who returned to New Orleans often reported feeling uncomfortable and unsafe.

Christina Kucera, the Planned Parenthood organizer with whom I evacuated, observed, "Issues of safety and shelter are intricately tied to gender. This has hit women particularly hard. It's the collapse of community. We've lost neighbors and systems within our communities that helped keep us safe." Kucera, a passionate advocate, listed some of the problems:

> There have been reports of rapes and assaults before evacuation and in the shelters. And that's just the beginning. There are continuing safety and health care needs. There are women who were planning on having children who now no longer have the stability to raise a child and want an abortion, but they have no money, and nowhere to go to get one. Six of the thirteen rape crisis centers in Louisiana were closed by the hurricane.

In early 2006, Shana griffin, a Black feminist, mother of a sixteen-year-old, social justice activist, and researcher based in New Orleans, co-founded the Women's Health & Justice Initiative (WHJI) and the New Orleans Women's Health Clinic, both INCITE affiliates. Partly in response to the story of a local musician's rape in the days after the storm, she wrote the following powerful message: "We have to have some form of community accountability for the sexual and physical violence women and children endured. I'm not interested in developing an action plan to rebuild or organize a people's agenda in New Orleans without a gender analysis and a demand for community accountability."

TRUTH AND RECONCILIATION

What actually happened in the days and weeks after the storm? We need our version of South Africa's Truth and Reconciliation Commission—a grand project with resources and funding to sort through the many narratives to find a larger truth and begin the process of both healing and justice.

We don't even know exactly who died. After September 11, 2001, the *New York Times* launched "Portraits of Grief," an ongoing series dedicated to documenting everyone who had died in the World Trade Center on the day the buildings fell. *Times* writers attempted to contact the relatives or friends of each of the 2,749 people who are thought to have died in the collapse of the towers. They wrote 2,310 full portraits until the last page ran in March 2003. This was a massive dedication of staff and time and resources. New Orleans received no such effort; no team of researchers was assigned to find out who died and what their stories were.

It is estimated that at least 1,800 people died due to Hurricane Katrina. Most of these deaths were in New Orleans, including 1,000 people killed in the Lower Ninth Ward alone.[15] But there is no agreed-upon method as to which deaths are counted. People who died outside of the Gulf Coast from injuries related to the storm and its aftermath are often not included in the totals. Suicides and other deaths related to the evacuation are also generally not counted. Most importantly, the recovery of bodies was so slow and incomplete that there are doubtless some who have not been counted because their bodies were never found. For all these reasons, the numbers of those who died are approximate.

New Orleans has an elected coroner—an eighty-year-old who trained as a gynecologist and has been in office since 1974—who was, by most accounts, unprepared to deal with a disaster of this magnitude. However, even the best-funded and most experienced coroner would have had difficulty managing hundreds of bodies all at once. And with this task, as with every other aspect of the city's recovery, the federal support and funding were not there, nor did they come. Decades of attacks on the very idea of government had paid off. The government could no longer be relied on to provide even the most basic kind of social aid—the very purpose for which it was designed.

A 2005 Gallup poll reported that, even adjusting for differences in income, white and Black New Orleanians experienced this disaster in deeply different ways. Blacks were more likely to have feared for their lives (63 percent vs. 39 percent), to have been separated from family members for at least a day (55 percent vs. 45 percent), to have gone without food for at least a day (53 percent vs. 24 percent), and to have spent at least one night in an emergency shelter (34 percent vs. 13 percent).[16]

When former FEMA director Michael Brown's emails from that period were made public, they revealed in stunning detail how little the agency cared about what was happening in New Orleans. "If you'll look at my lovely FEMA attire you'll really vomit. I am a fashion god," reads a characteristically lighthearted and gossipy email from the day after the hurricane hit. Other emails showed Brown and his staffers to have been more concerned with his dinner reservations in Baton Rouge and arranging for a dog sitter at his house than with anything happening in New Orleans.[17]

Two weeks after the storm, I was back in the city, traveling around freely with the aid of white privilege and a press pass, while Black residents of the city were being harassed daily by the police and National Guard. Entire neighborhoods of the city were still wet, but the natural high ground by the Mississippi River had not flooded.

Walking through the streets, I saw more city buses rolling through poor areas of town than I had ever seen pre-hurricane. Rather than serving the community, however, these buses were filled with soldiers. New Orleans provided a blueprint for this militarized style of relief. Thousands of soldiers patrolled the streets, yet no one, it seemed, was performing vital, basic tasks such as cleaning up. A Midcity resident complained to me, "Why don't they send some of these troops with tools to rebuild instead of just weapons? I guess they don't want it rebuilt."

THE NUMBERS IN THE NEW NEW ORLEANS

In those initial months, it seemed that almost everyone had left. Although the city had been evacuated quickly, with tens of thousands of people given one-way tickets to destinations across the United States, there was no corresponding big rush of people back into the city. But incrementally, day by day, people came back. Often it was a protracted, multi-phase process. For example, first a homeowner might return for a visit to look at their house. Then they would start arranging repairs, set up a trailer to live in while rebuilding their house, perhaps spending most nights in Baton Rouge or another city in the region, and commuting in for a day of house gutting. The whole time they would have to battle intransigent insurers and loan companies as well as FEMA and other federal agencies. Then, if they were able to win those battles and get the money to repair their home, and if a contractor didn't take their money and run, perhaps a year later (if they were lucky) they might finally be back living in it.

As of the writing of this book, the 2010 census had not yet been completed. The New Orleans population numbers are still disputed (and may not be fully resolved by the census results). But here is what is known: pre-Katrina, according to census figures, there were about 455,000 people in the city (others set the figure a bit higher). After lobbying from Mayor

Nagin and others, the U.S. census repeatedly reevaluated and raised their estimates of New Orleans's post-Katrina population from 239,000 to as high as 355,000 in a 2010 report (estimating for July 2009). Using even these highest estimates leaves a difference of about 100,000 residents. However, that number doesn't take into account the many current residents who were not here pre-Katrina. In the absence of definitive statistics, observers estimate that new residents could number 50,000 or more, which would mean that 150,000 pre-Katrina residents have not returned—about a third of the population.[18]

Add to that figure the New Orleanians who are in the city, but are still not home. They fall into the category that international human rights organizations describe as internally displaced, and no study that I'm aware of has attempted to count their numbers. The guiding principles of internal displacement, as recognized by the international community, entail more than to simply return. UN Principles 28 and 29 call for, in part, "the full participation of internally displaced persons in the planning and management of their return or resettlement and reintegration." The UN Principles also state, "They shall have the right to participate fully and equally in public affairs at all levels and have equal access to public services," as well as to have their property and possessions replaced, or else receive "appropriate compensation or another form of just reparation."[19] In other words, they call for a return that includes restoration and reparations. Civil rights attorney Tracie Washington explained the concept in simpler terms: "I'm still displaced until the conditions that caused my displacement have been alleviated. I'm still displaced as long as Charity Hospital remains closed. I'm still displaced as long as rents remain unaffordable. I'm still displaced as long as schools are in such bad shape."

Denny LeBoeuf, director of the Capital Post-Conviction Project of Louisiana noted,

> These people have the right of return. This humanitarian principle is good for our NOLA folks as well as for Rwanda refugees. After the war, and the air clears, people have the right to return to their home. Poor people of color occupy 100 percent of the Calliope [public housing development] and other dwellings where return has been refused. These folks make our culture what it is—whether through music, or food, or other venues—they connect us to this authentic, thriving culture.

ORGANIZING AMONG THE DISPLACED

Organizing was present wherever evacuees ended up. I heard stories of committees formed spontaneously in hotels, shelters, and trailer parks. In spring 2006 I visited Renaissance Village, an evacuee community of more than five hundred trailers, located north of Baton Rouge on land owned by a youth prison. I had heard about the organizing happening there and wanted to offer support.

Residents I spoke to were aching to come home. "Last year I was a middle income American, a homeowner—I never imagined I'd come to this," said Hillary Moore Jr., a former city employee and New Orleans property owner exiled in a small trailer in the middle of the complex. An older man, quiet and polite but with a passionate streak, Moore didn't want to be thrust into the role of struggling for basic rights. He would prefer to be living in his own home, peacefully approaching a comfortable retirement. Living alone, Moore barely fit in his trailer. When he talked about the family of five living next door, I couldn't imagine how they could possibly all squeeze in. Visiting Moore, I stood the whole time, as there was nowhere to sit.

As with all the residents I encountered, Moore was unhappy in his trailer home. "Why would they buy this for as much money as they paid? This thing is designed for a weekend—can you imagine someone trying to live in here for six or seven months?"

I asked him why he had agreed to move in. "When you've been living in a gymnasium with a hundred-plus people, a travel trailer sounds like a mansion to you, and when they tell you sign here so you can end standing in line to get a shower, you don't question anything, you sign and you jump at the opportunity." An over-capacity housing market from Baton Rouge to New Orleans made other options scarce.

On that day in 2006, at a community meeting in a large tent near Moore's trailer, residents voiced some of their recent complaints, most involving the logistics of living in an isolated, underserved community. Many of the occupants had no means of transportation. The only bus service was to Wal-Mart and back.

Not long after moving in, Moore and others initiated a residents' council. "We got tired of a lot of things Keta [the contractor company managing the park] was doing and we decided to organize because we realized there is strength in numbers," he told me. The residents' council formed an elected board and held open meetings every week. The struggle was uphill, but their organizing did win some concessions from FEMA and Keta. As the years went on, those who were able to find something better moved out of the park as soon as they could. Those who remained were those in the most need of help, often facing hunger and homelessness. In May 2008, Renaissance Village was torn down, and the last residents were evicted. By this point, the trailers had been revealed to have toxic levels of formaldehyde—they had never been intended as long-term accommodations.

A year after the storm, more than 100,000 people from the Gulf Coast were living in FEMA trailers, with an additional 33,000 living in apartments paid for by FEMA.[20] By 2009, almost all the sites like Renaissance Village had been shut down, the trailers had been removed, and the former residents had been kicked out. The trailers sat empty, as companies debated reselling them despite the toxic chemicals (there was a brief effort to sell them to Haiti in the aftermath of the 2010 earthquake, but activists in both countries fought against this effort at disaster profiteering). No one, as far as I'm aware, has tracked how many of Renaissance Village's three thousand residents made it back to New Orleans. I fear the worst.

For those who had been dispersed around the country, safety and community were even harder to come by. An article in the October 9, 2005, *New York Times* reported on a community of displaced New Orleans residents in rural Oklahoma, where local residents were "glad to see them go." "With each passing day," the *Times* reported, they "could feel the sympathy draining away."[21] The problem stemmed from the perception that being torn from one's home, community, livelihood, and culture—and in many cases also losing family members and loved ones, as well as enduring physical and mental trauma—was somehow a simple issue that could be solved with a place to stay in another state, some hand-me-down clothes, and a few meals.

New Orleanians were also kept from the resources of the very organizations that purported to be helping them. Jenka Soderberg, an Indymedia reporter and volunteer at the Common Ground Relief Collective, reported in 2005 on her experience at a FEMA compound. Inside the FEMA base camp for the city of New Orleans, she was told by contractors, "The tents [for FEMA workers] are pretty empty, not many people staying here." However, "we don't combine with the evacuees—we have our camp here, as workers, and they have their camps."

Soderberg stated,

> It made me feel sick to my stomach. We walked around this absolutely surreal scene of hundreds of enormous air-conditioned tents, each one with the potential of housing 250 people—whole city blocks of trailers with hot showers, huge banks of laundry machines, portajohns lined up 50 at a time, a big recreation tent, air-conditioned, with a big-screen TV, all of it for contractors and FEMA workers, none of it for the people of New Orleans.

Soderberg, thin and white and often wearing a utilitarian outfit holding many tools, was one of the volunteers who came to Common Ground inspired by their vision of reinventing relief. She spent her time in New Orleans hard at work on many projects, from setting up a pirate radio station to recording stories of police violence.

Soderberg continued:

> Thousands of New Orleans citizens could live there while they rebuilt and cleaned their homes in the city. But instead, due to the arrogance of a government bureaucracy that insists they are separate from the "evacuees," and cannot possibly see themselves mixing with them and working side by side on the cleanup, these people are left homeless, like the poor man I talked to earlier in the day, living under a tarp with his mother buried under the mud of their house. Why can't he live in their tents?[22]

The inequalities in the city's recovery were obvious. Some areas had electricity, gas, and clean streets, and some areas were untouched. Medical volunteer Catherine Jones wrote on her blog that driving the streets at night, "I felt like I was in the middle of a checkerboard. The Quarter lit up like Disneyworld; poor Black neighborhoods a few blocks over so dark I couldn't even see the street in front of me."[23]

The *Washington Post* reported in October 2005 that although both the overwhelmingly white Lakeview neighborhood and Black Ninth Ward neighborhood were devastated by flooding, "It now appears that long-standing neighborhood differences in income and opportunity...are shaping the stalled repopulation of this mostly empty city."

While military checkpoints were still keeping Lower Ninth Ward residents from even looking at their homes, "Lakeview, where 66 percent of children go to private school and 49 percent of residents have a college degree, was pumped dry within three weeks of the storm. Memphis Street (in Lakeview) smells now of bleach, which kills mold, and resounds to the thwack of crowbars and the whine of chain saws. Insurance adjusters have begun making rounds."[24]

With housing scarce and insurance rates rising, rents were going up by as much as 100 percent in some neighborhoods. Many activists also complained that church groups or Common Ground volunteers, were taking up the small amount of usable housing, leaving less available for returning residents. On a single day in November 2005, 335 evictions were filed in New Orleans courts—the amount normally filed in an entire month. There were reports of landlords throwing tenants' property out on the street without notice. Human rights lawyer Bill Quigley gave the first report on the situation. Quigley, a white, Catholic professor at Loyola Law School, played a central role in the battle for housing in the city. Even before the storm, Quigley had a national reputation as a tireless advocate for human rights locally and internationally. In the years after the storm, he became a hero to many who were fighting for the rebuilding of the city.

Discussing the evictions, Quigley reported:

> Fully armed National Guard troops refuse to allow over ten thousand people to even physically visit their property in the Lower Ninth Ward neighborhood. Despite the fact that people cannot come back, tens of thousands of people face eviction from their homes. A local judge told me that their court expects to process a thousand evictions a day for weeks. Renters still in shelters or temporary homes across the country will never see the court notice taped to the door of their home. Because they will not show up for the eviction hearing that they do not know about, their possessions will be tossed out in the street. In the street their possessions will sit alongside an estimated 3 million truck loads of downed trees, piles of mud, fiberglass insulation, crushed sheetrock, abandoned cars, spoiled mattresses, wet rugs, and horrifyingly smelly refrigerators full of food from August.[25]

During a Sunday service on January 29, 2006, in an African American church in the Central City neighborhood, the Reverend Jesse Jackson asked the five hundred people present—almost all of them African American—to raise their hands if they had evacuated. Every hand went up. He then asked who still had family and loved ones who had not returned, and again every single hand in the room went up.

THE FIRST POST-KATRINA MARDI GRAS

The lead-up to the first Mardi Gras after the storm generated complex feelings and conflicting schools of thought. Should we celebrate, to show that we were coming back? We have historically been a city that mourns through celebration, but was this tragedy too great, and still too fresh? Royce Osborn, a local filmmaker from a New Orleans Creole family who made the classic film about Black Mardi Gras cultural traditions *All on a Mardi Gras Day*, told me days after the storm that he was aching to come back, and was already looking forward to Mardi Gras 2006. "If we see the Indians out on the streets in the next Mardi Gras, then I'll know there's hope for New Orleans," he said.

At the same time that some looked forward to this Mardi Gras as a "return to normal," others felt it was too soon to invite out-of-towners to come in and party on our streets. A past leader of the Zulu Mardi Gras krewe sued Zulu (unsuccessfully) to stop them from parading. I understood the impulse. Celebrating Mardi Gras felt inappropriate that year to me as well. But at the same time, I was also looking forward to the opportunity to escape from thoughts of devastation for a short while.

Mardi Gras was smaller that year, and certainly whiter. It also felt more local—almost everyone at the parades seemed to be either a current New Orleans resident or a displaced person back to visit.

Soon after that first Mardi Gras, on April 22, 2006, voters went to the polls to choose among twenty-four mayoral candidates, as well as to vote for criminal sheriff, city council, and other positions. For races in which no candidate received over 50 percent, a run-off between the two candidates with the highest votes was held on May 20. Elections have traditionally been a big deal in the state that gave the nation Clinton campaign manager James Carville and Gore campaign manager Donna Brazile. Because the storm and recovery were still attracting international attention, this particular election became a national news story. And in the context of mass displacement of a Black population, the election became, at least in part, a spectacle about race.

When, on Martin Luther King Day of 2006, Mayor Nagin made an offhand remark about New Orleans becoming a "chocolate city once again," it became international news and fueled the fire of a racial debate. In New Orleans, there was a sea of white anger at Nagin, who was seen as having turned against the white voters who had elected him. Throughout the French Quarter, souvenir shops sold t-shirts depicting Nagin as Willy Wonka. Conservative talk radio was filled with attacks on the mayor, many of which seemed tinged with racial resentment.

Peggy Wilson, a white former city councilwoman regarded as one of the leading mayoral candidates, blatantly sought to appeal to the worst impulses of white New Orleanians. While Nagin promised that Black New Orleanians would come back, she seemed to long for them to stay away. Her lack of subtlety would almost have been refreshing if it hadn't been so offensive. Phrases other white politicians might let slip accidentally in an unguarded moment were her main talking points. With relentless racially coded attacks on public housing residents, depicting them as "drug dealers," "pimps," and "welfare queens," she sent a clear message about what she and her potential constituents saw as the real themes of the election.

Wilson was clearly betting on the Black vote being suppressed. "I figured the demographics might have changed now and I could run," she told the *Times-Picayune* shortly before the election. Businessman Ron Forman, whose agenda was similar to Wilson's but with a more polite face, seemed unconcerned with Black displacement and refused to engage in conversation about whether race might be a factor in the election. Although he polled at only one percent among the Black electorate, Forman was seen as a front-runner, and received the endorsement of the *Times-Picayune*.

Candidate Tom Watson, a Black reverend and outspoken advocate for evacuees and criminal justice reform, was more honest about the themes of the election, saying in one debate, "I live in a mixed neighborhood uptown, and white people won't talk to me. I walk my dog, and they'll talk to my dog and not to me."

Since Iraqis living in the United States had been given the right to vote in the Iraqi elections, people asked why displaced New Orleanians could not vote at satellite voting stations. A voting rights coalition that included the ACLU of Louisiana, National Association for the Advancement of Colored People (NAACP), Association of Community Organizations for

Reform Now (ACORN), and others stated that the guidelines for absentee voting "are unclear, complicated, and conflicting." One advocate from the coalition told me, "You practically need a legal consultation to figure out how to vote. It would be easier if they just instituted a poll tax." Congressman John Conyers called the lack of voting rights for the displaced "the largest disenfranchisement in the history of this nation."

Shortly before the mayoral election, Reverend Jesse Jackson and others led thousands of people in a civil rights march across the Crescent City Connection, the bridge connecting New Orleans to the white-flight suburbs on the west bank of the Mississippi River. One of the issues of the march was voter disenfranchisement. Mayor Nagin joined the front of the march, and in doing so carried an implied endorsement from the civil rights leaders.

Due in part to this implied support, as well as anger over the racist nature of many of the attacks Nagin faced, displaced New Orleanians voted in large numbers and reelected Mayor Nagin. Obviously, the vast majority of white voters had issues with Nagin that went beyond race, and those who voted for him did so for a wide range of reasons, but the racial split in voting—along with an inequitable recovery—added to the feeling of a divided city.

From his "chocolate city" comments and participation in the march, C. Ray Nagin might seem—especially to a national audience unfamiliar with his policies—to be a spokesperson for racial justice. The truth is more complicated.

Nagin is an economic conservative—during his first term he was dubbed "Ray Reagan," and after the storm he was a supporter of tearing down public housing and dismantling the school system. When first elected, in 2002, Nagin won (against another Black candidate) with 80 percent of the white vote and about 40 percent of the Black vote. At the time, he was seen as the more conservative, "pro-business" candidate, and represented a break with the Morial family dynasty that had held the office for sixteen of the past twenty-four years. Nagin is also a consummate politician who knows how to charm an audience. Tall and handsome, with a shaved head and a relaxed demeanor, he is a very charismatic man who always seems to be speaking honestly, off the cuff, as if to a friend.

When Nagin won reelection in 2006 (in a runoff against Mitch Landrieu, who is white), the ratio had reversed. He won with about 80 percent of the Black vote and about 20 percent of the white vote.[26] He was endorsed in the runoff election by arguably the most "left" candidate (Tom Watson) as well as by the most conservative (white Republican Rob Couhig).

Nagin's popularity decreased through his second term, until it had dipped to a 40 percent approval rating among Black voters and to less than 5 percent among white voters. While Nagin was in many ways a terrible mayor, he wasn't the real problem. New Orleans needed tens of billions, perhaps hundreds of billions, of dollars to rebuild—and long-term commitment to redressing its systemic problems. What New Orleans needed was simply beyond what any mayor could give.

In 2010, Mitch Landrieu ran again (Nagin was prevented by term limits from running for a third term) and easily defeated all candidates in a campaign in which he scarcely seemed to put in much effort. The media said voters had "buyers' remorse" after the last four years of Nagin, while many advocates pointed to the continued displacement of Black voters and a lack of compelling candidates. Either way, it pointed to a new era.

New Orleans's population had been nearly 70 percent African American, but by the 2006 election it had shifted down substantially (absent a census count, no one was sure by how much), and this difference was reflected in the changing landscape of electoral politics statewide. In 2007, while Republicans were losing across the rest of the United States, Christian Coalition candidate Bobby Jindal was easily elected governor of Louisiana. The following year, New Orleans's congressional seat shifted to Republican hands (though some factors in that race, like former Congressman Jefferson's ongoing legal troubles, had little to do with New Orleans's changing demographics). That same year, the New Orleans City Council changed to a white majority after decades of a Black majority.

Among the new city council members was self-proclaimed "political reformer" Stacy Head, a white lawyer elected to the city council in 2006. Head, a Democrat, was elected to the district that includes the Central City neighborhood, traditionally represented by a Black city council member. This was seen as an early sign of the loss of Black political power in the city. Head had campaigned against corruption and positioned herself as an outsider challenging the status quo.

In 2009, Councilwoman Head was caught up in a very public drama when civil rights attorney Tracie Washington released some of Head's email exchanges, which had been obtained through a Freedom of Information Act request. For weeks, the local media gave almost daily updates on the continuing battle over whether Washington had the right to publicize the emails, whether the public official who released them to Washington had the right to, and finally, over the content of the emails (which were, at a minimum, impolite). The messages revealed secret coordination for the 2008 election of Republican Congressman Joseph Cao and complaints against Head's fellow council members and city activists, such as civil rights organizer Jerome Smith (whom she misidentified as "Gerome Wilson").[27]

Head also disparaged the very New Orleanians she had been elected to represent, such as a woman in front of her in line at a supermarket:

> Pisses me off 100 percent of the time. I have been shopping carefully, looking at the per serving cost of all items. This chick in front of me is buying pre made croissant and egg, canned soups, solft driinks, pre made beef pattie (who eats that???), pre made RICE KRISPYs!!! Precut sweet potatos (didn't know those existed) and is payong with a food stamp card. I am voting for the freak mccain and his trash bag vp. I am sick of it. [all spelling *sic*].[28]

From her unflooded home, it seemed Head had never experienced life without a proper kitchen or even a working stove, which often necessitates buying pre-made and prepared items.

In other emails, Head attempted to have the value of Washington's home reassessed so the civil rights lawyer would have to pay higher taxes, and filed official complaints about Washington to the IRS and the Louisiana State Bar. Finally, Head complained to an aide, "EVERY FUCKING THING IS ABOUT RACE IN THIS SHITHOLE OF A CITY!"

Head, Jindal, Landrieu, Cao, and the other new faces in elected office embodied the demographic changes in New Orleans. Some pundits claimed that these new politicians indicated that the city had moved beyond race and into a post-racial era. But the divides remained—while Landrieu won clear majorities of white and Black voters in 2010, Head proved a much more racially divisive candidate. In a district that was 40 percent white, running against an underfunded candidate (the son of former mayoral candidate Tom Watson), she won her election with 98 percent of the white vote and 30 percent of the Black vote.[29]

But there was no electoral choice that could have provided New Orleans with the reconstruction it needed, after the federal government had made it clear it was not committed to the repair and revitalization of New Orleans. What was required was not different faces at the top, but a grassroots movement that could create real change.

ONE YEAR AFTER

Safe Streets/Strong Communities co-founder Xochitl Bervera, upon the one-year anniversary of Katrina, expressed both the tragedy we lived in and the resistance that inspired us. Her words, originally forwarded via email, are so eloquent and accurate I prefer to let her speak directly:

> Friends from around the country ask us: "How are things in New Orleans? Are things getting better?" I always have to pause, surprised that people haven't heard. I forget that the national media has abandoned us, that George Bush flew into town for five minutes to make promises of federal support, which gave the rest of the country and the world permission to look away. I am stunned that people don't know how much worse it is in New Orleans today for our organization, for our members, for our community than it was even six months ago.
>
> When people ask, I have to tell them: It's worse than you think. It's not what people want to hear, but it's the truth that isn't being reported in the mainstream media, so I have to keep telling them. And every time, I draw on a renewed commitment on the part of FFLIC and many others in New Orleans and around the country to hold onto faith and to the knowledge that the spiritual and material power of people who believe in and work for justice will one day prevail—and so we keep moving forward. Because it is always darkest before dawn and New Orleans, a year after Katrina, is due for the brightest of dawns....
>
> Undeniably, organizing has taken root in the city. From neighborhood associations to workers rights, environmental justice, and public safety reform groups, people are beginning to come together and use their people power, their power to disrupt, to shame, to confront elected officials and demand that they do what they were elected to do: serve the people of this city....
>
> If we and the many others in New Orleans who have begun, keep on organizing, we have hope that we may soon be able to answer the question differently, "So how are things in New Orleans?"[30]

YOUTH ACTIVIST KNOWLEDGE IS BORN LEADS SECONDLINE
TO PROTEST SCHOOL-TO-PRISON PIPELINE, APRIL 2009.
PHOTO BY ABDUL AZIZ.

CHAPTER FOUR

Wonder How We Doin':
The Blank Slate

If ya wonder how we doin'
Short version is we gettin' there
If ya wonder how we doin'
Short version is we gettin' mad

From "We Gettin' There" by Dr. John

Weeks after the storm, with the city evacuated, the schools closed, and no students, parents, teachers, or community members to interfere, suddenly the New Orleans public school system was up for grabs. Instead of gradual reforms being made to an existing system, the system itself was eliminated, and there were virtually no rules or limits as to what could take its place. "The framework has been exploded since the storm," explained New Orleans-based education reform advocate and Parents Organizing Network founder Aesha Rasheed. "It's almost a blank slate for whatever agenda people want to bring."

This opportunity was noticed by more than just local residents. As Naomi Klein noted, conservative economist Milton Friedman wrote in the *Wall Street Journal* not long after the storm, "This is a tragedy. It is also an opportunity to radically reform the educational system."[1] Days after the storm, the Heritage Foundation, a right-wing think tank based in Washington, D.C., sent out a press release advocating for vouchers and "market solutions" to the city's education problems.

Before the storm and displacement, the New Orleans school system comprised 128 public schools, 60,000 students, and about 8,500 employees, including at least 4,000 teachers.[2] There is no doubt that the system, widely regarded as being in crisis, was in desperate need of change. In the 2004–2005 school year, 63 percent of public schools in New Orleans were deemed "academically unacceptable" by Louisiana accountability standards (compared to only 8 percent of public schools across all of Louisiana). Within the New Orleans public education system, schools were largely segregated along racial lines. A few high-performing, selective-admission public schools had most of the system's white students; the rest of the school system was almost 100 percent African American. On the 2004 Louisiana Educational Assessment Program (LEAP) standardized test, white students from the public school system scored more than 50 points higher in both English and math than did African American students—a gap twice as large as that between white and Black students across all of Louisiana—and three-quarters of public school eighth-graders failed to score at the basic level on state English assessments.[3] A passing grade on LEAP, which scores students on a percentage scale from 1 to 100, is required for graduation and for advancement in some grades.

Forty percent of children in New Orleans lived below the poverty line. Seventy-seven percent of students in the public school system were participating in free or reduced-price lunch programs. Ten school superintendents in ten years had been fired or quit. Parents who could afford to, white parents in particular, had pulled their kids out of the system—almost half the city's students were enrolled in private or parochial schools. Advocates accused the public school system of functioning as little more than a warehousing program for Black youth. In spring 2005, headlines announced that the school system was facing bankruptcy.

In broad terms, there were two competing explanations for what was wrong with the pre-Katrina school system. On one side, grassroots advocates argued that the crisis went beyond the school system itself—that its dysfunction stemmed from larger issues that needed to be addressed, such as poverty, inadequate housing, high crime, and lack of job opportunities in the city, as well as low teacher pay, crumbling infrastructure, and an overall dearth of funding for public schools. On the other side, many local business elites and national education reformers felt that the most pressing problems were a corrupt school board, principals who were bureaucrats rather than innovators, and a powerful teachers' union that kept incompetent teachers from being fired and prevented reformers from taking bold actions. Their proposed solution was to take the schools away from the school board and the teachers' union and build something entirely new.

After the storm, these so-called reformers, like Tulane University President Scott Cowen and state schools superintendent Paul Vallas, got their wish. In 2003, the state had formed the Recovery School District as a vehicle for taking over troubled schools from the city. Before Katrina, five public schools had been taken over. In November 2005, less than three months after the storm, the state legislature passed a law enabling the Recovery School District to take over an additional 107 schools, removing them from local control, perhaps permanently. The state began the process of converting those schools under its control to a charter system.

Nationwide, the fight over charter schools has transcended the traditional boundaries of left and right. Some progressives support them as a potential tool for greater community control and as an opportunity to try education strategies that would not be possible given the bureaucracy common to public schools. Opponents see charter schools as a back-door strategy used by conservatives to undermine the public education system by creating a two-tiered "separate but equal" hierarchy within the public school system, while also opening up the management of schools to for-profit businesses.

Another contentious issue tied up in the dispute over charters was the role of the teachers' union—previously the largest and strongest in the city. In fall 2005, while the city was still evacuated, the school board voted to lay off nearly all of the system's 8,500 employees, and in June 2006 let the teachers' union contract expire with little comment and no fanfare.[4] Teachers subsequently hired by newly transformed charter schools reentered the job force without any union protection or representation.

To some, the teachers' union represented an influential Black-led political base advocating within the education system. "Elites of the city may prefer the teachers don't come back because they represent an educated class of Black New Orleans, with steady income, seniority, job protection," explained community advocate Jacques Morial, a key fighter on issues of reconstruction. Morial was especially active on health care and the fight to save Charity Hospital, which faced demolition as part of what advocates saw as an overall attack on the idea of public services.

The fired teachers, most of whom were Black, were in many cases replaced by young, mostly white, recent college graduates from Teach For America (TFA). TFA, which recruits college students to teach after graduation for two years in "troubled" American schools, has been criticized as a tool for replacing experienced—and often unionized and better paid—teachers. Detroit teachers' union president Keith Johnson called TFA teachers "educational mercenaries" who "ride in on their white horses and for two years share the virtue of their knowledge as a pit stop on their way to becoming corporate executives."[5]

The debate over what form the New Orleans educational system would take became entwined with the larger issue of who would (or could) return and when. At forums, at neighborhood meetings, and throughout the city and its diaspora, families were anxious. From Houston to Atlanta, displaced parents questioned whether their kids would have a school if they returned to New Orleans.

By the start of the spring semester, the city's private schools had seen almost 90 percent of their students return, while only 20 percent of public school students were back. Those that reentered public school encountered a system completely different from the one they had left, referred to by some as a "grand experiment in school reform." Thirty-five out of the fifty-six schools open in fall 2006 had been transformed into charters. In other words, the system was now a majority of publicly funded schools free from the oversight and many of the rules that had previously applied to New Orleans public schools.

According to Tulane professor Lance Hill, "New Orleans has experienced a profound change in who governs schools and a dramatic reduction of parent and local taxpayer control of schools." Hill identified dozens of different school operators and separate charter boards, some with multiple schools, each with its own "policies, including teacher requirements, curriculum, discipline policies, enrollment limits, and social promotions. Publicly accountable schools in which parents have methods for publicly redressing grievances are limited to only five schools (5.6 percent of the total)."

Advocates were concerned that the new administrations were inexperienced and unprepared to take over the New Orleans system. "They say this is an experiment," said attorney Tracie Washington about charter school plans. Referencing the notorious forty-year syphilis study in which white researchers deliberately withheld medical treatment from poor Black men in Alabama, she added, "Tuskegee was an experiment. We have reason to be suspicious of experiments."

According to activists fighting for a non-charter system, students whose parents are able to actively advocate for them have been able to enroll in improved public schools, but options are reduced for those whose parents have difficulty managing the applications and red tape. "Suffice it to say that the old system worked for people with higher education, with more resources," explained Mtangulizi Sanyinka, project manager of New Orleans's African American Leadership Project. "It wasn't that the system didn't work at all; it didn't work for poor people."

Pre-Katrina, thousands of kids didn't have to pre-register—they simply showed up at their neighborhood school on the first day, and the school found them a place. Now, most of those neighborhood schools didn't exist anymore, and those that did were no longer obligated to place students who just showed up. For the first few years, the changes happened far more rapidly than many parents and kids could follow, and there was virtually no system in place to communicate the changes.

Although some schools have improved, advocates claim that the charter transformation has been fundamentally unfair. The problem is not just that New Orleans's school system has two tiers. Perhaps it is inevitable that every large school system will have both good schools and bad schools (though no system should have schools as nonfunctioning as New Orleans's worst). The problem lies with the flawed premise—often unstated, yet still underlying the decisions made—that the best schools should go to the "best" students.

Some students have decided to fight the unequal treatment. At John McDonogh High School, a city school under state supervision, students formed an activist group called the Fyre Youth Squad (FYS) in 2006 to fight what they saw as unfair treatment and an unequal system. "Our school has 34 security guards and 21 teachers," a student told me. "How do we learn in that environment? Do they even want us to learn?"

FYS members later widened their base beyond John McDonogh, representing the most under-resourced schools, and they have refused to give up, continuing to fight fiercely for a better educational environment for themselves and their peers. FYS organized demonstrations and press conferences to focus public attention on the plight of students in the most underfunded schools. They brought a large group of students to Baton Rouge for a meeting of the Louisiana Board of Elementary & Secondary Education, the state administrative body with jurisdiction over the public schools. About a hundred FYS students and adult allies joined in a march through Midcity New Orleans to protest "high stakes testing," which the students said caused their teachers to focus on "teaching to the test" rather than providing a real education.

One of the FYS founders is a tall, thin, and handsome young man with an easy smile and endless charm who calls himself Knowledge Is Born. He continued his involvement with FYS even years after he graduated. Knowledge credits his involvement with the group—as well as the support of adult allies and his own belief in himself—with turning his life around.

He had failed the state's mandated standardized tests multiple times and was unable to graduate high school. He spent time in Orleans Parish Prison and was shuffled from school to school for infractions like fighting and marijuana possession. Knowledge kept retaking the Graduate Exit Exam (GEE) test and became an outspoken leader in the school reform movement, related at a demonstration his history of failing the test. According to a *Times-Picayune* profile, he told the crowd "that he had failed the GEE six times—an experience he called heartbreaking. 'Only by the grace of God, I never found myself tired of fighting.' Today, he said, is when we will stand up and say, 'We deserve better.'"[6]

Beginning with the school system, much of the change in post-Katrina New Orleans has been led by an influx of principals, teachers, planners, architects, developers, and other reformers who have relocated to the city. Often self-identifying as "YURPs"—Young, Urban, Rebuilding Professionals—they work in schools, nonprofits, foundations, and other businesses. Many in this community regard New Orleans as a blank slate on which they can project and practice their ideas of reform, whether in education, architecture, urban planning, or health care.

New Orleans's new professionals have often come here with the best intentions, with a love for this city and a desire to help with the recovery. However, activists criticize what they see as token attempts at community involvement and a paternalistic attitude among many of the new decision-makers. The YURP approach tends to overlook the people who lived here before, who are the most affected by the changes, and who have the least say in how those changes are carried out. "It wasn't a blank slate, it was a cemetery," said poet and educator Kalamu Ya Salaam. "People were killed, and they're building on top of their bones."

Attorney Tracie Washington, who served as an adult ally to the Fyre Youth Squad, questioned the motives and methods of many of the school reformers. "If you kick me out of my kitchen because you say you can cook better than me," she said, "then your gumbo better taste better than mine."

The national media expressed excitement and admiration for the new New Orleans school system, hailing it as a success story.[7] For the school reformers, this was a dream come true. They had media support; federal, state, and city officials on their side, and a massive influx of cheap, young, and idealistic labor. Teach For America supplied 112 teachers to New Orleans in 2007, 250 in 2008, and about 500 in 2009, while tens of millions of dollars in funding flowed in from sources such as the Gates and Walton foundations. School funding also increased from the state itself. According to the *Times-Picayune*, in the last full school year before Hurricane Katrina, the Orleans Parish district spent $7,877 per student. In the 2007–2008 school year, the Recovery School District spent, conservatively, about $12,900 per student—not including disaster-related capital costs. Some of these increases were only temporary, having come from Katrina-related federal funds that ran out soon after.[8]

Serious questions remain as to the true extent of the charter schools' much-heralded success. The new schools did frequently see higher scores, but they have also had access to the best facilities and, using state standardized tests for admission, have hand-picked a select student body (resulting in 40 percent fewer special education students.) Yet even using their own questionable standards, such as scores on the high-stakes LEAP exam, the reports of massive gains seem overstated. G.W. Carver School, the subject of a fawning 2008 *New York Times* article,[9] received an 88 percent failure rate for English and an 86 percent failure rate for math on state standardized tests in the 2008 school year. In fact, a comparison of scores across the district indicates that the schools with the best standardized test scores were the ones with the greatest number of senior teachers.[10] Unfortunately, these senior teachers—who were fired in mass numbers—are now in short supply.

There is no doubt that some students receive an excellent education in the new schools, but this revolution has been overwhelmingly led from outside, with little input from the parents, students, and staff of the school system. Poet and educator Kalamu Ya Salaam described the new system as representing "an experimentation with privatization, and everything that implies"—namely, that profit and expedience come before the public good.

In addition to school reformers, many of the newly arrived YURPs were architects and urban planners whose blank slates were represented by the neighborhoods of the city. Their arrival coincided with a rise in the profile and influence of the New Orleans neighborhood associations. The associations, most of which existed pre-Katrina, saw their membership numbers and involvement level multiply along with their influence as they filled a void left by governmental indifference and ineptitude in the weeks and months after the storm. The neighborhood associations became clearinghouses—resources of energy, ideas, and information—where everyone from politicians to architects, designers, and planners to foundations and other funders could go for input and to lend support. However, with hundreds of thousands of mostly Black New Orleanians still displaced, the post-storm membership of the neighborhood associations shifted in favor of the disproportionately white returning population.

As scholar Jason Neville described, "Almost everyone living in post-flood New Orleans has become, by definition, a planner and an activist, because the government has done very little to support the recovery of the neighborhoods....It has been the everyday residents of New Orleans struggling to rebuild their neighborhoods who have done the fundamental work of recovery planning, not merely agitating from the outside." Neville and co-writer Geoff Coates, both New Orleanians, also quoted New Orleans blogger Alan Gutierrez, who explained:

> We don't protest. We catalog and coordinate. We write and administer grants. We gut houses. We sit in attendance and listen carefully. We go to planning meetings because we are investing in a house whose value depends on the recovery of the neighborhood. We attend a school planning charade while [the] superintendent is bulldozing the schools under his control....We attend Housing Conservation District Review Committee meetings because the city has made clear its intention to demolish our homes without notifying us, compensating us, or giving us a process for appeal. To call a resident of New Orleans an "activist" is akin to calling a person in physical therapy to recover from a spinal injury a "health nut."[11]

This increased civic involvement was an encouraging development, as the neighborhood associations represented a potential for direct democracy and community involvement. They have had some definite successes—designing their own plans for rebuilding and resisting the destruction of their neighborhoods, as well as restarting basic functions like trash collection and other municipal services. The associations also made efforts to help their neighbors return, setting up systems of support and filling in where the government had let people down.

The rebuilding planning process was chaotic and confusing. Legions of planners from around the country came down independently to collaborate with neighborhood groups, while the mayor and city council hired separate planners. Several simultaneous processes were underway at the same time, with none having any real hope of being funded.

In November of 2005, the Urban Land Institute (ULI) issued its report, followed by Mayor Nagin's Bring New Orleans Back Commission (BNOB), which released its report in January 2006. The ULI report and BNOB's plan represented a validation of many New Orleanians' fears of a conspiracy to take their homes and keep them out of the city. Like an urban planning version of the triage at Memorial Hospital, both plans recommended focusing on rebuilding less-damaged areas first. The BNOB plan was published on the front page of the *Times-Picayune* and featured "green dots," representing future green spaces, such as parks, placed over several population-dense neighborhoods, including parts of New Orleans East, the Lower Ninth Ward, and even the multi-racial neighborhood of Broadmoor, where the Landrieu family had a home.

At public forums, the outrage was intense. "I don't know you, but I hate you," said New Orleans East resident Harvey Bender, directing his remarks at local developer and BNOB commission member Joseph Cannizzaro at an unveiling of the plan. "You've been in the background scheming to take our land."[12]

Meanwhile, individual neighborhood groups held *charrettes*—extended meetings, generally for a weekend or longer, with architects and urban planners—sponsored by leading planning and design firms from around the world. Soon after came the city council's Lambert Plan, named for Miami-based planner Paul Lambert, which attempted to incorporate some of this independent neighborhood planning. The Lambert plan was soon discarded, most likely due to political jostling between the mayor and city council.

The amount of community involvement during this time was astounding. The various rebuilding visions ran along a spectrum from full rebuilding—better than before—to a "downsized" New Orleans that abandoned or eliminated entire neighborhoods and sections of the city.

One of the tragedies of this period is that much of this energy and passion was squandered on plans that ultimately led nowhere.

After months of infighting and turf battles, Nagin and the city council agreed at the end of 2006 to hire Ed Blakely, an internationally recognized expert on rebuilding, as city Recovery Czar. Blakely moved forward on a less ambitious but in some ways more inclusive rebuilding plan, which, unlike the BNOB plan, entailed strong support for the Lower Ninth Ward and New Orleans East. However, even Blakely's modest agenda proved unachievable. Early on he promised, memorably, that we would see "cranes in the sky" by the fall of 2007. Sadly, 2007 ended with almost no construction occurring, other than private citizens rebuilding their own homes with very little help from any government agency.

In 2008 city voters approved the development of a Master Plan, endowed with the "force of law" before the plan was even completed, meaning that the mayor and city council had limited power to advance or block specific projects that did not conform to this still-to-be-developed plan. The rationale was that the plan needed to be legitimized even before it began, in order for interested parties to participate in its crafting. Many community members viewed this move as yet another a way the government was circumventing public control, by forcing public approval of a plan before the community had a chance to see it—indeed, before it even existed. A draft of the plan, prepared by a team of consultants hired by the City Planning Commission, was presented to community members in mid-2010. It remains to be seen if this rebuilding plan will have different and tangible results, but evidence seems to suggest that, regardless of the plan, no one in government has the political power or will to bring in the tens of billions of dollars a real reconstruction would take.

In June 2009, Blakely resigned, with little progress having been made during his tenure, and still no cranes to be seen. "Cranes is a metaphor for starts," he told an interviewer. "I didn't mean that necessarily literally."[13]

RIGHT OF RETURN

For some, Katrina represented a lifting of a capitalist veil, demonstrating that New Orleans was not just a victim of domestic racism but of U.S. imperialism as well. "One thing I learned, this is what disaster opportunism looks like," community advocate Greta Gladney reflected in 2009. "When the U.S. is at war with someone, and then they pour all this money into rebuilding, this is what it looks like."

In the week after I evacuated, I received emails from people I didn't know in Ghana, Cuba, Peru, and Lebanon. In New York City on September 9, 2005, a group of artists, initiated by Def Poetry Jam star and Tony Award–winning Palestinian poet Suheir Hammad, organized a benefit called "Refugees for Refugees" to raise funds and collect clothing for Katrina survivors. The benefit title beautifully embodied the spirit of solidarity and words of support that immediately flowed in from international allies.

Some Black New Orleanians spoke forcefully against being called "refugees," and civil rights leaders including the Reverends Jesse Jackson and Al Sharpton joined this call. To them the term "refugees" denied the victims' citizenship, and set them apart as an other. During this period, right-wing commentators seemed to be using the term for precisely this distancing purpose—to imply that New Orleanians didn't deserve sympathy because they were not "like us." However, some progressives and radicals chose to use the word "refugee" at the time for the specific reason that it explicitly linked what was happening in New Orleans with what people faced in other, more impoverished countries around the world.

A human rights framework proved helpful for dealing with the crises in the city. Social justice organizers took inspiration from an earlier generation of activists, such as Malcolm X, who had urged the movement to take their case to the UN and other international bodies, saying, "We have injected ourselves into the civil rights struggle, and we intend to expand it from the level of civil rights to the level of human rights." In his famous "The Ballot or the Bullet" speech, Malcolm parsed the difference between the two: "Civil rights means you're asking Uncle Sam to treat you right. Human rights are something you were born with."[14] In addition, groups that worked with recent immigrants found that civil rights campaigns—which are generally predicated on citizenship—excluded many of their members.

Advocates for Environmental Human Rights (AEHR), an environmental justice law firm co-directed by Monique Harden and Nathalie Walker, collaborated with local organizers to bring a human rights analysis to the grassroots, discussing human rights laws and treaties with community organizations. AEHR also presented their case to the UN, arranging for local residents to testify in Geneva about the U.S. government's human rights violations in New Orleans, and coordinating local visits from UN representatives.

In 2007, a broad coalition of grassroots organizations gathered in Atlanta for the U.S. Social Forum (USSF). Part of a global revolutionary process called the World Social Forum, gatherings like the USSF are meant as a counterbalance to international gatherings of the wealthy and powerful, such as the World Economic Forum, and are intended as a tool to amplify the voices of those who are excluded from the traditional corridors of power. Attended by almost fifteen thousand people, the Social Forum in Atlanta brought together grassroots, people-of-color-led, base-building projects with a radical, international analysis. A plenary on post-Katrina issues was a central event of the 2007 USSF, and hundreds (perhaps thousands) of activists and organizers from the Gulf Coast traveled to Atlanta by bus, plane, car, and train. Throughout the weeklong forum there were panels and workshops focusing on the experience of New Orleans and its residents.

The 2007 USSF was a turning point for New Orleans organizing. In the months leading up to the forum, New Orleans activists held monthly meetings—convened by Kimberley Richards from the People's Institute for Survival and Beyond (PISAB) and AEHR's Monique Harden—to build and coordinate local attendance. Individuals that had rarely been in a room together beforehand were able to build connections and alliances that still exist today. In fact, the monthly meetings that began as part of the USSF planning now serve as a general gathering for activists in New Orleans. These gatherings, called the Organizer's Roundtable, are seen as an important tool for building unity in the city's social justice community.

In 2009, after consulting with several communities around the United States, including New Orleans and San Antonio, it was announced that a host city had been chosen for the second USSF, in 2010: Detroit. New Orleanians can learn a great deal from Detroit's experience of economic devastation. New Orleans and Detroit are the two U.S. cities with the largest percentage of vacant or unlivable housing,[15] yet most of our housing was emptied overnight, while the so-called Rust Belt emptied over a span of decades. Out of economic desperation, both cities have turned to gambling, with major casinos in both downtown business districts. Both cities have also explored wide-scale urban gardening as a means of finding productive use for thousands of undeveloped lots.

Most importantly, both cities are sites of inspiring resistance. Elders in Detroit, such as Grace Lee Boggs and others who came out of the labor movement, are contemporaries of the movement veterans of New Orleans. Both cities became majority African American because of "white flight" to the suburbs, and the cultures of both cities made major contributions to the musical lifeblood of the United States. Walking the streets of Detroit, you can see and feel history all around you, as locals point out the childhood homes of Motown stars or the beautiful mural by Diego Rivera near blocks of empty houses and massive abandoned factories.

Another site of Leftist struggle has parallels to New Orleans: Palestine. From the central role of displacement to the ways in which culture and community serve as tools of resistance, there are illuminating comparisons to be made between these two otherwise very different places.

In the New Orleans Black community, death is commemorated as a public ritual (it's often an occasion for a street party), and the deceased are often also memorialized on t-shirts featuring their photos embellished with designs that celebrate their lives. Worn by most of the deceased's friends and family, these t-shirts remind me of the martyr posters in Palestine, which also feature a photo and design to memorialize the person who has passed on. In Palestine, the poster's subjects are anyone who has been killed by the occupation, whether a sick child who died at a checkpoint or an armed fighter killed in combat. In New Orleans, anyone with family and friends can be memorialized on a t-shirt. But a sad truth of life in poor communities is that too many of those celebrated on t-shirts lost their lives to violence. For both New Orleans and Palestine, outsiders often think that people have become so accustomed to death by violence that it has become trivialized by t-shirts and posters.

While it's true that these traditions wouldn't manifest in these particular ways if either population had more opportunities for long lives and death from natural causes, it's also far from trivial to find ways to celebrate a life. Outsiders tend to demonize those killed—especially the young men—in both these cultures as thugs, killers, or terrorists whose lives shouldn't be memorialized in this way, or at all. But the people carrying on these traditions emphasize that every person is a son or daughter of someone, and every death should be mourned, every life celebrated.

Also reminding me of Palestine is the resistance to displacement shown by New Orleanians. As Palestinian scholar and activist Mazin Qumsiyeh said, "*Sumoud* [steadfastness] by itself is resistance. Simple acts like getting married, going to school, reading a book become acts of resistance. When a student comes to my class at eight in the morning after passing numerous checkpoints—that is resistance."[16] Similarly, with all the obstacles facing poor and Black New Orleanians, the fact that so many have returned to their city is itself a kind of civil disobedience.

After Katrina, New Orleans organizers with an international perspective noticed and spoke out about these similarities—displacement, and a people's struggle to maintain their existence against a process of forced erasure. In the days and weeks after Katrina, conservative commentators stated that people shouldn't be living in New Orleans anyway, that they should not mind being dispersed around the country, and—as Barbara Bush so blithely suggested—would probably be happier elsewhere. Palestinians have faced the same argument for decades: there are fifteen Arab countries they could move to, so why do they need a Palestinian state?

The PHRF designed their first logo with a key to represent the right of return for New Orleanians, intentionally using the same key design Palestinians have historically used (based on the keys many Palestinians still hold, belonging to homes they were forced to leave in the mass displacement of 1948). When the Israeli bombardment of Lebanon began in summer 2006, a wide spectrum of New Orleans organizations rallied and spoke at a demonstration in front of a federal building downtown, including AEHR, Loyola Law Clinic, Common Ground Relief Collective, and INCITE.

INCITE's principled stance on Palestine, incidentally, caused them to lose a large grant from the Ford Foundation in 2004, a development that inspired *The Revolution Will Not Be Funded*, an essential and prescient book that helped give organizers in New Orleans a framework to critique the role of nonprofits in New Orleans's recovery.

On the second anniversary of Katrina, PHRF held a People's Tribunal, with Georgia congresswoman Cynthia McKinney among the sixteen judges, and governmental representatives from nine countries: Algeria,

Brazil, France, Guadeloupe, Haiti, Martinique, Mexico, South Africa, and Venezuela. This tribunal was a crucial historical moment. The judges heard testimony of firsthand experience with police and white vigilante violence in the days after the storm. They heard stories from the evacuee camp on Causeway and from the shelters and trailer camps to which residents had been displaced. They heard from public housing residents who had been kicked out of their homes. They heard about schools and health care and the environment. They heard powerful evidence of the systemic nature of the disaster faced by the people of New Orleans. Also of great importance: the testimony—which went on for multiple days—was videotaped; typed transcripts were also produced. The Tribunal organizers created an invaluable archive of evidence.

The connection to Palestine and other countries of the global South was reiterated throughout the tribunal proceedings, but the most eloquent and forceful statement was made by Louisa Hanoune, Deputy in the National Assembly of Algeria for the Workers' Party. Hanoune declared:

> I stand in solidarity with you because I come from Africa, a continent that is sinking into chaos and whose survival requires the united efforts of all women and men of good will. I stand in solidarity with you because throughout the testimonies presented to this Tribunal we heard war cries and words that recall the plight of the Palestinian people. They, like their counterparts here in the Gulf Coast, have the inalienable Right to Return....
>
> As a women's rights activist, I am in solidarity with the Black women because they are, like their counterparts in Palestine, among the most vulnerable. They have been deprived of all they possess in life, even their role in binding their families together. I will go back to sound the alarm against the oppression of the women in New Orleans, which is no less heinous than the oppression and double discrimination faced by the Palestinian women....
>
> If you agree, I will be your spokesperson in my country and beyond—in the Maghreb and the Middle East. I will report the facts that were delivered here, the testimonies presented, and the disaster that we witnessed first hand. The Workers Party Parliamentary Group will organize parliamentary hearings on the Katrina Tribunal in Algeria....To conclude, I would like to quote the Lebanese thinker and writer Jibran Khalil Jibran who wrote the following at the beginning

of the last century: "Woe be it to any nation where one single component claims to represent the entire nation."[17]

One connection between Palestine and New Orleans that resonates for
me personally is the subject of volunteer support. I was deeply involved in a
project in Palestine called the International Solidarity Movement. Beginning in 2001 and reaching a peak during the Israeli invasions of the West
Bank in the spring and summer of 2002, thousands of direct-action activists
converged on Palestine. From this experience, I learned the many ways in
which volunteers can be helpful; I also saw the ways in which they could do
harm, mostly by assuming they knew more about what should be done to
bring justice than the people they were ostensibly coming to help. I saw this
same dynamic—in terms of both positives and negatives—repeated in New
Orleans. The similarities were striking. I am quite sure this pattern repeats
in most situations involving outside volunteers, and therefore, as concerned
individuals and as a movement, we must examine and learn from these successes and failures.

THE VOLUNTEERS

From the first days after the disaster, people around the world wanted to
come to help New Orleans. It's estimated that during the first two years
after Katrina, well over a million volunteers came through New Orleans.[18] Some came for a few days; others never left. For revolutionaries
and progressives, there were two main organizations that recruited based
on an openly radical political analysis and encouraged mass numbers of
volunteers: the People's Hurricane Relief Fund and Oversight Committee (PHRF) and the Common Ground Relief Collective.

PHRF began as a broad coalition seeking to unite the multiple efforts
in the city in order to redefine disaster response. In the weeks after the
storm, almost every grassroots organizer in the city had affiliated with
PHRF, and they spoke of a desire to bring major nonprofits like Red Cross
under community control. The folks that initiated PHRF reached out to
their networks, inviting Black nationalists, civil rights movement veterans,
socialist parties, unions, and others. This outreach soon broadened to incorporate other networks, such as high school and college students. They
welcomed mass numbers of volunteers—including hundreds of students
from historically Black colleges—and engaged them in direct organizing.

During my first years in New Orleans (before Katrina changed the pace of life), I often visited the home of Curtis Muhammad, former SNCC organizer and PHRF founder. I would sit on Curtis's porch and listen as he talked about the lessons he'd learned from social movements, particularly the grassroots "botom-up" model advocated by activists like Ella Baker, who played a formative roll in SNCC. Ella had demanded that the civil rights movement leadership listen to the needs of the community and the ideas of young people, saying, "My theory is, strong people don't need strong leaders." Curtis told me that activists and organizers had become blinded by the divisions imposed by foundation funding, that virtually no one in the Left was willing to walk into communities and listen to the people most affected to find out what they really wanted—they were too focused on the pursuit of foundation money, and had become accountable to foundations rather than the people at the grassroots. In addition, Curtis believes that white activists, for the most part, have not dealt with white supremacy, and when they have been called out on that subject by Black organizers, they have retreated to any other movement—labor, Latin American or Palestine solidarity, anti-corporate activism—that will allow them to be active without challenging their racism.

Many of the founders of PHRF viewed direct aid—the primary function of most other projects active on the Gulf Coast—as inherently flawed. Their perspective was that the only relief responsible allies could deliver was in fighting to change the system that had caused the problems. PHRF advocated bringing in a model of international human rights standards (rather than the limited "rights" offered by legislation like the Stafford Act) and spoke of a Right of Return that encompassed not just the physical return of people to their homes but reparations for victims of both the current crisis and past crimes of structural racism and exploitation. They believed that all direct aid projects—like the massive efforts by the major nonprofits to provide housing and medical aid to some portion of the hundreds of thousands of displaced people, as well as the efforts by the federal government—should be brought under popular control. PHRF's slogan was "Nothing about us without us is for us."

Common Ground Relief Collective shared PHRF's critique of the relief model and was formed with the aim of inventing a new paradigm. Common Ground's slogan was "Solidarity, not charity." These two missions could have been compatible, and ideally these two collective efforts could have complemented each other. Unfortunately, tensions between the two groups arose from the very beginning. Many young Common Ground volunteers considered PHRF too deliberately paced and viewed themselves as the only ones in the city truly taking action. Some PHRF organizers viewed many of Common Ground's volunteers as unaccountable young white people with a savior complex, acting without thought as to the consequences of their actions and without learning the context of the situation in which they were operating.

Common Ground quickly made arrangements with displaced residents to clean out and temporarily occupy many homes and buildings, including a church school called St. Mary's in a devastated and mostly empty part of the Upper Ninth Ward, not far from the former Desire housing projects. Cleaned up by Common Ground volunteers, St. Mary's soon served as the main volunteer housing location, with up to hundreds of people at a time staying for free on sleeping bags packed into classrooms, showering in solar showers set up outside, eating in a communal kitchen, and volunteering for any one of dozens of cleanup crews or working groups. The majority of work consisted of gutting houses, but other projects included an education working group, a media team, a cop-watch project, and more. Most volunteers stayed for two weeks or less, but some stayed for months and many former Common Ground volunteers still live in New Orleans today. Some were conscientious and responsible in their efforts, and some took advantage of the free housing and food and skipped the volunteer work, instead partying in Bourbon Street clubs or Bywater bars.

By December 2005, when Common Ground co-founder Scott Crow wrote a widely circulated open letter that accused PHRF of having done nothing of value in New Orleans, there was overt animosity between the groups. ACORN president and founder Wade Rathke wrote a similar letter around the same time, comparing Curtis Muhammad of PHRF to Ahmed Chalabi. Chalabi, an Iraqi national who collaborated with the Bush administration, had been widely mocked for styling himself a leader of the Iraqi people despite having no real base, and Rathke's implication was that Curtis also had no base in the community. These attacks set the stage for a pattern of distrust that hindered large-scale organizing on a number of issues.

In 2006, the schisms within the organizing community worsened when the leadership of PHRF had a very public internal split. Curtis left to start a new initiative called the People's Organizing Committee (POC). At the time POC released a statement accusing PHRF of lacking community accountability and being unwilling to cede leadership to the communities they served. The New Orleans Workers' Center for Racial Justice, an organization founded as a PHRF working group aimed at linking Black and Latino worker struggles in the city, joined POC in the split. The Workers' Center later severed ties with POC as well, facing similar accusations from Curtis as those he had leveled against PHRF.

I don't believe it's productive to attempt to sift through all the charges and counter-charges that were flying around at this time. I believe there were best intentions and brilliant and dedicated organizers on all sides. In addition, many people involved were still dealing with personal loss, and I think they took their trauma and feelings of helplessness out on each other. It was a sad time of division, conflict, and frustration.

PHRF had represented a revolutionary hope for many leftists. Each new conflict and split was heartbreaking. The vision that Curtis and others articulated, of revolutionary change led by those most affected, was contagious and exciting. Any meeting chaired by Curtis felt like going back in time, to Freedom Summer with Ella Baker, fighting racism and building a new world, upending old values and structures. Thousands of young people who met Curtis through volunteering with these organizations left the experience feeling that their lives had changed direction, that they had joined a movement.

Although the conflicts and splits had left PHRF far from the all-encompassing coalition that had seemed possible in the beginning, it still retained a wide core of activists, as well as international allies. Kali Akuno, who came from a national organization called the Malcolm X Grassroots Movement, relocated to New Orleans from California in 2006 and took over much of the day-to-day running of PHRF. The lasting legacies of this time, such as the People's Tribunal, were among the organization's most vital and successful undertakings. Kali, a dedicated visionary, worked hard to repair rifts in the community, while maintaining a balance between PHRF's local presence and international perspective.

Malcolm Suber, who was born in South Carolina and moved to New Orleans from Chicago more than three decades ago, came to organizing from a revolutionary communist perspective. A longtime activist on a number of issues, especially struggles with police violence, he was one of the initial founders of PHRF. Suber continued with the group after Curtis left, working tirelessly to keep the organization together while at the same time repairing his flood-damaged Gentilly home. Suber is another unsung hero of New Orleans, someone who has spent decades fighting at the grassroots level, seeking neither fame nor glory, and always standing for principles.

While PHRF received much of its support from the Black Left, Common Ground drew from a mostly white support base. This disparity was an unfortunate reflection and continuation of the segregated history of the United States, but it was also the result of different strategies of outreach and organizing.

As people fled in the chaotic days after Katrina, former New Orleans Black Panther Malik Rahim refused to leave the city and invited concerned individuals from around the country to join him. In this racially charged situation, white vigilantes were patrolling the streets of New Orleans, in particular Rahim's Algiers neighborhood. Rahim's call was specifically aimed toward white allies to stand in support and protection of Black community members. The call went out initially as an email, which was widely forwarded and republished as an article in print and online publications. Within days after the storm, while much of the city was still flooded, the first volunteers arrived and Common Ground Relief Collective was formed.

Rahim's house was a campsite of volunteers: mostly white, young, and anarchist. As word continued to spread, more volunteers arrived, bringing supplies, abundant energy, and a wide array of skills. While many of the city's residents were being kept out and soldiers still manned checkpoints at most entries to the city, these activists were able to get in using press passes, medical ID, other certification (real or forged), or simply a clever story; in many cases, white privilege enabled them to pass through security unquestioned. Soon the nascent collective had transformed the neighborhood mosque, with which Rahim was active, into a free community health clinic. Other volunteers set up a wireless Internet zone, a solar-powered shower, and more projects from one day to the next.

Rahim is an incredible man. His deep voice, weighted with experience, projects an air of wise authority. He is tall, with kind eyes and gray dreadlocks that seem to emphasize his years on this earth. When he speaks, the room becomes silent, and people tend to hang on his every word. It makes sense that Common Ground grew based on Rahim's reputation and presence. Young people, for most of whom the Black Panthers had been just a vague legend, naturally wanted to stay and follow him. To many, Rahim seemed to be the only person really doing something in a time and place when all the government and mainstream aid organizations had failed. He is a revolutionary with a vision of redefining relief, in the way that the Black Panther Party redefined revolutionary party work by mixing radical politics with social programs like free milk for schoolchildren. Rahim welcomed the young white activists into this revolutionary tradition. And unlike PHRF (which also took in white activists, though far fewer) Common Ground, led mostly by outsiders, seemed content to overlook issues of race.

For years before Katrina, I jumped at any chance to listen to Rahim, to try to learn from his wisdom and experience. So I felt a kinship with the Common Ground volunteers who came to New Orleans. Many were part of the anticorporate global justice movement that had shaped much of my political development. As revolutionaries, we believe we can do better than the government and corporations. We believe we can fill the needs of people in crisis in a more effective and compassionate way, informed by radical values. Common Ground seemed to be our movement's opportunity to show that we could build a better world. Many young activists felt that this mission lent their efforts a sort of trump card—they must be doing the right thing if they were working with Rahim and had the best of intentions.

Within a month after the storm, mass numbers of volunteers were flowing into New Orleans. The newly formed Common Ground had a distribution network bringing food and supplies to sixteen thousand people in the area and a free health clinic serving hundreds of patients, many of whom had not seen a doctor in years, even decades. By November, they issued a wider callout for volunteers, with at least three hundred mostly young, mostly white activists coming through on the week of Thanksgiving, hundreds more arriving in the weeks that followed, and thousands by the following spring. By summer 2006 they had gutted hundreds of houses, started a newspaper and radio station, helped reopen the Martin Luther King Jr. charter school in the Lower Ninth Ward, and more.

By 2007, the health clinic had paid staff and a board of directors, and had legally (and amicably) separated itself from the rest of Common Ground. By 2009, the clinic had an operating budget of over one million dollars per year, more than fifteen staff members, and a state-of-the-art electronic medical record system.

The achievement of the clinic alone stands as a great credit to Common Ground. But within the organization there were problems. Casey Leigh, a young, white activist who volunteered with them, rose quickly to the rank of volunteer coordinator at St. Mary's. She came out of the experience with heavy critiques of what she saw from some white activists:

> Through my role as volunteer coordinator and interactions with people at St. Mary's, I was always amazed by people's sense of entitlement to experience in volunteer work. It was always a point of conflict when people were told that we didn't take volunteers for less than a week. Most [white] people are certain that their help is always needed and valuable. I do not exempt myself from this judgment. While it was in operation as a housing site, St. Mary's left a huge footprint in the 9th Ward—through sheer volume of people, noise, vehicles, equipment, trash, people drinking in the neighborhood, ex-volunteers setting up squats in houses around the school, etc. It is not okay that this revolving group of predominantly white people moved into the school and made it home, brought all of our cultural baggage with us, and even worse, felt entitled to be there.

For Leigh, the root of the problem was the short-term volunteers, because they were not from the community and came without an understanding or analysis of the intersection of race and other power dynamics:

> Records and community contacts/relationships were rarely passed on. Problems and conflicts were repeated over and over. Leadership of the organization and of projects within it needed to be transferred into the hands of local residents. It is not sustainable, nor accountable, to run an organization based on a revolving-door volunteer base.[19]

Ingrid Chapman, a white organizer with the Catalyst Project, an antiracist project based in the Bay Area, volunteered with Common Ground, PHRF, and other organizations. She came out of the experience with a similar analysis of the role of white, short-term volunteers:

Another example of racism was found in the attitude that relief work is superior to long-term organizing. Many volunteers were dismissive of long-term organizing efforts, while some white people who saw the importance of organizing acted competitively toward Black organizers and attempted redundant organizing efforts in the same communities. Many white middle class folks started projects without establishing any system of accountability to the people the projects impacted and/or sought to serve. They failed to build solid relationships in which feedback and direction comes from those who are most impacted and then incorporated into the work. Not prioritizing accountability leads to unspoken assumption that white people know what is best for the community, and cuts off processes for honest feedback. Also many of these projects started by folks from out of town lasted for very short periods of time and when they left town, they often took with them the resources they had originally brought in and or gained while they were there. When white people got feedback that they were acting in racist and disrespectful ways, they most often got defensive and dismissed those claims. Unfortunately for the Left, this is not an isolated incident. The same story happens almost every time organizations—large or small—comprised primarily of white folks, do not take the time to be self-reflective, build accountable relationships both internally and with people of color most impacted, and do not seriously prioritize anti-racism throughout all aspects of their work.[20]

New Orleanian Greta Gladney described the situation simply: "A lot of privileged folks were able to come here and start a project and not complete it."

A group of young, mostly white Common Ground volunteers who felt compelled to respond to the racism among other volunteers in the organization formed the Anti-Racist Working Group (ARWG). Through workshops, caucuses, discussions, potlucks, and other gatherings, as well as interventions at the point of arrival for new volunteers, ARWG delivered an analysis of racism and white supremacy to thousands of out-of-town activists. Rachel Luft, a professor of sociology at the University of New Orleans, worked with ARWG and brought wisdom and patience to a generation of activists struggling with these issues. Organizers from Catalyst Project spent several months in New Orleans over the years after trina and also helped shape this work.

By coming to their endeavors with an antiracist analysis, these white activists performed vital work. In the current U.S. context, where racism is still a significant factor in everyday life, white folks need to acknowledge and address issues stemming from their privilege. Not just because it's morally correct, but also to be effective in social justice work.

Common Ground and PHRF became the radical initiatives in New Orleans with the widest reputation across the United States, at least in part because they were the projects most welcoming to mass numbers. Volunteers also came through town to put in time with Habitat for Humanity, ACORN, and church-based groups. During the busiest times, such as spring break 2006 and 2007, tens of thousands of volunteers could be seen throughout the most damaged parts of the city, gutting homes or building new ones—or sometimes just taking photos and touring the damage.

Although many histories of the rebuilding highlight the mass numbers of white volunteers that came here, radical women-of-color networks came to New Orleans and not only supported crucial projects, but also were frequently more conscious of, and supportive toward, local efforts. Volunteers worked with grassroots, pre-Katrina organizations such as INCITE! Women of Color Against Violence, Critical Resistance, and arts and community projects including the Ashé Cultural Arts Center. Activists who came to New Orleans pre-Katrina for INCITE's national conference in spring 2005 returned after the storm to support the Women's Health & Justice Initiative (WHJI) and the New Orleans Women's Health Clinic, local affiliates of INCITE! New Orleans founded shortly after the storm.

Nationally, INCITE activists spoke out about the intersecting oppressions that shaped the disaster, initially forwarding the statement via email and on their website:

> INCITE! Women of Color Against Violence is stunned by the catastrophe and tragic loss in the wake of Hurricane Katrina. In New Orleans and in many other communities along the Gulf, people are experiencing unimaginable devastating conditions. We are especially alarmed for the people who have the fewest resources, who were unable to evacuate New Orleans because of poverty, who were—and in some cases still are—trapped without food, water, and medical attention. Because of racism and classism, these people are also overwhelmingly folks of color, and because of sexism, they are overwhelmingly women of color—low income and poor women, single mothers, pregnant women,

women with disabilities, older women and women who are caregivers to family and community members who were unable to leave the city. Women living at the intersections of systems of oppressions are paying the price for militarism, the abandonment of their communities, and ongoing racial and gender disparities in employment, income, and access to resources and supports....

Though we are also very distressed about reports of violence—including sexual and physical violence against women and children—in the area caused largely by widespread chaos and desperation, we condemn the current mass militarization of the area. There have been numerous accounts of vicious police brutality experienced by men and women who have survived untold horrors only to be subjected to abuse by the law enforcement officials sent to "save" them.... A militarized response is another piece of a racist pattern of dehumanizing poor people of color. Instead of seeing poor Black people driven desperate by the appallingly weak and unacceptably slow response of the federal government, the media and the government frame these primary victims as criminals or blame them for bringing the circumstances on themselves by "disobeying" mandatory evacuation orders when they had no means to comply.

We demand that there be no further criminalization of survivors of the hurricane as rescue, recovery, and rebuilding efforts go forward.[21]

Through its local affiliate, the Women's Health & Justice Initiative (WHJI)—and, later, through the New Orleans Women's Health Clinic—INCITE worked on multiple fronts after the storm. WHJI was established as a radical feminist of color organization dedicated to improving the social and economic health and well-being of women of color and their communities. Their first project, the New Orleans Women's Health Clinic (NOWHC), was created to attend to the immediate health care needs of low-income and uninsured women in the city. In addition to providing comprehensive, affordable, and safe sexual and reproductive health care, the clinic combined health services with social justice organizing in order to address the root causes of health disparities, as well as sexual and reproductive oppression.

According to NOWHC's co-founder Shana griffin,

The clinic was about more than service provision and care delivery. Its formation was about working from an intersectional framework of community development and health justice to increase women's access to high-quality, non-coercive, unbiased, and comprehensive sexual and reproductive health care—while integrating an understanding of the systemic and structural ways in which racism, gender oppression, and poverty make themselves known on the bodies and in the lives of our community.

In great frustration to its organizers, WHJI's work with its sister organization NOWHC was undermined in many ways. While the clinic was still in its planning stages, Common Ground heard about the project and promptly started their own women's clinic. This move was seen as a concerted attempt by Common Ground director Brandon Darby to sabotage the work of INCITE and WHJI organizers. In the larger scheme, organizers reported feeling marginalized by a social justice community that didn't prioritize the work of women of color, and by a medical community that disparaged the organizing aspect of their mission. Despite these obstacles, the New Orleans Women's Health Clinic provided services and health advocacy information to an estimated 8,820 women from 2007 through 2009, including direct medical services to 620 women, 430 of whom made repeat visits.

Through the support of WHJI, the New Orleans Women's Health Clinic did more than bring health care to women who otherwise might not have had it—they also contributed to an urgent dialogue on the nature of assistance and how organizing intersects with providing services. This was one of the most important issues raised during the post-storm era.

New Orleans organizations benefited from direct support offered by principled allies from across the country. For example, Malcolm X Grassroots Movement (MXGM), a national organization dedicated to the liberation of Afrikans in the United States; the Advancement Project, a legal and communications project; and Southerners On New Ground (SONG), a Southern queer initiative that seeks to bring an analysis of race and class to the queer movement, all volunteered and brought aid and funding. Crucially, these organizations came prepared to follow the leadership of folks on the ground, rather than arriving with their priorities already set, which was the model of corporate relief providers from the Red Cross on down.

Also supporting the struggle were Internet activists ColorofChange, who were inspired to action by Katrina. They sought to funnel online outrage into racial justice activism. One of their first outreach projects was selling a t-shirt that proclaimed "Kanye Was Right," referring to musician Kanye West's legendary TV appearance in which he stated, "George Bush doesn't care about Black people." ColorofChange later branched out beyond New Orleans, but continued to highlight issues in Louisiana, from activism at Angola prison to the case of the Jena Six.

Common Ground began with a very well-informed critique of the massive failures of the Red Cross and other aid agencies, and their defined goal was to work with the community, to support people's being in charge of their own rebuilding. Common Ground's efforts could be viewed as a multi-year experiment in what a radical model of assistance could look like. In 2006 and 2007, they even undertook to remake the idea of public housing by attempting to purchase a massive, privately owned low-income housing complex on New Orleans's West Bank called the Woodlands. For several months, as they tried to raise the money to purchase the complex, Common Ground volunteers worked to fix the property and support the tenants—attempting to redefine the tenant-landlord paradigm as one of cooperative ownership and management. The Woodlands experiment ultimately ended in heartbreak for both the tenants and the volunteers who had put in hundreds of hours of work when the Woodlands' owners suddenly, inexplicably severed their negotiations with Common Ground and evicted all the tenants.

Common Ground and PHRF are case studies in two kinds of disaster response. Sadly, the efforts of both proved unsustainable. This was due in part to the fact that both organizations were largely built from an activist base with a limited attention span (often only the length of a spring break from college). No doubt the general stress of operating in post-Katrina New Orleans also played a role.

Both PHRF and its offshoot, POC, formally closed their doors—PHRF in December of 2007 and POC about a year later. Curtis Muhammad expressed his disappointment with the U.S. Left and publicly departed from the country. He issued a public statement, gave a farewell interview on *Democracy Now!*, and moved to Jamaica, where he opened an organizer training institute called the International School for Bottom-Up Organizing. He still comes to New Orleans, but he has said that he doesn't believe the U.S. Left is ready for the kind of revolutionary change that is needed, and has decided to focus his work on supporting third world struggles in other parts of the Americas.

In late 2008, the reputation and legacy of Common Ground was diminished when it was revealed—first through a newspaper article, then through his own admission in an open letter—that one of the founders was an FBI informant.[22] Brandon Darby, a charismatic, shaved-head white militant in his early thirties, had been involved in numerous fractious conflicts within Common Ground, including the ejection of scores of volunteers for "dissent," the systematic ignoring of a wave of sexual harassment and assault against young female volunteers, and messy public conflicts with INCITE and PHRF, as well as with individuals such as Mama Dee, an influential community leader in the Seventh Ward neighborhood. Some community members had been suspicious of Darby from the beginning. Steve Bradberry, director of the New Orleans chapter of ACORN, was unsurprised to hear the accusations. "It's like when I heard Milli Vanilli were lip-synching," he said. "Number one, why is everyone surprised? Number two, who cares?"

Yet Darby's high profile and passionate advocacy had deceived many. He appeared in numerous television and radio interviews, seizing a prominent role in *Right of Return*, Academy Award–winner Jonathan Demme's documentary about New Orleans, which also secured Darby an appearance on Tavis Smiley's TV show. He was romantically involved with many young volunteers, who felt betrayed when they discovered this impassioned advocate of revolutionary upheaval was in fact on the FBI payroll.

This revelation has shaped the way many people view the legacy of Common Ground. Malik Rahim lived through the schisms caused by the U.S. government's COINTELPRO activity at its high point during the '60s and '70s, which involved the extensive use of government infiltration to foment and sustain distrust within movements. Rahim had trusted Darby deeply and implicitly. The revelations broke his heart.

It would be a mistake to judge Common Ground by Brandon Darby, or to judge PHRF and POC by their conflicts or sudden dissolutions. Whatever failures these organizations had, they also grappled very directly with fundamental issues that we as a movement must face: How do we engage in relief responsibly? If we cannot rely on our government or other state actors, if churches and the Red Cross and other charities are using flawed models, where do we turn for successful paradigms? Each time a disaster comes, whether natural or man-made (or, more likely, both), concerned people everywhere want to help. We want to rush to the site and volunteer or send money. If neither of these models is effective, what can we do? It's easy—and accurate—to say that we need to change the system that caused these disasters or allowed them to happen. However, when the next flood comes, and people are on roofs, starving, crying out for help, we need to find a way to give aid while also working to change the system and following the leadership of the people most affected.

Solidarity is a great idea, but what does it look like in practice? Activists from wealthy countries (or people from this country who are privileged beyond those they intend to help) often bring their privilege with them when they try to join in solidarity with other movements. A New York collective called Rethinking Solidarity phrased the discussion this way:

> Accountability is a process, one that moves in both directions and requires more thoughtful reflection of our position in this country in relation to others. This point is lost among those who believe that solidarity means forever assuming the posture of charitable support ("What can we do for the folks down there?"). And while at face value we may ask for nothing in return, few can deny the cachet that comes with having traveled abroad, the almost consumptive pleasure of immersing yourself in the culture of another's political movements. This is the pitfall of activist tourism—the privilege of visiting other counties and movements and informing oneself with a firsthand account without the responsibility of full engagement, of being a stakeholder. So long as social movements remain something to go and see as opposed to something we live, then despite our best intentions, we find ourselves only taking up space and inserting ourselves in communities in a way that reflects our internalized colonial attitudes and privileges.[23]

The same problems that arose among international solidarity activists also manifested in the post-Katrina landscape. In many cases, activists who had traveled to Palestine or Latin America were some of the same people who came to New Orleans.

Overall, most New Orleanians have love and appreciation for the volunteers that came down here after the storm. These questions of solidarity have no easy solution. But for our movement to progress and succeed, we need to keep asking these questions. The Rethinking Solidarity collective formulated some advice for moving forward:

> Being in solidarity with the people of the Global South means building relationships and strong communities of resistance here; by doing so we are linking to those standing up to the vast, global systems of control. This may seem vague, even counterintuitive, for how can you be in solidarity abroad by focusing within? But think of the converse logic of those from the United States claiming to be in solidarity with others, when their homeland is very much a "backward" country in many ways. Indeed, few can deny that when it comes to building strong social movements, those in the United States are in need of desperate aid from the Global South. Activists in the United States are still suffering from the way social movements have been crushed and "professionalized" over the past thirty years. We have lost touch with the basics, the foundation of movement building, which is about building relationships and sustainable communities while breaking out of the confines of single-issue organizing.
>
> This doesn't mean that we stop sending necessary support and resources to those abroad who need it. But our accountability lies in what we do within our own communities here. If our own communities are not strong enough to stand up to neoconservatives, then the work of those who promulgate war without end, the dictatorship of the free market, and the stealing of indigenous land will be made all the easier.
>
> What's more, focusing on communities here in the United States compels us to understand First World "privilege" as not purely nation-bound (i.e., if you reside here, you've got privilege). On the contrary, privilege is layered by histories of slavery, colonization, patriarchal control, etc. Our solidarity struggles must therefore find ways to address these inequalities within. This involves learning from the struggles of the Global South as well as offering what we can from within the US, including the perspectives and learned lessons of oppressed peoples in the US.
>
> The political moment calls for the kind of intercommunal solidarity that Huey P. Newton had in mind.... Today's movements fully recognize that sustainable power has always been located in communities seeking to do the "impossible" (at least what's considered impossible here in the United States)—that is, the literal building of new societies

that may provide alternatives to the nation-state model. Solidarity is to attempt the impossible wherever you might stand.[24]

As for attempting the impossible, New Orleans organizer James Perry and professor Melissa Harris Lacewell provided concrete numbers that illustrated the huge scope of the effort and the exponentially larger task at hand: "Millions of volunteer hours...have put more than 2,000 units of housing back into commerce. While noteworthy, the success pales when one considers that more than 80,000 units of housing were damaged."[25] Volunteer efforts cannot replace the damaged infrastructure of an entire city. At best, volunteers can contribute by reinforcing a safety net and by supporting local projects that bring a systemic analysis. The problems are structural, and any solution must address this larger context.

I believe that we should follow the example of the Zapatistas, who say, "Walking, we ask questions." In other words, we should keep moving forward and not become paralyzed by our doubts. At the same time, we must continue to ask the hard questions. What are we trying to do? Are we doing the right thing, and in the right way?

Reflecting on white activist responses to Katrina, Curtis Muhammad said to poet and journalist Walidah Imarisha:

> Every white person who shows up has the disease called white supremacy, and if they don't confront it and work on it, they are going to continue to have it. That's just the reality of racism.... [White activists] are not runaway slaves. They aren't now and they weren't during the Underground Railroad days. They can help us, feed us, house us, but they are not the slaves. They can't lead us.[26]

Stephanie Guilloud, a white organizer with Project South, wrote in a similar vein: "Confronting white supremacy is not an existential activity. The lesson here for our U.S. movements is about understanding how to challenge the dynamics of privilege and oppression while also building large, wide, and deep movements that are led by and rooted in the experiences of people who know injustice and exploitation—currently and historically."[27]

Many volunteers learned crucial lessons just from being here. First, they witnessed the nature of this disaster—they saw disaster capitalism close-up, in action, and the brutal faces of racism and profiteering exposed. Second, they were able to see and be inspired by local, grassroots resistance.

The experiments of Common Ground and PHRF were powerful learning and teaching experiences—and, more importantly, they gave vital help and support to people that needed it the most. Thousands received concrete aid, whether through house gutting, rebuilding, legal support, health care, or in countless other areas. Common Ground has not disbanded; in fact, they are still active, mostly in the Lower Ninth Ward and Algiers neighborhoods. The health clinic Common Ground started has been rated among the nation's best free health clinics and offers an exciting example of radical politics in action. While PHRF ceased to exist, their work was continued by former PHRF staff including anti–police brutality activist Malcolm Suber and rapper Sess 4-5.

WHJI, the INCITE affiliate, is still active as well. The New Orleans Women's Health Clinic was forced to close, mostly due to lack of funding. However, WHJI went on to be important leaders in the struggle from public housing, and through their ongoing public education campaigns, research projects, and organizing, they have been key in framing the health care debate. Beginning in 2008, WHJI sponsored a series of institutes to facilitate community-building conversations between social justice organizers and health practicioners, with an overarching goal of developing grassroots strategies that could equip those people most disenfranchised by the medical industry to exercise their agency and take control of their bodies, reproduction, and sexuality.

The extended impact of these initiatives lies in the experiences and lessons taken home by the volunteers. A new generation of student leaders, activists, and organizers will have had their views shaped by their work here. During the peak of activity of PHRF and Common Ground, they welcomed thousands of young people to bear witness. These volunteers made films, took photos, wrote articles, and told the stories of what they had experienced to millions of people—friends as well as strangers. The devastation of a U.S. city, abandoned by its own government, and the desire of the people of that city to return and rebuild despite all odds, will no doubt stay with those volunteers for their entire lives. They experienced—if only for a few days or weeks—the culture of New Orleans and the resistance that culture is built on. The legacy of struggle in New Orleans will live on in the movements they will lead.

PERCENT OF PEOPLE
LIVING BELOW
TWICE THE POVERTY
THRESHOLD BY
CENSUS BLOCK
GROUP IN ORLEANS
PARISH.

% living below twice the poverty threshold

0% - 21%
22% - 38%
39% - 55%
56% - 73%
74% - 100%
Neighborhood boundaries

Lake Pontchartrain

see inset
for rest of
N.O. East

Jefferson
Parish

Mississippi River

Miles
0 1 2 4

St. Bernard
Parish

Jefferson Parish

Miles
10

Greater New Orleans
COMMUNITY
Data CENTER

Feb 3, 2004 <www.gnocdc.org>

PROTEST TO STOP THE DEMOLITION OF CHARITY HOSPITAL,
SEPTEMBER 2009. PHOTO BY TASLIM VAN HATTUM.

CHAPTER FIVE

Dollar Day in New Orleans: Money and Relief

Listen, a million poor since 2004
And they got -illions and killions to waste on the war
And make you question what the taxes is for
Or the cost to reinforce, the broke levee wall
Tell the boss, he shouldn't be the boss anymore
Y'all pray amen
God save, these streets
One dollar per every human being
Feel that Katrina Clap...

—From "Dollar Day" by Mos Def

The video grabs your attention immediately. Young people in the Lower Ninth Ward hold up signs that read: "Looter," "We're still here," and "America did this." Amid empty lots and damaged houses, poet Nik Richard delivers this message straight to the camera: "Hurricane Katrina was the biggest national disaster to hit American soil, and nearly two years later, this area is still devastated. But you know what? We made sure we preserved it strictly for your tourism. For about seventy-five dollars, you can take one of these many tour buses."

Buses and cars drive by, and tourists with cameras stare in curiosity. Richard looks into the camera and says, "It looks like there's more money to be paid in devastation than regeneration. If y'all keep paying your money to see it, should we rebuild it?"

The award-winning short film *New Orleans for Sale* was made by 2-Cent Entertainment, a collective of young Black media makers. The group, which has a revolving membership of about ten members, made the film to convey the frustration felt by New Orleanians as their city became a national spectacle and a backdrop for politicians' stump speeches while rebuilding aid failed to arrive. The film received a 2008 NAACP Image Award and has been widely viewed online. In spite of these successes, 2-Cent is yet another unfunded project in New Orleans—a quintessential example of the brilliant grassroots undertakings that funders pass over. 2-Cent has no paid staff members and next to no budget for any of their pieces.

For 2-Cent, raising money or seeking the praise of the corporate media is beside the point. The collective's target audience is their community. Working at the intersections of art and justice, entertainment and enlightenment, 2-Cent has attracted a wide and growing fan base. They have collaborated with PHRF, produced shows on local television and radio stations, and created mix CDs and scores of short videos, including an ongoing collaboration with the socially conscious rapper Dee-1 and the FreedomLand project, which featured an all-star lineup of local rappers addressing issues of post-Katrina injustice. Above and beyond the creation of inspiring and provocative work, 2-Cent members also seek to pass on their skills to the next generation by teaching media making and presenting their videos in local high schools and colleges, as well as through their own summer camp.

"Huey Newton said the young people always inherit the revolution," quoted Brandan "B-Mike" Odums, 2-Cent's founder. "And that's what 2-Cent is, it's how our generation responded to that call." The collective formed in 2004, when Odums gathered a group of friends—most of them fellow students at the University of New Orleans—to produce a TV show with a message. "A lot of TV promotes a monolithic way of thinking, saying there's only one way to be, or promoting ignorance as cool," added Odums. "We say it's hot to stand up for yourself and speak for yourself."

Kevin Griffin, another founding member, joined because he shared Odums's desire to change the images and messages delivered to today's youth. "We were seeing the images that BET and others were putting out," Griffin said. "And we wanted to do something different, more positive."

In addition to being a media activist, Griffin is also a leader in a citywide movement, spearheaded by the Juvenile Justice Project of Louisiana, to close New Orleans's youth prison, the Youth Study Center. The Juvenile Justice Project has led campaigns to shut down other youth prisons around the state, including the notorious youth prison in Tallulah, Louisiana, and they are also working to create more options for young people who face jail time. For Griffin, these campaigns have personal meaning. "At the age of ten, I was sent to the Youth Study Center," Griffin explained. "A year later I was moved to Tallulah, which was known as the worst youth prison in the country. I was eleven. The next youngest person was seventeen, so I was a child among adults. And I was there for five years."

When he was released, Griffin was determined to turn his experience into something positive. "I could have stayed on that path that was laid out for me," he said. "But I didn't want to become that." He credits his family for helping support him when he got out. Griffin has also worked as a producer at WBOK, a Black-owned talk radio station. Art and commerce run in his family—his uncle, Mannie Fresh, the music impresario of the Cash Money record label, produced music that made New Orleans hip-hop famous.

2-Cent videos are notable for both their humor and style. "We liked a lot of the messages you would see on public access TV," explained Griffin. "But we wanted to make something with better production." This meeting of form and content, a mix of the serious and the comic, characterizes the 2-Cent style.

"We take education and comedy and we mix it all together," said collective member Amanda Rose, aka Manda B, a recent college graduate with a quick wit who writes and acts in the group's videos. "We can trick people into learning. We built it off a foundation of 'edutainment.' Even with our most crazy and bizarre scripts, we have a meaning."

These young media activists praise Gil Scott Heron, who declared famously that the revolution will not be televised, but for 2-Cent, media is a tool to be claimed and used for the mission of social change. "Other generations marched, and we march too," said Odums. "But in this age we have a whole new range of weapons, and we're trying to use those weapons. I think Martin Luther King Jr. would want to be on YouTube, to have his speeches distributed that way. Malcolm X would love to make mix tapes, have those out on the streets. The same reasons they boycotted and had protests in that era are our reasons too. We're coming from that same mindset, but we're using new tools, trying to get our inheritance."

This is New Orleans cultural organizing. In New Orleans, social justice work and the arts are interconnected, and are often one and the same. Neither gets the respect it deserves from politicians or from funders.

Dancers Stephanie McKee and Ausettua Amor Amenkum convey stories of struggle through movement, incorporating Black cultural traditions, such as Mardi Gras rituals and African dance, in their work. Sculptor and painter Willie Birch, who grew up in New Orleans public housing and participated in sit-ins against segregation during the '60s, has become known worldwide for his stunning creations—ranging from sculpture and mixed-media work to paintings with acrylic and charcoal—that are weighted with meaning and history. Musicians Troi Bechet, Tenth Ward Buck, and Rebirth Brass Band are not only master performers, but also continually seek new ways to reach out to young people, pass on their artistic skills, and share their time.

Theatre companies Artspot and Mondo Bizarro have been unafraid to challenge conventional ideas of what theatre is. Although these projects are staffed mostly by white artists, they engage directly in antiracist efforts and work in coalition with, and in support of, powerful Black-led projects such as Junebug Productions, John O'Neal's organization dedicated to continuing the work of the Free Southern Theatre.

Musicians and other artists played key roles in the post-Katrina resistance. Glen David Andrews, a trombone player and vocalist, grew up in the Treme neighborhood as part of a beloved and brilliantly talented musical family that also includes Troy "Trombone Shorty" Andrews and trumpeter James Andrews. Although under thirty, he has already become known as one of the most talented jazz musicians in the country. He is also socially involved, speaking out and performing at marches for health care and playing many benefits.

Andrews became an unintentional spokesperson against the criminalization of New Orleans culture when he was arrested for secondlining without a permit. He came back to play again the next night, still without a permit. "I got to be here," he told a reporter. "Because I have to stand up for what I believe in."[1] Andrews also spoke and performed in front of thousands of people who gathered at a 2009 demonstration to save Charity Hospital—a city institution, founded in 1736, dedicated to providing free health care to New Orleanians—from demolition. "They want us to say goodbye to Charity Hospital," said Andrews. "We ought to be saying goodbye to Bobby Jindal. We ought to be saying goodbye to Ray Nagin and the whole City Council."

After Katrina, the city was changing rapidly, and the institutions and traditions that made it unique were under threat. Musicians and artists fought back, not only performing at benefits but also speaking at demonstrations and even organizing campaigns. Sess 4-5, a young hip-hop artist, joined the staff of the PHRF, organized Katrina memorial demonstrations, and later joined the staff of the Juvenile Justice Project of Louisiana. Hot 8, regarded as one of the best brass bands in New Orleans (and, consequently, as one of the best in the entire United States) worked with Finding Our Folk, a project initiated by Omo Moses, the son of SNCC veteran Robert Moses. Hot 8 toured the Southern states with other musicians and performers, including poet Suheir Hammad and actor Danny Glover, as part of a campaign to organize the Katrina diaspora.

Tamara Jackson, president of the Social Aid and Pleasure Club Task Force, the alliance of all the city's secondline clubs, joined forces with marches to support expanding access to health care. Hip-hop artist Truth Universal was among those who joined with PHRF organizer Kali Akuno in forming a New Orleans chapter of the Malcolm X Grassroots Movement, playing a key role in events such as the city's annual Katrina commemoration march. A group of poets banded together as Artist In Action to coordinate their involvement in social justice work. One of those poets, Chris "One Eye" Williams, also worked for Ashé Cultural Arts Center and took part in a revived community organization, led by Kool Black, called Black Men United for Change, Equality and Justice, which sought to present a unified front of Black men organizing against violence in their communities. Filmmaker and photographer Broderick Webb dedicated his time to supporting the work of the Fyre Youth Squad.

This spirit of resilience inspired activist-artists from across the country and around the world to come to New Orleans. The dance group Urban Bush Women brought performances and established a summer leadership institute in New Orleans for artists and activists. Artist Paul Chan collaborated with the Classical Theater of Harlem to mount a free, site-specific, outdoor production of *Waiting for Godot*, featuring New Orleans native Wendell Pierce, in the Lower Ninth Ward and Gentilly. With the presentation of *Godot*, a "shadow fund," matching the production budget of the play, was donated to local cultural and rebuilding efforts. A duo of poet-artist-performers called Climbing PoeTree created a brilliant performance piece, *Hurricane Season*, with which they crossed the country in a van on a fifty-city tour, connecting local struggles across the United States with struggles in New Orleans.

Prospect.1, described as the largest biennial of international contemporary art ever held in the United States, displayed the work of hundreds of artists in multiple venues throughout New Orleans in 2008, helping to draw tourists back to the still-devastated city and bringing millions of dollars to the local economy.[2] Many New Orleans cultural workers complained that projects like Prospect.1, run by outsiders and appealing largely to cultural elites, took funding and attention away from local artists. Even so, these projects and others helped re-center New Orleans as an important arts and cultural destination.

COMMUNITY SPACES

For a year after the storm, a short street named Bayou Road in the Seventh Ward neighborhood of New Orleans was full of shuttered storefronts. Then, together, almost every shop reopened one day in late 2006. The Community Book Center, in the middle of the block, even managed to re-open despite having no front windows and a floor in major need of repairs. "Step carefully," Vera Warren-Williams, the owner, warned guests as they entered the store during the reopening celebration.

Originally established in 1983 as a bookstore in the home of Warren-Williams's parents, the Community Book Center is a welcoming place to visit and shop, where you can always find conversations about important issues if you're looking. The current location, which Warren-Williams bought shortly before the storm, is a large, open space filled with shelves of books as well as artwork and other items. Warren-Williams, a former substitute teacher, founded the store because she realized that Black youth had no place to find stories that reflected themselves and their history.

Neighborhood spaces such as the Community Book Center have long been a vital part of New Orleans organizing, serving as a gathering place for people and ideas. The revitalization of Bayou Road is just one more example of the community pulling together—friends and strangers stopping by and helping gut houses, cook food, or clear debris.

Although the Community Book Center is a crucial cultural and educational resource, spaces like it have received little outside support. Vera

Warren-Williams and her colleague Jennifer Turner have run Community Book Center for almost three decades with virtually no help from funders, before or after Katrina.

At Sportsman's Corner, a small corner bar in New Orleans's Central City neighborhood, community activists and organizers affiliated with Safe Streets/Strong Communities gather regularly to celebrate victories and holidays. This is also one of the main spots where the city's Social Aid and Pleasure Clubs gather and celebrate, where Mardi Gras Indians practice, and it is a stop on most uptown secondlines. When, after years of organizing, protesting, and lobbying, Safe Streets won municipal funding for an independent monitor over the city's notoriously corrupt and violent police department, the victory party was held at Sportsman's Corner. The community takes care of these spaces, but after Katrina, outside funders ignored them.

WHJI co-founder Shana griffin explained, "Organizing here looks like neighborhood get-togethers, potlucks, block parties, and conversations on a neighbor's porch. It's about culture and community." Black-owned businesses also often function as community spaces, nurturing the city's traditions while supporting local organizing. Barbershops and bookstores traditionally serve as community gathering spaces in Black neighborhoods around the United States, and this also holds true in New Orleans.

But years after Katrina, many of New Orleans's community spaces, vital resources for the revival of the city's culture and neighborhood activity, remain shuttered. Conventional sources of support, such as foundations and charities, have largely ignored this aspect of New Orleans life, and these spaces have received little outside assistance.

Community spaces were generally located in poorer neighborhoods, which sustained the most damage during Katrina. The Marcus Garvey Resource Center, a community space for African American youth located near the former Magnolia housing projects, took in more than five feet of water. Flooding destroyed not just the space but many of the resources inside, such as a rare listing of Black-owned businesses in New Orleans in 1940 and original copies of *The Negro World*, the weekly newspaper founded by Marcus Garvey in 1918.[3] The Resource Center, founded by the cantankerous community activist Louis Harding, has not reopened. As another example, for almost sixty-five years, the legendary Creole restaurant Dooky Chase had operated as a community anchor across the street from the Lafitte projects.

Martin Luther King Jr. held strategy meetings with local community organizers there. Its walls featured stunning paintings by Black artists, and regulars included artists and celebrities like James Baldwin and Ray Charles. Flooded by Katrina, the restaurant closed for repairs, with periodic announcements that it might reopen in 2006—then 2007. After months of rebuilding and with the support of prominent national allies, Dooky Chase was finally able to reopen in 2008, although only on a limited schedule.

Rising rents and costly repairs forced out the Neighborhood Gallery, a Central City–based venue for everything from theatrical productions and art installations to dance parties and community meetings. Their space was always open to any community event, from local spoken word shows to a touring exhibition of Palestinian art.

More than a victim of storm damage, the Neighborhood Gallery was a casualty of a real estate market that was no longer hospitable to small, community-oriented businesses. With entire neighborhoods still blighted, real estate speculators snapped up non-flooded properties and affordable spaces in the city became scarce. Black-owned stores and community spaces found themselves in crisis, as a decimated local population and diminished tourism meant that business suffered. Neighborhood Gallery never fully recovered. Co-directors Sandra Berry and Joshua Walker could no longer afford the rent on their Central City location, and had to move the gallery to their house.

Before closing in 2006, the Neighborhood Gallery had been open in various locations for over twenty years. "Every neighborhood we've gone into, we've enhanced it," co-director Berry said. "We take the arts to the 'hood. We've taken artists to a deserted field and built a playground." After losing their space, Berry and Walker began curating events at schools, coffee shops, and other venues. "We must have spaces that support all of us," Sandra explained. "We have to spread the art, support the culture. From prisons to church. Wherever there are people, we need to be."

Many of the proprietors of community spaces complain that, although their neighborhoods, stories, and images were used by big nonprofits in reports and fundraising appeals, they, as community anchors, never received any support. "They made us the poster child," said Ronald Lewis, who runs a cultural center in the Lower Ninth Ward called the House of Dance and Feathers, "but we got none of the benefits."

A SKY FILLED WITH MONEY

Living in New Orleans in the first years after Katrina, it was as if the sky were filled with money. I imagined it thirty feet up in the air, clearly visible but out of reach. The federal government alone had earmarked more than a hundred billion dollars for hurricane relief and reconstruction in the initial months after the storm.[4]

Yet no one from New Orleans seemed to be able to get his or her hands on that cash. Federal appropriations ended up in the hands of Blackwater, Halliburton, and other private contractors—or got stuck in legislative limbo between Washington and Baton Rouge. Corporate charities like the Red Cross had high administrative overhead that drained much of the money. The conditions they attached to the benefits available to families often kept support from reaching those most in need. Progressive foundations used relief funds to conduct studies, hire experts, and pay for their staff to stay at high-end hotels. Wherever the money went, it didn't go toward making it possible for the displaced to return.

Despite the attention New Orleans received from the Left, progressive resources have been comparatively scarce. Liberal foundations and nonprofits earmarked millions of dollars toward the Gulf, but most of that money did not go to New Orleans–initiated projects. According to local advocates, much of the money went to the same East and West Coast nonprofits that have traditionally received the majority of foundation grants. According to a 2009 report from New York City's Foundation Center, of the top twenty-five recipients of Gulf Coast–earmarked aid, thirteen were located outside the Gulf, including organizations like Teach For America, America*Speaks*, the RAND Corporation, and the Red Cross.[5] Some of these recipients, such as Oxfam America and the Ms. Foundation for Women, then set up their own programs to pass along that money to New Orleans organizations, with varying degrees of accountability and transparency. Even in the best-case scenarios (many activists have praised both Oxfam and the Ms. Foundation), this added another well-paid filter between the aid and the people who needed it.

Post-Katrina, local collectives without grants or paid staff immediately began crucial rebuilding work with almost no funding or outside attention. New Orleans residents sacrificed to rebuild their lives and their city. During this period, they watched as national organizations visited, conducted interviews, wrote reports, and received grants, yet did little to help the city. There are thousands of stories of groups and individuals that came through New Orleans with lots of promises, only to disappear soon after.

A dramatic disparity was established between paid and unpaid workers in post-Katrina efforts. In the days after the storm, the people who did most of the rescuing in New Orleans were not affiliated with any charity or government agency. They were neighbors helping each other out. For example, the Soul Patrol—a group of young Black men in the Seventh Ward neighborhood organized by longtime community leader Mama Dee—began rescue and relief work days after the storm. The only funding they received came, months later, in the form of small cash donations. Local institutions like Social Aid and Pleasure Clubs, which took on much of the responsibility for bringing people home by tracking down their members, helping to hold together the community that makes New Orleans special, also received almost no support.

The reality is that many of the community groups that do the most crucial work every day don't know how to—or don't have time to—write press releases, grant proposals, or fundraising emails, or design and maintain websites. Other organizations may write eloquent mission statements and speak very well in presentations, coming across as utterly committed, but without roots in the community, they're often misguided and do very little that is concrete. New Orleans has been inundated with top-down, well-funded organizations that are unaccountable to the community, from giants like Red Cross and Save the Children to smaller nonprofits that received funding based on their proposals and mission statements even though they had no plans to do any real work on the Gulf Coast.

In an open letter to funders and national nonprofits released in December 2006, a broad alliance of New Orleans's grassroots organizers, artists, and activists declared, "From the perspective of the poorest and least powerful, it appears that the work of national allies on our behalf has either not happened, or if it has happened it has been a failure."[6]

I helped draft this letter. In conversations with advocates, health care providers, educators, and media makers, I heard many stories of diverted funding and unmet needs. While some signers stressed that they had had significant positive experiences with national allies, few had received anything close to the funding, resources, or staff they needed, and most were still working unsustainable hours while living in a devastated city.

Research backs up the anecdotal reports. A January 2006 article in the *Chronicle of Philanthropy* argued that the $130 million in aid from private and corporate foundations given to New Orleans in the first months after Katrina was "small-potato giving for America's foundations, which collectively have $500 billion in assets." The article also asserted, "Just as deplorable as the small sums poured into the region are the choices foundations have made about where the money should go."[7] In other words, very little of the money went to projects directed by or accountable to New Orleanians. Advocate and lobbyist Russell Henderson called this phenomenon the "Halliburtonization of the nonprofit sector."

Despite widespread accusations of racism and mismanagement on the ground in New Orleans and in shelters across the South, the Red Cross raised more than two billion dollars from Katrina appeals. A February 2006 report from the Foundation Center pointed out that the Red Cross "ranked as by far the largest named recipient of contributions from foundation and corporate donors in response to hurricanes Katrina and Rita," receiving almost 35 percent of this aid. At the time of the report, an additional 35 percent of the money designated by foundations for Katrina aid had not been spent. The Bush-Clinton Katrina Fund, the Salvation Army, and United Way combined received another 13 percent. The remaining 17 percent was mostly spread among other national organizations.[8]

According to the *Chronicle of Philanthropy* article, foundations "seem to have been preoccupied with the issue of accountability. Many foundations wondered how they could be certain that grants to local groups would be well spent and, therefore, publicly accountable."[9] While that is a reasonable concern, it also reveals a double standard. The *Chronicle* writer went on to state, "The question of accountability didn't seem to bother the large foundations that gave so generously to the Red Cross, which had a questionable record of competence to begin with and attracted even more criticism in the aftermath of Katrina over its unwise use of funds, high administrative costs, and lack of outreach to minorities."[10] Meanwhile, the concern for accountability only traveled one way: foundations rarely discussed ways in which they would be accountable to the people most affected by the disaster. Instead, they asked how the organizations they funded would be accountable to the foundations, their funders.

The message from major funders was that New Orleanians could not handle the money appropriately. "Twenty-seven years running a business, and they don't trust us with money," commented Jennifer Turner of the Community Book Center. "They think we're all stupid or corrupt." She and owner Vera Warren-Williams have inspired me in myriad ways over the years, not least with their kindness. But if you want to see Turner get angry, ask her about foundations and funders.

She's not alone with this sentiment. Among community activists in New Orleans, the nerve is still raw. "A lot of that money goes to the West Coast or other places," said Deon Haywood, director of the New Orleans health care organization Women With A Vision (WWAV), referring to the money raised by nonprofits and foundations. "They see the South as too hard. They don't believe change will come here."

Many feel that media depictions of New Orleans and the bias and racism reflected therein were in part to blame for the reluctance of major funders to give money directly to the people most in need. In other words, the popular view of the people of New Orleans was as looters and criminals, or at least as too helplessly poor and ignorant to be trusted as partners in the rebuilding of their own city. "They figure if they give poor people money they'll buy crack and cigarettes," summarized PHRF co-founder Curtis Muhammad.

Years after the storm, news stories about post-Katrina New Orleans continued to focus on FEMA payments that were misused or obtained through fraud, rather than on the bigger stories of corporate profiteering or the tens of thousands of displaced people who received no aid whatsoever. Even progressives I know from the East and West Coasts repeated the same old biases about people from the South being backward and corrupt.

For a region of the country that has been historically underfunded, these issues are nothing new. "I'm very much afraid of this 'foundation complex,'" civil rights organizer Ella Baker said back in 1963, referring to the changes happening to the structure of grassroots movements, which were already becoming more beholden to those with the money than to those at the grassroots.[11] Fannie Lou Hamer, civil rights leader and co-founder of the Mississippi Freedom Democratic Party, echoed and expanded on

Baker's words: "I can't see a leader leading me nowhere if he's in New York and I'm down here catching hell."[12]

Going back even further: Marcus Garvey warned, in 1922, "The Negro who lives on the patronage of philanthropists is the most dangerous member of our society because he is willing to turn back the clock of progress at any time when his benefactor asks him so to do."[13]

Indeed, many foundations were established with the explicit goal of subverting and ultimately co-opting social movements. In 1970, John D. Rockefeller's Commission on Foundation and Private Philanthropy reported its mission this way:

> The spirit of dissent has spread its contagion across our student population and from there to other sectors of American life....If they are not to reach their climax in a war of all against all, we are summoned by this turmoil to carefully consider the ways in which we can convert dissent into a force for constructive action and civil peace....We must evolve more responsive processes through which our young and disenfranchised can secure a fair piece of the social action, whether or not they can acquire a piece of the affluent economic action.[14]

Foundations have fostered competition for scarce funding and resources rather than cooperation for a common goal of liberation. They have encouraged an environment where the "responsible" organizations, with moderate goals, are pitted against the "irresponsible," which demand wider, more systemic change. They have helped convert the job of an organizer into a career like any other, with all the hierarchies and bureaucracies of any corporate path. They have taken revolutionary dissent and redirected it into reform.

In *What Lies Beneath*, an anthology about New Orleans post-Katrina, members of INCITE wrote, "Though hundreds of nonprofits, NGOs, university urban planning departments, and foundations have come through the city, they have paid little attention to the organizing led by people of color that existed before Katrina and that is struggling now more than ever."[15]

The INCITE authors—who, through their work on the New Orleans Women's Health Clinic, experienced these issues firsthand—posited that successful organizing is rooted in the community and takes a long time to bear fruit. Mainstream funders don't appreciate this, and "a look at who and what gets funding in New Orleans, from foundations to support work, reveals the priorities of these foundations and the entire nonprofit system. Organizations that represent their work through quick and quantifiable accomplishments are rewarded by the system. Foundations are not only drawn to them but are pressured by their own donors to fund them."[16]

For many in the national nonprofit field, Katrina has been an opportunity for career advancement. While New Orleans groups were too overwhelmed by tragedy to think of applying for grants, a few well-placed national organizations and individuals did not hesitate to move to the front of the line. Although some had no connection to New Orleans, they often had prior relationships with the major foundations, as well as resources that translated into easier access to funding—development staff, website designers, and professional promotional materials.

Of course, foundations are not to blame for the continuing crisis in New Orleans, nor do they have a special responsibility to help the city. However, many foundations claim to this day that they supported the post-Katrina recovery. Because of these boasts, their actions (and alleged results) deserve added scrutiny from those they claim to have helped. Further, foundations exist in part to exploit a tax loophole, which allows wealthy individuals and families to establish foundations rather than paying money to the U.S. government in taxes. In this way, it is actually U.S. tax dollars the foundations are spending, and so they should be accountable to us all.

Foundations are an integral part of the current structure of U.S. nonprofits, a system that INCITE has dubbed the "nonprofit industrial complex" (NPIC), to emphasize the intersecting, interdependent, and corporatized structure of the system. In the NPIC, projects are frequently pitted against each other for grants from foundations. Community involvement is effectively discouraged—there is often more money to be had by parachuting into another community. The priorities of any given "mission" are guided by those with money, as accountability to those in need has become increasingly rare. The directors of nonprofit organizations may be aware of these problems but are so dependent on the foundations that they are afraid to make waves. Sometimes they are even afraid to be quoted on the record with their critiques of the system.

One of the major lessons to be learned from Katrina is that the structures of U.S. movements are in serious crisis. As INCITE members observed, incorporating as a 501(c)(3) nonprofit has become a crucial step for organizations, and the resulting paperwork and fundraising have made MBA graduates more desirable than visionaries. Many groups are also held hostage by work plans developed as part of grant applications and have lost the flexibility needed to respond to crises.

Shortly after Katrina, Safe Streets/Strong Communities co-director Xochitl Bervera posed the question,

> What's wrong with the 501(c)(3) structure that everyone could come down for a five-day tour but no one could come to actually do the work for a month? What's wrong with a 501(c)(3) structure where everyone is already so under-resourced and then tied to projects and promised outcomes that the biggest disaster this nation has seen in decades occurs and no one can stop what they are working on to come down and help? What's wrong with the foundation world that they have to produce 207 fancy glossy interview reports to their board in order to shuffle a few thousand dollars our way?

The current paradigm simply doesn't work. With accountability to funders but not to the community in need, aid projects are weakened and sometimes counterproductive. In *What Lies Beneath*, INCITE members argued that the structures of the NPIC prevented organizations from responding capably to the disaster as it occurred, and that a movement responsive to local communities would have been more effective. "Community organizing and community–based accountability are the things we have left when the systems have collapsed," they concluded.[17]

New Orleanians told me that in dealing with foundations, they were expected to be responsive to the foundations instead of to the concrete needs on the ground. "It's not just that you have to jump when they tell you to jump," the director of an education project told me, "you also have to act like you wanted to jump anyway."

"Whenever you deal with foundations," observed WWAV director Deon Haywood, "it's not about us or our communities' needs. It's about what is in their president's head that day."

The *Chronicle of Philanthropy* article encouraged foundations to play a role in "strengthening nonprofit organizations that serve low-income people and African Americans, as well as other minorities....America's foundations need to move from a policy of neglect of the nation's most vulnerable organizations to one of affirmative action, an approach that will mean changing the way many foundations do business."[18]

When asked for solutions, activists called for allies to bring a deeper respect for the experiences of the people on the ground. Others expressed an overall need for movements to move away from reliance on foundations and large donors.

"What's wrong with our movement and our organizations," asked Bervera, "that they couldn't collaborate and coordinate and offer us some organized plan of assistance instead of asking us to do more and more to help them help us? What's wrong with funders that they couldn't coordinate, the way they ask us to, so that they could come down once, together, and not on fifteen separate trips?"

The excuses for a lack of federal support for New Orleans are similar to the critiques levied against countries in the global South. For example, it was often claimed that the local New Orleans government was too corrupt and would squander any aid—the same kind of charge often unleashed on recipients of international aid. In Haiti, for example, the vast majority of post-earthquake aid went to nongovernmental organizations, further undermining the government's sovereignty.

As part of a scathing indictment of NGOs in Africa, Tajudeen Abdul-Raheem, the secretary general of the Pan-African Movement, wrote, "I am sure that many NGO workers really have come to Africa because they believe they are doing something good and right. However, it is also true that many are here because of their careers. Our misery is their job. Where will a disaster manager work if there are no more disasters?"[19]

THE RESPONSIBILITY OF RELIEF ORGANIZATIONS

Just outside New Orleans, past the Lower Ninth Ward in the eastern part of the city, is St. Bernard Parish, a mostly white community that was completely devastated by flooding. Thirteen percent of households lived below the federal poverty line, and every home there took in water. This was an area that needed help and needed it badly. However, in the journey toward recovery, St. Bernard pursued a path of racial discrimination that complicated relief efforts. In fact, elected officials deliberately worked to keep African Americans, many of whom had been displaced from New Orleans and were seeking nearby housing, from moving into St. Bernard.

Racial discrimination has a long history in St. Bernard politics. Judge Leander Perez, a power broker who dominated politics in St. Bernard (and neighboring Plaquemines Parish) for almost fifty years until his death in 1969, was known nationally as a spokesman for racial segregation. In a tirade typical of his rhetoric, Perez blamed the civil rights movement on "all those Jews who were supposed to have been cremated at Buchenwald and Dachau but weren't, and Roosevelt allowed 2 million of them illegal entry into our country."[20]

The main road through the parish was named for Perez, and his legacy still has a hold on the political scene. Lynn Dean, a member of the St. Bernard Parish Council, told journalist Lizzy Ratner, "They don't want the Blacks back....What they'd like to do now with Katrina is say, we'll wipe out all of them. They're not gonna say that out in the open, but how do you say? Actions speak louder than words. There's their action."[21]

The "action" Dean referenced was a "blood relative" ordinance the St. Bernard Parish Council passed in 2006. The law made it illegal for parish homeowners to rent to any person not directly related to the renter. In St. Bernard, which was 85 percent white before Katrina hit, this effectively kept Black folks from moving in, and coded language from city officials confirmed that result was exactly the point. The Greater New Orleans Fair Housing Action Center sued the parish on the grounds that the ordinance violated the 1968 Fair Housing Act.

St. Bernard's parish council agreed to a settlement, but the story didn't end there. That illegal ordinance was followed by another, this one blocking the construction of multi-family housing in the parish. By September 2009, U.S. District Judge Ginger Berrigan had found the parish to be in contempt of court three times, saying, "The Parish Council's intent...is and was racially discriminatory," and threatening to fine the parish ten thousand dollars a day if it didn't change its behavior. An editorial in the *Times-Picayune* agreed, saying, "This ruling strips off the camouflage and reveals St. Bernard's actions for what they really are: an effort to keep lower-income people and African Americans from moving into the mostly white parish."[22]

Despite the illegal and troubling laws and policies of the parish, some mainstream relief and recovery organizations declined to take a public position on the controversy. A dispute ensued, stemming from a question asked by activists concerned about racial justice in the rebuilding process: Are reconstruction projects responsible for speaking out against injustice in their community?

Several national organizations and thousands of volunteers came through St. Bernard to volunteer time and donate money, including United Way, the Salvation Army, and the Greater New Orleans Foundation. An organization called the St. Bernard Project, founded in 2006 by two transplants from Washington, D.C., became one of the highest-profile initiatives in the region, with millions of dollars in corporate and individual donations and thousands of volunteers. In 2008, CNN named St. Bernard Project co-founder Liz McCartney its Hero of the Year. On the 2009 Katrina anniversary, President Obama mentioned the organization in his weekly address, saying, "The St. Bernard Project has drawn together volunteers to rebuild hundreds of homes, where people can live with dignity and security."[23] The next week, the Broadway tour of *The Color Purple*, produced by Oprah Winfrey, announced that the production tour would be raising money for the St. Bernard Project, and that author Alice Walker would be personally participating in the fundraising.

This national acclaim and support increased criticism by activists of the implicitly racist rebuilding work happening in the parish. Professor Lance Hill first raised his voice on the issue in 2006, after the "blood relative" ordinance was passed. Hill was quick to point out that he was not against rebuilding housing in the parish. However, he added, "If they chose to rebuild homes that Blacks and Jews would be barred from, at a minimum they have a moral obligation to inform volunteers of the policies of the parish. To not do so is to mislead volunteers and donors and to become complicit with racism."

Hill was also among the signatories of an open letter released shortly after the *Color Purple* announcement, which expressed deep concerns over rebuilding efforts in the parish. "Regrettably, many relief and volunteer organizations chose not to respond to the 'blood relative' law, remaining silent on this issue," the letter stated. "With the benefit of hindsight, we now know that St. Bernard Parish officials interpreted silence as consent, which has now emboldened this rogue government to pursue other means to defy the Fair Housing Act."[24]

The letter was intended to pressure organizations to think about larger issues of injustice as they worked in the region. "It is time that we take a stand against housing discrimination in St. Bernard and throughout the Gulf Coast," the letter continued, "and make clear what the moral imperatives are for all organizations that seek to rebuild the Gulf Coast as a fair and just society."[25] Among the more than fifty signatories of the letter were human rights organizations such as the National Economic and Social Rights Initiative and U.S. Human Rights Network, the regional groups Moving Forward Gulf Coast and Louisiana Justice Institute, local housing rights groups MayDay Nola and Survivors Village, and high-profile individuals such as historian and author Douglas Brinkley.

Zack Rosenburg, the co-founder of the St. Bernard Project, was angered by the allegations of Hill and others. "We are not an advocacy group and we're not commenting on that," he told me, referring to the laws of the parish. "We're helping people get home." Rosenburg added that at least 30 percent of the families they had worked with had been African American, and he asked me to "think about the Black families who are living in FEMA trailers and want to move home, before writing this."

Advocates responded that rebuilding without challenging systemic injustices—in this particular case, injustices newly introduced by the local government—actually exacerbated the problem. They pointed out that the number of houses rebuilt for African Americans in the community—perhaps two hundred at the most, including the work of all the nonprofits in the area—paled in comparison to the thousands of Black New Orleanians excluded by the laws of the parish.

"This is why this issue in St. Bernard has troubled me so much," added Hill. "Exclusion is at the core of the injustices of Katrina. The deliberate efforts to prevent people from returning and the denial that these policies and practices were in place have been the central issues. The exclusionary ideology that was widespread in the white community in New Orleans became law in St. Bernard."

Ultimately, the aim of an open letter was to explicitly challenge groups like the St. Bernard Project and their model of working on reconstruction while studiously ignoring the larger context. Multiple levels of pressure challenged the elected officials in St. Bernard Parish and made clear that their policies would not stand. Through a combination of the efforts of or-

ganizers and legal action taken by the Greater New Orleans Fair Housing
Action Center, the laws were overturned and new, non-discriminatory
housing was built. Beyond that, organizers hoped victory would help create
a prototype for challenging aid organizations in the future. "Our silence
doesn't help anybody," said Hill. "It destroys more than the relief groups
can ever dream of building."

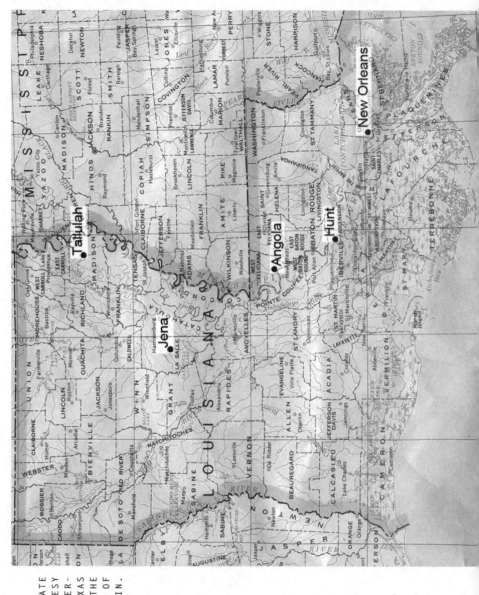

LOUISIANA STATE
MAP, COURTESY
OF THE UNIVER-
SITY OF TEXAS
LIBRARIES, THE
UNIVERSITY OF
TEXAS AT AUSTIN.

SECONDLINE TO PROTEST SCHOOL-TO-PRISON
PIPELINE, APRIL 2009. PHOTO BY ABDUL AZIZ.

CHAPTER SIX ·

Behind Them Penitentiary Walls: Organizing in Prison

To all my people on them corners I consider as dogs
I wish I could break a package down and send it to y'all
I know ya feelin me behind them penitentiary walls
Put me on the visit list and I'll be in to see y'all
Talk to 'em—your mayor ain't your friend, he's the enemy
Just to get your vote, a saint is what he pretend to be
Fuck him! Ah–listen to me, I got the remedy

From "Get Ya Hustle On" by Juvenile

The United States has the largest incarcerated population of any nation on earth—the people imprisoned in this country represent 25 percent of all prisoners around the world.[1] Nationwide, more than seven million people are in U.S. jails, on probation, or on parole, and African Americans are incarcerated at nearly ten times the rate of whites.[2] Our criminal justice system has become an insatiable machine—even when crime rates go down, the prison population keeps rising.[3]

The state of Louisiana has the highest rate of incarceration in the United States—816 sentenced prisoners per 100,000 state residents. By comparison, Texas places a distant second with 694 per 100,000. African Americans make up 32 percent of Louisiana's population but they constitute 72 percent of the state's prison population.[4]

Prison makes us all less free—by breaking up families and communities, by dehumanizing the imprisoned both during and after their sentences, by perpetuating a cycle of poverty, and by making all citizens complicit in the incarceration of their fellow human beings. Since so many New Orleanians live in prisons around the state, the stories from Louisiana State Penitentiary at Angola, Orleans Parish Prison, and all the other prisons of this state are central to the narrative of New Orleans's poor and dispossessed. Angola or a similar "lifers' prison" is frequently the final stop on an unjust journey that begins with children born into substandard health

135

care and housing; then shuttled into a school system that treats them like criminals from a young age; then left with few job options in a tourism-based economy in which corporations profit while the residents are left out; and finally entangled in a criminal justice system that treats them as guilty until proven innocent. This is the "cradle-to-prison pipeline," and nowhere is it more entrenched than in New Orleans.

For many poor Black youth growing up in New Orleans, the education system has functioned to train them for a life under state control. From metal detectors at the front door of their elementary schools to police officers patrolling the halls, students can view their time in school as preparation more for incarceration than for a career.

Pre-Katrina, thirty-eight percent of the city's children were living in poverty[5] and a majority of students in public schools were being raised in single-parent households. After the storm, families and communities were broken up further, and advocates reported that many students were being raised by siblings or foster parents, and a surprising number were living on their own. The principal at John McDonogh High School estimated in 2006 that twenty percent of his students were living without their parents.[6]

In New Orleans, 95 percent of the detained youth in 1999 were Black. At least 78 percent were locked up for nonviolent offenses. The detention center in Jefferson Parish reported that 96 percent of the minors held there in 2000 were incarcerated for nonviolent offenses. At least a third had been sentenced to three or more years.[7]

While New Orleans is in some ways culturally separated from the rest of the state, we are ultimately still under its control. Lawmakers in Baton Rouge make the policies that affect us, and the state controls more of our schools than does the city. And tens of thousands of New Orleanians spend their lives out of the city, locked in prisons upstate.

In 2004, Louisiana spent $96,713 to incarcerate each child in detention, compared to $7,877 to educate each student in the public schools.[8] The state ranked forty-eighth in the country for teacher salaries.[9] New Orleans had a 40 percent illiteracy rate in 2004 (that number includes people at "level one" literacy, meaning the person is unable to find an address on a map or address a letter), and it was estimated that over 50 percent of Black ninth graders would not graduate from high school in four years.[10] Every day, the equivalent of more than two classrooms of young people dropped out of Louisiana schools and about fifty thousand students were absent.[11]

According to a report by Human Rights Watch:

> The state of Louisiana has one of the highest rates in the country of children living in poverty and children not in school or working. Large numbers of children, especially Black children, are suspended from school each year, sometimes for the whole year. Approximately 1,500 Louisiana children are confined in secure correctional facilities each year.... In response to the question, "what would you most like to change here?" virtually every child at all of the facilities responded that they would like the guards to stop hitting them and that they would like more food. Children consistently told us that they were hungry.[12]

The prison industrial complex is also a system of gender violence. Not only are women the fastest growing prison population, but they are also victimized by this system in other ways—as one main example, many women are left to raise children alone when their partners are taken to prison. In a joint statement with Critical Resistance, members of INCITE noted the lack of attention paid to the system's impact on women: "Prison and police accountability activists have generally organized around and conceptualized men of color as the primary victims of state violence. Women prisoners and victims of police brutality have been made invisible by a focus on the war on our brothers and sons."[13]

Nearly everyone agrees that our criminal justice system needs to change, yet there is sharp disagreement over what in particular the problem is, and these divisions often fall along lines of race and class. Privileged residents, who have little personal experience with false arrest or the loss of family members to the criminal justice system, often think that even more people should be locked up. Those who have interacted directly with the system are more likely to view the solution as more complicated than simply putting an ever-increasing number of people behind bars. And in the United States, personal experience with the criminal justice system is definitely divided by race.

A 2009 article in the *New York Review of Books* detailed this division and its development:

> In the 1950s, when segregation was still legal, African-Americans comprised 30 percent of the prison population. Sixty years later, African-

Americans and Latinos make up 70 percent of the incarcerated population, and that population has skyrocketed. The disparities are greatest
where race and class intersect—nearly 60 percent of all young black
men born between 1965 and 1969 who dropped out of high school went
to prison at least once on a felony conviction before they turned thirty-
five. And the incarceration rate for this group—black male high school
dropouts—is nearly fifty times the national average.[14]

New Orleans youth groups address these issues directly, using popular education and arts to organize among young people around these issues. Fyre Youth Squad (FYS), initiated by young people from John
McDonogh High School, organized a secondline in 2009 to protest the
cradle-to-prison pipeline. Their members speak out and organize regularly on criminal justice and educational issues, and often work with other
groups like Young Adults Striving for Success, a youth-organizing project
affiliated with the Juvenile Justice Project of Louisiana and coordinated
by rapper and activist Sess 4-5.

Another youth collaboration committed to this issue is ReThink,
which has gathered kids together from city public schools to report on
conditions and make demands for change. They have worked in coalition
with FYS as well as with members of the Vietnamese American Young
Leaders Association (VAYLA), which is active mostly among the Vietnamese community in New Orleans East, but is concerned about the same
issues and generally eager to work in coalition with other groups.

Kids from ReThink, working collectively, wrote a poem reflecting
their experiences with the issue, called "School to Prison Pipeline":

> Metal detectors are what we want to eliminate
> And respect is what we want to gain
> The security guards think it's just a game
> School to prison is just not fair
> Our school just doesn't care…
> The principal don't care about our dignity and freedom
> They just think we're gonna be on the streets like all the rest
> We can prove that we can be leaders like the best

In 2009, ReThink asked Louisiana State Superintendent of Schools
Paul Vallas to end the use of metal detectors and to lessen the atmosphere
of policing in the schools. They requested that, instead, the school system

train student intervention teams to greet their classmates at the beginning of the day as a means of utilizing youth leadership to avert conflict. Vallas refused to consider ending the use of metal detectors; he did, however, implement several other student proposals, and the ReThink project became an important tool for bringing young people's voices into the decision-making process.

ORLEANS PARISH PRISON DURING THE STORM

When the storm hit, there was no evacuation plan for the 8,500 prisoners, including about 150 children, in the New Orleans city jail, generally known as Orleans Parish Prison (OPP). To city officials tasked with overseeing the evacuation of the city, and even to the sheriff who was responsible for the welfare of the jailed population, these people didn't matter.

Prisoners were abandoned in their cells as the water rose around them. They were then subjected to a heavily armed "rescue" by state prison guards that involved beatings, mace, and wading through five feet of water to get to a nearby highway overpass, where they were left in the sun with no water or food for several days. The prisoners were then taken to upstate prisons, from which most were then transferred to parish jails across the state.[15] Officials did not want this story to be told, and the media was not interested in telling it. But people at the grassroots were determined that these stories get out.

In a 2006 press conference outside Orleans Parish Prison (OPP), Critical Resistance New Orleans activist Tamika Middleton spoke out about the people in OPP who had been left behind as the floodwaters rose. "Katrina's aftermath reflects the way we as a nation increasingly deal with social ills: police and imprison primarily poor Black communities for 'crimes' that are reflections of poverty and desperation," she observed. "Locking people up in this crisis is cruel mismanagement of city resources and counters the outpouring of the world's support and concern for all survivors of Hurricane Katrina." Middleton was part of a coalition demanding an independent investigation into the evacuation of OPP and amnesty for the so-called "looters," those arrested for trying to feed and clothe themselves post-Katrina, while calling for real public safety in a rebuilt New Orleans.

Critical Resistance, along with Human Rights Watch, the ACLU, and other national organizations, worked with local activists—especially members of Safe Streets/Strong Communities such as Ursula Price, who spent months documenting these accounts—to bring out the truth of what happened during Katrina. Eventually these stories made it into mass culture, through books like Dave Eggers's *Zeitoun*, which told the story of a Syrian business owner who was falsely arrested and "disappeared" into the post-Katrina prison system, and the HBO series *Treme*, which has featured the search for a young man trapped in OPP during the storm as one of its main storylines.

Exposure of this abuse brought national attention to the condition of prisoners in Louisiana, and invited comparison to prison abuse scandals from Attica to Abu Ghraib, but local government officials dodged accountability and continued with business as usual. The stories were shocking:

Raphael Schwartz, a twenty-six-year-old Missouri man arrested and imprisoned for public intoxication on August 27, was sprayed with mace and abandoned by officers in a locked cell with seven other prisoners. According to papers filed by the ACLU of Louisiana, the men had no ventilation and nothing to eat or drink for four days.[16]

Quintano Williams, a thirty-one-year-old office manager picked up on marijuana charges just before the storm hit, testified in ACLU papers to being abandoned for days and then relocated to Elayn Hunt Correctional Center, where he was left with thousands of detainees on a football field. There he witnessed stabbings and fights. But, he said, prison staff "did not interfere with anything that was going on as long as people did not try to get out of the area."[17]

Rachel Francois was arrested in mid-August 2005, and as far as her family was able to discover, never had charges filed against her. "We tried to bail her out," explained her mother Althea Francois, a grassroots organizer and former Black Panther. "It was the day before Katrina, and the bail bonds places were all closed. If they had been open, she would have been released that day. Instead, we could not get her released until two months later." Althea Francois searched for two weeks before she found out where her daughter was being held.

Rachel and other women had been taken to Elayn Hunt and then to Angola, two all-male institutions. For Althea, who had spent much of the past three decades building outside support for her Black Panther comrades imprisoned in Angola, the news was especially devastating.

"When I found out she was at Angola prison, just the idea really broke my heart," Althea said. "She didn't have a bed until the last few days she was there. She had no food for four days. She saw them throw food at the men like they were animals, but even then they didn't give the women anything. The women were having panic attacks and were in fear for their lives."

Most of the people trapped in this brutal web of governmental abuse and neglect would have been released within a few weeks even if convicted. Lost in the system in the aftermath of the storm, however, they remained locked in maximum-security prisons such as Angola, or in parish jails across the state for, on average, more than a year.[18]

Civil rights attorney Mary Howell has been a leading critic of the practices of the city's criminal sheriff. "[In the year before the storm], eighty thousand people came into OPP as arrestees," said Howell. "Very few were eligible for rehabilitation programs. This prison has mostly been warehousing people. We've suffered under a policy where the city builds a huge jail that is then required to be filled with human beings, or else it's a waste of money."

Before Katrina, OPP was the eighth-largest jail in the country, comprised of several buildings located in Midcity New Orleans. The population of the jail was predominantly lower-income people, the vast majority of whom were African American. The jail also rented out cells to the federal government to house immigration detainees and other federal prisoners. Most of the prisoners left behind as the jail flooded were being held presentencing; they had not been convicted of any crime. Lawyers and researchers working on behalf of the prisoners stated that most were accused of misdemeanors, such as minor drug possession, parking violations, and public drunkenness.

At the time of the storm, Ursula Price was a staff investigator for A Fighting Chance, doing research on behalf of indigent defense cases in Louisiana. A brilliant Black woman in her early thirties with an easy and distinctive laugh, Price is a true hero of New Orleans's recovery. She worked around the clock for months despite having lost everything she owned in the flooding.

"Investigating what happened to these prisoners and where they are is not supposed to be our job. This should be the city's concern," she noted.

But Price made it her concern. She went on to co-found Safe Streets/Strong Communities, devoted to community-based organizing for criminal justice reform, in order to continue this work.

In 2006, Safe Streets interviewed more than a hundred prisoners who had been locked up prior to Katrina and then, after the storm, were spread across thirteen prisons and hundreds of miles. They found the average length of time people had been locked up without a trial was 385 days. One person had been locked up for 1,289 days. None of them had been convicted of any crime.

Listening to the stories Price told me of what prisoners were put through in those days, weeks, and months after the storm, I felt a chill. "I grew up in small-town Mississippi," she told me. "We had the Klan marching down our main street, but I've never seen anything like this."

Only a few individuals managed the defense of these prisoners. One of them, Phyllis Mann, a lawyer from rural Alexandria, Louisiana, found that many of the OPP prisoners had been moved to a prison near her, so she started visiting them. According to Price, Mann dropped everything in her private practice to dedicate herself to their legal defense—and offered her home to twelve former prisoners who, upon their release, had nowhere else to go.

Even today, years later, we do not have a solid accounting of what happened in OPP during and after Katrina. "Immediately after the flooding, the governor issued an order suspending the clock on court proceedings," Price told me. The state no longer had a time limit—formerly sixty days—under which to present charges or release prisoners. "It stopped due process," Price continued. "Almost all of the public defenders were laid off. Meanwhile, in trying to defend these folks, we had massive travel costs and almost no funding."

Ross Angle, who was moved from OPP to Elayn Hunt to St. Francis Parish Prison, told Human Rights Watch that his captors blamed the Department of Corrections (DOC) bureaucracy. "Picture waking up every day in a prison somewhere—you don't even know where you are—knowing you were supposed to be free, not knowing how long they were going to keep you there. Not knowing if it would ever end. After they moved me, I kept asking for someone to look at my case, and they just kept telling me, 'We're waiting on the DOC guys, we don't know anything.' If my lady wasn't seven months pregnant, calling them every day and yelling, then I would probably still be there....It made me feel worthless."[19]

Samuel "Nick" Nicholas was imprisoned in OPP on a misdemeanor charge and was due to be released on August 31, 2005. Instead, after a harrowing journey of several months, he was released in February 2006. A handsome Black man in his forties, Nick does building work. He is also part of a Social Aid and Pleasure Club in his neighborhood and plays drums at secondlines and on Mardi Gras Indian holidays.

I met up with Nick and his good friend Benny Flowers at Central City's Sportsman's Corner bar. Despite his best efforts to move on, Nick told me he still shudders when he thinks of those days in OPP. "We heard boats leaving, and one of the guys said 'Hey man, all the deputies gone,'" Nick described. "We took it upon ourselves to try to survive. They left us in the gym for two days with nothing. Some of those guys stayed in a cell for five days. People were hollering, 'Get me out, I don't want to drown, I don't want to die.' We were locked in with no ventilation, no water, nothing to eat. It's just the grace of god that a lot of us survived."

Benny Flowers, shorter and quieter than Nick, was clearly even more disturbed by the experience. On a work release program, he was locked in a different building in the sprawling OPP complex. By his count, there were about thirty incarcerated youth in his building, some as young as fourteen years old.

> I don't know why they left the children like that. Locked up, no food, no water. Why would you do that? They couldn't swim; most of them were scared to get into the water. We were on work release, so we didn't have much time left. We weren't trying to escape, we weren't worried about ourselves, we were worried about the children. The guards abandoned us, so we had to do it for ourselves. We made sure everyone was secured and taken care of. The deputies didn't do nothing. It was inmates taking care of inmates, old inmates taking care of young inmates. We had to do it for ourselves.

Benny Hitchens, another former inmate, had been imprisoned for unpaid parking tickets. "They put us in a gym, about two hundred of us, and they gave us three trash bags. Two for defecation and one for urination. That was all we had for two hundred people for two days."[20]

State DOC officers eventually transported thousands of inmates from OPP to the Elayn Hunt Correctional Center, in rural St. Gabriel, Louisiana (near Baton Rouge), where the evacuees were kept under guard in a field. They were outside day and night, with no shelter and little or no food and water. "They didn't do us no kind of justice," Flowers told me. "We woke up early in the morning with the dew all over us, then in the afternoon we were burning up in the summer sun. There were about five thousand of us in three yards."

Nick was taken from Elayn Hunt to Oakdale Prison. "At Oakdale, they had us on lockdown twenty-three hours, on Friday and Saturday it was twenty-four hours. We hadn't even been convicted yet. Why did we have to be treated bad? Twenty-three and one ain't nothing nice, especially when you ain't been convicted of a crime yet. But here in New Orleans you're guilty 'til you're proven innocent. It's just the opposite of how it's supposed to be."

From reports that Ursula Price of Safe Streets received, some prisoners had it worse than those in Oakdale. These prisoners were sent to a notorious former youth prison in Jena, a town far upstate that would become front-page news in another case of injustice almost two years later. For years children from New Orleans had been shipped to the Jena facility, infamous among Louisiana criminal justice advocates for its brutal conditions. The abusive youth prison had been shut down in 1999 after legal action by the Juvenile Justice Project of Louisiana.[21]

"I have no idea why they thought it was acceptable to reopen it with the same staff," Price continued, referring to the use of the Jena prison for Katrina evacuees. "People were beaten, an entire room of men was forced to strip and jump up and down and make sexual gestures towards one another. I cannot describe to you the terror that the young men we spoke to conveyed to us."

"This ain't just started, it's been going on," Nick told me. "I want to talk about it, but at the same time it hurts to talk about it. Someone's gotta start talking about it. It's not the judge, it's not the lawyers, it's the criminal justice system. Everybody who goes to jail isn't guilty. You got guys who were drunk in public treated like they committed murder."

"If you ask anyone living in New Orleans, the police, the justice system, may be the single most influential element in poor communities," Price stated. "It's what breaks up families, it's what keeps people poor."

"One thing I can't forget is those children," Benny Flowers told me. "Why would they leave those children behind? I'm trying to forget it, but I can't forget it."

Pre-Katrina, the New Orleans public defender system was already dangerously overloaded, with only forty-two attorneys and six investigators for several thousand clients. In the year after the storm, New Orleans had only six public defenders and one investigator. And these defenders were not necessarily full-time, nor were they committed to their cases. One of the attorneys was reported by advocates as spending his days in court doing crossword puzzles instead of talking to his clients. All the public defenders were allowed to take on an unlimited number of additional defendants for pay, and it was reported that they did a more vigorous job on behalf of their paid clients. Orleans Parish Criminal District Court judge Arthur Hunter complained in 2007 that "Indigent defense in New Orleans is unbelievable, unconstitutional, totally lacking the basic professional standards of legal representation, and a mockery of what a criminal justice system should be in a western civilized nation."[22]

Before the storm, according to the Safe Streets report, some detainees were brought to a magistrate court shortly after being arrested, "where a public defender was appointed 'solely for the purposes of this hearing.' The assigned attorney did not do even the most cursory interview about the arrestee's ties to the community, charges, or any other information relevant to setting a bond. Other interviewees were taken to a room where they faced a judge on a video screen. These individuals uniformly reported there was no defense lawyer present."

The report continued:

> After appointment, [defense attorneys] by and large did not visit the crime scene, did not interview witnesses, did not check out alibis, did not procure expert assistance, did not review evidence, did not know the facts of the case, did not do any legal research, and did not otherwise prepare for trial…with few exceptions, attorneys with the Orleans Indigent Defender program never met with their clients to discuss their case. Appointed counsel did not take calls from the jail, did not respond to letters or other written correspondence, and generally did not take calls or make appointments with family members…. [Defenders] frequently did not know the names of their clients.[23]

By exposing these conditions and pressuring city officials, Safe Streets was able to win reforms that transformed the city's public defender system. It was a notable victory, but only scratched the surface of the changes needed.

A September 2009 report from the U.S. Department of Justice (DOJ) found that, four years later, little had changed in the city jail. "Conditions at OPP violate the constitutional rights of inmates," the DOJ reported. "Inmates confined at OPP are not adequately protected from harm, including physical harm from excessive use of force by staff." The report documented "a pattern and practice of unnecessary and inappropriate use of force by OPP correctional officers." This included "several examples where OPP officers openly engaged in abusive and retaliatory conduct, which resulted in serious injuries to prisoners. In some instances, the investigation found, the officers' conduct was so flagrant it clearly constituted calculated abuse."[24]

CAMP GREYHOUND

After the hurricane, incarceration was the first city function to return. Due process and civil liberties were almost nonexistent for new arrestees, who were put in metal cages the authorities had constructed in a makeshift prison at a Greyhound bus station, and given no access to phones or lawyers. When ACLU attorney Katie Schwartzmann went to observe the proceedings, a sheriff's deputy at first refused her access, then later took and read her notes.

Hundreds of people passed through "Camp Greyhound," set up by warden Burl Cain of the Louisiana State Prison at Angola. "The one thing that works," Cain said, just over a week after the storm, while the city was still flooded and mostly empty, "[is] to have a jail. They realize you can't have the security until you have a jail.... We've arrested over 233 people that have been brought through here.... Without a jail, no reconstruction."[25]

Camp Greyhound was used as a tool for the mass incarceration of men and women of color, poor people, and anyone else who happened to be in the wrong place at the wrong time. Merlene Maten, a seventy-three-year-old African American grandmother and church elder, had evacuated to a hotel in the New Orleans suburb of Kenner, Louisiana, following the flooding of her home in the city. She was among those caught up in this web.

According to one report:

As a Black woman taking shelter from the storm in a predominantly white suburb, she was profiled by police as having committed or participated in a break-in at a nearby deli when in fact, at the time of her arrest, she was retrieving food she had brought with her from her car. Witnesses confirm that Ms. Maten never entered the store in question. Although witnesses tried to explain the situation to police, the officers refused to listen and characterized the women as "emotional." Ms. Maten was held for over 16 days, first in the local jail, and then in the state penitentiary, on charges that she took $63.50 in food from the deli.[26]

During that time, new arrestees were offered a choice—either plead guilty and be put to work on city cleanup crews, or plead not guilty and face months in Angola or another upstate prison, with no access to a lawyer.

TORTURE AT ANGOLA PRISON

The Louisiana State Penitentiary at Angola, also known as "the Farm," is a former slave plantation where little has changed in the last two hundred years.

Visitors are often overwhelmed by the prison's size. At twenty-six square miles, the Farm is roughly the same size as Manhattan, and its vast acreage contains a golf course (for use by prison staff and some guests), a radio station, an arena where the prison holds a rodeo in the spring and fall, and a massive farming operation that ranges from staples like soybeans and wheat to other traditional Southern plantation crops.

Safe Streets co-founder Norris Henderson spent twenty years at Angola—a relatively short time, given that officials estimate 97 percent of Angola's 5,100 prisoners are expected to die behind its walls.[27] "Six hundred folks been there over twenty-five years," Henderson explained. "Lots of these guys been there over thirty-five years. Think about that: a population that's been there since the 1970s. Once you're in this place, it's almost like you ain't going nowhere, that barring some miracle, you're going to die there." Nationally, one in ten incarcerated people are serving life sentences; in Louisiana, the rate is almost twice that. Louisiana is one of seven states that offer no possibility of parole for people serving life, and one of three that extends that no-parole policy to juveniles.[28]

Prisoners at Angola still do the same work as the enslaved Africans did when the Farm was a slave plantation. "Angola is a plantation," Henderson explained. "Eighteen thousand acres of choice farmland. Even to this day, you could have machinery that can do all that work, but you still have prisoners doing it instead." Many white guards at the Farm are descended from families that have lived on the grounds since the plantation days.

Nathaniel Anderson, a current inmate who has served nearly thirty years of a life sentence, agrees. "People on the outside should know that Angola is still a plantation with every type and kind of slave conceivable," he says. The work at Angola can be brutal, with long days in the hot sun, working in the fields. In 1952, thirty-one inmates cut their Achilles' tendons as a protest against brutality at the prison.

The torture of prisoners in U.S. custody is not limited to military prisons in Iraq, Afghanistan, and Guantanamo. In 2008, a death penalty trial in St. Francisville, Louisiana, exposed widespread and systemic abuse at Angola. Even in the context of such officially sanctioned torture, the behavior documented at Angola stands out both for its brutality and for the significant evidence that abuse was condoned and encouraged from the very top of the chain of command.

In a remarkable hearing, twenty-five inmates testified to having experienced overwhelming violence in the aftermath of a 1999 escape attempt at the prison. During the escape attempt, one guard was killed and two were taken hostage. A team of officers, including Angola warden Burl Cain, rushed in and began shooting. Inmate Joel Durham was killed by officers. Another inmate, David Mathis, was wounded.

The twenty-five inmates who testified were not accused of involvement in the escape attempt. Nevertheless, according to their testimony, they were kicked, punched, beaten with batons and with fists, stepped on, left naked in a freezing cell, and threatened with death. They were threatened by guards that they would be sexually assaulted with batons. They were forced to urinate and defecate on themselves. They were bloodied, had teeth knocked out, were beaten until they lost control of bodily functions, and were beaten until they signed statements or confessions presented to them by prison officials. One inmate had his jaw broken and another was placed in solitary confinement for eight years.[29]

Angola has no official guidelines for dealing with escape attempts or other crises, a policy that seems designed to allow, if not actually encourage, the violent treatment documented in this case. Richard Stalder, then secretary of the Louisiana Department of Public Safety and Corrections, was also on an official visit to the prison at the time. Yet despite—or perhaps because of—the presence of the prison warden and head of corrections for the state, guards were allowed to engage in brutal retribution. Warden Cain later told a reporter after the shooting that Angola's policy was not to negotiate. "That's a message all the inmates know," he said. "They just forgot it. And now they know it again."[30]

Five prisoners, including David Mathis, were charged with murder, and are still facing the death penalty—a decision based in part on testimony that was obtained through the beating and torture of other inmates.

The St. Francisville hearing was requested by Mathis's defense counsel to demonstrate that, in a climate of violence and abuse, inmates were forced to sign statements through torture, and therefore their statements should be inadmissible.

Twentieth Judicial District Judge George H. Ware Jr. eventually ruled that the documented torture and abuse were not relevant. However, the behavior detailed in the hearing raised strong doubts about the cases against the defendants, who have become known as the Angola Five. Even more important, it provides direct insight into the kinds of treatment common at facilities like Angola.

The hearing revealed a pattern of systemic abuse so open and regular that the traditional excuse of "bad apples" is negated. Inmate Doyle Billiot testified to being threatened with death by the guards. "What's not to be afraid of? Got all these security guards coming around you every day looking at you sideways, crazy and stuff. Don't know what's on their mind, especially when they threaten to kill you." Another inmate, Robert Carley, testified that a false confession was beaten out of him. "I was afraid," he said. "I felt that if I didn't go in there and tell them something, I would die."

Inmate Kenneth "Geronimo" Edwards testified that the guards "beat us half to death." He also testified that guards threatened to sexually assault him with a baton, saying, "That's a big black...." (Edwards was unable to say the word). "Say you want it," the guards taunted him.

Later, Edwards continued, the guards "put me in my cell. They took all my clothes. Took my jumpsuit. Took all the sheets, everything out the cell, and put me in the cell buck-naked....It was cold in the cell. They opened the windows and turned the blowers on." At least a dozen other inmates testified to receiving the same beatings, assault, threats of sexual violence, and overnight "freezing treatment."

Some guards at the prison treated the abuse as a game. Inmate Brian Johns testified at the hearing that, "one of the guards was hitting us all in the head. Said he liked the sound of the drums—the drumming sound that—from hitting us in the head with the stick."

Despite prison officials' denials of the policy of abuse, the range of prisoners who gave statements, in addition to medical records and other evidence introduced at the trial, presented an incontrovertible argument that abuse was a standard policy at the prison. Without admitting liability, the state agreed to settle two civil rights lawsuits filed by thirteen inmates. Several of the prisoners received seven thousand dollars in settlement. The inmates will have to spend that paltry sum behind bars—none of them are expected to be released.

Two of Angola's most famous residents, political prisoners Herman Wallace and Albert Woodfox, have become the primary example of another form of abuse common at Angola—the use of solitary confinement as punishment for political views. The two men have each spent nearly forty years in solitary. Woodfox and Wallace—who together with former prisoner Robert King are known as the Angola Three—have filed a civil suit against Angola, arguing that their confinement has violated both their Eighth Amendment rights against cruel and unusual punishment and their Fourth Amendment right to due process.

Statements by Angola warden Burl Cain have made clear that Woodfox and Wallace are being punished for their political views. At a 2009 deposition, attorneys for Woodfox asked Cain, "Let's just for the sake of argument assume, if you can, that he is not guilty of the murder of Brent Miller." Cain responded, "Okay. I would still keep him in [solitary]…I still know that he is still trying to practice Black Pantherism, and I still would not want him walking around my prison because he would organize the young new inmates. I would have me all kind of problems, more than I could stand, and I would have the Blacks chasing after them….He has to stay in a cell while he's at Angola."[31]

Louisiana attorney general James "Buddy" Caldwell has said the case against the Angola Three is "personal" to him.[32] These statements by Caldwell and Cain indicate that this kind of vigilante attitude not only pervades the DOC, but that the mindset, in fact, comes from the very top.

The problem is not limited to Louisiana State Penitentiary at Angola—similar stories can be found in prisons across the country. American Friends Service Committee reported that on any given day in the United States, up to two hundred thousand men and women are held in solitary confinement. At California's Corcoran State Prison, guards "set up fights among prisoners, bet on the outcome, and then often shot the men for fighting, seriously wounding at least forty-three and killing eight just in the period 1989–1994."[33] The director of the ACLU's National Prisoner Project, Elizabeth Alexander, told reporters, "If you look at the iconic pictures from Abu Ghraib, you can match up these photos with the same abuses at American prisons, each one of them."[34]

Torture and abuse are illegal under both U.S. law and international treaties that the United States is signatory to, from the 1948 Universal Declaration of Human Rights to the International Covenant on Civil and Political Rights, ratified in 1992. We have a constitutional prohibition against cruel and unusual punishment. Despite our laws and treaties, U.S. prison guards have rarely been held accountable to these standards.

Advocates have long argued that once we pronounce abuse or torture acceptable against "the worst" prisoners, the next step is for it to be used against the wider population. A 2008 legal petition filed by Herman Wallace stated, "If Guantanamo Bay has been a national embarrassment and symbol of the U.S. government's relation to charges, trials, and torture, then what is being done to the Angola Three…is what we are to expect if we fail to act quickly…. The government tries out its torture techniques on prisoners in the U.S.—just far enough to see how society will react. It doesn't take long before they unleash their techniques on society as a whole."[35] If we don't stand up against this abuse now, it will only spread, he argued. The vigilante violence enacted on the streets of New Orleans after Katrina—condoned and carried out in part by the police—is one example of the truth of Wallace's predictions.

Despite the hearings, civil suits, and additional documentation, the guards who performed the acts of torture at Angola remain unpunished, and the system that enabled this treatment remains in place. In fact, several of those guards have been promoted, and retain a supervisory capacity over the same inmates they were documented to have beaten mercilessly. Warden Burl Cain still oversees Angola, and, in fact, was named National Warden of the Year in 2003.

PRISON ORGANIZING

In 1971, the Black Panther Party that Warden Cain is determined to punish was viewed as a threat to this country's power structure in the inner cities and in the prisons. At OPP, for one day the entire jail population refused to cooperate, in solidarity with New Orleans Panthers, who were on trial at that time. "I was in the jail at the time of their trial," Safe Streets director Norris Henderson told me. "The power that came from those guys in the jail, the camaraderie....Word went out through the jail, because no one thought the Panthers were going to get a fair trial. We decided to do something. We said, 'The least we can do is to say the day they are going to court, no one is going to court.'"

The action was successful and inspired prisoners to take more action. "People saw what happened and said, 'We shut down the whole system that day,'" he recalled. "That taught the guys that if we stick together we can accomplish a whole lot of things."

Herman Wallace and Albert Woodfox were inmates from New Orleans who had recently become members of the Black Panther Party and as activists, they were seen as threats to the established order of the prison. They organized among the other prisoners, conducting political education and mobilizing for civil disobedience to improve conditions.

Robert Hillary King (addressed by friends as King) had joined the Black Panther Party while incarcerated at OPP. He was transferred to Angola and immediately placed in solitary confinement (known as Closed Cell Restriction or CCR)—confined alone in his cell with no human contact for twenty-three hours a day. He later found out that he had been transferred to solitary because he was accused of killing another prisoner. However, the attack had happened at Angola before King was moved there.

In March 1972, not long after they began agitating for reform from behind bars, Wallace and Woodfox were accused of killing a correctional officer. This was the justification given for moving them to solitary, where each of them remained for nearly thirty-six years. In March 2008, they were moved out four days after a congressional delegation, led by Congressman John Conyers, arranged a visit to the prison. This move was only temporary, clearly an attempt by prison authorities to avoid congressional oversight. Within weeks, Wallace and Woodfox were placed back in solitary, and the next year Wallace was moved to Elayn Hunt. Legal experts have said this case marks the longest time anyone in the United States has spent in solitary. Amnesty International declared, "The prisoners' prolonged isolation breached international treaties, which the U.S. has ratified, including the International Covenant on Civil and Political Rights and the Convention against Torture."[36]

King, Wallace, and Woodfox became known internationally as the Angola Three—Black Panthers held in solitary confinement because of their political activism. King remained in solitary for nearly twenty-nine years, until he was exonerated and released from prison in 2001. Since his release, King has been a tireless advocate for his friends still incarcerated. "I'm free of Angola," he often says, "but Angola will never be free of me."

Wallace and Woodfox have the facts on their side. Bloody fingerprints at the scene of the crime do not match their prints. Witnesses who originally testified against the two have recanted, while others have stepped forward to testify that Woodfox and Wallace were nowhere near the scene of the crime. There is evidence of prosecutorial misconduct, such as purchasing inmate testimony. Even the widow of the slain guard has spoken out on their behalf. In early 2008, the two prisoners received a visit from Representative Conyers, head of the U.S. House Judiciary Committee. Cedric Richmond, chair of the Louisiana House Judiciary Committee, also spoke out on their behalf. Finally, in summer of 2008, the magistrate in Woodfox's case recommended the reversal of his conviction.

Woodfox and Wallace's supporters form an international coalition of allies, who have tried every method conceivable to fight for their friends' freedom. Supporters have made films, exhibited art, lobbied Congress, and written articles. Community organizers (and fellow New Orleans Panthers) like Althea Francois and Marion Brown kept in contact and continued building support during decades when no one else would pay attention. Malik Rahim, another former Panther, has also fought to spread the word about their case, as has Shana griffin of INCITE.

Mwalimu Johnson, who was held at Angola from 1977 to 1992, is one of many former prisoners who have kept Woodfox and Wallace's struggle alive, and his inspiring presence stands as testimony that freedom from Angola is possible. The executive secretary for the Capital Post-Conviction Project of Louisiana, Johnson is among the kindest people I have met. He has been confined to a wheelchair since 1975, when he was shot by FBI agents who later admitted that they had shot the wrong person—they were pursuing the suspect in a bank robbery Johnson had nothing to do with. Johnson lives life by a code of generosity and concern for others. "Negative experiences are a kind of cancer," he said. "And my choice as a human being is either to encourage the spread of that cancer or to arrest it and apply a solution. I opt to be part of the solution, part of the healing. Forgiveness is not a matter of doing anything heroic or exceptional, it's just about being natural."[37]

But this is more than the story of courageous men struggling to prove their innocence. The story of the Panthers at Angola is a battle for liberation in the hardest of situations. "They swam against the current in Blood Alley," said Nathaniel Anderson, a current inmate at Angola who has been inspired by Wallace and Woodfox's legacy. "For men to actually have the audacity to organize for the protection of young brothers who were being victimized ruthlessly was an extreme act of rebellion."

The efforts of King, Woodfox, Wallace, and other Panthers in prison initiated real change and represented a fundamental challenge to the dehumanization of the prison industrial complex. They stopped sexual assault and built alliances among groups of prisoners that had previously been pitted against each other over petty differences.

"They were part of the Panther movement," Norris Henderson explained. Henderson was introduced to organizing by Black Panthers, becoming a leader of prison activism and a jailhouse lawyer during his time at Angola. "This was at the height of the Black Power movement, we were understanding that we all got each other. In the nighttime there would be open talk, guys in the jail talking, giving history lessons, discussing why we find ourselves in the situation we find ourselves. They started educating folks around how we could treat each other. The Nation of Islam was growing in the prison at the same time. You had these different folk bringing knowledge. You had folks who were hustlers that then were listening and learning. Everybody was coming into consciousness."

The work of Wallace, Woodfox, and King had an effect that continues to this day. Henderson emphasized that prison activism coupled with outside support for activists behind bars can be tremendously powerful. "In the early 1970s, people started realizing we're all in this situation together. First, at Angola, we pushed for a reform to get a law library. That was one of the first conditions to change. Then, we got the library; guys became aware of what their rights were. We started to push to improve the quality of food, and to get better medical care. Once they started pushing the envelope, a whole bunch of things started to change. Angola was real violent then, you had inmate violence and rape. The people running the prison system benefit from people being ignorant. But we educated ourselves. Eventually, you had guys in prison proposing legislation."

The 1970s were a time of reforms and resistance in prisons across the United States. Uprisings such as the Attica prison rebellion in New York State received popular support and resulted in real change. Today, many of the gains from those victories have been overturned, and prisoners have even less recourse than before. "Another major difference," Henderson explained, is that "you had federal oversight over the prisons at that time, someone you could complain to, and say 'my rights are being violated.' Today, we've lost that right."

Working against injustice benefits us all. "Most folks in prison are going to come out of prison," said Henderson. "We should invest in the quality of that person. We should start investing in the redemption of people."

After decades of efforts from their lawyers and activists, Wallace and Woodfox have won some legal victories and some improvements in their conditions, including a brief release from solitary confinement, but their incarceration continues. In 2009, as mentioned, Woodfox was transferred to Elayn Hunt Correctional Center, where he remains in solitary, a move seen as an attempt to break up the solidarity movement that has built up around the men. The two remaining members of the Angola Three are still behind bars, punished for standing up against an unjust system that has grown even larger and more deadly. And the abuse does not end there. "There are hundreds more guys who have been in [solitary] a long time too," Henderson added. "This is like the first step in a thousand-mile journey."

NEW ORLEANS POLICE ON BOURBON STREET, 2010.
PHOTO BY ABDUL AZIZ.

CHAPTER SEVEN

Serve and Protect:
Criminalizing the Survivors

We was high school students
And they searching our coats
They ain't find nothing
But scarlet-lettered study notes
Students in the hood don't matter to the fuzz
Came from nothing so they thought that's what we was
Set up not to win, pigs never lock the pen
Could have been our last day breathing oxygen
When I think back the action was kinda subliminal
To make us think that we would grow up to be criminals

From "Serve and Protect" by Truth Universal

After Katrina, young Black men in New Orleans were portrayed solely as perpetrators of violence. This distortion of events obscured the greater, systemic violence that was perpetrated against both men and women by law enforcement, prison officials, and government leaders. Vigilante killings, police brutality, neglect and abuse of prisoners, and the forced displacement of tens of thousands of New Orleanians are crimes that were barely mentioned in (or were omitted completely from) news coverage in the days and weeks after the storm. When they were mentioned, it seemed the United States wasn't listening, because these stories didn't fit with the narrative the nation had already chosen to believe.

In the context of Katrina, women were both victims of violence and the justification for its furthering. Reports of rape in the Superdome were used to justify the need for a militarized version of relief. But the violence that women faced by being displaced and made homeless was not discussed, even though the majority of lease holders in public housing—all of which was emptied and much of which was later demolished, with no replacements built—were mothers. Systemic violence against women was ignored, while Black communities continued to be criminalized.

The stories the corporate media have left untold are not only those of state and law enforcement violence. They are also not interested in the stories of communities coming together to solve problems without state intervention. In New Orleans our real "first responders" were the folks who lived in the communities that took the most flooding. The young Black men from these neighborhoods, who were later demonized as criminals, were out in the days after the storm rescuing people and distributing food.

The untold heroes of the city's reconstruction, ignored in the official accounts, are the grassroots organizers, on the front lines, working in their communities and building a movement for a just reconstruction that includes everyone, not just those at the top. These organizations and individuals fought against the ways in which the disaster was framed as primarily a policing and military issue. For years, as the media ignored them, they rallied to change the debate. Activists documented police and vigilante killings in the aftermath of the storm. They canvassed neighborhoods and waited outside prison gates to gather stories of survivors. They organized community meetings, released reports, held press conferences, and collaborated with sympathetic journalists.

Finally, more than three years after the storm, the tide began to turn. Today, the story of police violence against unarmed survivors of the storm is a widely known fact. This is a victory for those who fought to get the story out. But this success did not come easily, and the struggles are far from over.

On September 1, 2005, Governor Kathleen Blanco sent in National Guard troops with the words, "They have M-16s and they are locked and loaded.... These troops know how to shoot and kill, and they are more than willing to do so if necessary, and I expect they will."[1] Her statement set the threatening, punitive tone that was adopted by law enforcement for months, even years, to come. That tone, coupled with media repetition of images of "looters," served to criminalize Black New Orleanians in the minds of many people across the nation.

There are essential connections to be drawn from televised dehumanization of "criminals" and "welfare mothers" to laws that criminalize the poor; from the glamorization of torture to the standardization of the practice in U.S. prisons; from brutality in foreign prisons to vigilante gangs patrolling the streets of a U.S. city with the tacit permission of local police.

These links do not imply direct cause and effect. There were vigilante gangs, like the Klan, operating in the South for decades before television even existed. Yet each of these is a symptom, increasingly severe, of the underlying cause. Until we confront the underlying pathology—that is, public approval of violence against those who are seen as "deserving" of it—our society will continue to get sicker.

The justification for violence against those seen as "deserving" was amplified for decades through Hollywood depictions and then perfected by the Bush administration, which made explicit the arguments implied by TV shows like *24* and films like *Die Hard* and *Death Wish*—we need cops (and soldiers and federal agents) to break the rules. The message was this: the rules are the problem. There are good people and there are bad people, and we don't need to worry about how the evildoers are treated. Further, the job of keeping us safe is necessarily dirty, and the police will need to break some rules to do the job right. "Tough on crime" politicians like former New York mayor Rudolph Giuliani contributed to this environment by discarding decades of reforms and practices meant to offer opportunities for rehabilitation, pushing instead for more police, arrests, and prisons.

The Giuliani model, adopted by police departments around the country, is known as the "broken windows" theory. The idea is that if you don't stop small crimes—loitering, breaking windows, illegal sidewalk merchants—they create an environment in which major crimes—drug dealing, robbery, murder—can flourish. According to this theory, police departments should devote significant resources to these petty crimes, which had often been ignored by major city police forces before the Giuliani paradigm swept the nation.

The New Orleans Police Department has embraced this practice. NOPD arrest more than fifty-eight thousand people every year. Of those, nearly 50 percent are for traffic and municipal offenses.[2] According to the 2003–4 report from the Metropolitan Crime Commission, 95 percent of those brought to the New Orleans Criminal District Court were arrested for a nonviolent offense.[3]

This approach dovetailed with a similar rise in the criminalization of poverty—for example, arresting homeless folks for loitering. This trend was on the rise during both the economic rise of the '90s and the recent market collapse, according to a study by the National Law Center on Homelessness and Poverty.[4]

This philosophy has led to tens of thousands of people locked up for small infractions every year, and has been used as justification for racial profiling and harassment. The NOPD can point to a massive number of arrests and claim they are doing their part to fight crime in the city. Meanwhile, the people most at risk of being victims of crime carry as much distrust of the NOPD as of the murderers in their neighborhoods, and are therefore reluctant to help in any investigation.

THE SOUND OF THE POLICE

Distrust of the police by the New Orleans Black community, especially the working-class Black community, has deep roots in the city's longstanding racial tensions, and has at times exploded in violence. In 1900, a young Black man named Robert Charles shot twenty-seven white people, including seven policemen, killing four. The reaction set off a white race riot and mass killing of Black New Orleanians.

In 1972, Mark Essex, a young Black man who had military training and Black nationalist political leanings, began shooting at white people, focusing in particular on cops. Perhaps the greatest testimony to the depth of anger felt by the city's Black community toward the police is the fact that many in the community openly celebrated his actions, some of them drawing connections to the previous shooting by Charles. As white antiracist activist David Billings described:

> [Twenty-three]-year-old Mark Essex…went on a shooting spree that ended on the top of a Howard Johnson's hotel across from the New Orleans City Hall. Essex…held off the entire police department and National Guard of New Orleans (at that time still almost totally white in an already black-majority city). Essex killed five police officers, including the Deputy Chief Louis Sergo. Black people watched from chairs they set up across the street from the Howard Johnson's. They were not afraid since they knew Mark Essex was not shooting at them. When Essex was finally killed, 200 bullets were found in his body.[5]

The white-flight suburbs around the city have a history of open hostility to Black New Orleanians. During the 1980s, Jefferson Parish sheriff

Harry Lee famously ordered special scrutiny for any Black people traveling in white sections of the parish. "It's obvious," Lee said, "that two young Blacks driving a rinky-dink car in a predominantly white neighborhood? They'll be stopped." Lee, the son of Chinese immigrants, was an immensely popular public figure—he served as sheriff of Jefferson Parish for almost thirty years, until his death in 2007.

In 1987, Sheriff Lee built barriers at the border between a white neighborhood in Jefferson Parish and a Black neighborhood in Orleans Parish called Pigeon Town. Civil rights protests followed, with Pigeon Town residents calling for New Orleans's Black mayor to "tear down our Berlin Wall." Over the protests of white suburban residents, Mayor Sidney Barthelemy sent in a crew to demolish the wall.[6] The move was later upheld in a court decision, which found that Lee's action had "improperly blocked entrance to a state highway."

In 1994, according to New Orleans's *Gambit Weekly*, "After two Black men died in the Jefferson Parish Correctional Center within one week, [Sheriff] Lee faced protests from the Black community and responded by withdrawing his officers from a predominantly Black neighborhood. 'To hell with them,' he'd said. 'I haven't heard one word of support from one Black person.'"[7]

In April 2005 Jefferson Parish officers were found to be using as target practice what critics referred to as "a blatantly racist caricature" of a Black male. Sheriff Lee laughed when presented with the charges. "I'm looking at this thing that people say is offensive," he says. "I've looked at it, I don't find it offensive, and I have no interest in correcting it." These accusations of "target practice" gained force a few weeks later with the May 31, 2005, killing of sixteen-year-old Antoine Colbert, who was behind the wheel of a stolen pickup truck with two other teens. One hundred ten shots were fired into the truck, killing Colbert and injuring his passengers. In response to criticism from Black ministers over the incident, Lee responded, "They can kiss my ass."[8]

In 2006, the sheriff of St. Tammany Parish, a suburban New Orleans community on the far side of Lake Ponchartrain, said, "I don't want to get into calling people names, but if you're going to walk the streets of St. Tammany Parish with dreadlocks and chee-wee hairstyles, then you can expect to be getting a visit from a sheriff's deputy."[9]

Even a brief summary of the recent history of police abuse in New Orleans conveys a shocking catalogue of violence:

In 1980, a police officer named Gregory Neupert was found shot to death on a levee in the West Bank neighborhood of Algiers. According to community activist M. Endesha Juakali,

> [The police decided that] someone in the black community killed one of them and they intended to get some payback. Almost immediately, the entire Black community in Algiers was under siege. People were beaten, kidnapped, and tortured. Based upon the information received from the use of torture, police raids led to the murder of four people in Algiers, three men and one young mother who was shot through the eye with a 357 magnum revolver and in the chest with a shotgun loaded with double ought buckshot. She was shot while naked, unarmed and in front of her 4 year old son. During that same period unarmed Black men were killed in the French Quarter and the Desire community. In fact, in a very short period of time, 11 people had been killed by the police, in different parts of the city, following the death of Officer Neupert.[10]

In 1990, a man named Adolph Archie, who had been accused of killing a cop, was brutally murdered by a mob of police in an action that the *New York Times* called "a lynching."

> When the car carrying Archie arrived at a hospital, a mob of screaming officers was there to meet it. No superior officers dispersed the mob. The screaming intensified. For some, Archie's death would not be sufficient. They also wanted his genitals mutilated. These were New Orleans' officers of the law. The keepers of the peace. For reasons that have never been satisfactorily answered, Adolph Archie was not taken into the hospital, but was driven to a station house in the precinct of the officer he had killed. There he was fatally beaten.
>
> The issue is not whether Adolph Archie deserved to die, but whether police officers can be trusted to uphold the law. Large numbers of officers in New Orleans have proved again and again that they cannot. And in New Orleans, as in many other cities, the nefarious activities of the police are routinely covered up, rationalized, and even encouraged by other public officials.
>
> In the Archie case, the coroner of Orleans Parish, Dr. Frank Minyard, filed an autopsy report that protected the police. Based on Dr. Minyard's findings, Archie could have died in an accident—a bad fall,

for example. In fact, Archie had suffered massive injuries. His skull was fractured and his teeth kicked in. Most of the bones in his face were broken. His larynx was fractured. And there was severe hemorrhaging in his testicles.[11]

In a September 2000 report, the Progressive Policy Institute detailed,

> A 1994 crackdown on police corruption led to 200 dismissals and upwards of 60 criminal charges, including two murder convictions of police officers. Investigators at the time discovered that for six months in 1994, as many as 29 New Orleans police officers protected a cocaine supply warehouse containing 286 pounds of cocaine. The FBI indicted ten officers who had been paid nearly $100,000 by undercover agents. The investigation ended abruptly after one officer successfully orchestrated the execution of a witness.[12]

In the end, six hundred NOPD officers were arrested, fired, or disciplined, or resigned while under investigation.

Two former NOPD officers are serving life sentences for murders committed during this time period. A 1998 report from Human Rights Watch described the case against one of the officers:

> Officer Len Davis, reportedly known in the Desire housing project as "Robocop," ordered the October 13, 1994, murder of Kim Groves, after he learned she had filed a brutality complaint against him. Federal agents had Davis under surveillance for alleged drug-dealing and recorded Davis ordering the killing, apparently without realizing what they had heard until it was too late. Davis mumbled to himself about the "30" he would be taking care of (the police code for homicide) and, in communicating with the killer, described Groves's standing on the street and demanded he "get that whore!" Afterward, he confirmed the slaying by saying "N.A.T.," police jargon for "necessary action taken." Community activists reported a chilling effect on potential witnesses or victims of brutality considering coming forward to complain following Groves's murder.[13]

New Orleans has a shockingly high murder rate. A population of fewer than five hundred thousand was expecting three hundred murders in 2005, most of them centered on just a few Black neighborhoods.

After Katrina, despite most of the population being displaced, the murder rate in New Orleans actually went up—to nearly one murder for every thousand people. By comparison, New York City had just under six hundred murders in 2006. If New York had matched the murder rate of New Orleans, about eight thousand people would have been killed.

Before and after Katrina, murder suspects have rarely been convicted. Often, a few days after a shooting, the attacker might be shot in revenge. Distrust of the police is so high that even when murders happen in front of large crowds, officers often can find no witnesses. For the 162 murders in 2006, the DA's office had only one conviction.[14]

Also out of the view of the media were incidents of police violence that specially targeted women. Less than a week before Hurricane Katrina, NOPD officer Keith Griffin was booked with aggravated rape and kidnapping. According to a *Times-Picayune* report, "Griffin is accused of pulling over a bicyclist under the guise of a police stop in the early morning hours of July 11. The two-year veteran officer allegedly detained the woman, drove her to a remote spot along the Industrial Canal near Deslonde Street, then sexually assaulted her."[15]

In April 2005, officer Corey Johnson was booked with aggravated rape. Johnson identified himself as an officer in order to enter a woman's Treme home at 4:30 in the morning and then demanded sex.[16]

Times-Picayune columnist Jarvis Deberry reported that "Officer Christopher Buckley was investigated in 2001 and 2003—once for raping a child and once for raping two children," and kept on the force until 2008, when he faced a third rape charge, this time for the rape of a thirteen-year-old girl.[17]

"CRIMES AGAINST NATURE": THE CRIMINALIZATION OF SEX WORKERS

Tabitha has been working as a prostitute since she was thirteen. Now thirty years old, she can often be found working on a corner just outside of the French Quarter. A small and slight white woman, she has battled both drug addiction and illness and struggles every day to find a meal or a place to stay for the night.

These days, Tabitha, who asked that her real name not be used, has yet another burden: a stamp printed on her driver's license labels her a sex offender. Her crime? Offering sex for money.

New Orleans city police and the district attorney's office regularly use a state law written for child molesters to charge hundreds of sex workers like Tabitha as sex offenders. The law, which dates back to 1805, declares it a crime against nature to engage in "unnatural copulation"—a term New Orleans cops and the district attorney's office have interpreted to mean anal or oral sex. Sex workers convicted of breaking this law are charged with felonies, issued longer jail sentences, and forced to register as sex offenders. Of the 861 sex offenders registered in New Orleans as of January 2010, 483 were convicted of a crime against nature. And of those convicted of a crime against nature, 78 percent are Black and almost all are women.

This law impacts those convicted in both small and large ways. Tabitha has to register an address in the sex offender database. She also has to purchase and mail postcards with her photo to everyone in the neighborhood informing them of her conviction. If she needs to evacuate to a shelter during a hurricane, she must evacuate to a special shelter for sex offenders, which has no separate safe spaces for women. She is even prohibited from ordinary activities in New Orleans like wearing a costume at Mardi Gras.

"This law completely disconnects our community members from what remains of a social safety net," said Deon Haywood, director of Women With A Vision (WWAV), an organization that promotes wellness and disease prevention for women who live in poverty. Haywood's group formed a coalition of New Orleans activists and health workers that organized to fight the ways that police abuse the 1805 law.

Haywood views police use of this law as part of the NOPD's overall policy of criminalizing poverty. "What this is really about is over-incarcerating poor and of-color communities," agreed Rosana Cruz, associate director of VOTE, who is also a part of the coalition.

Although some women have tried to fight the sex offender charges in court, they've had little success. The penalties they face became even harsher in 2006 when Congress passed the Adam Walsh Act, requiring tier-1 (the least serious) sex offenders to stay in the public registry for fifteen years.

There's also an added danger to fighting the charges, according to Josh Perry, a former attorney with the Orleans Public Defenders office. "The way Louisiana's habitual offender law works, if you challenge your sentence in court and lose, and it's a third offense, the mandatory minimum is twenty years. The maximum is life," Perry explained.

Many of the women Haywood's group works with are engaged in the highest-risk types of sex work. They meet customers on the street and in bars. Most are dealing with addiction and homelessness, and many are not eligible for food stamps or other public assistance because of felony convictions on their record. "I'm hoping that the situation will look different because of this coalition," Haywood said. "I can't tell you how overwhelmed we've been from the needs of this population."

Miss Jackie is one of those women. A Black woman in her fifties, she was arrested for sex work in 1999 and charged as a sex offender. Her name was added to the registry for ten years. When the registration period was almost over she was arrested for possession of crack. She says the arresting officer didn't find any drugs on her person, but the judge ruled that she needed to continue to register as a sex offender for another fifteen years—the new federal requirement—because her arrest was a violation of her registration period. "Where is the justice?" she asked, speaking through tears. "How do they expect me to straighten out my life?" Struggling with basic needs like housing, Miss Jackie added, "I feel condemned."

Advocates and former defendants claim that the decision as to who is charged under what penalty is made arbitrarily, at the discretion of police and the district attorney's office, and that the law disproportionately affects Black women as well as transgender women. When asked about the allegations of abusing the crime against nature statute, NOPD spokesman Bob Young responded, "Persons are charged according to the crime they commit."

Wendi Cooper's story, however, paints a different picture. In 1999, Cooper had recently come out as transgender. A Black transwoman, she worked in prostitution a few times and quickly discovered it wasn't for her. But before she quit, she was arrested. At the time, Cooper was happy to take a plea that allowed her to get out of jail and didn't think much about what the "crime against nature" conviction would mean on her record. As she got older and began work as a health care professional, the weight of the sex offender label began to upset her more and more. "This is not me," she said. "I'm not that person who the state labeled me as…it slanders me."

Cooper appealed to the state to have her record expunged and talked to lawyers about other options, but she still must register as a sex offender until 2015 and potentially longer. "I feel like I was manipulated, you know, pleading guilty to this crime…. And it's hard, knowing that you are called something that you're not," she said. She is also afraid now that the conviction will prevent her from getting her license as a registered nurse, or from being hired.

Although Cooper only worked in prostitution briefly and has not resumed since her arrest, she still faces harassment from the police. When they run her ID through the system and find out about the prostitution charge, they threaten to arrest her again or sometimes, she alleged, they demand sex. "Police will see that I been to jail for the charge," she said. "And then they'll try to have me, forcefully, sexually…. One I had sex with, because I didn't want to go to jail."

Thinking about her experiences with police over the years, Cooper got quiet. "Sometimes I just wanna do something out the ordinary, and just expose it, you know?" She sighed. "They hurt me, you know?"

Sex workers accused as sex offenders face discrimination in every aspect of the system. In most cases, they cannot get released on bond, because they are seen as a higher risk of flight than people charged with violent crimes. "This is the level of stigma and dysfunction that we're talking about here," said Perry. "Realistically, they're not getting out."

Jennifer, a twenty-three-year-old white woman who also asked that her real name not be used, has been working as a prostitute since she was a teenager, and also works as a stripper at a club on Bourbon Street. She recently broke free of an eight-year heroin addiction. Unless the law changes, she will have the words "sex offender" on her driver's license until she is forty-eight years old.

Deon Haywood of WWAV observed that stories like this show that the law has the effect of forcing women to continue with sex work. "When you charge young women with this—when you label them as a sex offender—this is what they are for the rest of their lives," she said.

Jennifer said it has affected her job options. "I'm not sure what they think, but a lot of places won't hire sex offenders," she said.

Haywood said the women she sees have few options. Many of them are homeless, sleeping in abandoned houses or on the street, or trading sex for a place to stay. "The women we work with, they don't call it sex work," she said. "They don't know what that means. They don't even call it prostitution. They call it survival."

LAW ENFORCEMENT VIOLENCE
AGAINST TRANSWOMEN

On a weekday evening in 2009, a group of transgender women met in the Midcity offices of Brotherhood Incorporated, an organization that provides healthcare and fights the spread of HIV and AIDS in low-income Black communities. When the conversation turned to the police, the mood in the room turned to outrage, as each woman had a story of harassment and abuse. Tyra Fields, a health worker who facilitated the meeting, told a story of being arrested without cause one night as she walked into a gay bar. "They never give us a reason they are arresting us," she said, explaining that being Black and transgendered is often enough reason for arrest, generally on prostitution-related charges.

A young and soft-spoken transgendered woman named Keyasia told a story of being persecuted by police who followed her as she walked down the street, rushed into her apartment, and arrested her in her own home. "Within the last four or five months, I've been to jail eight or nine times," said Keyasia. "All for something I didn't do. Because I'm a homosexual, that means I'm a prostitute in their eyes." Expressing the frustration in the room, she added, "I want to go to the French Quarter and hang out and have cocktails just like everyone else. Why can't I?"

Diamond Morgan, another of the women, described a pattern of harassment from police that begins, she said, "Once they discover my transgender status." She said she has been arrested and sexually assaulted by police and by employees of Orleans Parish Prison, who are under the auspices of the New Orleans Office of Criminal Sheriff. She detailed her own personal experience of assault, and that of friends, adding that OPP is a site many women speak of as especially abusive. She said that sexual assault of transgender women is common at the jail, and other women in the room agreed.

Tracy Brassfield, a transgender sex worker and activist also at the meeting, has dedicated herself to fighting against discrimination. Originally from Florida, Brassfield moved to New Orleans because she fell in love with the city. "But when I got here," she said, "I started running into problems with the police." These problems included what Brassfield called deliberate harassment from officers who target Black transgender women not because of any crime they've committed, but just because of who they are. "They say, you're transgendered, you're a fag, you're a punk, you're going to jail," she said.

Brassfield decided to fight back and organize. "I was raised in an activist family," she said. "I know my civil rights." She contacted local social justice and legal advocacy organizations such as WWAV, Critical Resistance, the ACLU of Louisiana, and the Orleans Public Defenders, seeking allies in her struggle. She also reached out in the community of transgender women. "My thing is put it out there, get it exposed," she explained. "This is not just about me, this is about everyone."

Members of the city's larger gay community complain of unwarranted arrests and a criminalization of sexuality, with police specifically targeting bars in the Black gay community. "If a gay man wants consensual sex, the undercover officer lies and says money was offered," said John Rawls, a gay civil rights attorney who has spent decades in New Orleans fighting on these issues.

Advocates and community members also assert that once gay men or transgender women are arrested for offering sex, they are also more likely than others arrested in similar circumstances to be charged under the "crime against nature" statute.

Wesley Ware, a youth advocate at Juvenile Justice Project of Louisiana, said that harassment against those who are perceived as gay or gender-noncomforming begins at a young age, and can include hostility from their parents, fellow students, and often from school staff. According to Ware, this leads many of these youths to bring weapons to school to defend themselves. "Gay and bisexual boys and young men are four times more likely to carry a weapon to school," he said. "Of homeless youth, 50 percent identify as lesbian, gay, bisexual, or transgender. Of kids in youth detention, 13 percent are LGBT." Ware added that many of these youth face an unsympathetic court, including judges who think that they will help "cure" gay youth by sending them to juvenile detention. "Ninety-nine percent of the kids in youth detention in New Orleans are black," added Ware. "So obviously what we're talking about is youth of color."

"This community is facing systemic discrimination in pretty much every system they deal with," said Emily Nepon, a staff member of the Sylvia Rivera Law Project, a legal organization that fights for transgender racial and economic justice. According to Nepon, women in this community deal with intersecting forms of oppression. "High levels of employment discrimination, housing discrimination, overpolicing, profiling that leads to higher incarceration rates, and higher levels of abuse within prisons."

Back at the meeting at the Brotherhood Incorporated offices, Brassfield urged women to stand up and fight back. "We need to document," she said. "What you want to do is illustrate a pattern of harassment and abuse." She handed out flyers and phone numbers for WWAV, Critical Resistance, and a sympathetic lawyer. "We have to look out for each other," she said. "I want to organize, just what we're doing now. The girls got to stick together."

POLICE AND VIGILANTE VIOLENCE AFTER THE STORM

During Katrina, the actions of the local and regional police departments were among the biggest dangers to public safety. The town of Gretna, part of Jefferson Parish across the Mississippi from New Orleans, stationed armed police officers on the bridge leading out of New Orleans in the days after Katrina. Under orders from the Gretna chief of police, the officers blocked the main escape route for the tens of thousands suffering in the Superdome, Convention Center, and throughout the city, even firing "warning shots" above the heads of those trying to escape the flooded city. This incident ranks among the cruelest examples of state violence in our time, yet no one was ever punished for it. In fact, those responsible were praised for their actions.

As the *Los Angeles Times* reported on September 16, 2005, "Little over a week after this mostly white suburb became a symbol of callousness for using armed officers to seal one of the last escape routes—trapping thousands of mostly Black evacuees in the flooded city—the Gretna City Council passed a resolution supporting the police chief's move. 'This wasn't just one man's decision,' Mayor Ronnie C. Harris said Thursday. 'The whole community backs it.'"[18]

In Baton Rouge, less than an hour from New Orleans, police were apparently under orders from their supervisors to make the city inhospitable to displaced New Orleanians. In the weeks after the storm, the behavior of the Baton Rouge police was so blatantly racist, violent, and illegal that state police from Michigan and New Mexico, who had come to Baton Rouge as volunteer reinforcements, left after just two days, lodging formal complaints with the city. As many observers noted at the time, it takes serious crimes for fellow police to break what is known as the "blue wall of silence."

State troopers described a pattern of violence and racial discrimination that pervaded the Baton Rouge force, including widespread beatings, search and seizure, spraying of mace, and arrests—all of which were apparently random and unprovoked. Troopers said that "Baton Rouge officers referred to black people as 'animals' that needed to be beaten down." Another state trooper reported that "Each time [Baton Rouge Police Officer Chad King] would make contact with a Caucasian person he would be friendly and pleasant. But when he spoke to a black person he was very loud, rude, and demeaning." A Michigan cop said that "officers offered to let him beat a prisoner as a thank-you for helping out with relief efforts."[19]

During the days after the storm, crews of white vigilantes were patrolling both sides of the Mississippi River, targeting Black people.

Donnell Herrington reported being shot by a gang of armed white vigilantes in the Algiers neighborhood. In interviews by a team that included journalist A. C. Thompson, neighbors of one of the vigilantes, a forty-seven-year-old man named Roland Bourgeois Jr., reported hearing him promise to shoot anybody with skin "darker than a brown paper bag."[20]

This story was an open secret. Chilling reports made it into interviews with survivors, an independent film, the People's Tribunal convened by PHRF, and independent media such as the radio program *Democracy Now!* Herrington was even featured in Spike Lee's documentary *When the Levees Broke*. But the corporate media, including New Orleans's own daily paper, ignored the story for almost four years.

Finally, investigative journalist A. C. Thompson, writing for ProPublica and *The Nation* in December 2008, documented the shooting of Herrington and the deliberate killing of other Black men fleeing the storm by these vigilantes with the endorsement and even the participation of local police.[21] Thompson had been urged by writer Rebecca Solnit to investigate the story. Solnit, in turn, had heard about the accusations of vigilante violence—and the lack of an official investigation—from community activists such as Malik Rahim.

Shortly afterward, a delegation of civil rights activists from New Orleans met with members of the Black Congressional Caucus and Justice Department staffers under then-newly appointed Attorney General Eric

Holder, and asked the DOJ to investigate both the vigilante killings and the other incidents of police violence. Between the investigative work of Thompson and the Justice Department—plus the *Times-Picayune*, which had been shamed into investigating the story it had ignored—the truth finally began to emerge. One by one, officers were charged with a wide range of crimes, including killings and their cover-ups, which had occurred in the days after the storm. More details began to emerge about the work of the Algiers vigilantes as well (as of this writing, none of the vigilantes have been charged with any crime). Even more important, DOJ oversight of the police department promised some systemic changes.

In 2009, working with a team of reporters from the *Times-Picayune* and the television show *Frontline*, Thompson documented at least ten shootings by police in the aftermath of Katrina. In every case, local police mounted little if any investigation into the incidents. Police told the family members of Matt McDonald, a young man who was killed by an officer, that their son had been killed by a civilian. His parents didn't find out a New Orleans cop had killed their son until a reporter called them four years later.[22]

Mardi Gras Indian chief Kevin Goodman was among those who witnessed the police violence. Although he had told his story to an Austin newspaper in the weeks after the storm, it took years for the killing he witnessed to receive a serious investigation.

> I was at the [New Orleans] Convention Center three, four days without food. People sick, sitting out on the curb in their wheelchairs, using the bathroom on themselves. Babies dehydrated. No nurses, no medical attention, no doctors. By Friday night I was laying down trying to sleep, but I couldn't stand the smell of myself or the filth around me. So I got up and walked around. I saw a police car go by and some guys started walking toward the police car. One guy's trying to get their attention, and he waved like this. Next thing I know I hear, "Boom!" A shot come out of the police car and they drove off. Killed a man and left him. Gone. Everyone watched him die, gasping for breath. I bet it didn't get reported, that the police killed a man. I never seen nobody die before.
>
> The police cars say, "Protect and Serve." Wasn't no protecting and serving going on. We protected ourselves and served ourselves. The sick, the poor, the helpless. About 2 hours later, the police passed by

again and ran over the dead man they killed. And kept going. I raise
my right hand to God.[23]

On September 2, 2005, four days after Katrina made landfall, Henry
Glover was shot by one officer, then was apparently taken hostage by other
officers who either killed him directly or burned him alive. His burned remains were found weeks later in the back of a car with a bullet wound in
his skull. Sometime between the discovery and the coroner's report, the
skull disappeared and the case was not flagged by the coroner's office as a
potential homicide.[24]

Six days after Katrina, seven officers killed two unarmed New Orleanians—a mentally challenged man named Ronald Madison was shot in
the back—and injured several more in a hail of gunfire on the Danziger
Bridge. This bridge crosses the Industrial Canal, connecting New Orleans
East with the rest of the city, and was one of the only routes survivors from
that part of town could travel to escape the floodwaters.

Madison was shot by officer Robert Faulcon. Officer Kenneth Bowen
then rushed up and kicked and stomped on him, apparently until he was
dead. The officers involved arrested Madison's brother Lance under false
pretenses and later had secret meetings at which they conspired to invent
a cover story, including planting a gun, hiding evidence, inventing witnesses, and writing coordinated statements, rewritten multiple times to
be believable.[25]

Madison's family members and the families of the others shot that
day kept the case alive for years while the media dismissed them and local
law enforcement, including Republican U.S. Attorney Jim Letten, refused to investigate. When the Justice Department became involved in
2009, they found evidence of a wide-ranging conspiracy conducted so
openly that one officer, Sergeant Arthur Kaufman, felt comfortable
shouting out to a room full of cops, "Hey, somebody give me a name," as
he invented a witness and testimony on the spot. In response, another officer shouted back, "Lakeisha."[26]

This and the other cases of police shootings in the wake of Katrina
could not have remained undisclosed for so many years without active participation by many parties. The corporate media refused to investigate; the
city coroner covered up evidence; the Bush Justice Department and U.S.
Attorney Jim Letten ignored the pleas of family members and others; the

staff of city DA Eddie Jordan bungled their investigation; and the police department, from the rank and file to the very top, looked the other way. Police Superintendent Warren Riley said he never read the report on the events at Danziger Bridge.[27]

"We have a coroner who always finds police were justified," said former PHRF director and longtime police accountability activist Malcolm Suber. Suber was referring to eighty-year-old Frank Minyard, who has been city coroner since 1974. Minyard has been the frequent subject of complaints from activists, who've charged that he has mislabeled police killings. "We've had independent coroners, forensic doctors come after him," said Suber, "and we found that basically all of his findings were bogus. Just made up."

As further evidence of Minyard's complicity in police violence, Suber described a case from the summer of 2005. Witnesses said police beat Raymond Robair to death. He was unarmed and not accused of any crime. In a report that evokes parallels to the Adolph Archie case, the coroner ruled that he "fell down or was pushed." This "fall" broke four ribs and caused massive internal injury, including a ruptured spleen.[28]

"If you ask any attorneys who have handled cases of police killings," Suber continued, "when they have hired independent doctors to go after our coroner, nine times out of ten he's wrong."

Suber also pointed out that the city's current district attorney, Leon Cannizzaro, has been slow to pursue cases of police violence. "The district attorney just does not file charges," said Suber. "When it's involving police, he just finds no crimes committed." U.S. Attorney Jim Letten has failed, too, said Suber. "A number of community groups have gone and met with him, asked him to investigate [Danziger Bridge and other cases], and he didn't do anything."

The law enforcement violence continued in the months following the storm. On Saturday, October 8, 2005, three NOPD officers—Lance Schilling, Robert Evangelist, and Stewart Smith—and two FBI agents were caught on video beating sixty-four-year-old Robert Davis, an African American teacher who was walking through the French Quarter. The incident received more attention than most law enforcement violence because it came a month after Katrina. However, news reports took pains to point out the "high levels of stress" NOPD officers were under.[29] Smith was suspended for 120 days while Schilling and Evangelist were eventually fired.

In 2009 a state appeals court ordered the department to rehire Evangelist. Lance Schilling later committed suicide.

The violence persisted. A small sampling of further incidents:

On December 30, 2006, Ronald Coleman, a young Black man who was the national legislative campaign coordinator for ACORN, was beaten and handcuffed by a group of seven plainclothes officers who mistook him for a pickpocket. After beating him up, they ran his ID and apparently realized their mistake—they had been looking for a "Black man wearing black," and Coleman was wearing blue.

On Mardi Gras of 2008, a group of Black city transit employees went to the Beach Corner Bar, a Midcity hangout popular with police officers. The bar apparently also had an informal "whites only" policy. The Black city workers were attacked and arrested by white off-duty cops, who also shouted racial expletives and planted a gun on one Black worker.[30] District Attorney Leon Cannizzaro's daughter was present and reportedly involved in the brawl; later, one of the cops who had been fired for his participation in the fight was hired by Cannizzaro's office.

In the summer of 2008, off-duty officer Ashley Terry, upset at being caught in the traffic of parents picking up their kids from camp, waved her gun in the air while leaning out of her car, frightening children and others at Jerome Smith's Tambourine and Fan summer camp at the Treme Community Center. Smith brought the fight to city hall. Speaking in front of city council members, with dozens of Treme community members present in support, he placed the incident in a larger context of police behavior toward the Black community. In response, City Council Representative Stacy Head called Smith "racist" and threatening, and tried to have his summer camp defunded.

On January 1, 2009, in the first hours of the new year, twenty-two-year-old Adolph Grimes III was killed by fourteen police bullets, twelve of which hit him in the back. He had been sitting in his car, waiting for a friend. Nine officers participated in the killing, which was termed an assassination by community members. Even the *Times-Picayune*—not known to be especially critical of local police—called for an investigation. Outraged local ministers also called for accountability.[31]

"The disclosures around Danziger and other cases of police violence after the storm represent a real opportunity to raise some fundamental questions about the nature of police and what they do," said Malcolm Suber. For Suber, the various federal investigations and office of police monitor have not gone far enough. While he is glad for the few reforms that have been won, he will not be satisfied by anything less than real community oversight over the department. Discussing the DOJ involvement, he said, "I don't think we can call on a government that murders people all over the world every day to come and supervise a local police department."

Suber isn't the only one who thinks the changes need to go deeper. "How you gonna get the wolf to watch over the chicken coop?" asked Adolph Grimes, Jr., the father of Adolph Grimes III. "It's the system itself that is corrupted."

LEADERSHIP BY THOSE MOST AFFECTED

Many of the leaders most active and effective on criminal justice issues are survivors of this pipeline. Robert Goodman, a staff member of Safe Streets, was born and raised in the schools and prisons of Louisiana. A large yet gentle man with a shaved head and a slow, deliberate gait, Goodman has worked to educate himself and transform his life. He entered jail for the first time at thirteen, and started using heroin at fourteen. He was incarcerated—and still using heroin—until he was thirty-two, and wasn't able to quit using until he was forty-two. On May 9, 2006, when Goodman had been clean for ten years, his brother Ronald was killed in an encounter with the NOPD. It was Goodman's fight for justice for his brother that led him to start organizing.

Goodman became an activist, working with Safe Streets and joining community organizer Kool Black in an organization called Black Men United for Change, Equality and Justice. But escape from the cradle-to-prison pipeline is not easy, as Goodman discovered. The police locked him up in 2009 on a thirty-five-year-old charge. Fortunately, he received support from friends and allies, including legal support from Carol Kolinchak of Juvenile Justice Project of Louisiana, and was released a few months later.

For Goodman, the post-Katrina demonizing and criminalizing of the survivors came as no surprise. He explained that the primary crisis of New Orleans is a discriminatory and corrupt school system that funnels young men into a brutal and unfair criminal justice system. "Every time a Black child is born in Louisiana, there's already a bed waiting for him at Angola

State Prison," he stated. "When I went to prison, I was illiterate," Good-man added. "I didn't even know anything about slavery, about our history."

Safe Streets has had a fundamental influence on the city's framing of the debate around criminal justice. Because of their work, journalists and politicians began—one by one—to confront systemic issues and examine the roots of the problems. Safe Streets's methods have been as important as their considerable victories, including the appointment of an independent monitor over the city's police department and a complete overhaul of the Indigent Defense Board. They have inspired active participation and leadership by the people most affected by reforms. The goals, struggles, and successes of Safe Streets have been grounded in the community and in the activism of people like Goodman, who know the problems of the criminal justice system firsthand.

For those who have been victimized by law enforcement violence, standing up and talking about what they have faced has already been transformative. "I can't imagine where my family would be if it weren't for Safe Streets," Goodman tells me. "We would have been pushed to the side. This organizing inspired my mother to live another day."

Organizers like Goodman have worked closely with advocates, researchers, and others to bring about these much needed changes. Also of vital importance are the lawyers, especially those who fight death penalty cases, such as the dedicated defenders with Innocence Project New Orleans and the Louisiana Capital Assistance Center; as well as the investigators of A Fighting Chance and NOLA Investigates, who provide the thousands of hours of effort it takes to win on these cases.

These lawyers have represented those whom the system has abandoned, from kids caught up in notoriously brutal youth prisons to indigent people on death row (Louisiana has executed about one person per year since 1983, and has 84 people on its death row).[32] These are the truly compelling stories of criminal justice in New Orleans post-Katrina, yet you can be sure these local voices will not be covered in the media or depicted on television. Even on *The Wire*, which has been justly praised for getting so much right about the systemic nature of the problems with the criminal justice system, the one character who was the least complicated, and most purely evil and unsympathetic, was also the only defense attorney depicted on the show. The New Orleans–set HBO show *Treme* (by the creators of

The Wire) took a step toward addressing this imbalance by basing a character on New Orleans criminal defense attorney Mary Howell (portrayed by actor Melissa Leo).

KOOL BLACK

Whenever law enforcement violence is reported, the media and politicians tell us that there are no other solutions to our societal problems. We are told that abusive police and wrongful convictions are necessary hardships we must accept in order to live in safety. However, communities have found other ways to provide safety. In the Jim Crow period, the police served as a tool for enforcing white power, and Black communities needed to find their own ways to provide safety for their neighborhoods. Some of today's community activists seek to continue that tradition.

Raised in the St. Thomas housing development in the Tenth Ward, Robert "Kool Black" Horton is a dedicated community organizer and father, as well as a former hip-hop artist and current gospel choir singer. He began his career as a founder of Black Men United for Change, Justice and Equality, a grassroots, community-based collaboration that initiated local responses to community problems. For fifteen years, he has been a trainer in antiracist organizing with the People's Institute for Survival and Beyond (PISAB). He also worked as campaigns and project director for Critical Resistance, the national prison-abolition organization, before he felt a pull to return to more local activism and went back to organizing full-time with Black Men United.

Kool first became a full-time organizer in the St. Thomas development around 1992. "Black Men United for Change was part of a larger effort," Kool said.

> To do grassroots organizing and educate people about what was happening in their neighborhoods, to deal with issues around teenage pregnancy prevention, the high risk of HIV in the community, and also issues around tenants' rights as public housing residents. These meetings would go beyond conversation on these issues, into dialogue about housing issues, the murder rate, police brutality, drugs, employment— those kind of basic things people need for their survival. So because this community was already pretty organized, we had one or two retreats and Black Men United for Change was established.

Kool's story is a remarkable, concrete example of a community-led
project effecting real change:

> We started by bringing employers to the table to help brothers get
> jobs. We acted as a job referral, and we had about sixty or seventy
> people connected with our organization that we were able to find
> work for.
>
> Then we started working on these issues of crime and policing. The
> murder rate was so crazy. There were two areas in particular, one was
> called Death Alley, and the other one was called Cutthroat. You didn't
> want to be in these neighborhoods after dark. The murders were occur-
> ring, and there was no intervention. The police would come out and lay
> the yellow tape down and draw the chalk lines but this was after the
> blood was spilled, and we felt it was too late by then. We realized that,
> had someone stepped in sooner, we could save lives.
>
> So Black Men United for Change developed a community-policing
> model called the St. Thomas Peacekeepers, which was conflict resolu-
> tion based on the relationships we had with folks in that neighborhood.
>
> A person would get killed, for instance, on a Tuesday evening. But
> it didn't start then. It was initiated a few days earlier, on a Friday or
> Saturday night at the neighborhood block party or a dice game. And
> because no one said anything then, it was allowed to filter over later.
>
> We had a large presence wherever there were community events or
> large gatherings. We would be present in the neighborhood, and be-
> cause we had relationships with the people involved, we knew how to
> approach them and get them to at least listen and come to some sort of
> reasoning. There were times where the situation was too complicated
> for us to get involved, or we were too close to the situation, then we
> would bring in an outside, neutral party.
>
> As a result of our work, we began to watch the murder rate drop in
> St. Thomas, from thirty-one murders to zero, in a three-year period.
> The murder rate was about thirty-one people when we began—that's
> thirty-one killed in one year, just in the St. Thomas development. That
> went down to fourteen the next year, then to six, then zero.
>
> We were also able to address police brutality. There were rumors
> that people were being targeted and gunned down by the New Orleans
> police department. There was this group [of police] called the head-
> hunters, who rode around with black baby doll heads on the hood of
> their police car. We were able to deal with that matter and have those
> officers removed from out of not only St. Thomas, but the entire 6th

District police area, because they were terrorizing not only St. Thomas, but also the other public housing sites in that district....

Folks are being criminalized by the police here. When the issue of race in particular comes into play, the New Orleans police department is not unique. When you look historically, the police department has been one of the biggest terrorists in our neighborhoods, and that's across the country, and those relationships haven't changed much. The faces of politicians have changed, that's it.

From the initial moments after the city flooded, there have been two very different visions competing to define the recovery. One is of the "security" exemplified by Governor Blanco, who sent in National Guard troops while business elites contracted with Blackwater's armed guards and corporate disaster profiteers.

The other is one that seeks both justice and liberation. It involves building new work opportunities and providing health care and housing for people, rather than offering them minimum-wage, dead-end jobs, crumbling infrastructure, and more prisons. Community projects such as Black Men United offer tangible alternatives to the deadly "security" proffered by law enforcement.

This latter vision is supported by the efforts of grassroots activists and organizers. We are building a movement that is focused not on tearing down prisons but on creating and sustaining something better, a world in which safety comes from within the community. We are building a world in which the very idea of prisons will become obsolete. A world in which "prison" is an arcane word for our descendants to invoke as a reminder of the distant past. In this future, they will wonder how we as a people could ever have thought it was permissible to take away life, freedom, and humanity from our brothers and sisters.

In 2001, the city tore down the St. Thomas development where Black Men United had demonstrated such remarkable success, scattering the former residents around the city. This demolition happened a few years before Katrina, but it set a precedent for a much larger struggle—one that would in many ways define the post-Katrina landscape of New Orleans.

ORLEANS PARISH,
PRISON EXPENDITURES
PER NEIGHBORHOOD IN
THOUSANDS OF DOLLARS,
2007. PRODUCED BY
LAURA KURGAN AND THE
SPATIAL INFORMATION
DESIGN LAB AT GSAPP,
COLUMBIA UNIVERSITY,
AS PART OF A PROJECT:
JUSTICE REINVESTMENT,
NEW ORLEANS, 2007

PRISON ADMISSION DATA
WAS PROVIDED BY THE
LOUISIANA DEPARTMENT
OF PUBLIC SAFETY AND
CORRECTIONS.

FROM A 2008 YOUTH EVENT ORGANIZED BY JJPL AND SESS 4-5.
PHOTO BY ABDUL AZIZ.

CHAPTER EIGHT

You Don't Want to Go to War: The Struggle for Housing

You don't want to go to war
With New Orleans
Just give us our homes; it'll be all right

Protest chant, adapted from the song "You Don't Want to Go to War,"
by Rebirth Brass Band and Soulja Slim

I met Charhonda Thomas when we worked together as union organizers in 2000. Born and raised in New Orleans, Charhonda is in her early thirties now and has two kids. Although she has "9th Ward for life" tattooed on her leg, Charhonda lives in Houston now, and for me, her continued displacement represents a lot of what is wrong with the new New Orleans.

Over several years, through hundreds of hours of conversation and time spent together, Charhonda introduced me to this city I love. When I'm dancing to a brass band at a secondline or sitting on a stoop on a spring day with the scent of barbeque in the air, I think of her. Charhonda taught me everything I know about community organizing—she's the best organizer I've ever met. She has a gift for immediately connecting with people, which is not surprising for someone from New Orleans, where you hug people when you're first introduced to them and everyone—of any age or gender—is known affectionately as "baby." She is brilliant both intellectually and interpersonally, with the kind of skills and experience this city badly needs.

Charhonda was the first of many amazing people who welcomed me to this city. She is also one of the thousands of people kept from returning by the government policies enacted after Katrina.

When I came back to New Orleans, one of my first stops was Charhonda's house. It was empty, as were most houses in the city at that time. I left a note on the door, then went to her mother's house, also empty, and left a note there. I hoped that she would come back to the house, even if just to see the state it was in, and that when she did she would see my note. Charhonda is one of my best friends, and I had no other way to reach her. Her phone, and her mother's phone, were disconnected. Her email address was disabled. Her former employer didn't know how to reach her.

A year passed before I reconnected with Charhonda. On the anniversary of Katrina, I went to a memorial march sponsored by the PHRF. "I knew you'd be here," she said, and it was as if we had never been separated. In those months after the storm, each gathering, from secondlines to protest marches to neighborhood meetings, was another chance to find and reconnect with friends and neighbors who had disappeared.

When I saw her that August day in 2006, I asked what I could do to get her to move back. I offered to help her find employment, housing, and a babysitter for her two young children. Charhonda explained why she couldn't come back. As a single mother of two kids under three years old, she needed childcare. Family members in Houston, especially her mother, were able to watch her kids while she was at her job. With any job she got in New Orleans, she'd be spending too much of her money on childcare, unable to afford other expenses. She also didn't want to leave her children with strangers all day. In addition, she saw that the city's school system and health care system were in a shambles. For Charhonda, New Orleans was not only unaffordable, it was also no longer safe, especially for her kids.

In the months after the storm, there had been a lot of empty promises from politicians about people being able to come back. Yet there were also architects, urban planners, think tanks, and politicians—in their unguarded moments—talking of a "smaller footprint."

There is a racial divide on the issue of return. According to a 2009 poll conducted by James Carville, 64 percent of white New Orleanians said the city should "shrink its footprint"—which meant keeping Black neighborhoods like New Orleans East and the Lower Ninth Ward from rebuilding—while 74 percent of Black respondents were opposed to the idea.[1]

Since Katrina, I've seen many friends leave, beaten down by a city they love and where they wanted so badly to stay. With every loss the city has been diminished.

Housing is a human right. There can be no fairness or justice in a society in which some live in homelessness, or in the shadow of that risk, while others cannot even imagine it. Since the housing market bubble burst and foreclosures exploded in 2007, the U.S. government, which has spent decades getting out of the service of providing housing, has been reluctant to do anything about it. The free market ideology so dominant in our country dictated that the only solution was to give the banks hundreds of billions of taxpayer dollars, even if a more obvious solution would have been to help the people being evicted to stay in their homes, and to help those with no home to secure one.

New Orleans experienced a different, earlier housing crisis due to Katrina. Eighty percent of the city had been underwater. Even houses that didn't flood often had wind damage or needed other repairs. Many homeowners who had predatory loans discovered this problem as they attempted to rebuild. Five years after Katrina, about one in four residential addresses remain vacant or unoccupied.

Many initiatives came here to build houses. Actor Brad Pitt's work with his organization Make It Right has shown an impressive amount of flexibility and a real desire to rebuild in a way that is accountable to local residents. Pitt invited high-profile architects to meet with neighborhood associations to get their feedback on the designs of homes. He also donated his own money and raised money from wealthy contacts. While it is completely reasonable to be suspicious of Hollywood philanthropy in general, Pitt may be directly responsible for more rebuilding in the Lower Ninth Ward than any government aid, organizational support, or individual act of charity. This reflects well on him, but more pertinently, it reflects very poorly on our government.

No amount of volunteerism or donations from movie stars could even approach the massive level of reconstruction needed. The damage was in the tens of billions of dollars. In terms of recovery, the Lower Ninth Ward ranks far behind other neighborhoods, with only 11 percent of its pre-Katrina number of households, as of 2009. Since the devastation of the city, rents have gone up an average of 46 percent citywide (much more in some neighborhoods), while city services like public transportation remain very limited.[2]

Of all the many issues surrounding housing, one battle in particular embodied the way in which some people were kept out while others were invited back in: the struggle over the public housing developments. Immediately after Katrina, politicians, developers, and planners announced their intent to tear down all the remaining public housing in New Orleans despite the fact that most of the buildings had come through the storm without significant damage. As Baton Rouge Congressman Richard Baker gloated shortly after the hurricane hit, "We finally cleaned up public housing in New Orleans. We couldn't do it, but God did."[3] Activists countered that what the city needed was to have the existing housing repaired or new housing built. We didn't need good, solid buildings that had survived the storm to be torn down as part of an ideological attack on the idea of low-income housing.

Only months after the storm, City Council President Oliver Thomas (who later went to prison for a corruption scandal involving bribes related to a city contract for a parking lot), declared publicly that many of the public housing residents should not be allowed to return. Employing the stereotype that people are poor because they don't want to work, Thomas declared, "There's just been a lot of pampering, and at some point you have to say, 'No, no, no, no, no.'" He also stated, "We don't need soap opera watchers right now."[4]

At the city council meeting at which Thomas made those remarks, Nadine Jarmon, the appointed chief of the Housing Authority of New Orleans (HANO), declared that Thomas's position reflected HANO's policy, adding that if "they don't express a willingness to work, or they don't have a training background, or they weren't working before Katrina, then [we're] making a decision to pass over those people."[5]

These statements were made six months after the hurricane. Thousands of undamaged housing units were empty, thousands more homeless New Orleanians faced eviction from FEMA hotels and trailers, and tens of thousands of tenants whose rental homes had been damaged had nowhere to go. In the midst of this crisis, Council President Thomas, two other council members, and the chief of HANO blamed the victims. What about single parents and caretakers? What about the elderly, injured, or disabled? Didn't they deserve housing, even if they didn't have training or an extensive job history? Why was "intent to work" demanded only of public housing tenants? And what was so wrong with the actual housing that it needed to be torn down? In a city in which so much property was damaged or destroyed, why tear down homes that were undamaged or only slightly damaged?

INCITE has put forth an analysis that issues of war, displacement, law enforcement violence, and housing are linked—and all are both racialized and gendered. When public housing is closed and 99 percent of its residents are Black—as is the case in New Orleans—then the issue of housing is also one of race. Since women make up the majority of public housing tenants in New Orleans, discrimination against those tenants also becomes a gender justice issue.[6]

Working-class Black women were the most demonized in the attacks on public housing residents and faced the most difficulties in returning. The gendered nature of these attacks crystallized into outright eugenics when Louisiana state representative John LaBruzzo of Metairie proposed mass sterilization of public housing residents and other women receiving public assistance. "What I'm really studying is any and all possibilities that we can reduce the number of people that are going from generational welfare to generational welfare," he told a *Times-Picayune* reporter.[7]

While LaBruzzo's proposals were too extreme even for the far-right-wing Republicans in the Louisiana legislature, his comments reflected the attitude held by many toward poor residents. "LaBruzzo talks about poverty as though it were an infectious disease," responded members of the Women's Health & Justice Initiative (WHJI), "rather than a condition people are condemned to by Louisiana's lack of investment in education, employment, affordable housing, and quality health care programs, services, and resources."

Before the evacuation, New Orleans had more than 9,000 families in Section 8 housing and 7,700 public housing apartments. Five thousand one hundred and forty-six of those units were occupied and the others were empty, supposedly waiting for repairs and refurbishing. In total, more than 14,000 families were receiving some form of housing assistance from HANO. Most of the five thousand still-occupied units were in the so-called Big Four, the four largest developments remaining in the city: Lafitte, B. W. Cooper, St. Bernard, and C. J. Peete. These developments did not consist of large, anonymous towers like the housing projects of Chicago or New York. The New Orleans public housing had porches and balconies on two- and three-story houses, with pedestrian walkways, courtyards, and in the case of Lafitte, large oak trees.

The Lafitte development stood near the intersection of Claiborne and Orleans, the epicenter of Black Mardi Gras and often described as the heart of New Orleans's Black community. It was part of the greater Treme neighborhood, the oldest free Black community in the United States. Across the street was Dooky Chase, the legendary Black Creole restaurant where civil rights leaders and famous Black musicians had gathered while white restaurants would not let them in. Built in 1941 as a Black-only development (the nearby Iberville was white-only at that time), the Lafitte had 896 units. People spoke with pride of the Treme craftsmen who had built the sturdy and attractive structures.

The B. W. Cooper complex—located on Calliope Street and sometimes called the Calio—was home to 1,400 African American working-class households in 1,546 units on 56 acres of land. It was the third-largest housing development in Louisiana and the largest tenant-managed housing development in the country. In some circles it's famous thanks to rapper Master P and the artists of his No Limit record label, many of whom not only came from this development but also talked about it nonstop throughout their albums. Built in 1941 and expanded in 1954, the Calio was given over to full resident control in 1998, and had been "considered by many to be a national model of how the quality of life in a housing development can be improved when it is tenant-managed."[8] Situated at the crossroads of the neighborhoods of Central City, Gert Town, and the Central Business District, it offered housing that was centrally located and affordable.

The C. J. Peete, also known as the Magnolia or Nolia, was name-checked in many rap songs (including Juvenile's "Nolia Clap") and was the birthplace of several artists from the notorious Cash Money record label, as well as the artists Soulja Slim and Jay Electronica. It is also the birthplace of an earlier generation of artists and culture makers, including many Mardi Gras Indians and painter/sculptor Willie Birch. Located in the heart of the Central City neighborhood, the Nolia had 1,403 units at its peak, many of which had already been torn down or abandoned at the time of Katrina. It was fairly close to the Calio, as well as to the smaller Guste development, which had been mostly torn down and redeveloped by 2005.

The St. Bernard was located in the Gentilly neighborhood, in New Orleans's Seventh Ward. It was not far from Mayor C. Ray Nagin's house or from the city's fairgrounds, which host Jazz Fest every spring. The St. Bernard had been considered one of the safest developments in the city. However, when the Desire and St. Thomas developments were torn down a few years before Katrina, many of the residents from those developments were moved to St. Bernard, destabilizing the community. Prior to Katrina, it had 1,300 units, only 963 of which were occupied.

A few hundred residents also lived in the Iberville, just outside the French Quarter, in the neighborhood that had once housed Storyville—the early twentieth-century "red light district," often credited as the birthplace of jazz. With its prime location, Iberville was the most coveted by real estate developers. Near the high ground of the Mississippi, the area had experienced very little flooding and many residents had never evacuated, making it harder to lock them out and keep them from returning.

People who lived in the Big Four developments were not as fortunate as the Iberville residents. Most had evacuated; shortly afterward, their apartments were sealed and plans began for their homes to be torn down. The U.S. Department of Housing and Urban Development (HUD) soon announced a plan to tear down more than 4,500 apartments—almost all the remaining units in the Big Four—to be replaced by fewer than 800 units.[9] Only a fraction of this 800 would be set aside for former residents.

The battle had begun, and the city would never be the same.

At a housing demonstration at the St. Bernard development in April 2006, shortly after Oliver Thomas's widely publicized remarks about "soap opera watchers," I spoke to former St. Bernard resident Pamela Mahogany. She mentioned the city's sudden feigned concern about unlivable conditions in public housing. "We've been having mold, mildew, and backed-up sewers for years," she told me. "I've been here forty-two years and it's been a hazard the whole time. They never cared before. This is part of their goal to tear our development down."

Community is what Mahogany missed most about her home in St. Bernard. "They say it's unsafe here. When I lived here I didn't have a burglar alarm. Now I have one, 'cause I don't know the people around me. They say people here didn't have jobs. Guess what: I'm a nurse. I go to work every day."

At that same demonstration, several former residents of the St. Bernard housing development expressed their desire to return to their homes. A few had made the trip all the way from their exile in Houston. One resident proclaimed that he was going to move back in as a form of civil disobedience. Although his conviction was inspiring, the idea that civil disobedience would be required to move back into one's own undamaged home was profoundly disturbing. In the following months, many former residents, as well as activists who wanted to stand with them in solidarity, moved into these supposedly unlivable homes. Some people lived there for months, without electricity—in the C. J. Peete complex, for example—until the situation became untenable. Activists also moved into the Lafitte and St. Bernard developments but were quickly arrested.

People of this city who have made vital contributions to U.S. culture, but who have always been left out of the profits, were once again placed last in line. Loyola Law Clinic director Bill Quigley noted this inversion of justice. As he said, "What if we turned the priorities upside down, instead of saying that we are going to start with building up the high ground, what if we prioritized restoring housing and justice for those who had the least to begin with?"

LOOTERS WITH KEYS

Rebecca G. Brown lived on Erato Street in the B. W. Cooper complex for twenty-four years. Her neighbor, Dorris Johnson Frohm, said Ms. Brown had the "the loveliest house on the block, and always welcomes you in."

One day in early January 2006, Ms. Brown stood in her doorway crying. Her home had been destroyed—not by flooding or wind damage, but by theft. Two beautiful mirrors that hung in her stairwell were gone. The computer that her son used in college was gone. Her TV and two DVD players were also gone, along with most of her pictures and valuables.

Nearby, Yasmond Perry, thirteen, and his twelve-year-old brother Deseon stood outside their home at 3201 Erato with their mother, Josephine. "We haven't been inside yet," she said. "I'm kind of scared. Everyone's been calling me saying that they are taking all of our stuff—furniture and all. We were only here once right after the storm—but I'm hearing people have been in here since."

Inside the home, the boys stared in astonishment. "Oh my God, they took everything!" Surveying her home, Josephine went down the long list of furniture items that were missing—sofa, loveseat, television, table, and chairs—all gone.

"How did they have time to take all this?" exclaimed Josephine, who had been home a few weeks after the storm to check on her house. "It was fine really then. Not much different than I'd left it." During that visit, she described, "Yasmond was standing on the porch and the National Guard pulled up within five minutes pointing guns at him." She ran outside and showed the military proof that she lived there. "So, if they are here in minutes pulling a gun on my boy, how do people have the time to unload whole households without any notice? And it's not just me. It's my whole block!" Upstairs, the rooms were turned upside down, with drawers and boxes emptied. In shock, the boys each grabbed two personal items and walked downstairs. "This is all I need I guess," said Deseon with a grim look, "everything else is messed up."

Most of the Calio was not damaged in Hurricane Katrina or the subsequent flooding. After Katrina, HANO posted a general notice in the projects informing residents that they could not move back, and some Calio tenants received notice to clear out their possessions. HANO hired a Las Vegas company named Access Denied to install sixteen-gauge steel plates over windows and doors at various city projects. As one resident observed, "They finally invested money in the projects, and of course it's to keep residents out."

In interviews, HANO spokespeople expressed concerns about "looting," "troublemakers," and "squatters." Although it was true that there had been massive theft from homes in these projects, visits to at least twenty homes that had been burglarized revealed that most had their locks intact. The apartments had been broken into by someone with keys and access. Residents placed the robberies as having occurred around December 2005—long after Mayor Nagin began urging people to return to the city, and weeks after the National Guard had finished breaking into homes to check for bodies. People that lived in the B. W. Cooper complex had no doubt that someone from HANO—the only people who had the keys to all the apartments—had robbed them. This fit a pattern of HANO officials robbing the people they served. The Authority's Section 8 housing director, Dwayne Muhammad, was later convicted of illegally using Section 8 vouchers for himself, despite the fact that he made well over $100,000 a year and the city had an extensive waiting list for the vouchers.

At the stripped Perry home, Yasmond and Deseon said they desperately wanted to return to New Orleans. "The kids in Houston don't like us. They treat us funny. I just want to come home." Josephine, a cook, had a meeting at her previous job. "They are offering us something to come back. I'd be happy to come back. I just don't have nowhere to live." Before the storm Josephine held down two jobs. "I don't mind working, as long as the kids have a solid home."

Ruth Hayes, the assistant manager of the development, confirmed, "We are experiencing a high volume of burglary. People are coming home and what they expected to be there is not there," she said. Hayes had no other information on the robberies. Another B. W. Cooper management representative told local activist Elizabeth Cook that residents "gotta change their attitude before we let them back in."

Rebecca Brown's neighbor, Dorris Johnson, spent that December day in 2005 sifting through her wrecked home. "They trashed my house—look at this. The storm didn't do this! I called HANO to find out what was going on. They told me to get my stuff out or it was going in the dumpster. Good thing I have a good son who could bring me all the way here." Johnson wanted her house back. "There's nothing wrong with these houses. We could all be back living here." Johnson's house, like every other apartment on the river side of Galvez Street, did not take in water. Only half the development, located on the far side of Galvez—commonly called "back-a-town"—had any flooding damage.

Approximately two thousand people lived on the dry side of the complex, estimated Johnson. "That's two thousand people that could have housing tomorrow." Johnson and her son sifted through their apartment in search of pictures and memorabilia. "This is what I came for," holding up her granddaughter's graduation picture. "It was clean around here," motioning to her area. "No kids sat on these steps. This was a family area. No drugs around here."

Johnson lamented the neglect of her neighborhood and community and summed up her anger toward those who robbed her apartment. "I know that I come into this world with nothing and leave with nothing—but let me decide what I get to keep in the meantime. I worked hard for those few things."

During this period there was an enormous outcry from politicians and continued coverage in the media about "looting." Yet with all this talk of security, somehow there was no real protection or concern for the poor majority the way there was for businesses and the wealthy neighborhoods.

We may never find out who broke into all those homes in the Calio, since they have now been torn down. If residents had been allowed to return, this massive theft would not have happened. The Calio certainly had problems, but it did offer community, and that community brought with it a kind of security and comfort that is now notably absent from the city. Proponents of tearing down the public housing insisted that it would make the city safer, yet in the months after the storm, with the housing developments empty and most of the former residents still displaced, the crime rate went up.

Another B. W. Cooper resident, Ms. Trymore, stared at her wall. Her framed picture of Rosa Parks was missing. "We saved to get that picture, you know," said Trymore. "It cost like $200. We didn't have that kind of money. But, we admire that woman, you know. Now it's gone. Who would steal that?"

A HISTORICAL STRUGGLE OVER PUBLIC HOUSING

The effort to tear down the city's public housing developments had begun before Katrina, and was part of a national trend. From 2000 to 2008, HUD demolished one hundred thousand units of housing in the United States and replaced only forty thousand.[10] Across the United States, the government had abandoned its commitment to affordable housing. In New Orleans, public housing had been under threat for decades, facing declining services and demonization from the media. But the projects were also a site of much value for many in the city—offering a tight-knit community that cultivated a great deal of music and other culture, as well as grassroots resistance.

In 1966, the Free Southern Theater (FST), the theatrical arm of the civil rights movement, moved into a supermarket flooded by Hurricane Betsy near the Desire Public Housing Development in the Ninth Ward neighborhood. FST became an integral part of the community and produced a play called *Ghetto of Desire,* which laid bare the struggles of Desire residents. According to a web history of the FST, the *Ghetto of Desire* "exposed the gross inequalities people living in the Desire projects faced on a daily basis. In the play, the problems getting in and out of the project due to the railroad tracks and canals that surrounded the area, the inadequate recreational facilities for kids, and the poor condition of the roads within the development came under scrutiny. When CBS decided to broadcast the play...the Housing Authority of New Orleans went up in arms, demanding its cancellation."[11]

The New Orleans Black Panthers, who started in the St. Thomas development in 1970 and soon after moved to the Desire projects, continued this tradition of community organizing and outreach in the public housing developments. The chapter had a public education program that reportedly attracted 150 youth at any given time, a free breakfast program, and community patrols to protect against police violence.[12]

In 1982, Desire residents took over the HANO central office to demand better services. The Afro-American Liberation League, which led anti–police brutality protests in the '80s, were another group active in the public housing developments, especially the Fischer development on the West Bank.

In 2003, the Desire housing development was torn down and scheduled to be succeeded by new "mixed-income" housing, which would accommodate a small portion of the former residents. At the time of Katrina, the former Desire was in the process of being replaced with flimsy houses, now called Abundance Square. The storm easily destroyed these new houses, and HANO announced plans to rebuild again, using the same flimsy design. The Guste development—also called the Melpomene (or Melph) and the birthplace of several bounce music stars, including Katey Red—was torn down and redeveloped during this time, scattering most of its former residents. The Fischer development, on the West Bank, was also demolished.

Pre-Katrina, the biggest housing fight in the city had been over the fate of the St. Thomas development in the Tenth Ward, uptown. Activists and developers battled for years over what would happen to this neighborhood. The St. Thomas was a hard and violent place to live. But Kool Black and Black Men United had built a base in their community, and made a major difference in solving problems that afflicted the development. Ultimately, though they were able to deter violence in their community, they were up against systemic issues they couldn't affect. From Reagan through

Clinton to Obama, the policy toward public housing has stayed the same: tear it down. In the '80s and '90s, HUD seemed to be trying to make public housing as unlivable as possible in order to bolster their case for tearing it down. Repairs were never made. Apartments were left empty for years to be squatted by drug dealers and others. Social services were cut. Schools in the neighborhoods of the projects looked more like prisons. If the government had spent half the money it took to tear down the St. Thomas on making repairs, supporting groups like Black Men United, and creating job opportunities and better schools, the St. Thomas could have become a model community. Instead, the writing was on the wall.

According to Kool Black:

> People were being blamed for crime in the neighborhood. They say that crime is a public housing issue. Ask yourself, where did the dollars for housing go? We saw our greatest deterioration in public housing and downsizing of funding and staff in the 1970s and '80s. This was a backlash to integration. Fifty percent of St. Thomas was vacant. The money was pulled out of public housing. The staff was downsized.
>
> "Hope VI" [the federal program to transform public housing] is a joke. This country is getting out of the public accommodation business. Look at health care; look at charter schools and the privatization of schools. The country is downsizing from public responsibility. Public education was developed for white people initially. In the '60s, people of color integrated the system, and it became time for the government to get out of that service.

After years of resistance, St. Thomas was torn down and the neighborhood was renamed River Garden. The redeveloped area features shiny, new cookie-cutter houses—only a small percentage was reserved for former residents—several vacant lots, and a Wal-Mart. Some of those kicked out of public housing no doubt moved into non-subsidized housing. But it's likely that most former residents relocated to other developments, were shifted to Section 8 apartments, moved in with relatives, or were left homeless.

In 2007, I spoke with Pres Kabacoff, the CEO of HRI Properties, which he describes as an "inner-city revival company."[13] Tall and thin with white hair, a goatee, and wire-rimmed glasses, Kabacoff is a charismatic, confident, and somewhat bohemian spokesperson for the vision of a smaller, wealthier city. He moves comfortably between the worlds of high-level politics and—via his girlfriend Sallie Ann Glassman, a white "voodoo priestess"—the downtown arts scene.

A key power broker in New Orleans, Kabacoff was on Mayor Nagin's Bring New Orleans Back Commission, and is a major proponent of the demolition of public housing. A story on NPR portrayed him as a liberal visionary determined to create a Paris on the Mississippi,[14] and other liberal media followed suit. He is an influential city leader, as was his father, who was a chief figure in the tourist development of New Orleans and also established the city's first television station.

Critics say Kabacoff is reshaping the city into a place more hostile toward poor people, both through his development projects and his political role in the battle over public housing. He also earned notoriety as one of the forces behind a lawsuit that tried to keep the 2006 post-Katrina mayoral election from being delayed, which was seen by advocates as an effort to disenfranchise voters by rushing the election at a time when many poor, Black, and displaced voters would not be able to participate.

Kabacoff was the key player behind the redevelopment of the St. Thomas, an undertaking he described as "the template for all of the revitalization that now the Housing Authority is doing with all of their housing projects." One major element Kabacoff brought to the St. Thomas was the idea of replacing the development with not just housing, but also what he has touted as the country's first inner-city Wal-Mart. The Wal-Mart has been successful, but many former residents found the promises of new and better housing to be a mirage.

For years, Kabacoff advocated for demolition, especially of the centrally located Iberville. On the subject of public housing, he said the main problem is poor people crowded together. "When you get that concentration, usually what you get is crime, usually bad schools around it, crack cocaine, child abuse. You get a breakdown, a societal breakdown, so the federal government decided in the early '80s that they would start to get out of the public housing business, privatize it, turn it over to developers." He described public housing developments as "all poor, usually mothers—not fathers—mothers with children," declaring the St. Thomas was "[b]asically 5,000 mothers with children in 1,200 to 1,500 units in a hundred buildings…. You've got grandmothers taking care of infants. Three generations of people that haven't worked."

The St. Thomas development had 970 units in 1937 and expanded to 1,510 units in 1952. It was originally one of several "white-only" developments, later integrated by the Civil Rights Act of 1964. Many white families moved to the suburbs in response to the integration of housing and schools; soon after, the federal government began to cut funding for maintenance of the developments and to evict people for having incomes that were too high. By the time Kabacoff got involved with the St. Thomas, the federal government had been clearing it out for nearly twenty years, mostly by leaving apartments empty when families moved out. This high level of vacancy, of course, undermined the St. Thomas's sense of community and created a vicious cycle of bad living conditions.

These systemic attacks made the neighborhoods poorer and more dangerous, which led to further cuts and vacancies, and ultimately left the developments in such bad shape that they had few defenders when they were finally demolished. "By the time we got involved," said Kabacoff, "there were probably 600 families. All of those families were relocated when the project was torn down."

Advocates were angered by Kabacoff's decision and the disregard he had for former residents. "How many of the 1,510 families who used to live in St. Thomas have been allowed to move back in?" lawyer Bill Quigley asked. "About a hundred. A few of these families have had to force their way in with litigation by the Greater New Orleans Fair Housing Action Center. The demolition of St. Thomas is hailed as a mostly-good outcome by developers.... What do the 1,400-plus families who were moved out and not allowed to return think? Don't ask—no one else is."[15]

Kabacoff countered that by bringing back more public housing residents, "You would have been right back to where you started with a devastated, dangerous ghetto."

Although Kabacoff is perhaps the city's leading proponent of demolishing public housing, he's acknowledged some of the social ramifications. "This is not nirvana. When you upset a neighborhood, you upset family structures. Even though it was a hellhole to live in, at least you knew the people around you and you had family relationships. That's, many times, destructive to a family to get dislocated." However, Kabacoff has no apologies for the social engineering of forcing people out of their homes and scattering them around the city. In the projects, he said, residents "live in a neighborhood where really no one had a job, or very few people had a job, and you didn't even really know people who had a job. Unless you were Michael Jordan or Einstein, your life probably was going to be a pretty miserable one from birth to death.

"I think we made a wise social choice in saying this is really not help-ing the people living there," he said. "You're condemning them to...well, you know what it's like."

Ultimately, Kabacoff feels he has gotten his way in this post-Katrina era. "I am optimistic about this city," he said, describing poor people as probably happier in their displacement across the United States, where he believes they have likely found better economic opportunities. "I think we'll have a wealthier, smaller city."

Former St. Thomas resident Kool Black still feels betrayed by what happened to his old home and neighborhood. "St. Thomas was a painful ex-perience for me. It helped me understand this thing called community or-ganizing, so that's positive. But it is painful because of the end results. They said they would turn our community into a mixed-income community. Community folks that participated didn't know the scope of what they were dealing with. Developers ended up gentrifying and developing the commu-nity out of existence."

Advocate Bill Quigley described the St. Thomas's replacement, River Garden, as a collection of "cute gingerbread pastel houses," in place of the sturdy, well-built housing that once stood there. Today, according to Quigley, fewer than forty of the former St. Thomas residents have found homes in the new development.

Activists who came to New Orleans after Katrina often assumed that elites wanted to tear down affordable housing because there was money to be made—that high-priced condos or luxury hotels and boutiques would be built in its place, as has happened in other major cities, from the Bay View area in San Francisco to Cabrini-Green in Chicago to the tenements of the Lower East Side in New York City. But New Orleans's housing market never had that kind of strength—there is not much demand here for more luxury housing or hotels. The Lower Ninth Ward was never likely to be turned into a golf course or condominiums.

The truth is, elites simply didn't want these poor people back in the city. Not because profits could be made from selling their homes and land, but simply because they were seen as criminals and parasites, and those in power wanted them gone. From the very day they evacuated, public housing residents faced determined opposition to their return. Politicians, business leaders, and the daily paper were united in calling for an end to the big housing developments. Most white residents of New Orleans wanted to see public housing destroyed and a significant percentage of the Black community did as well.

For advocates, it was a difficult position to be in. We believe in decent, affordable housing for all. Yet for decades, political attacks on public housing have succeeded in halting most repairs and upkeep, making the housing less and less desirable. Then, when the demolition orders come, our choice is either to defend housing that is affordable but no longer decent—or to accept the destruction of the housing.

The proponents of demolition use this conundrum to their advantage. Defenders of public housing are accused of wanting poor people to live in substandard conditions. Promises are always made that new affordable housing will be built. Current tenants are recruited who are willing to tell the media they are in favor of demolition, that no one would want to live in the present housing, and that it should be torn down.

In New Orleans, when public housing residents took on a leadership role in the struggle, they were attacked. Tenants who planned to move back into their homes in order to demonstrate the housing's viability were threatened by HANO representatives with the loss of their Section 8 benefits and were demonized in the local media. The *Times-Picayune* seemed to be among the biggest champions of the plan to tear down the developments. In one news article, the paper mocked a resident for complaining about her Section 8 housing, unfavorably contrasting the resident's complaints about a leaky sink and warped back door with a photo showing her large-screen TV and wood floors. The article barely addressed her main grievance, which was that under Section 8, unlike with HANO, there was no mechanism by which to hold landlords accountable.[16]

When people who had not lived in public housing stood up in support of the cause, the movement was painted as being "led by outsiders." The truth is that the movement to save public housing was led by its former residents. The core leaders were some of the most inspiring organizers in New Orleans, including former public housing residents Shana griffin (Iberville), Kool Black

(St. Thomas), Reverend Marshall Truehill (B. W. Cooper/Calliope), Sess 4-5 (Desire), Mandisa Moore (Lafitte), and Stephanie Mingo (St. Bernard).

Others who came to stand in solidarity with them often had deep connections to the issue, like M. Endesha Juakali, who had lived next door to the St. Bernard development, Willie "J. R." Fleming, a former public housing resident from the Cabrini-Green projects in Chicago, and Bob Tannen, an artist and architect who lived not far from the Lafitte. Rapper Sess 4-5 put together a *Stop Da Demolitions* mixtape, featuring local hip-hop artists like T.L. and Truth Universal.

Another truth is that, although the housing in these projects may have been substandard, it was still a better option than homelessness, which was what many residents faced. It was also unlikely that the promises to rebuild would be fulfilled. In fact, in examples around the country, as well as with the St. Thomas development, the demolition of public housing had resulted in most former residents being excluded.

Housing activists also faced antagonism from within. Much of this internal hostility came from a small collective that operated under multiple names, most frequently C3 or Hands Off Iberville. Although the membership varied, two members were constant—Tulane University academic Jay Arena and a French Quarter fortuneteller named Mike Howells. Their positions were often principled—as revolutionary communists, they employed an analysis of class dynamics and a critique of the overall capitalist system that resonated with many activists. Both had been active for decades, especially around police brutality, public housing, and the antiwar movement. Unfortunately, their primary methods often involved attacking anyone on the Left who deviated from their line even slightly. They also maintained that the primary root of every problem was capitalism, and paid little to no attention to the dynamics of race or gender. Arena and Howells were often critiqued as two middle-aged white men who spent an inordinate amount of time attacking progressive and radical women and people of color, and the internal conflicts they stirred up created a toxic environment that drove many people away.

But issues with C3 were far from the only problem. There were other sharp fault lines between people active in the movement. PHRF organizer Kali Akuno cited the collective trauma people had just lived through as making them less likely to trust each other. "Stress that hadn't been dealt with brought out major inconsistencies in people's analysis," said Akuno. "As a social movement, we ignore this issue at our peril."

For two and a half years after Katrina, the public housing movement used many tactics, from protests to lawsuits to direct action. Several organizations in the city worked on the issue, each with specific goals and approaches, and frequently with overlap in personnel. M. Endesha Juakali was one of the main organizers with Survivors Village, a group mostly of former residents of the St. Bernard development. Residents of Public Housing was another group, loosely affiliated with the People's Organizing Committee (POC) and especially active around the C. J. Peete development, although they also had members and actions affiliated with all the complexes.

Each of these groups—including C3—carried out important work and secured some real victories on housing issues. An early victory that Kali Akuno pointed to involved the Lower Ninth Ward, which, he maintained, housing activists kept from mass demolition in the months after the storm. "In January of 2006, they were going to bulldoze the entire neighborhood," said Akuno. "That would have been much worse." Akuno said that legal action, combined with the direct action of activists moving into a house near the levee break, helped prevent the demolitions. "There was a lawsuit by Ishmael Muhammed and the Praxis Project, plus the Common Ground people had moved into a house in the neighborhood. ACORN played a role as well, with their placards in the neighborhood saying 'No Bulldozing.' The placards got attention on TV. In early meetings, people were saying, 'I didn't know my house was in danger until I saw that story on TV.'" The fact that people still live in Iberville, which continues today to be under threat of demolition, stands as another important victory from these efforts.

Akuno felt that much of the work to preserve the housing was strategically solid. For him, the larger problem was the circumstances surrounding the organizing, with many of the poorest, those with the most at stake, displaced. "Understand, in a political sense, what this displacement has meant," Akuno explained. "It's a different city now. We have 100,000 less people. It's hard to sustain actions like this while much of your base is in Houston."

In the days after the storm, it seemed that public housing residents had few allies. But over the months and years that followed, it began to feel as if the tide was turning, and support came from surprising areas. In the

New York Times, architecture critic Nicolai Ouroussoff spoke out against the demolition. He singled out the Lafitte development, saying of HUD:

> In its rush to demolish the apartment complexes—and replace them with the kind of generic mixed-income suburban community so favored by Washington bureaucrats—the agency demonstrates great insensitivity to both the displaced tenants and the urban fabric of this city....
>
> In arguing to save the buildings, preservationists point to the human scale of the apartment complexes, whose pitched slate roofs, elegant brickwork and low-rise construction reflect a subtle understanding of the city's historical context without slavishly mimicking it.
>
> Tellingly, neither housing agency has closely examined alternatives to demolition, like renovating some buildings in the complexes and replacing others....
>
> The housing agencies' tabula rasa planning mentality recalls the worst aspects of the postwar Modernist agenda, which substituted a suburban model of homogeneity for an urban one of diversity. The proposal for "traditional-style" pastel houses, set in neat little rows on uniform lots, is a model of conformity that attacks the idea of the city as a place where competing values coexist.[17]

Activists and lobbyists fought in the state legislature and in Congress. Representative Maxine Waters was a leader in passing House Bill 1227, "The Gulf Coast Hurricane Housing Recovery Act of 2007," which would have saved much of the housing or at least provided for one-for-one replacement. The bill was ultimately killed in the Senate, largely due to the opposition of David Vitter and Mary Landrieu, Louisiana's two senators.

The public relations battle was intense. HANO stated publicly that it was cheaper to tear down the developments than to rebuild, but research told another story. Attorney Bill Quigley wrote:

> The Housing Authority's own documents show that Lafitte could be repaired for $20 million, even completely overhauled for $85 million while the estimate for demolition and rebuilding many fewer units will cost over $100 million. St. Bernard could be repaired for $41 million, substantially modernized for $130 million while demolition and rebuilding less units will cost $197 million. BW Cooper could be substantially renovated for $135 million compared to $221 million to demolish and rebuild fewer units. Their own insurance company reported that it would take less than $5,000 each to repair the CJ Peete apartments.[18]

Even faced with this evidence, housing officials continued with the same story. "It's clear that HUD and HANO have been routinely and regularly lying to the public," Quigley told a reporter. "The discussions that they've had internally and with each other are completely different from what they've been saying publicly."[19]

Quigley and civil rights attorney Tracie Washington waged a valiant legal defense, challenging the demolitions on multiple fronts. They were aided by the Advancement Project, a national legal project that dedicated a huge amount of resources to Gulf justice, as well as by other allies in New Orleans and nationally. They succeeded in winning delays, buying time for activists to organize, but in the end all legal strategies were exhausted.

There were solidarity protests at HUD offices around the United States, including in California, Minnesota, and Washington, D.C. White activists from the Anti-Racist Working Group and Catalyst Project chained themselves to the offices of HANO. Residents risked arrest to break into their own homes, clean them up, and live there, proving with their own bodies that the housing was safe and not damaged by the storm.

During this time, homelessness was on the rise. Advocates estimated that more than twelve thousand homeless folks lived in the city—almost five percent of the city's estimated population at that time.[20] A new initiative formed, founded and led by homeless folks. They called themselves Homeless Pride and set up an encampment in the park across from city hall. The camp should have served as a daily reminder to the city's politicians of the results of their policies. However, no one from the mayor's office or city council seemed to have a change of heart. Instead, they closed the park. When Homeless Pride members set up a new encampment under a highway overpass a few blocks away, officials worked with UNITY for the Homeless, the city's main homeless advocacy alliance, to quietly place the people from the encampment in temporary housing. Although this brought immediate improvement to the lives of many of the people living under the overpass, it also served to silence the larger debate about the need for systemic solutions.

After decades of struggle, the future of New Orleans public housing came down to a meeting at city hall, a few days before Christmas of 2007. Activists were pessimistic about what would happen, but even with low expectations, the events of the day were traumatic.

I was one of those who arrived early, but not early enough, and so was faced with locked doors and a line of police. The few activists allowed into

the building were stopped when they tried to speak. When they kept trying, many were tasered and arrested. Hip-hop artist and activist Sess 4-5,
organizer Kool Black, New Black Panther Krystal Muhammad, and several others were dragged to jail. Outside, activists chanted to be let in and
pushed against locked gates. When the gates started to give, police rushed
forward with pepper spray and tasers. The protest grew louder.

But the drama inside was over quickly. The final city council vote to
tear down public housing was unanimous, with no visible hesitation from
any of the council members. Cynthia Hedge Morrell and Cynthia Willard
Lewis, the Black city council members who, between the two of them, represented the devastated neighborhoods of the Lower Ninth Ward, New
Orleans East, and Gentilly, had for a long time been reliable opponents of
affordable housing in their district—not just public housing, but also Section 8 and low-income developments. And this position tended to be generally popular among their base of middle-class and wealthier Black voters.
James Carter, a more politically progressive Black city council member
(representing an area including the French Quarter, Treme, and the West
Bank neighborhood of Algiers), had seemed more open to the arguments
on behalf of the residents, but in the end, he offered no dissent to the council's consensus.

As one activist described the vote and its consequences:

> On Thursday, December 20th 2007, the New Orleans City Council
> voted unanimously to demolish more than 4500 units of public housing
> in the city....
>
> Outraged and desperate to defend their homes, the collective of
> public housing residents and their allies locked outside of City Hall's
> gates broke through the fence twice, demanding entrance. Both times
> they were turned back with pepper spray and tasers by the NOPD. In-
> side the chamber pro-housing activists were tackled and dragged out
> after disrupting the meeting to demand the gates be opened and
> empty seats filled.
>
> The Times-Picayune published...a congratulatory story about the
> vote entitled "Unanimous." Over the next 2 days more than 190 com-
> ments were made by readers of the Times-Picayune in response to the
> following question: "Were police reckless?"
>
> Most of these comments reveal the deep and vicious racism that lies
> beneath support for demolition of public housing....Much of the sup-

port for demolition rests on openly racist notions of public housing residents as "animals," and "welfare queens" and visions of the "projects" as
nothing more than environments that serve to "breed a particularly bad
criminal element." There is zero recognition that as tough as it was to
live in a hyper-segregated working class neighborhood, these were still
communities, these were still affordable homes.

Many commentators call for using "attack dogs" and "water cannons"
on protesters without any apparent irony.[21]

While hostility from racist white folks, such as those who comment on
the *Times-Picayune's* website, was perhaps to be expected, the unanimous
city council vote was a brutal blow. The cumulative weight of fighting intensely for such a long time and losing so definitively hit people hard. Some
organizers never quite recovered from the experience and still talk about
that day with a mixture of sadness and anger. Other folks moved away or
disappeared for months in a self-imposed temporary retirement.

Within weeks, the public housing developments across the city were
being torn down. Many people avoided driving by the former neighborhoods because the sight of the rubble was too much for them. The devastation was enormous. At a glance, you could see teddy bears and clothes
and furniture, the personal possessions of thousands of people, mixed in
with piles of bricks and concrete.

HOMELESS AND STRUGGLING

Crawling through a hole in a fence and walking through an open doorway, Shamus Rohn and Mike Miller led the way into an abandoned
Midcity hospital located next to the American Can Company building.

Rohn and Miller are outreach workers for UNITY for the Homeless,
and they do this all day long—searching seemingly empty houses and
buildings for homeless people—so they can offer services and support. "We
joke about having turned criminal trespass into a full-time job," said Rohn.

Up a darkened stairway and through the detritus of a building that
looked like it had been scavenged for anything of value, Rohn and Miller
entered a sundrenched room. Inside was Michael "Mickey" Palmer, a fifty-
seven-year-old, white former construction worker and merchant seaman
who had made a home in the abandoned hospital. Palmer was in some
ways lucky. He'd found a room with a door that locked. He salvaged some

furniture from other parts of the hospital, so he had a bed, a couch, and a rug. Best of all, he had a fourth-floor room with a balcony. "Of all the homeless," he said, "I probably have the best view."

When I visited him in the summer of 2009, Palmer had been living in the hospital for six months. He'd been homeless since shortly after Katrina, and this was by far the best place he'd stayed in the meantime. "I've lived on the street," he said. "I've slept in a cardboard box." He is a proud man, thin and muscled, with a fresh shave, clean clothes, and a trim mustache. He credited his grooming to a nearby church, which let him shave and shower.

Palmer would like to be able to pay rent again. "My apartment was around $450. I could afford $450. I can't afford $700 or $800, and that's what the places have gone up to." Keeping himself together, well-dressed and fresh, Mickey was trying to get back to the life he had. "I have never lived on the dole of the state," he said proudly. "I've never been on welfare, never collected food stamps." Before Katrina, Palmer did repairs and construction. "I had my own business," he said. "I had a pickup truck with all my tools, and all that went under water."

Palmer is one of thousands of homeless people living in New Orleans's storm-damaged and abandoned homes and buildings. At the time I visited, the Greater New Orleans Community Data Center counted more than sixty thousand abandoned residential addresses in the city, and that number didn't include any of the blighted non-residential buildings, such as the hospital Palmer was staying in. Overall, about a fourth of the addresses in the city were still vacant or abandoned, the highest rate in the nation. UNITY for the Homeless has been the only organization surveying these spaces, and Miller and Rohn are the only full-time staff on the project. By the time we met, in summer of 2009, they had surveyed 1,330 buildings—a small fraction of the total number of empty structures. Of those, 564 were unsecured. Nearly 40 percent of them showed signs of use, involving a total of 270 bedrolls or mattresses.

UNITY estimated there were at least six thousand squatters out of the estimated twelve thousand homeless individuals in the city. The alliance received funding from the federal government in early 2009 for 752 housing vouchers, specifically to help house the city's homeless population. UNITY created a list, prioritizing those homeless people in greatest need, some of whom were in danger of dying if they didn't get help. However, the vouchers were slow to arrive, and at least sixteen people on the list died during the wait. "The stress and trauma that these people have endured cannot be overstated," said Martha Kegel, executive director of UNITY. "The neighborhood infrastructure that so many people depended on is gone."

UNITY staff noted that not all people living in abandoned homes are squatters. In the previous three months alone, they had found nine homeowners living in their own toxic, flood-damaged, often completely unrepaired homes. These were people living in buildings that they or extended family members owned, which had been identified as abandoned and not fit for human habitation.

The abandoned-building dwellers Rohn and Miller found were generally older than the overall homeless population, with high rates of disability and illness. The average age of folks they found was forty-five; the oldest was ninety. Over 70 percent had reported or displayed signs of psychiatric disorders, and 42 percent showed signs of disabling medical illnesses and problems. "Disabling" means "people that are facing death if not treated properly," said Shamus Rohn. "We're not talking about something like high blood pressure."

"This leg here bent backwards, and the muscle came up," explained Naomi Burkhalter, an elderly Black woman in a wheelchair, sitting outside of the abandoned house she lives in and gesturing to her badly twisted leg. She was injured during Katrina and can't walk now. She stays in a flood-damaged house in the Gert Town neighborhood, without electricity or running water. She said that the owner, who could not afford to repair the home, knows she lives there along with two other women. When they need water, they fill up bottles at neighbors' homes. When she needs to get in and out of her house, she crawls; very slowly dragging herself up and down the steps with her hands, leaving her wheelchair outside and hoping no one takes it.

Burkhalter was employed at a shrimp company and rented an apartment before Katrina. Now, between her injury and higher rents, she can no longer afford her former home. "My rent was $350," she explained. "But when I came back, my rent was up to $1200." Burkhalter has been homeless since then.

The demolition of public housing exacerbated homelessness in the city, not only taking away the community that for many people provided comfort and safety, but also making affordable rentals even harder to find. Section 8 subsidized housing was offered as a solution for those displaced from public housing and other poor renters, but the supply of landlords willing to accept Section 8 tenants is far smaller than the demand for such housing.

A 2009 study from the Greater New Orleans Fair Housing Action Center (GNOFHAC) found that 82 percent of landlords in the city either refused outright to accept Section 8 vouchers or added insurmountable requirements.[22] The study found that discrimination (both racial and gender-based) on the part of landlords and mismanagement by HANO were barriers to Section 8 renters. One prospective landlord told a Housing Action Center tester that he wouldn't rent to Section 8 holders "until Black ministers…start teaching morals and ethics to their own, so they don't have litters of pups like animals, and they're not milking the system." Ninety-nine percent of Section 8 voucher holders in Orleans Parish are Black. A large majority are women.

Mismanagement by HANO was also a big problem for prospective landlords. "I faxed HANO the needed information twelve times for the rent, but I was never paid," said one landlord. Another housing provider said, "I called every day for a month and never got a call back."

At the time the GNOFHAC report was released, more than a hundred members of STAND with Dignity, a grassroots membership project with the New Orleans Workers' Center for Racial Justice, protested outside of the offices of HANO, decrying the lack of action. A single mother named Ayesha told the crowd that she had been on the Section 8 waiting list for eight years and still hadn't received any help. She was paying 80 percent of her income for rent and had been forced to go months at a time without water, gas, or lights. George Tucker, another member of STAND—and, like Mickey Palmer, a former merchant mariner—told the assembled crowd his story of being evicted from his apartment because HANO lost his paperwork. Because of bureaucratic carelessness, he was homeless for thirteen months. "This governmental crookedness is not new," he said. "But it cannot continue without consequences."

When both houses of Louisiana's legislature unanimously passed a bill creating a statewide agency—to be almost entirely funded by the federal government—to address the issue of homelessness, Governor Bobby

Jindal vetoed the bill. He also vetoed funding for the New Orleans Adolescent Hospital, further reducing medical and mental health services in the city at a time when the need is increasing.

For people like Mickey Palmer, trapped in a city with few jobs, expensive housing, and ever-decreasing social services, there are not many options. "At one time, we were part of the city and part of the workforce," Palmer told me. "But people cannot afford the housing in New Orleans anymore. I find most of the people I know, my friends, they can't afford the rent."

Like most people in his position, Palmer has felt hopeless about his plight. "I try not to get depressed," he says, nervously flicking his lighter, "But this can get you depressed. I'm not a politician, and I'm not politically savvy, but I don't think they care."

People in public housing and those who are homeless are not the only ones who feel unsafe. Tenant protection laws in most of this country vary between limited and nonexistent. As the recent national housing crisis has demonstrated, even homeowners are often one missed payment away from catastrophe. Yet people in my own neighborhood were mostly silent in the debate over public housing, a silence echoed in neighborhoods around the city. If there is anything this experience should teach us, it's the importance of our coming together on the issue of housing, so that no one needs to fear losing the security of the roof over their head.

Although Homeless Pride disbanded after the encampments under the overpass and across from city hall were cleared out, there are still grassroots activists around the city engaged on this issue, and the group STAND with Dignity—also led mainly by current or recently homeless folks—has been a direct successor. There are inspiring groups in other cities taking direct action on this issue, too, such as the Poor People's Economic Human Rights Campaign, which set up a tent city during the 2008 Republican National Convention, and Picture the Homeless, a direct action–oriented, homeless-led collective in New York City.

Nationwide, one of the most inspiring stories is that of Max Rameau, the Haitian-born Miami resident who founded Take Back the Land in 2006. Take Back the Land moved people with no homes into empty houses owned by banks or the city. Although my cynical instincts expected these actions to be demonized by the media, in fact, Rameau received mostly positive press, including a front-page article in the *New York Times*.[23] This sympathetic coverage seemed to indicate a changing tide in this country, as anger at the banks and the investors that caused the national housing crisis has reached new heights. In early 2010, Take Back the Land expanded to form a national coalition, and Survivors Village from New Orleans was one of the organizations to join their call.

CENTRAL CITY DETAIL. PRISON EXPENDITURES PER BLOCK IN THOUSANDS OF DOLLARS, 2007. PRODUCED BY LAURA KURGAN AND THE SPATIAL INFORMATION DESIGN LAB AT GSAPP, COLUMBIA UNIVERSITY, AS PART OF A PROJECT: JUSTICE REINVESTMENT. NEW ORLEANS. 2007 PRISON ADMISSION DATA WAS PROVIDED BY THE LOUISIANA DEPARTMENT OF PUBLIC SAFETY AND CORRECTIONS.

IMMIGRANT RIGHTS DEMONSTRATION, MAY DAY, 2010.
PHOTO BY JORDAN FLAHERTY.

CHAPTER NINE

The Rest of the World Lives Here Too: Immigrant Struggles

Evacuated as if criminal
Rescued by neighbors
Shot by soldiers

Adamant they belong

The rest of the world can now see
What I have seen

Do not look away

The rest of the world lives here too
In America

From "On Refuge and Language" by Suheir Hammad

Race relations in New Orleans have often been narrowed to Black and white, especially pre-Katrina. According to the 2000 census, the city was about 67 percent African American, 27 percent white, 2 percent Asian, and 3 percent "Hispanic."[1] In a city with a deep history of racial tensions between Black and white, other people of color—and especially recent immigrants—often went unmentioned in discussions of city demographics.

That changed after the storm. While much of the Black community was displaced, a large Latino immigrant population arrived to work jobs in the city's reconstruction and consequently changed the demographics of New Orleans. These workers were hardly welcomed—on the contrary, they were demonized by everyone from Mayor Nagin to local talk radio hosts. Many had been lied to by contractors, who brought them to New Orleans with promises of housing and high-paying jobs that often did not exist.

Immigrants were also targeted by police and by thieves, two groups that knew this population had very little recourse. In 2008, in the nearby town of

Slidell, "Officer Jonathan Lutman stole as much as $3,000 from Hispanic motorists in at least four traffic stops between April and June."[2] In March 2009, NOPD officer Darrius Clipps was charged with "aggravated burglary, sexual battery, false imprisonment with a weapon, malfeasance in office, simple kidnapping, aggravated kidnapping, and unauthorized entry of an inhabited dwelling" in a crime spree that mostly targeted Latino immigrants.[3]

Pre-Katrina, most Latinos in New Orleans were long-term residents; there was very little in the way of social services and infrastructure specifically for the recent immigrant community. Weeks after the storm, a handful of volunteers initiated the Latino Health Outreach Project and began setting up clinics for Latino day laborers wherever they could be found—from hotels and campsites to a restaurant on Canal Street where workers gathered on Friday nights. The outreach team reported that some of the workers who arrived just after the storm were forbidden by their employers from talking to anyone or even from leaving their rooms at night. They were working in hazardous conditions for low pay and without proper safety protections. Many became ill and had no access to medical care.

Catherine Jones, a local doctor and activist who helped initiate the project while she was still a medical school student, wrote at the time:

> The stories we are hearing from workers are so monumental we don't know what to do with them. Some people are working in mold-infested houses with no masks or protective gear; some contract laborers are being imprisoned in hotels by their bosses, who won't let them leave the premises once they return from the day's work. People are working six and seven days a week, often for ten or more hours a day. We have talked to many day laborers who don't get paid after working for a day or even an entire week. These cold nights, many people are sleeping in tents while their bosses stay next door in heated trailers. Some people sleep under cars or bridges. Everyone is worried about flu, what it will mean to get sick in this climate where no job is guaranteed and a day's wage helps support as many as ten people back home.
>
> A friend who used to live near the clinic told us how one day, when he and some other people were going to work in Chalmette, they got stopped by the police at the checkpoint and the police asked them for their green cards. Our friend showed his Texas drivers' license and explained that he didn't have a green card since he's a US citizen. 'You

need a green card,' they said. They turned back the entire truck and told everyone they couldn't go to work that day.[4]

The New Orleans Workers' Center for Racial Justice began as a project of the PHRF. Under the leadership of Saket Soni, who arrived in New Orleans in 2006 specifically to help launch that project, the Workers' Center rapidly developed a national reputation. Saket and the other organizers eventually divided their work into three discrete but interconnected areas of focus. Through the Congress of Day Laborers they organized among day laborers; through the Alliance of Guest Workers for Dignity they supported immigrants who were in the United States temporarily on the H2B "guest worker" visa; and through STAND with Dignity they worked with a primarily low-income African American population. The Workers' Center organized in homeless camps and on day laborer corners, and even did community outreach in the workers' home countries of India and Mexico. The Alliance of Guest Workers for Dignity marched from New Orleans to Washington, D.C. with Indian guest workers—immigrants who were in the United States temporarily on the H2B "guest worker" visa—who had been hired to work on Gulf Coast shipyards. Through this local-international organizing, the march to D.C. became a major news story in India and put pressure on the Indian government to intervene. STAND with Dignity and the Congress of Day Laborers forced changes in law and policy from institutions including HANO and the NOPD as well as from the city government. Through their multiple projects, the Workers' Center brought principled, radical politics, a global perspective, and dynamic tactics to grassroots work.

Unfortunately, an attitude that demonized immigrants was established early on by Mayor Nagin himself. In October 2005, Nagin inquired of a gathering of businessmen helping to plan the city's recovery, "How do I ensure that New Orleans is not overrun by Mexican workers?"[5] Later, in a mayoral debate, he proclaimed, "Illegal is illegal, so I'm not supportive of illegal aliens or illegal immigrants working in the city of New Orleans." This inflammatory rhetoric, delivered while blatant violations of workers' rights were ignored, set the stage for the abuse that followed.

Progressive organizers in the Black community also expressed reservations about the new arrivals. "I'm not disputing the desirability of all oppressed peoples uniting against a common oppressor," Mtangulizi Sanyika, project manager of the African American Leadership Project, told me. "But right now this idea of Black-Brown unity is more of an idea than a reality.

"You have to put this into perspective," continued Sanyika. "Latinos are working in horrible conditions that ought to be illegal, and being exploited. At the same time, many Black people resent Latinos for coming in and working under those conditions. It's like when you have a strike and a group is brought in as strikebreakers.

"Who is to blame?" Sanyika asked, rhetorically. "Who is always to blame: those that control the money and power. When you see Blacks and Latinos on the street, they don't act antagonistic. It's not a personal antagonism. But there is an institutional antagonism."

A 2006 report by the Advancement Project, the National Immigration Law Center (NILC), and the coalition that would become the New Orleans Workers' Center for Racial Justice documented in vivid detail the ways in which Black and Latino workers in the reconstruction of the city faced a shocking catalogue of abuses, including wage theft, widespread and massive health and safety violations, racism and discrimination, law enforcement violence, and more.[6]

Through direct accounts, the report painted a detailed and dramatic picture of declining workers' rights in the city. Despite the huge demand for labor to rebuild the city and the billions of dollars spent, workers were pitted against each other for jobs while well-positioned businesses and contractors gorged on huge profits. Residents of the city continued to go without housing while corporate profiteers moved in and reaped the benefits.

Rosana Cruz, working at the time with NILC and the Workers' Center, expressed a sympathetic understanding of the apprehension from the Black community. "There are anxieties that are incredibly valid about a cultural genocide of this city," she tells me. "This is a city that was built on racism. The organizing we're doing is a counter to the racism dividing immigrants and African Americans against each other.

"It's a conversation that's so juicy," Cruz added, alluding to the media's complicity in framing the debate as Black versus Latino.

> Whenever white folks get to not be the bad folks, when communities of color are pitted against each other, it spreads like wildfire. When the boss starts making people compete, it's no accident. It's not immigrant workers who started this discourse of, "We like to work harder than

anyone else," it's the business community. It's not immigrant workers that left people on rooftops, didn't have an evacuation plan, and left the school system to decline. It's the elites of this city. Immigrants and people of color have been used throughout history to break unions. As long as people keep talking about Black-Brown tension, no one's talking about the real power brokers in this city.

"We have to redirect the conversation to white accountability," Cruz continued.

What it means to be an antiracist white ally is central to this discussion. There needs to be a focus on the real stakeholders here, the real players. We're talking about fundamental issues to our society. What are the sources of power, who is benefiting, and how can they be held accountable? It's not just about immigrant workers. Both immigrants and African Americans are dealing with a lot of the same issues, whether it's right of return or housing or voting or law enforcement violence, all these issues have connections. Trying to bridge this artificial divide is key.

On May 1, 2006, thousands of Latino workers demonstrated for immigrants' rights, filling several blocks of Canal Street in the heart of New Orleans's business, hotel, and tourist districts. Although the rally was small compared to the hundreds of thousands who marched on that same day in cities such as Dallas and Los Angeles, the march was still one of the largest the city had seen in decades. "Being part of the Latino community in New Orleans, we've always had issues of visibility around immigrants," said Cruz. "Now, for five thousand people to come out and do something so public and visible…it's amazing and beautiful."

Media, politicians, and contractors had tried to create conflicts between Black and Latino groups of workers. But the May Day march demonstrated that multiracial alliances are both possible and important. Civil rights movement veteran and Tambourine and Fan founder Jerome Smith came to speak at the demonstration to express his support for immigrants' rights. Smith told the crowd, "I heard from Houston evacuees they were excited by your walking out [of schools and jobs during the national day of action] and wanted to join but didn't know to get involved," he told the crowd. "I want you to know that your struggle is in the heart of my people."

"Cheap labor from Blacks has been integral to this city's history and still is," Smith told me later. "It's woven into the fabric of this city. And now corporations are benefiting from exploiting Latinos just like the old money of this city benefited from slavery."

By 2009, the city's attitude toward Latino immigrants had shifted dramatically. The majority of the city council, as well as the editorial page of the *Times-Picayune*, all spoke out in favor of reforms including tougher penalties on contractors who stole from workers. They also got a public agreement from then-police chief Warren Riley that offical department policy would be that Latinos who reported crimes would not be questioned about their immigration status. The efforts of organizers in the Latino immigrant community, especially members of the Workers' Center for Racial Justice, deserved much of the credit for these changes.

Through their various projects, the Workers' Center built concrete solidarity among these communities. For example, in May 2010, after Arizona passed SB1070, a notoriously anti-immigrant racial-profiling bill, the Workers' Center sent a delegation that included Black and Latino members to stand in solidarity with workers in Arizona. Members of STAND with Dignity discussed the similarities between the racial profiling faced by African Americans in New Orleans and that faced by Latinos in Arizona.

VIETNAMESE LEADERS

New Orleans's Vietnamese community of nearly ten thousand people is among the largest in the United States, with an annual Tet (Vietnamese New Year) celebration that is among the biggest outside of Vietnam. Most of the community came to New Orleans as refugees from the Vietnam War, and they have traditionally been Catholic and conservative.

Located in a tight-knit section of New Orleans East, the Vietnamese community raised their profile through post-Katrina efforts to bring back their neighborhood in the first months after the storm. Shortly after, organizers turned their energy to fighting a landfill project planned nearby. These grassroots protests developed into political power, helping to elect Anh "Joseph" Cao in December 2008 as the nation's first Vietnamese American congressman.

The U.S. Vietnamese population, with its anticommunist roots and "model minority" status, may not seem likely at first to be major players in the story of progressive organizing in post-Katrina New Orleans. The media played on these stereotypes in their coverage of the New Orleans Vietnamese community's response to the storm. As journalist and scholar Eric Tang noted:

> Local and national presses were thus quick to enlist the Vietnamese as symbols of survival amid despair.... The headlines and articles insisted on more optimistic themes: "We will rebuild;" "We never expected anything from government;" "We've been through worse." Thus, from Katrina's toxic floodwaters resurfaced the model minority, a much-needed elixir for those unable to stomach the hard truths coming from the regions' hardest hit Black communities.[7]

But the city's Vietnamese community has defied expectations and dodged prejudices. As Tang reflected, "The nuanced political and racial location that Vietnamese Americans of New Orleans occupy...doesn't quite conform to traditional left-to-right political ideologies." In fact, the Vietnamese community here has been among the most reliable supporters of a range of issues, from the campaign to close the Youth Study Center, a notorious youth prison, to environmental justice activism. As Tang described:

> Indeed, the Vietnamese Americans of New Orleans pride themselves on self-reliance, yet they also demand government accountability, especially when confronted with injustice. They seek to advance themselves politically and economically, yet seem to do so without sacrificing solidarity with other racial groups, particularly neighboring African Americans. Nowhere were these values more clearly on display than in the aftermath of Hurricane Katrina. Less than six weeks after the storm, the Vietnamese Americans of New Orleans East returned to their homes, doing so over the objection of local and federal officials. Their leader was Father Nguyen The Vien, a political firebrand and head of Mary Queen of Vietnam church. "Before the storm, I guess you could call us libertarians," Father Vien said. "Our attitude toward government was: 'you don't bother us, we won't bother you.' But Katrina changed all that. We had a responsibility to speak out." And so with each step of the rebuilding process, the priest and his congregation battled those who stymied their efforts: foot-dragging FEMA officials, the Waste Management Corporation that sought to dump Katrina debris in their backyard, city leaders all-too-eager to sell off New Orleans East to developers. Through it all, the priest was surrounded by a coterie of experienced community organizers, policy wonks and attorneys.[8]

One of the major initiatives in this community is the Vietnamese American Young Leaders Association (VAYLA), which has organized Vietnamese youth along several issues, especially education, and has collaborated closely with other youth groups in the city, including Young Adults Striving for Success, Fyre Youth Squad, and ReThink. The groups have formed a youth organizing collaborative to work together on arts and cultural efforts, such as spoken word events and *Through the Youth Lens*, a youth photography project. They are also committed to collaborative organizing through a series of youth convenings, aimed at bringing together young people in the city as a grassroots political force that crosses traditional barriers of race, background, and neighborhood.

NEW ORLEANS INTIFADA

In late 2008, as Israeli missiles were falling on Gaza, the Arab community of New Orleans decided to break their silence. A renewed wave of organizing brought energy and inspiration to a population that had been quiet. The movement is youth-led, with student groups arising on college campuses across the city, and also broad-based, with mass protests of more than a thousand people marching through the French Quarter.

Their aims, activists have stated, are to fight against what they see as a combination of silence and bias from local and national media, and—more broadly—to fight for a change in U.S. policy toward the Middle East. Activists from New Orleans's Arab population, which is largely Palestinian, have expressed hope that they can follow the examples set by the city's Latino and Vietnamese communities. According to Angelina Abbir Mansour, a student activist at the University of New Orleans, outrage over the December 2008–January 2009 devastation in Gaza was a catalyst. "When the Gaza massacre happened, the first thought that came to everyone's head was 'We can't be quiet anymore,'" she said. Young activists were also inspired by concurrent successes in other cities, such as a successful campaign at Hampshire College that pressured the college's board of trustees to divest from companies supplying the Israeli military, as well as sit-ins and building occupations on other campuses in the United States and Europe.

At Jackson Square, in the center of the French Quarter, more than a thousand people gathered on January 4, 2009, for one of the largest demonstrations this city had seen in recent years. Tracie Washington, co-director of the Louisiana Justice Institute, attended with her teenaged son. Addressing the crowd on a megaphone, she said, "My son asked me today about what is happening in Gaza. He asked, 'Is it like if I pinched you and you punched me?' I said to him, 'No, it's like if you pinched me and I shot you with an AK-47.'"

The cheers of the crowd were audible from several blocks away. Palestinian youth led raucous chants of "No justice, no peace," and "Gaza, Gaza, don't you cry, in our hearts you'll never die." Children held up signs that read, "This is what an Israeli target looks like."

The Louisiana Justice Institute is one among several local social justice and civil rights projects with which the Palestinian organizers have established ties. The Women's Health & Justice Initiative, Pax Christi, the Malcolm X Grassroots Movement, and Mayday Nola have all joined in collaboration. "I've seen a huge amount of support from the African American community," said Mansour, who is co-founder of a chapter of the General Union of Palestinian Students on the campus of the University of New Orleans. "Because they know more than anyone what it's like to face racism. Alliances between our communities make sense."

The January 4 march was the second of four mass demonstrations for Gaza during the Israeli bombing. The first, coordinated in less than twenty-four hours, drew more than three hundred people. Palestinian youth instigated and led the march, and entire families participated. The size of the demonstrations surprised even the organizers. "New Orleans is a small town," said activist Emad Jabbar, co-owner of several shoe stores. "For 1,200 people to come out with just a few days' notice—I'm speechless." Although every local TV station covered the demonstrations, the *Times-Picayune* refused to send a reporter. In response, activists announced a media justice demonstration the following week, bringing almost one hundred people to protest outside the paper's offices—a demonstration the *Times-Picayune* covered with just a photo, no article.

Organizing in New Orleans's Arab community is not new, going back at least to the first Intifada in the late 1980s, a time of increased activity in the Palestinian diaspora. Since then, activism has surged and receded in waves, with national organizations such as the Muslim American Society and US Campaign to End the Israeli Occupation offering support and training, especially in recent years. In 2003, I was part of a coalition of local activists that formed NOLAPS—New Orleans, Louisiana Palestine Solidarity—an action-oriented group dedicated to raising awareness about the situation in Palestine, as well as to building on connections between different antiracist and anti-colonial struggles.

NOLAPS started as a collective of white, Arab, African American, Latino, and Asian activists from a range of different ages and backgrounds, dedicated to building a grassroots, effective, and broad-based movement. During an intense wave of actions from 2003 through 2005, activists presented a breathtaking array of events—films, demonstrations, and speakers. They planned art shows, a Palestinian hip-hop concert, presentations in high school and college classrooms, and a regional conference called Local Organizing for International Change. Activists met with newspaper editorial boards, participated in radio shows, set up literature tables at busy public locations, and spoke at churches.

The two years before Katrina had seen mass action, coalition building, and education among local Palestinians and their allies. In some respects, today's movement is built directly on that work. Palestinian community activism went through a lull after Katrina, with a brief resurgence during the 2006 Israeli bombardment of Lebanon. A new wave began rising in 2007, reaching a fevered level of activity during the 2008–2009 bombing.

NOLAPS also arranged human rights delegations to the Middle East, sending nine delegates from diverse backgrounds and communities to Palestinian cities on the West Bank in the summer of 2004 (another New Orleans delegation of seven went to Gaza in 2009.) They self-published a book, *Harvesting Olives and Removing Roadblocks*, about New Orleans solidarity activists' experiences in Palestine, and printed a quarterly newsletter. One member, Rebecca Rapp, made and distributed a film called *Four Months and Ten Days: A Journey Through Palestine*, chronicling her time in the Palestinian city of Nablus. The group worked on art projects, a photography exhibition, and collaborated with PATOIS: The New Orleans International Human Rights Film Festival, a social justice media and education project of which I was director for several years.

Throughout 2004, NOLAPS met on the campus of Xavier University, a historically Black college, and had a core membership comprised of Muslims, Christians, Jews, and secular activists. Members collaborated closely with different sectors of the Arab and Muslim communities in the city—meetings were attended by representatives of New Orleans's Muslim Shura Council, the American-Arab Anti-Discrimination Committee of New Orleans, New Orleans's Palestine American Congress, and Stop the Wall, a local group of more than two hundred New Orleanians with family in the Palestinian village of Beit Anan, which is threatened by the Israeli Segregation Wall.

The coalition was multiracial, multi-generational, and eclectic. One of the main organizers was a young Palestinian hip-hop artist named Shaheed, who was also a pre-med student at Xavier University. Another core member was a white Episcopal minister who had traveled to Bethlehem and Jerusalem. Other members ranged from Palestinian Christians to Nation of Islam members to young Jewish activists. A woman who had been part of a pro-Israel delegation funded by the New Orleans Jewish Federation joined NOLAPS. She had returned from the Jewish Federation trip so disturbed by the Palestinian suffering she had seen that she broke with the Federation and became an activist for Palestinian rights.

The resurgent wave of activism fueled by the 2008–2009 massacre in Gaza has built on and expanded this history. Campus groups at Tulane and the University of New Orleans have held protests, cultural events, and educational sessions. A group of young Jewish activists has built an informal alliance to challenge the conservative New Orleans Jewish establishment by speaking out against racist Israeli policies. Palestinian youth have called actions across the city, including marches through downtown, a protest at an event organized by the Louisiana Department of Commerce to attract local investment in the Israeli state, and more.

As is often the case for immigrant communities, the city's Palestinian community is spread out yet insular. Families are located in various suburbs on the West Bank, but there isn't a particular neighborhood where most live. The community is rarely discussed in national coverage or even in the local media. "Growing up just outside of New Orleans, I didn't know there was a Palestinian community here," Angelina Abbir Mansour said. "I guess because we're a small population and we're not making headlines." Maher Salem, a young community leader and owner of a retail store on Canal Street, agreed. "The Palestinian community is a small minority in New Orleans. The city is mostly African American and white, then you have Latinos, then Vietnamese, and Palestinians are the smallest group. We're at the bottom of the list."

Many of New Orleans's Palestinians are originally from a handful of small towns and villages near Ramallah and Jerusalem, such as Silwad, Al-Bireh, Al-Mizra'a, and Beit Anan. They are often small business owners, running restaurants and other neighborhood establishments. If you walk into a convenience store or gas station in New Orleans, odds are pretty good that you'll find Palestinians behind the counter.

Although Katrina displaced many members of the city's Arab community, they still feel connected to the city. "I know guys that are in Dallas now," Salem said. "But every time we have a protest or something else happening they call and ask what happened. They miss living here."

For those who have returned, rebuilding has been difficult—as it has been for other New Orleanians, in this city where a fourth of all properties are still empty. Sandra Bahhur, a Palestinian-American woman originally from Al-Bireh, is a nurse and restaurant owner who has been a strong voice for social justice in New Orleans. She was a part of the original group that formed NOLAPS and helped organize many of the group's events, often hosting meetings, benefits, and out-of-town guests, such as Georgia congresswoman Cynthia McKinney, at her restaurant. She is a powerful speaker who is able to talk passionately about Palestinian cultural resistance.

Bahhur's home in the Lakeview neighborhood was so damaged by flooding that she couldn't get the doors to open. Her restaurant on Carrollton Avenue was destroyed, just days before it would have been ready to debut. She and her husband Luis had been working all day on the restaurant the day before the hurricane, as they often did. "We had just bought a new oven, new refrigerators, new kitchen equipment," she told me shortly after the storm. "Everything's destroyed. Our home is destroyed, the business is destroyed. We lost everything. Everything."

Like many New Orleanians, the Bahhurs love this city, and they refused to give up. After two years of rebuilding, their restaurant opened in late 2007 to positive press coverage and full houses. However, the Bahhurs were never able to fully recover from the rebuilding debt they incurred after the storm. With the nation's economic downturn, the restaurant hit hard times and closed permanently in early 2009. Despite all their efforts to stay, the Bahhurs ultimately decided to leave the city.

Realizing that the media ignores their work, Palestinian activists have had success in organizing events and actions through social networking sites, email, texting, and word of mouth. Dissatisfied with the lack of coverage from their local paper, they have created powerful media to document their own movement. Additionally, the young media creators from 2-Cent Entertainment made a pair of short videos that documented the activist uprising in response to the Gaza bombing, which were widely distributed online.

The students and other community members are determined to make their mark in the city through changing the media landscape and shifting public opinion. "We're a part of this city," said Emad Jabbar. "We identify with it. If you ask most New Orleans Palestinians where they're from they'll say New Orleans—especially the young ones." It was this spirit of solidarity that led dozens of Palestinians to join with African American community leaders in the annual Martin Luther King Day march. Maher Salem explained, "My cause, my goal is about the Palestinian people, Gaza, and freedom for everyone. However you describe me—businessman, father, community leader—what I am is someone who stands for justice."

As they move forward, Palestinian activists are excited by the possibilities. "People call me, come to me in the street and in the mosque, and ask me what are you up to, what's next," said Jabbar. "Our organizing in New Orleans is moving forward. People in the community are passionate, and have a lot of energy. We just need to keep stepping up."

MELISSA BELL AND JENA SIX SUPPORTERS, 2007.
PHOTO BY MAVIS YORKS.

CHAPTER TEN

Fight for What's Right:
The Jena Generation

I'ma ask you this one more time...
You don't see them folks in them boats?
The kids without shoes? Man, there's people dying.
What you gonna do, huh?
Shoot me in the head?
Just another dude dead cause of the words that I said
I ain't scared of you. Uh-uh. I ain't running.
I'ma fight for what's right or die for something.

Dee-1, From "Freedomland" produced by 2-Cent Entertainment

The story of the Jena Six began in September 2006, just after the first anniversary of Katrina.[1]

LaSalle Parish, where the town of Jena is located upstate, is 85 percent white. Jena is still largely segregated, from the white barber who refuses to cut Black people's hair to the invisible line separating the white and Black parts of town. LaSalle is also one of Louisiana's wealthiest parishes, with small oil rigs in many backyards contributing to the area's net worth. The parish is a major contributor to Republican politicians, and former Klansman David Duke received a solid majority of local votes when he ran for governor in 1991—in fact, he received a higher percentage of votes in LaSalle Parish than in any other part of the state.

Jena had been the site of a notoriously brutal youth prison, which was closed in 1999 after years of lawsuits and negative media exposure. The facility reopened in 2007 as a private prison for the growing business of immigrant detentions.

On August 31, 2006, a Black student at Jena High School named Kenneth Purvis asked during a school assembly if everyone had permission to sit under the tree in the middle of the school's front yard. It was a seemingly innocuous question, but no Black students had ever sat under the tree—it was understood as being for whites only. The school administrator replied that anyone could sit anywhere, and proceeded with the assembly. The following day, there were nooses hanging from the tree. Black students interpreted the action as a clear warning to stay in their place.

"It was in the early morning," said Robert Bailey, eighteen years old, one of the first students to see the nooses.

> I seen them hanging. I'm thinking the KKK, you know, were hanging nooses. They want to hang somebody….I know it was somebody white that hung the nooses in the tree. You know, I don't know another way to put it, but, you know, I was disappointed. Because, you know, we do little pranks. You know, toilet paper, that's a prank, you know what I'm saying? Paper all over the square, all the pranks they used to do, that's pranks. Nooses hanging there—nooses ain't no prank.[2]

Black students were upset by the nooses. They talked about it and thought about it in class and after school. Showing remarkable short-sightedness, LaSalle Parish school superintendent Roy Breithaupt termed the nooses a "harmless prank" and tried to move on. After a couple days, in response to the nooses and to the inaction by school officials, nearly every Black student in the school stood under the tree in a spontaneous and powerful act of nonviolent protest. According to Kenneth Purvis, "One person went, the next person went, everybody else just went."

The town's district attorney, Reed Walters, was called in by school administrators that same day. Flanked by police officers, Walters gathered the entire student body into a school assembly—which, like the schoolyard, had been divided by race for as long as anyone could remember. Black students were on one side of the auditorium and white students on the other.

Walters is a tough-on-crime prosecutor popular with the white residents of Jena. He has refrained from making any controversial public statements about race. However, his political mentor, a colorful relative of Huey Long named Speedy Long, had a close relationship with the Klan. According to locals, the Klan had been active in Jena into at least the '70s.

Walters told the Black students to stop making such a big deal over the nooses. Months later, in the course of a hearing, Walters said that, at the time, he had wanted the students to "work things out on their own." Directing his remarks to the Black students, Walters warned that if they didn't stop making trouble, "I can make your lives disappear with a stroke of my pen."

Tensions simmered in the school throughout the fall, occasionally exploding into fights and other incidents. According to Bryant Purvis, one of the Black students (also Kenneth Purvis's cousin), "There were a lot of people aggravated about it, a lot of fights at the school after that, a lot of arguments, and a lot of people getting treated differently."

In the first weekend of December, Robert Bailey was assaulted at a party by a group of white Jena High graduates. The next day, Matt Windham, a white graduate of Jena High School, threatened several Black students, including Bailey, with a shotgun. The students disarmed Windham and left with the gun. Windham received no charges, while Bailey was charged with theft of a firearm, second-degree robbery, and disturbing the peace.

The following Monday at school, white students taunted Bailey and a fistfight broke out. A young white student named Justin Barker was badly beaten and briefly lost consciousness. Barker was taken to the hospital, but seemed to have no major injuries, and was quickly released. That evening, Barker was out socializing with friends at a school ring ceremony.

School officials and police officers took statements from about fifty witnesses. The statements gathered by police and school officials did not paint a clear picture of who was involved. White students frequently referred to a group of "Black boys," or other non-identifying descriptions, and most testimonies seemed unclear as to the identities of who was involved.

Within hours, six Black students, ranging in age from fourteen to eighteen, had been arrested in the beating of Justin Barker: Theo Shaw, Robert Bailey, Bryant Purvis, Carwin Jones, Mychal Bell, and Jesse Ray ("Jody") Beard. We may never know if the accused youth were involved in the fight—the only Jena Six youth who (later) admitted to participation was Mychal Bell. It seems likely that some of the six were not involved, at least from my reading of the witness reports. However, all of those accused were known to have taken part in—or even to have instigated—the protest under the tree. Most of them had no history of discipline problems. "I think the district attorney is pinning it on us to make an example of us," Bryant Purvis told me. "In Jena, people get accused of things they didn't do a lot."

Soon after, at an appearance at the Jena courthouse, the parents of these six young men discovered that their sons were being charged with attempted murder. "The courtroom, the whole back side, was filled with police officers," Tina Jones, Bryant Purvis's mother, recalled. "I guess they thought maybe when they announced what the charges were, we were gonna go berserk or something."

In early December 2006, Jason Williamson, an attorney with the Juvenile Justice Project of Louisiana, sent an email to lawyers and activists in New Orleans that described the situation:

> ...the recent series of unfortunate events in Jena, LA, located in LaSalle Parish, resulting in the arrest of at least six African American high school students on charges ranging from aggravated robbery to attempted second degree murder. The circumstances surrounding these arrests paint a disturbing picture of a community mired in racial tension and a criminal justice system that seems intent on making an example out of the young Black men allegedly involved in the incidents.

It was from Williamson that many in New Orleans, myself included, first heard about the case. Not long after, Tory Pegram, a dedicated, young white activist who worked for the ACLU of Louisiana, traveled to Jena as part of a state tour on the issue of racial profiling. When she came back, she told me, "You need to come to Jena. There's a movement happening there."

It was the first week of May, several months after that initial email, before I was able to ride up to Jena with Pegram. The families of the six accused had been reaching out since December, but the only journalist to have written about the case was Abbey Brown at the *Town Talk,* a daily newspaper in nearby Alexandria. Caseptla Bailey, the mother of Robert Bailey, had written letters to politicians and newspapers and anyone else she could think of. Her daughter Catrina Wallace (Robert's half-sister) worked tirelessly by her side.

An outspoken twenty-something single mother with a wiry frame, Wallace threw herself into the work of building support for her brother and the other young men. The outside support that began to coalesce around the case brought her hope and energy. She was hungry for information and developed a close friendship with Pegram, who had made the Jena case her main focus. Pegram drove the four-plus hours from New Orleans up to Jena every couple weeks, often bringing CDs, radical reading material, or other gifts for Caseptla and Catrina. They spent hours each night talking about organizing, legal strategies, and how to win when it seemed the odds were against you. King Downing, an organizer with the national ACLU, often joined the discussion, as did a middle-aged, white Baptist preacher named Alan Bean. The parents of other Jena Six youth— among them Tina Jones, the mother of Bryant Purvis; Marcus Jones, the father of Mychal Bell; Theo Shaw, the father of Theo Shaw Jr; and John Jenkins, the father of Carwin Jones; also frequently stopped by. Jesse Ray (Jody) Beard's parents were less involved. Beard was a couple years younger than the other kids, and since he was under sixteen his case was, in some aspects, legally separate from the others.

A Black church was the only place in town that allowed the Jena Six parents to hold meetings. In a town where most people's employers were white, many Black residents felt pressure to stay quiet. In the face of opposition, however, the Jena families' voices grew louder. Without a network of support, this campaign was initiated and led by these courageous families.

Bean, the Baptist preacher, was among the earliest supporters of the Jena families and played a big role in spreading their story to the world. A Canadian by birth and Southerner by choice, Bean began his activism in 1999 in response to a string of false arrests in his then-hometown of Tulia, Texas. Nearly a third of the Black males in the small town of Tulia had been arrested on charges of drug dealing, all based on the testimony of a freelance undercover lawman, Tom Coleman, who traveled from town to town in Texas offering his services as a narcotics agent. Coleman's testimony was later exposed as having been entirely fabricated, and the convictions were overturned, but only after the accused had been subjected to several years of painful personal hardship.[3]

After that experience, Bean founded an organization called Friends of Justice and dedicated himself to supporting awareness around cases of criminal justice abuse in rural Texas and Louisiana. Small towns such as Jena do not generally have access to the kind of support and funding available to metropolitan areas. Bean's work has often been a game-changing intervention, providing experience, ideas, and resources, and helping to bring these cases to light.

This disparity in funding and attention has been a regrettable misstep on the part of social movements. Rural Southern towns were the front lines of direct action for the '60s civil rights movement. The Congress of Racial Equality (CORE) and Student Nonviolent Coordinating Committee (SNCC) were active throughout the rural South, and rural towns have been sites of vital, homegrown resistance. In 1964, the Deacons for Defense was formed in Jonesboro, Louisiana, just north of Jena and west of Tallulah, and the legacy of this armed self-defense organization inspired later radicals such as the Black Panthers. Today, many progressives seem to have ceded the rural United States to the right wing, preferring to focus on the cities instead. For people in small Southern towns, like the Jena Six families, this leaves few options or resources.

In addition to false convictions and ruthless prosecutions, violent confrontations with racial undertones still occur in many small Southern towns. Rural Louisiana had seen two big cases around the same time as the nooses were hung. Shortly after the incident in Jena, Gerald Washington of the small southwest Louisiana town of Westlake was shot, three days before he was to take office as the town's first Black mayor. An official investigation declared his death a suicide, but family members called it an assassination. Less than two weeks after that, shots were fired into the house of Earnest Lampkins, the first Black mayor of the northwest Louisiana town of Greenwood. Lampkins reported that he continued to receive threats throughout his term, including a "for sale" sign planted outside his house.

On my second day in Jena, there was a small rally for the accused youths. In front of the Jena courthouse, I listened to Alan Bean inveigh against injustice before a mostly local crowd. Bean was not the kind of fiery speaker you might expect of a Baptist minister, but his words carried the weight of his conviction. "The highest crime in the Old Testament," he declared, "is to withhold due process from poor people. To manipulate the criminal justice system to the advantage of the powerful, against the poor and the powerless." As with many protests in the rural South, religion was always a part of the landscape in Jena, and several supporters were ministers. Bean's Biblical study (and his white skin) helped him to reach out to a broad base of people in the town, and he discussed the case with many people in Jena before moving forward with publicizing it.

Before long, Bean had become too closely associated with the Black community in Jena for most white residents of the town to feel comfortable being honest with him, but when he first arrived, he was able to gather different perspectives on what had taken place. Bean offered this research as background material for reporters who came through in the following weeks and months, which led to later accusations from right-wing sources like the *Weekly Standard* that Bean had fabricated key elements of the story. In fact, most journalists who covered Jena gave only brief attention to Bean's resources. His crucial role was in sounding the initial alarm and serving as an early advisor to the families themselves.

As Bean spoke to the crowd, officers from the state police intelligence division watched from the side, videotaping Bean, the other speakers, and the audience. There were fewer than twenty of us at that early demonstration, but this small group was about to make history.

I had spent the night on the floor of a trailer owned by Catrina Wallace, Robert Bailey's sister. She had welcomed me and the other supporters from out of town, and gave us a place to stay. Before we went to the demonstration, officers from the state police had stopped by. They wanted to know what we had planned and who would be coming. They were specifically interested in knowing whether a New Orleans minister loosely associated with Al Sharpton's National Action Network was expected. They were very concerned about his "violent" message and that of other "radicals," which they said pushed the boundaries of free speech. To us the visit from the officers seemed to be an attempt at intimidation.

At the demonstration, I spoke with family members and allies about the issues at the center of the case. "I don't know how the DA or the court system gets involved in a school fight," Marcus Jones, Mychal Bell's father, told me. "But I'm not surprised—there's a lot of racism in Jena. A white person will get probation, and a Black person is liable to get fifteen to twenty years for the same crime." Jones had moved away from Jena years before, to Dallas, but had come back to fight for his son. As the only parent who lived in a larger city, in some ways he had developed more of an activist perspective than the others, and he later built closer bonds with some of the more radical supporters, such as Black nationalists who came to Jena in solidarity.

Jones questioned why the nooses and other threatening actions had not been taken seriously by the school administration. "What's the difference?" he asked me. "There's a color difference. There was white kids that hung up a noose, but it was Black kids in the fight."

Justin Barker's beating had been serious. He had briefly lost consciousness during the fight and was kicked while unconscious. But to most people observing the case, including legal experts, Barker's injuries were "school-fight-serious," not "attempted-murder-serious." Jones explained to me, on the day we met, a litany of reasons why the students should not be charged with attempted murder. "[Barker] did not have life-threatening injuries, he was not cut, he was not stabbed, he was not shot, nothing was broken. You talk about conspiracy to attempt second-degree murder; you think about the Mafia, you think somebody paid a sniper or something. We're talking about a high-school fistfight. The DA is showing his racist upbringing, and bringing it into the law."

In conversation with Jones, I thought about the fights I had seen in the (mostly white) schools I attended growing up in Florida and Massachusetts. I had seen people injured worse than Barker, but it was unimaginable that the police would have been called. The school-to-prison pipeline was not made for me or my peers.

As we stood near the courthouse, I asked Bryant Purvis how the case was affecting him. "One of my goals in life is to go to college, and not to go to jail, and that changed me right there," he told me. "That crushed me, to be in a jail cell."

Purvis's mother described the agony of having her son taken away from her without warning. "You wake up in the morning and your son is there. You lay down at night and he's there. Then all of a sudden he's gone. That's a lot to deal with."

I kept going back to Jena about once a month, along with Tory Pegram and a growing list of other allies, to stand with the families. Each time, the gathering grew larger; word about the case was spreading. The family members continued to meet, host rallies, send out press releases and letters, and make phone calls—anything that might possibly be of help. For months, they had stood nearly alone. Many of their friends and neighbors were afraid to speak out after some friends reported that they had been threatened with losing their jobs. Yet in the face of overwhelming obstacles, and with no organizing experience or friends in high places, the families continued to stand up against injustice. Now it was starting to pay off.

Abbey Brown's reporting in the Alexandria *Town Talk* is among the most authoritative records of the entire experience. She continued to attend each protest. Tony Brown, a Black radio DJ in Alexandria, also covered the story from nearly the beginning—every morning, the families tuned in to his radio show and got excited when he mentioned them. That spring, activists from *Community Defender*, a public access TV show from Lafayette, Louisiana, were the first reporters to give video coverage of the story.

My first report from Jena, published on May 9, 2007, by the *Indypendent* newspaper in New York City and *Data News* in New Orleans, as well as on several websites, was the first article about the case to reach a national audience. It was followed in the weeks to come by stories by reporters for the *Chicago Tribune* and *The Observer* in Britain, and a news report on the BBC. The story of the "Jena Six," a phrase coined by the family members, began to circulate on the web via email, blogs, and social networking sites. Along with the families, we kept track of each news report in those first months, getting excited as the story spread.

At the end of June, hundreds of activists were traveling to the U.S. Social Forum in Atlanta. I raised funds for the Jena families to go to the USSF as part of a strategy to build national awareness about their case. Unfortunately, Mychal Bell's trial was scheduled for the same time period.

On Monday, June 25, while jury selection for Bell's trial was underway, the charges facing him were reduced slightly. He now faced twenty-two years in prison for assault, rather than one hundred years for attempted murder. The grassroots pressure and international attention to the story already seemed to be having an effect.

On June 28, 2007, Bell was the first of the Jena Six to go to trial. He refused to take a deal in exchange for testifying against his friends. At Bell's refusal, his public defender, Blane Williams, became visibly angry, called no witnesses, and gave what observers have described as an extremely weak defense. Prosecuting the case was District Attorney Reed Walters, the same man who, months before, had told the Black students at assembly that he could "make [their] lives disappear."

An all-white jury quickly convicted Bell of aggravated second-degree assault and conspiracy to commit aggravated second-degree assault. DA Walters made the case that the assault qualified as "aggravated" because a dangerous weapon was involved. The dangerous weapon was Bell's sneakers. The conspiracy charge came because Barker was allegedly kicked by other students as he lay on the ground. It was explained that the young Black males who stomped Justin Barker were co-conspirators with Bell even if the group of them had never agreed to a coordinated attack.

Alan Bean was among those attending the trial and made a list of reasons that Bell's defense was inadequate. Among the highlights:

- The ten student witnesses who testified at Mychal Bell's trial were all white. In fact, most of them were part of a distinct minority within the high school's white student population who had previously attended all-white elementary schools in the county surrounding Jena.

- Justin Cooper was the only witness at trial to testify that Mychal Bell kicked Justin Barker as the victim lay unconscious on the ground. Since Justin Cooper was one of the boys who admitted to hanging the nooses at Jena High School at the beginning of the school year, he can hardly be seen as an objective or credible witness. Defense Attorney Blane Williams was apparently unaware of Cooper's connection to the noose incident.

- Jessica Hooter was one of four trial witnesses who identified Mychal as the person who threw the first punch at Justin Barker. Two days after the assault occurred, Jessica was unable to identify the initial attacker. But as she explained at trial, "After I thought about it more, I remembered more." In his closing remarks, Blane Williams never mentioned that she had embellished on her earlier testimony.

- Jessica Hooter's mother served on Mychal Bell's jury. Defense attorney Blane Williams asked hardly any questions during jury selection process.

- The single male juror graduated from high school with Justin Barker's father.[4]

When Mychal Bell was convicted, many supporters were shocked. The stakes suddenly became much higher. He now faced sentencing; it was expected that he would receive close to twenty years. Several activists told me later that despite their well-tested cynicism about the criminal justice system, they had truly believed there was no way Bell would be convicted. Bell's quick trial and quicker conviction brought the case and the injustice at play into starker relief.

Days after Bell's conviction, the TV/radio program *Democracy Now!* aired its first report from Jena. (I produced the report in collaboration with

Rick Rowley, Jacquelline Soohen, and Kouross Esmaili). In the week after the broadcast, the Jena Six families' defense fund, which until then had been nearly empty, received tens of thousands of dollars, almost all of it in small contributions mailed by *Democracy Now!* viewers and listeners. Suddenly the story of Jena exploded and it seemed that all the major national papers and networks were sending someone down to Louisiana.

During this time journalist and activist Jesse Muhammad wrote a cover feature about the Jena Six for *The Final Call*, the Nation of Islam's newspaper, which was seen globally. Jesse, a brilliant and charming young man driven by the cause of justice, did more than report the story. He and other members of the Houston branch of the Nation of Islam initiated organizers' calls with representatives from student governments, incorporating active participation from nearly every historically Black college and university in the United States. This mobilization ushered in a surge of grassroots energy around the case, which invited even more attention and support. Within weeks Reverend Al Sharpton had come to Jena; Reverend Jesse Jackson had called to offer support in rallying the Black Congressional Caucus; John Mellencamp had released a video inspired by the case; MySpace and YouTube were filled with Jena-related updates, opinions, and videos; and the corporate media were finally forced to pay attention.

ColorofChange, the web-based organization inspired to action by Katrina, also became involved and made the Jena case a major focus of their work for months. Aiming to channel online outrage into racial justice activism, ColorofChange followed a model similar to that of the liberal organization MoveOn.org—bringing people in through online petitions, then encouraging further activism and real-world involvement. ColorofChange co-founder James Rucker spent a lot of time in Jena during this period, and his organization represented an important part of the growing network of supporters of the Jena families.

On July 31, 2007, three hundred supporters, most from the immediate region, but some from as far away as California, Chicago, and New York, descended on Jena to protest DA Reed Walters's conduct and to call for dismissal of all charges against the youths. The largest groups were the Millions More Movement and Nation of Islam delegations from Houston, Monroe, and Shreveport, and nearly fifty members of Friends and Family of Louisiana's Incarcerated Children (FFLIC) from Lake Charles and

New Orleans. New Orleans was also heavily represented by the Women's Health & Justice Initiative, Critical Resistance, Common Ground, and the Malcolm X Grassroots Movement.

The demonstrators marched through tiny downtown Jena in the biggest civil rights march the town had ever seen. "Jena was so small," Jesse Muhammad said later, "that we started to march, and chanted 'No Justice, No Peac...' and before we could even finish the phrase we had already marched through all of downtown." After marching around the block and back to the courthouse, protestors delivered a petition with forty-three thousand signatures, gathered by ColorofChange, to the District Attorney's office.

In the two weeks after the demonstration, even more influential allies came on board. The Congressional Black Caucus—representing forty-three members, including then-Senator Barack Obama—issued a statement calling for charges to be dropped, and the city of Cambridge, Massachusetts, passed a resolution in support of the families of the Jena Six.

As national support grew beyond what any of us had imagined possible, we started to ask ourselves why. Grassroots activists had been crucial in getting the word out, and non-corporate and nontraditional media helped keep the story on the radar. But of all the outrageous cases we had seen, why had this one in particular been able to break through media apathy?

Some have labeled the Jena Six case a throwback to the past, to Jim Crow, but in fact, Jena presented a clear picture of the current state of our system. The Jena Six were living proof that there are still two systems of justice functioning in this country, one for Black people and one for white; one for rich and one for poor. The unpunished incidents in the days and months leading up to the fight were evidence that white students in Jena would never have faced charges if they had beaten up a Black student. Jena didn't become famous because it was so different from what happens elsewhere in the criminal justice system in our country, but because it was such a naked example of what happens every day.

Enlisting national support through their website, ColorofChange gathered sixty thousand signatures on another petition, this one addressed to Louisiana governor Kathleen Blanco, calling for her to pardon the accused and to investigate DA Reed Walters. Governor Blanco, a Democrat elected with the overwhelming support of Black residents of Louisiana, responded with a condescending statement, tersely informing petitioners, "The State

Constitution provides for three branches of state government—Legislative, Executive, and Judicial—and the Constitution prohibits anyone in one branch from exercising the powers of anyone in another branch."[5]

The sentencing in Mychal Bell's case was scheduled for September 20, and the Jena Six family members called for a protest. About three hundred people had come to the last demonstration. With the recent surge in national support, we wondered how many would come to this one. It was an almost unprecedented situation—a national demonstration called by a small group of families in a rural town. As the date got closer, the media attention multiplied. Black radio was key—Michael Baisden, a syndicated radio host not generally known for his political commentary, started talking about the case on his show every day. The families had media calls coming in from around the world, more than they could handle. Suddenly, everybody wanted to know about the Jena Six.

The Jena families released a statement of their demands:

1. Drop (or fairly reduce) all charges.
2. Reinstate school credits.
3. No juvenile records.
4. Investigate noose incident.
5. Remove Reed Walters from the District Attorney's office.
6. Conduct Undoing Racism workshops for LaSalle Parish school system staff, faculty, administrators, students, parents, and community members.

The corporate media, and even some civil rights leaders, chose to ignore these demands—an unfortunate dismissal, because these demands were visionary. Whereas many so-called allies of the families focused on whether or not charges should be filed against the kids who hung the nooses, the families did not seek that kind of vengeance in their demands. They didn't believe the existing system was a solution for anyone involved, white or Black. Instead, by demanding Undoing Racism training—workshops created by the People's Institute for Survival and Beyond—for people from the school and community, they were seeking to address the root of the problem.

The media, despite overlooking some of the story, did seem to grasp that something big was coming. On CNN, Anderson Cooper gave powerful coverage that amplified the date of the upcoming protest. Almost every major U.S. news outlet aired something Jena Six-related in the days leading up to the protest.

Mychal Bell's convictions were overturned in an appellate court on September 14, which gave a further sense that freedom for these young men was possible. Soon it seemed the whole world was coming to Jena.

On September 20, 2007, I witnessed something unlike anything I had seen in my life: a beautiful and enormous outpouring of energy and outrage.

At 5:00 a.m., buses were already arriving. A full bus from Chicago emptied out at a ball field in the Black section of town, some people brushing their teeth as they stepped into the slightly chilly pre-dawn air. They were just waking up, but quickly became charged and energized. Next came buses from Baton Rouge, Los Angeles, and Philadelphia. The ball field, one of several sites designated as a gathering point, was soon filled with hundreds of people, then thousands.

By 7:00 a.m., reports were coming in that hundreds of buses were lined up outside of town, some having been prevented by state police from entering—apparently because there was no place for the vehicles to go. Despite the reports, buses—as well as cars and motorcycles—were still pouring into Jena from east and west, and thousands more were massing in the streets outside the Jena courthouse. Jesse Muhammad later reported that when the bus he was on was stopped miles outside of town, he and everyone else got out and walked the rest of the way. As simultaneous rallies began at the courthouse and ball field—which were a few miles apart—a continuous stream of people flowed into the city.

By 9:00 a.m., there were by some estimates 50,000 people in this town of 2,500 residents. Almost every business in town was shut down, many roads were closed by police checkpoints, and an overflowing sea of protest filled the city for miles.

This demonstration had not been initiated by any national organization, and there was little coordination between the major groups that had become involved. The call had come from the families themselves, and most people had heard about the demonstration through local Black radio stations, especially syndicated programs like the Michael Baisden and Steve Harvey shows, as well as through informal online networks. One YouTube clip, made by an activist and recommended by Baisden on his show, was quickly viewed well over a million times.

As thousands of demonstrators gathered at the ball field for the rally, sponsored by the NAACP, thousands more marched from the courthouse to Jena High School, and tens of thousands continued to arrive and fill the streets of downtown. The decentralized quality was beautiful, although sometimes chaotic. Because the movement lacked a hierarchy of leadership, there were many agendas, and understandably some confusion. People were unsure when the march would begin—or if there was a march—and were generally unaware of parallel events, such as an afternoon hip-hop concert at the ball field, attended mostly by people from the local community. Participants seemed unconcerned about the lack of clarity, however, and marched on their own schedule, which lent a more grassroots feel to the day. Too many mass marches have become rote—for example, the demonstrations in Washington, D.C., called by a wide range of mainstream civil rights groups, have become so pre-programmed and predictable that they feel disempowering to many participants. The Jena demonstration felt improvised and real.

The t-shirts on display reflected the lack of central control—each community had made their own t-shirt, so there were literally hundreds of variations on the "Free the Jena Six" theme, often personalized to reflect their school or community. Hours of speakers delivered messages of solidarity and calls to action, from the Reverends Al Sharpton and Jesse Jackson to performers such as Mos Def and Sunni Patterson, while the enormous crowds marched, chanted, and basked in a truly historic outpouring of activism. Participants varied from children and teens attending their first demonstration to longtime activists and community leaders. People who had never before been to a demonstration ended up coordinating a delegation or booking a bus for this journey. Erika Murray, a spoken word poet from New Orleans, booked a bus and filled it with poets and their friends. It was one of at least ten buses from the city.

Although the vast majority of Jena's white community chose either to stay indoors or to leave town, hundreds of Black Jena residents proudly displayed their "Free the Jena Six" shirts, and continued to congregate in the ball field hours after most out-of-town visitors had departed.

Sadly, white activists from across the United States largely stayed away from this historic event. Perhaps one to three percent of the crowd was white, in what amounted to a disturbing silence from the white Left and liberals. This silence indicated that racial divisions among progressive communities in the United States are as pronounced as the divisions facing the country as a whole. White folks in this country who are serious about building an effective movement need to come to events like this and stand in solidarity. Silence implies complicity. Many of the white activists I did see there were people I knew from New Orleans. Many were former Common Ground volunteers, such as the members of the Anti-Racism Working Group, who had expressed a desire to work more consciously to support Black struggles.

The march was a generational moment—the kind of watershed event that could signal a turning point in our country. But what did the gigantic crowd in Jena mean? For some supporters, it felt like justice at last, after all those months the families had stood alone—finally, a moment when the world stood with them. It was also a moment for historically Black colleges and universities to shine. Student activists organized entire convoys.

The massive crowd represented a movement unconnected to any party or political affiliation. Revolutionaries and liberals, Black nationalists and anarchists, people from all over who are concerned about a criminal justice system that has locked up two million people and keeps growing. It was a moment for those concerned about education in the United States, especially the policing of our schools and the devastation caused by the cradle-to-prison pipeline. It was a moment for those who feel that the United States still has not dealt with our history of slavery and Jim Crow, or the present incarnations of white supremacy. As Al Sharpton said memorably that day, we now face "James Crow, Esq.," the cleaned-up descendant of Jim Crow.

In an article in Dissident Voice, criminal justice organizer Xochitl Bervera linked the Jena case, beautifully and painfully, to other young people she knew:

> I want to tell you about Emmanuel Narcisse. He was a tall, slim, handsome young man who was killed by a guard at the Bridge City Correctional Center for Youth—a Louisiana juvenile prison—in 2003. Apparently, he was "fussing" in line, talking back to a guard. The guard punched him in the face, one blow, and Emmanuel went down backwards, slamming his head on the concrete. He took his last breath there behind the barbed wire of that state-run facility. The guard was sus-

pended with pay during the investigation. No indictment was ever filed against him.

There is also Tobias Kingsley, [Name changed for purposes of confidentiality] sentenced when he was 15 to two years in juvenile prison for sneaking into a hotel swimming pool (his first offense). Tobias endured physical and sexual abuse inside the prison. He said that guards traded sex with kids for drugs and cigarettes, and sometimes set kids up to fight one another, making cash bets on the winner. His mama said he was never the same after he came home....

And there is Shareef Cousin, who was tried as an adult and sent to death row in the state of Louisiana for a murder that he didn't commit. Shareef spent from age 16 to age 26 behind bars, the majority of those years isolated in Angola's Death Row, because an overzealous prosecutor didn't care that the evidence didn't really add up. After all, it was only a young Black man's life on the line....

There are hundreds more. Thousands. Every day in the state of Louisiana (and in most states in this nation), injustices of epic proportions are taking place in our criminal and juvenile justice systems. We, those of us who live here, fight here, and organize here, know hundreds of families and young people—often our own—who've endured almost inconceivable levels of violence, abuse, neglect. And despite efforts to get someone, anyone to care and to act, these young people most often end up statistics in somebody's dismal report, or an anecdote in an article just like this...

So, Hallelujah! Almost overnight it seems, the nation is looking deep into the heart of Louisiana's criminal justice system and seeing what we've been shouting about all these years! The racism, the blatant and unaccountable abuse of power masquerading as "justice." The slavery-like, Jim Crow-like, Bush-era prejudice and exploitation that has been the bedrock of white supremacy here and all over the Deep South for decades. Young people of color and mothers across the country are rising up saying "We won't take it anymore! We demand justice!" The myth that the goal of the criminal justice system is protecting public safety is slowly unraveling as youth in Philadelphia, DC, Oakland and mothers in Chicago, Jackson, and Birmingham make that most important of realizations, "that could have been me," "that could have been my child."

Many are asking, "why now?" Why, of all the horrific incidents we've seen and exposed, is this the one that set off this fire of hope?...

Let me tell you what my heart tells me. What really matters is not why, but what we plan to do with this moment now that it has arrived. What will the leaders, the youth, the elders of our movement do now?[6]

Andre Banks, writing on the day of the demonstration, posed further questions, challenging supporters of the Jena Six to take the next step:

What would happen if every person who wore a t-shirt today or handed out a flyer or wrote a blog post woke up tomorrow and looked for the Mychal Bell in their own backyard? He, or she, won't be hard to find. What if our outrage, today directed at the small Louisiana town of Jena, extended to parallel injustices in Detroit or Cincinnati or Sacramento or Miami? What if we viewed this mobilization not as the end of a successful, innovative campaign, but as the moment that catalyzes us into broader and deeper action in every place where we are?[7]

For the corporate media, September 20 was the beginning of the end of the story. In the week before the demonstrations, Mychal Bell's convictions had been overturned and most of the other five saw their charges reduced. For months, media coverage had been generally sympathetic to the Jena Six families. As was inevitable, when that story had been exhausted, and when a real movement seemed to be building, the tide began to turn.

In a September 29 column in the Kansas City *Star*, Jason Whitlock led the counterattack. He seized on the fact that Alan Bean, the Texas preacher and activist, had announced his role in spreading the story, and accused the entire media of copying from Bean's narrative rather than properly researching the course of events. "Bean's story is framed—by his own admission—as an indictment of the criminal justice system and the people in power in Jena and, therefore, the story is unfairly biased," Whitlock wrote.[8]

The most shameful installment in media coverage came the next month, when the *Christian Science Monitor*, usually a much more intelligent news source, published an opinion piece by *Jena Times* editor Craig Franklin. The *Jena Times* is a small, weekly local paper with a staff of two: Craig—whose brother Scott is the LaSalle Parish sheriff—and his father, Sammy Franklin. The opinion piece, an embarrassing bit of propaganda that claimed to dispel "media myths" about the Jena Six case, could be summed up as "Everything is fine here, there's no racism, it's all outside agitators, move on."

Franklin claimed that Kenneth Purvis's question about who could sit under the tree at Jena High School was "to make a joke and to drag out the assembly and avoid class." And that the "crudely constructed nooses were not aimed at Black students. Instead, they were understood to be a prank by three white students aimed at their fellow white friends, members of the school rodeo team." The piece ended with the words, "Meanwhile in Jena, residents are getting back to their regular routines, where friends are friends regardless of race. Just as it has been all along."[9]

Family members of the Jena Six were very far from being "back to their regular routines." Their children still had major criminal charges hanging over their heads. Relatives and friends were harassed by local police. In addition, pressure brought on by the glare of the national spotlight had started to cause tension among the main family members involved. Several of the core organizers were no longer in regular touch with each other.

Suspicion against the outside supporters began to develop. Unfortunately, there were unscrupulous people who sought to profit from the families' hardships. This created an atmosphere of distrust and raised suspicion even of those supporters that had repeatedly demonstrated their trustworthiness.

This tension exploded into the public sphere when one of the parents said on the nationally syndicated Michael Baisden radio show that ColorofChange was taking money meant for the families—committing fraud. These allegations were later shown to be definitively false, but the damage had been done. Once the taint of corruption is in the air, it is very hard to dispel.

For me, one of the most difficult and saddest aspects of the Jena Six case was seeing the families—who had been unified for months under incredible pressure—endure the strain of the national attention. Even though most of this attention was supportive and with the best intentions, it still caused discomfort and conflict. I had seen similar problems in New Orleans after Katrina. In some cases, local activists felt they had to compete against each other for the attention and resources being offered. Fortunately, once the national glare had moved on, the Jena families seemed able to return to a level of trust and communication.

Unrelenting public scrutiny was hard for all the kids at the center of the case, but Mychal Bell likely had the hardest experience. He was arrested along with the other five in December 2006. Unlike the others, Bell's parents couldn't afford bail, so he was not released before his June 2007 trial. After his conviction, he remained in custody. Since his trial occurred before major national attention and resources came to Jena, his defense was sub-par, and he suffered accordingly.

When Bell's conviction was overturned by an appellate court in September, just days before the tens of thousands of protestors descended on Jena, he was briefly released. But District Judge J. P. Mauffrey Jr. ordered him back in prison soon after, on the grounds that the incident with Justin Barker had violated the terms of his probation for a previous conviction. "This is judicial revenge," said Al Sharpton, referring to Mauffrey's decision. "The judge was already defeated once by the appellate court, and now he's taking his frustrations out on Mychal Bell." Lawyers eventually succeeded in having Mauffrey removed from the remaining Jena Six cases.

In December 2007, Bell took a plea agreement that required him to spend eighteen months in custody, including time already served. Most of the remainder of his time was spent in a group home, rather than a jail.

This stress began to take its toll. Bell and the other youths reported that they felt the weight of people's media-generated expectations of who they were. One youth, who had left town for school, reported that he went by another first name when he met new people.

For Bell, the pressure became too much. He attempted suicide just before New Year's Eve of 2008, shooting himself in the chest with a gun. Thankfully, he was not seriously injured. In April 2009, almost three years after the event that started it all, Bell reflected on the incident and its repercussions in his own words:

> When I look back at the day that I got in a fight with Justin Barker at my high school, I now realize that I should have done what Dr. King preached, which was non-violence. A few months before the fight, I remember seeing nooses hung from a tree at my school, and none of the few Black students knew who was responsible. But, what came to my mind were images of Mississippi burning, seeing how Black people were hung and killed, and it felt very disrespectful. In the small town that I grew up in, I had always felt that Black people and white people didn't get along. After all, this was Louisiana.
>
> When I first entered prison, I was young, only 16, and I had been charged as an adult with attempted murder.... I spent over a year in

prison, before I took a plea bargain in juvenile court for a simple battery and was given time served and sent home. Since that time, my life hasn't been easy…a lot of people talk bad about me and the media has portrayed me as someone who I am not…I know the truth about who I am and I know I am not a bad person. The media pushed me to a point where I tried to kill myself…but that incident has made me a stronger person, and now I can finally see my dream in front of me.[10]

For the Jena Six families, the problems continued. In addition to continued police harassment, there were threats from white supremacist groups, who posted the families' phone numbers online.

In the summer of 2009, in a move that many in the Black community saw as an attempt at revenge for the successful defense of the Jena Six, the LaSalle Parish sheriff carried out a massive police action. Most of Jena's main Black neighborhood was cordoned off, and Catrina Wallace was swept up in mass drug arrests conducted by a SWAT team with a helicopter. Officers seemed to have initiated the raid despite a complete lack of evidence—no drugs were seized that day, despite armed police breaking down the doors of Wallace's home and others in the raid.

In June 2009, the remaining charges against the young men were quietly dropped. Each of the five remaining defendants pleaded "no contest" to the misdemeanor charge of simple battery. They were placed on non-supervised probation for one week and had to pay a five-hundred-dollar fine and, in most cases, an additional five hundred dollars in court costs. A civil suit filed by the family of Justin Barker was settled when the Jena Six defendants, including Mychal Bell, agreed to pay the Barker family an undisclosed settlement—rumored to be about twenty-four thousand dollars, plus any money made from selling their story of the case.

Our movements should be proud of our role in this struggle. We should celebrate this victory. The attention helped the students. All of them remained in school rather than going to prison. Without the world watching, the DA and judge could have done whatever they wanted. The massive exposure also eventually brought better legal representation than most Black youths entangled in the prison industrial complex will ever receive. Jim Boren, one of the best defenders in the South, Carol Kolinchak, legal director of the Juvenile Justice Project of Louisiana, and investigators including the team from NOLA Investigates all dedicated themselves to this case. Once this team of lawyers and investigators became involved, the young men's prospects improved dramatically. It's heartbreaking that something as basic as a competent legal defense is out of reach for so many, and astounding to see the difference it makes.

Regarding organizing and its relation to the media, the Jena Six case taught us two important lessons. The first is the power of independent media, which helped to nurture and promote this story until the major outlets could no longer ignore it. The second is the importance of accountability. It's not enough for media—or for our movements—to be supportive; we also need communication, collaboration, and empathy for those directly affected. There are lives at stake.

Continuing her crystal-clear analysis of Jena, Xochitl Bervera turned her sights to an indictment of the criminal justice system and laid out the next steps for our movements:

> Justice in Jena requires all of us across the country to rise up against the racism and exploitation of the criminal justice system....We must cast off once and for all, the fundamental lie that the system has anything to do with criminals or justice or public safety. We must not back down, as so many movements have, when we are "crime-baited," accused of defending rapists and murderers, accused of defending crime itself. We must not make excuses for some parts of the system while protesting others. Similar to opposing the war, the whole war, and not simply certain battles or certain strategies, we must oppose the system in its entirety. We must dismiss, once and for all, the urge to discuss what's wrong with the system—what's broken and needs to be fixed.
>
> There is nothing broken in this system. In fact, usually (when it is not disrupted by 50,000 protestors), it is quite efficient at doing precisely what it was created to do. In the Deep South, the criminal justice system as we know it was built after the abolition of slavery, as part of the terror machine which destroyed the briefly federally protected Reconstruction era. Without nuance or subtlety, the system was created by wealthy, land-owning whites to keep Blacks "in line," on the plantation, and working for next to nothing. Thanks to the Thirteenth Amendment which abolished slavery "except as a punishment for crime," laws and codes were invented that criminalized the very existence of Black people, police were hired to "enforce" those laws, and courts were mandated to send these newly created "criminals" to jail, or better yet, to be leased out to the very plantation

owners they had been "freed" from just months before. The "justice" that was once meted out by slave owners, who were "masters" of their property, was now taken care of by the law. The word "slave" was replaced by the word "criminal."[11]

The six young men who faced life in prison have made the best of their second chance that the movement helped win. All six are now in college, or on their way. Theo Shaw went to Louisiana Delta Community College in Monroe and was elected vice president of the school's student government association. Robert Bailey enrolled at Grambling State University, where his mother and grandmother graduated. Bryant Purvis and Carwin Jones went to colleges in Texas. Mychal Bell went to Southern University in Baton Rouge. Jesse Ray ("Jody") Beard, the youngest of the group, went to live with his lawyer Alan Howard and his family in Connecticut, where he enrolled in a private high school.

CONTINUING THE WORK
Xochitl Bervera and folks from Safe Streets/Strong Communities and FFLIC continued their proactive efforts, working in communities like Tallulah, a small town about ninety miles from Jena.

Tallulah is the prison town where Kevin Griffin of the video collective 2-Cent spent five years of his life. Within the city limits, the first sight after the "Welcome to Tallulah" sign is the town's prison, a large complex of thirty-three buildings surrounded by fence and barbed wire.

The prison has a long and notorious reputation. Minnesota senator Paul Wellstone visited in 1998, and incarcerated kids broke onto a roof to shout out complaints about their treatment. The *New York Times* ran several articles that same year, including a front-page report calling Tallulah the worst youth prison in the United States.[12] The U.S. Justice Department sued the State of Louisiana over the systematic abuse at the prison, where even the warden said, "It seemed everybody had a perforated eardrum or a broken nose."[13]

Journalist Katy Reckdahl chronicled both the abuse at the prison and the community organizing in response in an award-winning series of articles in the *Gambit Weekly*, starting in 2001.[14] Activists lined up local and statewide support to close the prison, holding protests and lobbying the state legislature.

The movement was successful, and Tallulah's youth prison was closed in 2004. But activists like Bervera aspired to do more. They had a vision of reversing the national pattern of closing schools and opening prisons: they wanted to close the prison and open a school.

As another northern Louisiana town struggling over whether to spend money to educate poor, mostly Black youth or to incarcerate them, Tallulah and its continuing organizing represented an extension of the movement begun in Jena, and an attempt to move the activism in a more proactive direction.

On a sunny, Saturday afternoon in fall 2007, I visited Mr. Hayward Fair, a civil rights movement veteran from Tallulah. Fair is a founder of People United for Education and Action, a grassroots alliance dedicated to transforming the former prison into a "success center" that would provide classes and job training.

When I met with Fair, he was going door to door with activists from FFLIC, Southern Center for Human Rights, and Safe Streets. At nearly seventy years old, with muscular arms and a shaved head, he showed no sign of slowing down. "I've been doing a little community organizing," he explained modestly. As he went from house to house, it seemed everyone in the city knew him, and each person had an opinion about both the prison and what Tallulah needed. Drawing respect for both his age and his local reputation, Fair was offering a vision for a new Tallulah. This meant a lot to residents who had watched the town die around them as it slowly changed from a regional cultural center to a place known mainly for its prison.

Fair is proud of Tallulah's civil rights history. In the spirit of the Deacons for Defense, which had started in nearby small towns, Tallulah embraced local armed self-defense. "We had some people here that went off to World War II, then they come back here and were second-class citizens," he explained. "They had to ride in the back of the bus. They said we're not going to put up with this. So we started a movement ourselves, to eliminate that."

Fair experienced intense white resistance to basic rights for Black people. "At one point, the Klan met about three miles outside of town and had a rally, and they was going to come into town that evening. They thought they were going to run all the Blacks out of town," Fair says. But resistance in Tallulah was strong. "When they came into town the streets was crowded. People were walking stiff-legged, with their shotguns down under their pants. We told the police we're going to take care of ourselves; we don't need you to take care of us. They thought they were going to scare somebody, but nobody here was afraid of them."

Speaking in a gravelly voice and walking with a deliberate step, Fair led me to the site of the prison. "When the prison came to town, most people weren't even aware of what it was going to be," he said. "It was something that produced jobs, and people needed jobs, so there wasn't no real resistance to it." Today, Tallulah's economy is devastated, and Fair blames the prison, at least in part. "It's killing the economy of the area, in my opinion," he said. "Prisons only bring money to the owners."

Standing near the prison, Fair gestured down the street. "We're about a block and a half from the junior high school, we're about five blocks from the senior high school. Our children have to walk out from the classroom and the next thing they see is all these bars and towers and all these big buildings. It had a psychological effect on the children and the adults as well. It really just devastated this whole city."

Tallulah, which is seventy percent Black, used to be a town with a thriving shopping district and nightlife that Black folks would travel from all around the region to visit. It even boasted the country's first indoor shopping mall, built in 1925. To demonstrate his point, Fair took me downtown, to a street of shuttered storefronts, with almost no people about. "On a day like this, on a Saturday evening, you could hardly walk down the streets of Tallulah, you'd be bumping into people. You had all businesses on this end of town," he gestured across the street. "All the way down, nothing but businesses: grocery stores, cafes, clothing stores, barrooms, you name it. The town was wide open, stayed open twenty-four hours a day, seven days a week."

I asked Fair how Tallulah fit into a wider picture.

All the eyes of the world is focused on the Jena Six. But every small community in the South, and in the North, has its Jena Six. Maybe you can't visualize it or maybe you don't want to visualize it, but this is not just small, rural towns. Look at New Orleans, during the storm. When the people was trying to cross the bridge to get out of the flood, there were people on the other side, armed, that would not let them cross. In the rest of the nation people are being treated the same way. Chicago, New York, it don't matter where you are.

The former prison at Tallulah is still run by the Louisiana Department of Corrections. However, in 2010, it was renamed the Louisiana Transition Center for Women and now offers GED programs and training for female prisoners within one year of release. Community members are still working to transform the facility into a full-fledged school, but they see this initial change as a leap forward from its former status.

Before leaving, I asked Fair what kept him in the struggle. "I ain't struggling, I'm free," he answered.

> I'm gonna do what I know is right, and I don't care who you are. I see the young people in the community that need help. That's what keeps me going. If you see something and you feel it ain't right, don't say they ought to change it, get in there, roll your sleeves up and say let's change it. That's the only way. You gotta keep a cool head and do the thing that's right. When you know right and fight for it, you're gonna win.

After Jena, activists around the United States asked why there was not more attention for cases like the Jersey Seven (later, after three of the women accepted plea bargains, the Jersey Four), a group of Black lesbians who faced "gang assault" and attempted murder charges for defending themselves against a man who attacked them on the street. There were attempts, in New Orleans and elsewhere, to brand cases as "the next Jena," although no case has captured attention in quite the same way or magnitude. Jena represented something new and exciting, a break with the past. From the grassroots spread of the information to the organizing rooted in the leadership of the families at the center of the case, to the outcome—a rare and complete victory—Jena will inspire those that took part, as well as those who followed from afar, to know that we can make a difference. There is a new generation, the Jena Generation, ready to stand up again, waiting for the right mix of inspiration and outrage.

If this momentum, this undirected and uncontrolled outrage, could be channeled toward real societal change, if outrages like Jena can finally bring about the conversation on race in this country that we were promised after Katrina, if this united movement to support these six kids can show that we can unite and win, then Jena will truly have been a victory. When that happens, we can say it all began with six families in Jena, Louisiana, who refused to stay silent.

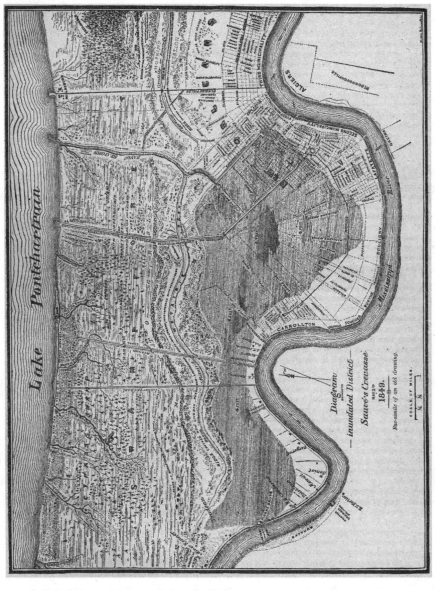

"DIAGRAM SHOWING THE INUNDATED DISTRICT SAUVÉ'S CREVASSE, MAY 3RD 1849. FACSIMILIE OF AN OLD DRAWING." FROM REPORT ON THE SOCIAL STATISTICS OF CITIES, COMPILED BY GEORGE E. WARING, JR., UNITED STATES CENSUS OFFICE, PART II, 1886. COURTESY OF THE UNIVERSITY OF TEXAS LIBRARIES, THE UNIVERSITY OF TEXAS AT AUSTIN.

KATRINA COMMEMORATION SECONDLINE, AUGUST 2009.
PHOTO BY ABDUL AZIZ.

Conclusion: Desire

I'm from a stock that pitch cocktail bombs and hand grenades.
We pour cayenne pepper around the perimeter of the building to keep
the police dogs at bay.
I'm the Panther Party in the Desire housing projects in New Orleans...

From "We Made It" by Sunni Patterson

Poet Sunni Patterson is among those displaced by the aftermath of Katrina. Her house in the Ninth Ward was cut in half by the floodwaters and has since been demolished. Although the house had been in her family for generations, her relatives had difficulty presenting the proper paperwork for state reimbursement of rebuilding costs—a problem shared by many New Orleanians. "We're dealing with properties that have been passed down from generation to generation," said Patterson. "The paperwork is not always available. A lot of elders are tired, they don't know what to do."

After the storm, Patterson traveled the country, performing poetry and trying to raise awareness about the plight of New Orleans. But her income was not enough—her post-Katrina rent was twice what she had paid before the storm, and she was also putting up money to help her family rebuild while taking care of her son, Jibril, born a few years after the storm. "I wound up getting evicted from my apartment because we were still working on the house," she said. "In the midst of it, you realize that you are not generating the amount of money you need to sustain a living," she sighed.

Now, like so many other former New Orleanians, she cannot afford to live in the city she loves. "I'm in Houston," she said, bewildered by her own words. "Houston. Houston. I can't say that and make it sound right. It hurt me to my heart that my child's birth certificate says Houston, Texas."

One of the hardest aspects has been the loss of her community. "In New Orleans, even if you don't know someone, you still speak and wave and say hello. In other places, there's something wrong with you if you speak to someone you don't know."

On the fourth anniversary of Katrina, as in previous years, Patterson was among the many who joined in the annual Katrina march and commemoration. This tradition was intitated in 2006 by PHRF and the ritual has been continued by many of the same activists who were part of that organization. Sitting with Jibril strapped to her torso, Patterson looked at the crowd assembled in Hunter's Field—a small park in the Seventh Ward where the commemoration activities concluded—and reflected on the state of the city's recovery. She described the responsibility for encouraging reflection, healing, and action that she feels artists hold within a community, pointing out that artists such as Sess 4-5 had organized the commemoration. "These artists came together and organized these events," she said. "You're not hearing of the city council putting together an event to facilitate healing of the people. I never heard of anything like that. But I have heard of poets gathering, I have heard of musicians gathering, I have heard of visual artists gathering to come together in a multidisciplinary kind of way, to heal and facilitate action in the people."[1]

Patterson wants to see the positive in the loss. "The good part is that New Orleans energy and culture is now dispersed all over the world," she says. "You can't kill it. Ain't that something? That's what I love about it. So we still gotta give thanks, even in the midst of the atrocity, that poetry is still being created."

In the first days after the storm, when Curtis Muhammad sent out a message announcing the founding of the People's Hurricane Relief Fund and Oversight Committee (PHRF), the words reverberated globally:

> Not until the fifth day of the federal government's inept and inadequate emergency response to the New Orleans disaster did George Bush even acknowledge it was "unacceptable." "Unacceptable" doesn't begin to describe the depth of the neglect, racism and classism shown to the people of New Orleans. The government's actions and inactions were criminal.[2]

I am still inspired by that call to action. Although PHRF no longer exists, Curtis's lessons have stayed with me. He always stood on principle with those most in need, he was an inspiring presence, and his departure was a loss for the city.

When the levees broke and the city flooded, outrage broke out across the country and around the world. Chokwe Lumumba, co-founder of the

Malcolm X Grassroots Movement (MXGM), said that Katrina represented "the Emmett Till of our generation," a moment of collective trauma so profound that it could inspire a new generation of activism.³ MXGM was among the scores of organizations that rushed resources and members to the Gulf Coast to be on the front lines. The fact that this outrage didn't lead to wider changes—or to a broad-based, sustaining movement—still feels like a wound to many who invested themselves.

New Orleans is now in a *post*-post-Katrina era. We are a smaller city. As many as two hundred thousand of our neighbors were kept from returning, most starkly evidenced by the demolition of public housing. The displacement was not just felt by poor folks. Middle- and upper-class Black communities in New Orleans East and Gentilly were devastated as well. The national economic downturn also took a disproportionate toll on those who struggled to rebound after the storm. According to a study, nearly one in four Black-owned companies in New Orleans and Biloxi had closed in 2008, a rate 52 percent higher than for white-owned businesses.⁴

Two years after Katrina, with public housing about to be demolished and much of the city still in ruins, the situation felt bleak. In an open letter to the movement, Curtis Muhammad wrote, in part:

> With this second anniversary of Katrina upon us, there are a few words I wish to speak. This letter is written to the progressive, left movement for justice in the USA. In the last two years, every left organization has been in New Orleans, but despite that there is still no sign of a mass movement. There is still no sign that most activists are willing to put their knowledge and resources at the service of the grassroots and take their leadership from the bottom. I have found myself wondering, have poor Black people been so vilified and criminalized that they are completely off the radar even of the so-called left? When Katrina happened, I hoped and expected that this would be the trigger to once again set off a true mass movement against racism and for justice in the US, led by those most affected: poor, Black working people. When it became abundantly clear that this was not happening, I found myself at the crossroads of hope and hopelessness, and began to wonder how to spend the last years of my life in the service of my people.
>
> The thing that I remind myself when I'm contemplating hopelessness is the beauty of humanity and the fact that people have always

fought for what was right even when they knew they couldn't win. They tried because they loved each other; I think it's because it's built into human beings for people to look out for each other. There is a drive in humanity to be just, to live in a society that is just, equal and respectful. I believe that ultimately people will achieve a just society; I believe humanity came out of a just society and will create it again....

This thinking, this logic has been the motivating factor in my life of movement work: the belief that there is a basic humanity that is inside the soul of most people. That this humanity can be harvested and organized into a movement for justice to free our people from slavery, bondage, oppression and exploitation. That the 80 percent of the world who live on an average of $2 a day can and will overcome the 1 percent and return us to a collective life organized around love, justice and equality....

If you are looking for me, look among the youth, the poor, and the struggling masses trapped in slave-like conditions throughout the world, for I am no longer available to an opportunistic and racist left. I now seek refuge among the poor.[5]

I feel similar frustration at the losses of these past few years, as do many others.

The election of Barack Obama has demonstrated that change at the top does not translate into systemic change. The current president's economic policies offer no break from the neoliberalism of his predecessors, and his international policies do nothing to challenge the Washington consensus of U.S. domination. For New Orleans, reconstruction has remained stalled. In August 2009, the Institute for Southern Studies surveyed more than fifty Gulf Coast community leaders and activists on the performance of the administration. Respondents gave the president's recovery efforts a grade of "D+"—only slightly higher than the "D-" the previous administration had received. [6]

As Cornel West told Amy Goodman on *Democracy Now!* in 2009:

The obsession is keeping track of Obama in the White House, a white house primarily built by Black slaves. What about those who are still locked at the bottom, when you have a policy team—neo-imperialist policy in foreign policy, neoliberal in economic policy—that's reproducing the conditions of those stuck at the bottom across race? And at this point, you see, you can't allow race and him being the first Black

president to hide and conceal the very ugly class realities of poor and
working people. And that's precisely, I think, why we're trying to generate some motion, some momentum and some movement....I think,
in terms of style, that the Obama administration is obsessed with the
wrong Lincoln. They are obsessed with the Lincoln who they think
moved to the right and was trying to create bipartisan consensus with
conservatives, whereas we know there's no Lincoln without Frederick
Douglass. There's no Lincoln without Harriet Beecher Stowe. There's
no Lincoln without Wendell Phillips or Charles Sumner. That was a
social movement.[7]

To make true progress, we need a social movement to challenge whoever is in office. "I can understand disappointment with Obama," said
PHRF organizer Kali Akuno, who is not an Obama supporter, "But apathy will only make it worse."

Thinking about the systems and policies that forced out Sunni Patterson and kept my friend Charhonda Thomas from returning makes me
sad and angry. All the money allegedly spent, all the investigative reports,
all the protests, all the fundraising in New Orleans's name—yet there is so
much more that needs to be done. What will it take to ensure that what
happened here doesn't happen again—anywhere? Can what we've been
through bring lessons and inspiration?

THE TRAGEDY IS REPEATED

When a catastrophic earthquake struck Port Au Prince in January 2010,
New Orleanians watched in horror, anger, and outrage as the patterns of
profiteering and victimization we had seen in New Orleans were repeated in Haiti: the criminalization of the survivors, the privatization
and militarization of relief, and the opportunism and profiteering of
business elites and unscrupulous NGOs. News of mass devastation and
the loss of perhaps three hundred thousand lives in the island nation hit
hard in the Crescent City. Almost every hurricane that has swept the
Gulf Coast has first visited devastation on our neighbors in Haiti, but we
share more than tropical storms: New Orleans and Haiti are related by
geography, history, architecture, and family. We are also linked by firsthand experience of the ways in which oppression based on race, class,
and gender interacts with and is magnified by these disasters.

Many New Orleanians have roots in Haiti, and the Haitian revolution (1791–1804) inspired uprisings in our city. The five hundred enslaved people who participated in the 1811 Rebellion to End Slavery were directly influenced by the Haitian revolution—one of the leaders, Charles Deslondes, had come to Louisiana from Haiti.[8] Even much of traditional New Orleans-style housing design, such as the Creole cottage and shotgun house, came here via Haiti.

According to historian Carl A. Brasseaux,

> During a six-month period in 1809, approximately 10,000 refugees from Saint-Domingue (present-day Haiti) arrived at New Orleans, doubling the Crescent City's population.... The vast majority of these refugees established themselves permanently in the Crescent City. [They] had a profound impact upon New Orleans' development. Refugees established the state's first newspaper and introduced opera into the Crescent City. They also appear to have played a role in the development of Creole cuisine and the perpetuation of voodoo practices in the New Orleans area.[9]

The parallels between these disasters are numerous and disturbing. In the days after Katrina, there was no rescue plan for the thousands of people trapped in Orleans Parish Prison. In Port Au Prince, the walls fell down around nearly 4,500 Haitians held in a prison built for 800. Many inmates died while others managed to free themselves. The corporate media used the fact that these prisoners had escaped death as an excuse for inciting fear of the earthquake victims. Once again, the survivors quickly were labeled as looters. Author Rebecca Solnit noted this pattern in an excellent article, "When the Media Is the Disaster," addressing the ways in which the media had demonized the people of Haiti and condemning "those members of the mass media whose misrepresentation of what goes on in disaster often abets and justifies a second wave of disaster."[10] Evangelist Pat Robertson even added a new twist to this old libel, accusing the people of Haiti of having made a pact with Satan for which they were now apparently being punished.

New Orleans's education, health care, and criminal justice systems were already in crisis before Katrina. Similarly, in Haiti, two hundred years of crippling debt imposed by France, the United States, and other colonial powers had drained the country's financial resources. Military occupation and periodic presidential coups, coordinated and funded by the United States, have obliterated any national governmental infrastructure.

Haitian poet and human rights lawyer Ezili Dantò elaborated:

> In more recent times, the uses of U.S. foreign aid, as administered through USAID in Haiti, basically serves to fuel conflicts and covertly promote U.S. corporate interests to the detriment of democracy and Haitian health, liberty, sovereignty, social justice and political freedoms. USAID projects have been at the frontlines of orchestrating undemocratic behavior, bringing underdevelopment, coup d'état, impunity of the Haitian Oligarchy, indefinite incarceration of dissenters, and destroying Haiti's food sovereignty, essentially promoting famine.[11]

Author Naomi Klein reported that within twenty-four hours of the earthquake, the Heritage Foundation was already seeking to use the disaster as an attempt at further privatization of Haiti's economy. The Heritage Foundation, as mentioned, issued similar recommendations in the days after Katrina, advocating free-market "solutions" such as school vouchers.

The Red Cross and other corporate charities were quick to fundraise for Haiti. But did their aid reach people on the ground? An Associated Press report broke down the allocation of aid as follows: for every one dollar of U.S. aid to Haiti, 42 cents went to disaster assistance, 33 cents to the U.S. military, 9 cents to food, 9 cents to transport the food, 5 cents to pay Haitians to help with recovery efforts, less than 1 cent to the Haitian government, and a half-cent to the government of the Dominican Republic.[12] Tracy Kidder of the Haiti-based organization Partners in Health/Zanmi Lasante put it succinctly: "There are 10,000 aid organizations in Haiti, and Haiti is still one of the poorest countries in the world—then something's wrong with the way things are, the way aid is being administered."[13]

Mercenary companies set up in Haiti almost immediately, according to journalist Jeremy Scahill, who reported that one military group set up a website to advertise their services in Haiti within hours after the earthquake.[14] "New Orleans was a masked military action," said PHRF organizer Kali Akuno. "Haiti is an unmasked military action."

Haiti's wealthy and international elites were spared much of the destruction. Describing "an extreme, almost feudal divide between rich and poor in Haiti," the *Washington Post* noted that "search-and-rescue operations have been intensely focused on buildings with international aid workers, such as the crushed U.N. headquarters, and on large hotels with international clientele. Some international rescue workers said they are being sent to find foreign nationals first."

The *Post* quoted a churchgoer who speculated that reconstruction dollars would likely be directed to businesses owned by Haiti's elite. "They only give the aid money to the same big families, over and over. So I ask, what is the point? They have given money to these families to help Haiti for 50 years, and look at Haiti. I say the Americans need to make up a new list."[15]

Once again, and on a much larger scale than the in aftermath of Katrina, there was no organization with the resources to track how many people had died in the earthquake, or who they were, and the numbers of those killed remain an estimate.

INCITE activists sent out a list of women-run organizations in Haiti, noting that women were especially victimized by Katrina and its aftermath and encouraging fellow activists to support relief that focused on those hit hardest by this disaster. Members of the Women's Health & Justice Initiative asked, "How can we intentionally support the long term sustainability and self determination of the Haitian people? When crises of this magnitude occur, we all understandably want to act quickly, but we must also figure out how to act thoughtfully in our efforts to develop a comprehensive, sustainable, and accountable transnational radical feminist response."[16]

It is imperative that we heed the lessons of Katrina and of the Haiti earthquake, because these patterns repeat with each disaster, and they will keep repeating until we break the cycle.

I NEED RED BEANS AND RICE ON A MONDAY NIGHT

New Orleanians are not done fighting. We love our city and refuse to give up. There is a great deal progressives can learn from the indomitable spirit of New Orleanians. Our failures as well as our victories offer many lessons for the next city or region affected by disaster.

Community, not foundations or government, has led this city's recovery. Bayou Road—the Seventh Ward location of the Community Book Center—is now home to more businesses than before the storm. Government assistance hasn't enabled these businesses to come back; it was the effort of community members working together. Local efforts also revived cultural institutions such as the network of Social Aid and Pleasure Clubs, the century-old Black community institutions that organize secondline parades almost every weekend throughout the year. These clubs worked to bring back members of their communities, aware that regardless of any politician's promises, they were on their own.

As a result of the 2007 U.S. Social Forum in Atlanta, a broad coalition of New Orleans activists began meeting monthly to combine their efforts. The Organizers' Roundtable, as the coalition is known, has become an important source of collaborations and community building.

All these efforts have been led by the people who cannot bear to leave this city. People keep on fighting to return—to their last breath and beyond. New Orleans funeral director Ceatrice Johnson told the *Times-Picayune* in 2009 that 30 percent of her business—up from 5 percent pre-Katrina—involves the shipment of bodies. "People are dying in other places and being shipped in," she told a reporter. "They want to get home one way or another. That's the way true New Orleanians feel."[17]

Each time I see a family moving back to the city, I am inspired by their act of resistance and courage. I love the dedication to community here, a commitment people feel to their neighbors and their city. Every day I see other small acts of resistance through secondlines and other cultural expressions. I see people going to what seems like the thousandth neighborhood-planning meeting and still sharing fresh ideas. I see people demonstrating in the streets. I see people being generous despite the cruelty of the city's elite who've tried to keep them out. I see people giving their neighbors food and places to stay.

The city's traditions didn't die. Almost all the Social Aid and Pleasure Clubs still exist. There's still a secondline nearly every weekend. Mardi Gras Indians still take to the streets on St. Joseph's Night and hold Indian practice in neighborhood bars all year around. Bounce music still fills the nightclubs. Jazz, spoken word, theatre, and art fill the community spaces.

"How do we even begin to wrap our heads around what it means for us to live here, considering what an enormous struggle it is every day?" asked performer Nick Slie. "It's both horrific and amazing at the exact same time."[18]

In 2009, the Essence Music Festival and the Bayou Classic had one of their biggest years ever. Incredibly stubborn and loyal people who love this city still live in the Lower Ninth Ward, Gentilly, New Orleans East, Desire, and all the other neighborhoods that seemed destined to be abandoned in those first months after the storm. People take to the streets to party, to protest, to barbeque. And even five years later, displaced New Orleanians are still moving back. "I don't like the food in Houston," more than one former resident has told me. "I need red beans and rice on a Monday night. I need gumbo. I need jambalaya."

In 2010, the New Orleans Saints football team—which had been so unsuccessful in years past that fans had started a gameday tradition of wearing paper bags over their heads in shame—won the Super Bowl, and the city was enveloped in an aura of ecstasy. Throughout the city, strangers were hugging, and everyone seemed in love with their neighbors—and their city. People were so excited for the Saints that they had scheduled a parade—the largest in the city's history—that was to take place even if the Saints lost. Thousands of people made plans to meet the team at the airport to celebrate them, *even if they lost*. Although the game was in Miami, hotel rooms in New Orleans were sold out because people wanted to celebrate here. When the team won, it felt like a vindication for the city. We felt like the nation was celebrating with us. It felt like the whole world was aware of what the city had been through, and people were cheering for our recovery. It felt like recovery really might be possible, and we could unite and rebuild together.

THE VICTORIES OF THE KATRINA GENERATION

Freedom for the Jena Six was a victory for and by all of us who are committed to a more just world. Our movements should share in the feeling of having defeated an injustice and taken a step forward.

The continuing strength of the culture of New Orleans is another victory—a survival against planned erasure. This is a culture built on two centuries of resistance, from the uprising of 1811 to the five hundred community members who stood in solidarity with the Black Panthers in the Desire housing projects, to the families of the Danziger Bridge victims and others killed by police violence, who spoke out and organized against systemic lies and corruption.

The tens of thousands of poor folks who have returned despite the obstacles all represent small individual victories and a large collective one. The million-plus volunteers who came through this city will no doubt go on to lead crucial battles, with many more victories, inspired by the lessons learned in New Orleans. And here, on the ground, many of the same folks who were fighting long before anyone was watching or paying attention are still here, still fighting the same battles we fought before Katrina—over health care, education, housing, workers' rights, and criminal justice. And sometimes we win.

In hundreds of small skirmishes, in grassroots organizing and demonstrations, the fight continues. Not just the fight to return, but to make this city a better, more just place. As director of Dillard University's Deep South Center for Environmental Justice, Beverly Wright has fought for a safe and fair return for New Orleans residents. She too lost her home to Katrina, and declared during a 2006 forum sponsored by the African American Leadership Project, "They've underestimated the determination of people like me to fight to our last breath."

I believe the next generation of New Orleans activists will continue and expand on this work. The young people from programs like Students at the Center and the members of Fyre Youth Squad, ReThink, the Vietnamese American Young Leaders Association, and Young Adults Striving for Success are already making their mark. In a few years they will be leading a movement for real change.

The issues discussed here are systemic. Reform is not enough. There is nothing wrong with striving for short-term improvements. But if our work doesn't include an analysis of how it intersects with—and challenges, rather than reinforces—the systems of white supremacy, patriarchy, homophobia, colonialism, and capitalism, then it is part of the problem. Our movement must break free of the nonprofit model and its dependence on foundations, which ignore the grassroots organizations and the individuals most in need of funding, in favor of reinforcing the status quo.

To effectively pursue justice and liberation, we first need to build a base of resistance. The tactics and traditions that are central to New Orleans organizing—potlucks, story circles, and freedom schools—have helped make our movement stronger by basing it in community.

Our artists are also community leaders, and arts and culture are integral to New Orleans organizing. Through dancing, singing, playing instruments, reciting poetry, creating, and celebrating we come together—using our whole selves to communicate.

We need to continue to question and reevaluate our strategies and tactics in order to evolve as we move forward. We should not abandon marches or direct action; nor, however, should we automatically repeat actions that may have worked in the past without assessing whether they would be effective in a particular situation. We need to build our base by reaching out to the people most affected by systemic injustice, and we need to construct our movement based on their knowledge and wisdom.

All of us interested in fighting for social justice need to examine issues of accountability. Whether an organizer, journalist, teacher, health care worker, or other ally, we need to ask how we are answerable to the people we are seeking to support. Good work, done with the best of intentions, but without accountability or a systemic analysis, ends up creating more problems than it solves. This is not to advocate chronic inaction, but rather thoughtful action.

We need to prioritize human rights for all, not civil rights for citizens. We need to share lessons, strategies, tactics, and targets with our international allies in order to build a worldwide movement that challenges the global systems of exploitation. In other words, we need to link rather than divide.

Community will sustain us when the cause seems hopeless. The people of New Orleans have demonstrated that. They stood together and fought back, joined by allies around the world and reinforced by a legacy of resistance. This culture, community, and generosity of spirit continue to inspire all those who love New Orleans. Bringing these elements together will help sustain us in this struggle and cultivate new generations for the next. The Jena Generation has just begun to fight.

Organizations in the Struggle for Post-Katrina Justice

Below are some of the initiatives that inspired this book. More information about most of these groups and their work is available elsewhere in these pages. This list is limited to organizations currently in existence at the time of publication, and is not meant to be definitive. Websites or addresses are listed when applicable.

NEW ORLEANS AND LOUISIANA SOCIAL JUSTICE ORGANIZATIONS

Advocates for Environmental Human Rights
Works for the cause of environmental justice as a human right. www.ehumanrights.org

A Fighting Chance/NOLA Investigates
Investigations for the defense in capital cases. www.nolainvestigates.com

African American Leadership Project
Agenda building, policy analysis, strategic dialogue, and consensus building. www.aalp.org

Agenda for Children
Policy work for children's rights. www.agendaforchildren.org

American Civil Liberties Union (ACLU) of Louisiana
Legal struggles for civil rights. www.laaclu.org

American Friends Service Committee of New Orleans
Organizing against the cradle-to-prison pipeline and other campaigns.
www.afsc.org/office/new-orleans-la

Black Men United for Change, Justice and Equality
Grassroots organizing among Black men from New Orleans.

Children's Defense Fund of Louisiana
National child advocacy organization—in New Orleans, conducts Freedom Schools, among other projects. www.childrensdefense.org

Common Ground Relief Collective
Short-term relief and long-term rebuilding support. www.commongroundrelief.org

Common Ground Health Clinic
Dedicated to providing free, quality health care for New Orleans. www.commongroundclinic.org

Critical Resistance New Orleans
Prison abolition organization. www.criticalresistance.org

Deep South Center for Environmental Justice
Environmental justice organization based at Dillard University. www.dscej.org.

European Dissent
White antiracist group in New Orleans, affiliated with the People's Institute for Survival and Beyond (PISAB).

Families and Friends of Louisiana's Incarcerated Children (FFLIC)
Organizes among family members of incarcerated youth. www.fflic.org

Finding our Folk
Raising the voices of displaced New Orleanians. www.findingourfolk.org

Fyre Youth Squad
Young people organizing for better schools. www.myspace.com/1fyreyouth

Greater New Orleans Fair Housing Action Center
Legal struggles against housing injustice. www.gnofairhousing.org

Innocence Project New Orleans
Represents innocent prisoners serving life sentences in Louisiana and Mississippi. www.ip-no.org

Institute for Women and Ethnic Studies
Sexual and reproductive health justice among youth, women, and people of color. www.iwesnola.org

International Coalition to Free the Angola 3
A collective working to free Herman Wallace and Albert Woodfox, the two members of the Angola Three who remain in prison. www.angola3.org

Juvenile Justice Project of Louisiana
Legal and organizing work to reform juvenile justice. www.jjpl.org

Louisiana Justice Institute
Legal advocacy for civil rights and facilitation of a wide range of social justice campaigns in New Orleans and across the state. www.louisianajusticeinstitute.org

Loyola Law Clinic
Legal clinic representing indigent clients. www.law.loyno.edu/clinic

Make It Right
Founded by Brad Pitt to rebuild housing in the Lower Ninth Ward. www.makeitrightnola.org

Mayday New Orleans
Organizing for public housing justice. www.maydaynolahousing.org

National Coalition of Blacks for Reparations in America (N'COBRA)
New Orleans chapter of national alliance working for reparations. www.ncobra.org

Nation of Islam—New Orleans
Rebuilding and antiviolence work in the city. www.noineworleans.org

Neighborhoods Partnership Network (NPN)
Network of neighborhood organizations in New Orleans. www.npnnola.com

New Orleans Food & Farm Network
Food access organization. www.noffn.org

New Orleans, Louisiana Palestine Solidarity (NOLAPS)
Organizing and activism for awareness of Palestine, linking struggles in New Orleans with the Middle East. http://nolaps.blogspot.com

New Orleans Workers' Center for Racial Justice
Building worker power, advancing racial justice, and organizing to build a social movement in post-Katrina New Orleans. www.nowcrj.org

NO/AIDS Task Force
Services and advocacy for HIV-infected individuals. www.noaidstaskforce.org

Parents Organizing Network
Supports parents in taking a powerful role in the creation of excellent public schools. www.nolaparentsguide.org

People's Institute for Survival and Beyond (PISAB)
Antiracist community organizers and educators dedicated to building an effective movement for social transformation. www.pisab.org

Resurrection After Exoneration
Works to reconnect exonerees to their communities and provide access to those opportunities of which they were robbed. www.r-a-e.org

ReThink: Kids Rethink New Orleans Schools
Students reforming the school system post-Katrina. www.therethinkers.com

Safe Streets/Strong Communities
Campaigns for a new criminal justice system in New Orleans. www.safestreetsnola.org

School at Blair Grocery
Dedicated to the growth and development of young minds in the Lower Ninth Ward of New Orleans. http://schoolatblairgrocery.blogspot.com

Stay Local! New Orleans
Supports local businesses. www.staylocal.org

Students at the Center

A writing and digital-media program for students in New Orleans public, non-charter high schools. www.sacnola.com

Survivors Village

Former public housing residents in New Orleans struggling for housing justice. www.communitiesrising.wordpress.com

Twomey Center for Peace Through Justice

Education for social justice consciousness. www.loyno.edu/twomey

UNITY of Greater New Orleans

A collaborative of sixty agencies working with homeless people in New Orleans. www.unitygno.org

Vietnamese American Young Leaders Association of New Orleans (VAYLA)

Empowering Vietnamese American youth through services, cultural enrichment, and social change. www.vayla-no.org

VOTE: Voices of Formerly Incarcerated Persons

Building the political power of people most impacted by the criminal justice system. www.vote-nola.org

Welfare Rights Organization

Welfare recipients organizing to help protect the rights of poor people. www.welfarerightsorganization.org

Women's Health & Justice Initiative (WHJI)

A radical feminist of color, anti-violence, justice-based organization. The New Orleans affiliate of INCITE! Women of Color Against Violence. www.whji.org

Women With A Vision

Health care justice for women from at-risk and socially vulnerable communities. www.wwav-no.org

ARTS, CULTURE, AND COMMUNITY ORGANIZATIONS AND SPACES

2-Cent Entertainment

Grassroots youth filmmaking collective. www.2-cent.com

Artspot Productions

Theatre and arts organization. www.artspotproductions.org

Ashé Cultural Center

Black-owned cultural and community space. www.ashecac.org

Backstreet Cultural Museum

Cultural center preserving the history and culture of Black Mardi Gras.
www.backstreetmuseum.org

Community Book Center

African and African American-centered bookstore and community space.
www.communitybookcenter.com

Craige Cultural Center

Community space and cultural center in the Algiers neighborhood.
1800 Newton Street, New Orleans, LA 70114

Guardians of the Flame Cultural Arts Collective

Preserving New Orleans's Black Mardi Gras cultural traditions.

House of Dance and Feathers

Lower Ninth Ward space dedicated to preserving New Orleans culture.
www.houseofdanceandfeathers.com

Iron Rail Bookstore and Infoshop

Anarchist infoshop and lending library. www.ironrail.org

Islamic Shura Council of Greater New Orleans

Organization of New Orleans's Muslim community.

Junebug Productions

African American Arts company, preserving the civil rights traditions of the
Free Southern Theatre. http://junebugproductions.blogspot.com

Lesbian, Gay, Bisexual and Transgender Community Center of New Orleans

Builds, strengthens, and unifies the Greater New Orleans area LGBTQ community.
www.lgccno.net

McKenna Museum of African American Art

Dedicated to New Orleans African American art. www.themckennamuseum.com

Mondo Bizarro

Creates original, multidisciplinary art and fosters partnerships in local, national, and international communities. www.mondobizarro.org

Neighborhood Gallery

Exposure and support for artists. www.theneighborhoodgallery.com

Neighborhood Story Project

Works with writers in neighborhoods around New Orleans to write and publish books about their communities. www.neighborhoodstoryproject.org

New Orleans Kid Camera Project

Uses photography training and support to help young people express themselves.
www.kidcameraproject.org

PATOIS: The New Orleans Human Rights Film and Arts Festival

Organizes events, amplifies local voices, and builds community at the intersection of arts and
social justice. www.patoisfilmfest.org

Porch Cultural Organization and Center

Community-based organization using the arts to effect social change. www.theporch-7.com

Social Aid and Pleasure Club Task Force

An alliance of the city's social aid and pleasure clubs.

Tambourine and Fan

Works with young people in the Treme community to pass on New Orleans art and culture.
Treme Community Center, 1600 St. Philip Street, New Orleans, LA, 70116

Tekrema Center for Art and Culture

African American community space in New Orleans's Lower Ninth Ward.
www.thetekremacenter.com

Zeitgeist Multi-disciplinary Arts Center

Film and arts space in Central City New Orleans. www.zeitgeistinc.net

OTHER SOUTHERN AND GULF COAST SOCIAL JUSTICE ORGANIZATIONS

Friends of Justice

Supports struggles against injustice in criminal cases across Texas, Louisiana, Arkansas, and
Mississippi. www.friendsofjustice.wordpress.com

Institute for Southern Studies

Nonprofit research center working to bring lasting social and economic change.
www.southernstudies.org

Miami Workers Center

Building working-class community power in Miami. www.theworkerscenter.org

Mississippi Immigrants' Rights Alliance (MIRA)

Advocacy organizing and education for immigrants' rights. www.yourmira.org

Mississippi Workers Center

Grassroots worker advocacy. 213 Main Street, Greenville, MS, 38701

Organizing in the Trenches

Founded by Caseptla Bailey and Catrina Wallace, family members of one of the Jena Six, to
continue struggles for social justice. PO Box 831, Jena, LA, 71342

Project South
Atlanta-based movement building organization. www.projectsouth.org

Southerners On New Ground (SONG)
Envisioning a world where the third-shift factory worker and the drag queen at the bar down the block see their lives as connected and are working together for liberation. www.southernersonnewground.org

Take Back the Land
Miami-based collective empowering the Black community to determine how to use land for the benefit of the community. www.takebacktheland.org

NATIONAL ALLIES

The Advancement Project
A civil rights law, policy, and communication "action tank." www.advancementproject.org

Catalyst Project
White antiracist collective based in California. www.collectiveliberation.org

Center for Constitutional Rights
Uses law for social justice struggles. www.ccrjustice.org

ColorofChange
Online resource for racial justice organizing. www.ColorofChange.org

INCITE! Women of Color Against Violence
A national activist organization of radical feminists of color advancing a movement to end violence against women of color and their communities. www.incite-national.org

Malcolm X Grassroots Movement
Defending human rights and promoting self-determination. www.mxgm.org

National Economic and Social Rights Initiative (NESRI)
Advocacy for a human rights vision in the United States. www.nesri.org

Rainbow Push Coalition
Religious and social development organization led by Reverend Jesse Jackson Sr. www.rainbowpush.org

Right to the City Alliance
Movement-building alliance of community-based organizations. www.righttothecity.org

US Human Rights Network
Building links between organizations to promote U.S. accountability to universal human rights standards. www.ushrnetwork.org

V-Day
Founded by Vagina Monologues author Eve Ensler to stop violence against women and girls. www.vday.org

LETTER FROM THE PEOPLE OF NEW ORLEANS TO OUR FRIENDS AND ALLIES

December 15, 2006

We, the undersigned, represent a wide range of grassroots New Orleans organizers, activists, artists, educators, media makers, health care providers, and other community members concerned about the fate of our city. This letter is directed to all those around the world concerned about the fate of New Orleans and the Gulf Coast, but is especially intended for U.S.-based nonprofit organizations, foundations, and other institutions with resources and finances that have been, or could be, directed towards the Gulf Coast.

In the days after the storm, there were promises of support from the federal government and an array of nongovernmental organizations, such as progressive and liberal foundations and nonprofits. Small and large organizations have done fundraising on our behalf, promising to deliver resources and support to the people of New Orleans.

Many organizations and individuals have supported New Orleans-led efforts with time, resources, and advocacy on our behalf, and for this we are very grateful. These folks followed through on their commitments and offered support in a way that was respectful, responsible, and timely.

However, we are writing this letter to tell you that, aside from these very important exceptions, the support we need has not arrived, or has been seriously limited, or has been based upon conditions that become an enormous burden for us.

We remain in crisis, understaffed, underfunded, and in many cases, in desperate need of help. From the perspective of the poorest and least powerful, it appears that the work of national allies on their behalf has either not happened, or if it has happened, it has been a failure.

In the days after August 29, 2005, the world watched as our city was devastated. This destruction was not caused by Hurricane Katrina, but by failures of local, state, and national government, and institutional structures of racism and corruption. The disaster highlighted already-existing problems such as neglect, privatization, and deindustrialization.

As New Orleanians, we have seen tragedy firsthand. We have lost friends and seen our community devastated. More than 15 months later, we have seen few improvements. Our education, health care, and criminal justice systems remain in crisis, and more than 60 percent of the former population of our city remains displaced. Among those that remain, depression and other mental health issues have skyrocketed.

While many nationwide speak of "Katrina Fatigue," we are still living the disaster. We remain committed to our homes and communities. And we still need support.

In 15 months, we have hosted visits by countless representatives from an encyclopedic list of prominent organizations and foundations. We have given hundreds of tours of affected areas, and we have assisted in the writing of scores of reports and assessments. We have participated in, or assisted in, organizing panels and workshops and conferences. We have supplied housing and food and hospitality to hundreds of supporters promising to return with funding and resources, to donate staff and equipment, and more. It seems hundreds of millions of dollars have been raised in our name, often using our words, or our stories.

However, just as the government's promises of assistance, such as the "Road Home" program, remain largely out of reach of most New Orleanians, we have also seen very little money and support from liberal and progressive sources.

Instead of prioritizing efforts led by people who are from the communities most affected, we have seen millions of dollars that were advertised as dedicated toward Gulf Coast residents either remain unspent, or shuttled to well-placed outsiders with, at best, a cursory knowledge of the realities faced by people here. Instead of reflecting local needs and priorities, many projects funded reflect an outside perception of what our priorities should be. We have seen attempts to dictate to us what we should do, instead of a real desire to listen, and build together.

We are at an historic moment. The disaster on the Gulf Coast, and especially in New Orleans, has highlighted issues of national and international relevance. Questions of race, class, gender, education, health care, food access, policing, housing, privatization, mental health, and much more are on vivid display.

The South has been traditionally underfunded and exploited by institutions, including corporations, the labor movement, foundations, and the federal government. We have faced the legacy of centuries of institutional racism and oppression, with little outside support. And yet, against massive odds, grassroots movements in the South have organized and won historic, inspiring victories with international relevance.

In New Orleans, despite personal loss and family tragedies, people are fighting for the future of the city they love. Many are working with little to no funding or support.

We are writing this open letter to you to tell you that it's not too late. The struggle is still ongoing. Evacuees are organizing in trailer parks, health care providers are opening clinics, former public housing residents are fighting to keep their homes from being demolished, artists and media makers are documenting the struggle, educators and lawyers are joining with high school students to fight for better schools.

We ask you, as concerned friends and allies nationwide, as funders and organizations, to look critically at your practices. Has your organization raised money on New Orleans's behalf? Did that money go toward New Orleans-based projects, initiated and directed by those most affected? Have you listened directly to the needs of those in the Gulf and been responsive to them? Have you adjusted your practices and strategies to the organizing realities on the ground?

We ask you to seize this opportunity, and join and support the grassroots movements. If the people of New Orleans can succeed against incredible odds to save their city and their community, it is a victory for oppressed people everywhere. If the people of New Orleans lose, it is a loss for movements everywhere. Struggling together, we can win together.

Cherice Harrison-Nelson, director and curator, Mardi Gras Indian Hall of Fame; Royce Osborn, writer/producer; Greta Gladney, fourth-generation Lower Ninth Ward resident; Corlita Mahr, media justice advocate; Judy Watts, President/CEO, Agenda for Children; Robert "Kool Black" Horton, Critical Resistance; Jennifer Turner, Community Book Center; Mayaba Liebenthal, INCITE! Women of Color Against Violence, Critical Resistance; Norris Henderson, co-director, Safe Streets/Strong Communities; Ursula Price, outreach and investigation coordinator, Safe Streets/Strong Communities; Evelyn Lynn, managing director, Safe Streets/Strong Communities; Shana griffin, INCITE! Women of Color Against Violence;

Min. J. Kojo Livingston, founder, Liberation Zone/Destiny One Ministries; Shana Sassoon, New Orleans Network Neighborhood Housing Services of New Orleans; Althea Francois, Safe Streets/Strong Communities; Malcolm Suber, People's Hurricane Relief Fund; Saket Soni, New Orleans Workers' Justice Project; Nick Slie, I-10, Witness Project, co-artistic director, Mondo Bizarro; Catherine Jones, organizer and co-founder, Latino Health Outreach Project; Jennifer Whitney, coordinator, Latino Health Outreach Project; S. Mandisa Moore, INCITE! Women of Color New Orleans ; Aesha Rasheed, project manager, New Orleans Network; Dix deLaneuville, educator; Rebecca Snedeker, filmmaker; Catherine A. Galpin, RN, FACES, and Children's Hospital; Grace Bauer, Families and Friends of Louisiana's Incarcerated Children; Xochitl Bervera, Families and Friends of Louisiana's Incarcerated Children; Bess Carrick, producer/director; John Clark, professor of philosophy, Loyola University; Diana Dunn, People's Institute for Survival and Beyond, European Dissent; Courtney Egan, artist; Lou Furman, Turning Point Partners; Ariana Hall, Director, CubaNOLA Collective; Gwendolyn Midlo Hall, historian, writer, and lecturer, New Orleans and Mississippi Pine Belt; Susan Hamovitch, filmmaker/teacher, NYC/New Orleans; Russell Henderson, lecturer, Dillard University and organizer, Rebuilding Louisiana Coalition; Ms. Deon Haywood, events coordinator, Women With A Vision Inc.; Rachel Herzing, Critical Resistance, Oakland; Rev. Doug Highfield, Universal Life Church, Cherokee, AL; Joyce Marie Jackson, PhD., Cultural Researcher, LSU Dept. of Geography & Anthropology, and co-founder of Cultural

Crossroads, Inc., Baton Rouge Elizabeth K. Jeffers, teacher; Dana Kaplan, Juvenile Justice Project of Louisiana; Vi Landry, freelance journalist, New Orleans/New York; Bridget Lehane, European Dissent and People's Institute for Survival and Beyond; Karen-kaia Livers, Alliance for Community Theaters, Inc.; Rachel E. Luft, assistant professor of sociology, Department of Sociology, University of New Orleans; Damekia Morgan, Families and Friends of Louisiana 's Incarcerated Children; Ukali Mwendo, hazardous materials specialist, NOFD, president, Provisional Government— Republic of New Afrika/New Orleans, LA, former resident of the Lafitte Housing Development; Thea Patterson, Women's Health & Justice Initiative; J. Nash Porter, documentary photographer and co-founder of Cultural Crossroads, Inc., Baton Rouge; Gloria Powers, arts project manager; Bill Quigley, Loyola Professor of Law; Linda Santi, Neighborhood Housing Services of New Orleans; Tony Sferlazza, director, Plenty International NOLA; Heidi Lee Sinclair, MD, MPH, Baton Rouge Children's Health Project; Justin Stein, neighborhood relations coordinator and community mediator, Common Ground Health Clinic; Audrey Stewart, Loyola Law Clinic; Tracie L. Washington, Esq., co-director, Louisiana Justice Institute; Scott Weinstein, former co-director of the Common Ground Health Clinic; Melissa Wells, New Orleans resident; Jerald L. White, Bottletree Productions; Morgan Williams, Student Hurricane Network, co-founder; Gina Womack, Families and Friends of Louisiana's Incarcerated Children

Pledge in Support of a Just Rebuilding of St. Bernard Parish, Louisiana, and the U.S. Gulf Coast

In September of 2006, the Parish Council in St. Bernard Parish, Louisiana, enacted a law that would have prohibited homeowners from renting homes to anyone other than a "blood relative." Since the Parish is overwhelmingly white and had few Jewish citizens, the law effectively made it a crime to rent to African Americans, Vietnamese Americans, Latinos, Jews, and other populations who did not live in the parish in large numbers pre-Katrina.

Many of us engaged in rebuilding and relief work were deeply troubled by the "blood-relative" law and similar policies that discouraged the return of African Americans and the poor in New Orleans and throughout the Gulf Coast. Regrettably, many relief and volunteer organizations chose not to respond to the "blood-relative" law, remaining silent on this issue.

With the benefit of hindsight, we now know that St. Bernard Parish officials interpreted silence as consent, which has now emboldened them to pursue other means to defy the Fair Housing Act. The parish and its leaders are openly disobeying a federal court order and considering a charter change that would require a public referendum on any proposal to construct affordable multi-family housing. Their actions have been repeatedly ruled illegal in federal court because they are discriminatory in intent and impact.

It is time that we take a stand against discrimination wherever it occurs, and make clear what the moral imperatives are for all organizations that seek to rebuild the Gulf Coast as a fair and just society.

As local and national relief organizations and volunteer groups, we recognize we have a moral obligation to work towards a just rebuilding of the Gulf Coast, and we pledge to speak out against injustice where we see it. This includes discriminatory housing policies, such as those pursued by elected officials in St. Bernard Parish, Louisiana.

Organizations Endorsing:
Action Coalition for Racial, Social, and Environmental Justice—University of New Orleans; Advancement Project; Advocates for Environmental Human Rights; C3/Hands Off Iberville; Caffin Avenue Church of God; Coastal Women for Change; Common Ground Health Clinic; Community Church Unitarian Universalist—New Orleans; Emerging ChangeMakers Network; Families and Friends of Louisiana's Incarcerated Children; Homeless Action Team of Tulane University (HATT); Jesuit Social Research Institute, Loyola University; Junebug Productions; Katrina Rita Diaspora Solidarity; Loyola University Chapter of the National Lawyers Guild; Louisiana Justice Institute; Lower Ninth Ward Center for Sustainable Engagement and Development; Lower 9th Ward Homeowners' Association; Mayday New Orleans; Mennonite Central Committee— New Orleans; Mississippi Center for Justice; Mondo Bizarro; Moving Forward Gulf Coast, Inc.; National Economic and Social Rights Initiative (NESRI); New Orleans Palestine Solidarity; New Americans Social Club (New Orleans Holocaust Survivors Organization); PATOIS: The New Orleans International Human Rights Film Festival; People's Institute for Survival and Beyond; Poverty & Race

Research Action Council; Pyramid Community
Parent Resource Center; Southern Institute for
Education and Research; Survivors Village; US
Human Rights Network; Zion Travelers
Cooperative Center

New Orleans Films

Below are some resources on film that further explore the themes raised in this book. This list is not at all definitive, but helps highlight some of the voices not generally heard in corporate media discussions of the city. With a few exceptions, this list focuses on post-Katrina works directed by New Orleanians, with a preference toward those films that highlight and explore the city's unique culture and grassroots resistance. Most, but not all, are documentaries.

All on a Mardi Gras Day
Perhaps the definitive film on New Orleans's Black Carnival traditions, in all their riotous, colorful, and spiritual glory. Directed by Royce Osborne (2003, 60 min)

Black Indians of New Orleans
Most likely the first documentary about Mardi Gras Indians, containing vital archival footage. Directed by Maurice Martinez (1976, 30 min)

By Invitation Only
An unprecedented look at the inner workings of the insular world of New Orleans's old-line Carnival society through the lens of one of its own. Directed by Rebecca Snedeker (2006, 57 min)

Cut Off
A film about the demolition of public housing in New Orleans and activist responses. Directed by Broderick Webb and Edward Holub (2008, 45 min)

The Farm: Angola USA
A devastating, Academy Award–nominated look inside the lives of prisoners at the Louisiana State Penitentiary at Angola. Directed by Liz Garbus, Wilbert Rideau, and Jonathan Stack (1998, 88 min)

Faubourg Treme
Writer Lolis Eric Elie tells the story of New Orleans through his neighborhood, Faubourg Treme, the oldest Black neighborhood in America and the birthplace of jazz. Directed by Lolis Eric Elie and Dawn Logsdon (2008, 68 min)

Finding Our Folk
The documentation of a tour of artists and activists through the post-Katrina diaspora, working to support the Right of Return. Directed by Omo Moses (2008, 56 min)

Freedom on My Mind
Academy Award–nominated documentary of the Mississippi Freedom Movement in the early 1960s, featuring People's Hurricane Relief Fund founder Curtis Muhammad (then named Curtis Hayes). Directed by Connie Field and Marilyn Mulford (1994, 110 min)

From the Mouthpiece on Back
The young men of the To Be Continued Brass Band and their struggle to return to New Orleans after Katrina. Directed by Colleen O'Halloran and Jason DaSilva (2008, 60 min)

Fullness of Time
Made in collaboration with local artists and youth, an experimental science fiction film with New Orleans's devastation as a backdrop. Directed by Cauleen Smith (2008, 56 min)

Glory at Sea
A fantastical short-fiction film about the post-Katrina mourning process. Directed by Benh Zeitlin (2008, 23 min)

Independent America: Rising from Ruins
A fascinating study of the plight of local businesses in New Orleans after the storm. Directed by Hanson Hosein (2009, 70 min)

I Won't Drown on That Levee and You Ain't Gonna Break My Back
A short advocacy video made by the organization Critical Resistance, focusing on criminal justice issues after the storm. Directed by Ashley Hunt (2006, 30 min)

Katrina: Man-Made Disaster
A short news piece about New Orleanians' struggles against displacement. Directed by Big Noise Films (2008, 26 min)

Katrina Story
A legendary New Orleans bounce musician's personal story of Katrina, featuring footage shot during and just after the storm, as he evacuated from New Orleans East to the Houston Astrodome. Directed by Tenth Ward Buck (2006, 35 min)

Katrina's Children
Explores the impact of Hurricane Katrina on nineteen children from different neighborhoods of New Orleans. Told from the point of view of the children themselves, through their stories, their play, and their art. Directed by Laura Belsey (2008, 83 min)

Land of Opportunity
Several years and hundreds of hours of footage went into making this comprehensive and powerful film about housing struggles in New Orleans after Katrina. Directed by Luisa Dantas (2010, 90 min)

Low and Behold
A powerful independent feature shot in New Orleans in the months after Katrina, following a young white insurance adjuster who is overwhelmed by the devastation he sees. Directed by Zack Godshall (2007, 90 min)

Mardi Gras: Made in China
New Orleans tourist Mardi Gras serves as a backdrop for an entertaining exploration of the issues of globalization. Directed by David Redmon (2005, 72 min)

Neo Black Leaders and Politics
Filmed mostly in the '80s in New Orleans, an abstract film about local social justice activism. Directed by Rudy Mills (2007, 30 min)

New Orleans Exposed
A semi-exploitational view of life in New Orleans's housing projects before the storm. Directed by Dwayne "Video Wayne" Morgan (2005, 62 min)

New Orleans: My Home, My Life, My Love
Tells the story of Katrina through several survivors, including John Keller's story of staying in New Orleans's American Can Company Building. Directed by Jamie R. Balthazar (2005, 60 min)

Race: The 2006 New Orleans Elections
A thorough telling of the first post-Katrina mayoral election. Directed By Katherine Cecil (2010, 60 min)

Recover and Restore
A multiple-part video advocacy project, focusing on issues from housing to health care to immigrant labor. Directed by Trupania Bonner (Ongoing)

Right to Return: New Home Movies from the Lower Ninth Ward
An Academy Award–winning director's effort to chronicle several New Orleanians' post-Katrina experience. Directed by Jonathan Demme (2007, 108 min)

Tootie's Last Suit
Explores the complex relationships, rituals, history, and music of New Orleans's vibrant Mardi Gras Indian culture while telling the story of Allison "Tootie" Montana, former Chief of the Yellow Pocahontas Hunters. Directed by Lisa Katzman (2006, 97 min)

Trouble the Water
Based on footage from just before, during, and after Katrina shot by New Orleans native Kimberley Rivers Roberts, a devastating firsthand portrait of the storm and its aftermath. Directed by Carl Deal and Tia Lessin (2008, 96 min)

Wade in the Water, Children
Filmed by a class of New Orleans high-school students in the first months after Katrina, an intimate and personal view of the struggles after the storm. Directed by Elizabeth Wood and Gabriel Nussbaum (2008, 73 min)

When the Levees Broke
The first major post-Katrina New Orleans documentary, and still one of the best, especially for audiences unfamiliar with the city. Directed by Spike Lee (2006, 255 min)

Ya Heard Me
The definitive film about New Orleans bounce music and the culture around it. Directed by Matt Miller and Stephen Thomas (2008, 77 min)

Notes

CHAPTER ONE: WE WON'T BOW DOWN

1. Jeffrey Kofman, "Katrina Weaker Than Originally Thought," *ABC News*, December 21, 2005, abcnews.go.com/US/HurricaneKatrina/story?id=1429373
2. Unless stated otherwise, quotes throughout this book come from direct conversations, interviews, public appearances, or (as in this case) e-mail communication.
3. Nine Times Social and Pleasure Club, *Coming Out the Door for the Ninth Ward* (New Orleans: Neighborhood Story Project, 2009).
4. Cornel West, "Exiles from a City and from a Nation," *Guardian* (UK), September 11, 2005, www.guardian.co.uk/world/2005/sep/11/hurricanekatrina.comment.
5. Susan Henry, *My Mother's House of Beauty* (New Orleans: Neighborhood Story Project, 2009), 36.
6. *New Orleans*, directed by Stephen Ives (PBS American Experience, 2007).
7. Katy Reckdahl, "St. Joseph's Night Gone Blue," *Gambit Weekly*, March 29, 2005.
8. Albert Thrasher, *"On to New Orleans!": Louisiana's Heroic Slave Revolt* (New Orleans: Cypress Press, 1995).
9. Malcolm Suber, speech sponsored by the Louisiana Museum of African American History, July 25, 2009.
10. Alissa Hall, "The Mysterious Marie Laveau: Voodoo Queen of the Bayou," *Dark Realms* (Summer 2006).
11. Mary Gehman, *Women and New Orleans: A History*, (New Orleans: Margaret Media, 1988).
12. Katy Reckdahl, "Long Road to Freedom," *Gambit Weekly*, July 26, 2005, www.bestofneworleans.com/gyrobase/Content?oid=oid%3A34895.
13. Leonard N. Moore, *Black Rage in New Orleans: Police Brutality and African American Activism from World War II to Hurricane Katrina* (Baton Rouge, LA: Louisiana State University Press, 2010).
14. Gary Orfield, *Reviving the Goal of an Integrated Society: A 21st Century Challenge* (Los Angeles: The Civil Rights Project, UCLA, 2009).
15. U.S. Bureau of the Census, "Population of the 100 Largest Urban Places, 1960"; "1970 Census of Population and Housing"; "Residential Segregation of Blacks or African-Americans: 1980–2000," www.census.gov.
16. John O'Neal, paper, nd.
17. Jim Randels, "After The Storm," blog, http://blogs.edweek.org/teachers/randels, October 28, 2005.

CHAPTER TWO: LIES ON THE NEWS

1. Elizabeth Mullener, "Ex-Marine John Keller Shepherded Hundreds to Safety Following Katrina," *Times-Picayune*, March 25, 2007.
2. Dan Berger, "Constructing Crime, Framing Disaster," *Punishment & Society* 11, no. 4 (2009): 501.

3. Susannah Rosenblatt and James Rainey, "Katrina Takes a Toll on Truth, News Accuracy," *Los Angeles Times*, September 27, 2005.

4. *Soul Patrol: Katrina's Own*, short film, directed by Taylor Gentry and Drew Annis, 2006.

5. Denise Moore, "What REALLY Happened in New Orleans: Denise Moore's Story," Daily Kos, September 6, 2005, www.dailykos.com/story/2005/9/6/211436/8987.

6. Wil Haygood and Ann Scott Tyson, "It Was As if All of Us Were Already Pronounced Dead," *Washington Post*, September 15, 2005.

7. Larry Bradshaw and Lorrie Beth Slonsky, "The Real Heroes and Sheroes of New Orleans," *Socialist Worker*, September 9, 2005, http://socialistworker.org/2005-2/556/556_04_RealHeroes.shtml.

8. Margaret Moser, "My Gang Don't Bow Down," *Austin Chronicle*, May 5, 2006.

9. John M. Barry, *Rising Tide* (New York: Simon and Schuster, 1997), 313.

10. Michael Homan, "Refugee or Concentration Camp at I-10 and Causeway?" December 6, 2005, http://michaelhoman.blogspot.com/2005/12/refugee-or-concentration-camp-at-i-10.html.

11. Leah Hodges, *Democracy Now*, December 9, 2005, www.democracynow.org/2005/12/9/new_orleans_evacuees_and_activists_testify.

12. Bob Moon, "Houston, We May Have a Problem," *Marketplace*, September 5, 2005.

13. Jodie Escobedo, "Baton Rouge Report," September 26, 2005, http://nihilistic-kid.livejournal.com/655611.html.

CHAPTER THREE: STILL GOT ME IN DISBELIEF

1. Sheri Fink, "The Deadly Choices at Memorial," ProPublica, August 27, 2009, www.propublica.org/feature/the-deadly-choices-at-memorial-826.

2. James Perry and Melissa Harris Lacewell, "Katrina Nation," Huffington Post, August 26, 2009 www.huffingtonpost.com/melissa-harrislacewell-and-james-perry/katrina-nation_b_267571.html.

3. Leslie Kaufman and Campbell Robertson, "In Gulf Oil Spill, Fragile Marshes Face New Threat," May 1, 2010.

4. Associated Press, "Gulf of Mexico Oil Spill Has Countless Livelihoods in Limbo," May 2, 2010.

5. Patrick O'Driscoll, "Cleanup Crews Tackle Katrina's Nasty Leftovers," *USA Today*, December 11, 2005.

6. West, "Exiles from a City and from a Nation."

7. Associated Press, "Halliburton's KBR Unit Gets Contract to Repair Gulf Coast Facilities," *Houston Business Journal*, September 6, 2005.

8. The Road Home Program, "Weekly Detailed Statistics as of May 24, 2010," www.road2la.org/newsroom/stats.htm.

9. Kalima Rose, Annie Clark, and Dominique Duval-Diop, *A Long Way Home: The State of Housing Recovery in Louisiana 2008* (New Orleans: PolicyLink, 2008), www.policylink.info/threeyearslater.

10. Vincanne Adams, Taslim Van Hattum, Diana English, "Chronic Disaster Syndrome: Displacement, Disaster and the Eviction of the Poor From New Orleans," *American Ethnologist* 36, no. 4 (2009): 624.

11. Bill Fletcher, "Can Richard Trumka Turn Organized Labor Around?" *Black Commentator*, October 8, 2009, www.blackcommentator.com/345/345_aw_trumka_labor.html.

12. Lance Hill, email to author, October 24, 2005.

13. Christopher Cooper, "Old-Line Families Escape Worst of Flood and Plot the Future," *Wall Street Journal*, September 8, 2005.

14. Jeremy Scahill, "Blackwater Down," *The Nation*, October 10, 2005, www.thenation.com/doc/20051010/scahill.

15. Rowan Moore, "Brad the Builder in New Orleans," *Guardian* (UK), March 24, 2010.

16. David W. Moore, "Katrina Hurt Blacks and Poor Victims Most: Differences Larger By Race Than Income," Gallup poll, October 25, 2005, www.gallup.com/poll/19405/katrina-hurt-blacks-poor-victims-most.aspx.

17. CNN, "'Can I Quit Now?' FEMA Chief Wrote as Katrina Raged," November 4, 2005, www.cnn.com/2005/US/11/03/brown.fema.emails.

18. Statistics and reports compiled by the Greater New Orleans Community Data Center were a great help in this research, and all research on the city's neighborhood demographics; Sam Roberts, "New Orleans Grows; Florida Cools," *New York Times*, March 20, 2008, www.nytimes.com/2008/03/20/us/20census.html.

19. United Nations, *Guiding Principles on Internal Displacement*, available at www.amnestyusa.org/pdf/UN_guidingpriciples_intdispl.pdf.

20. Shaila Dewan, "Storm Evacuees Remain in Grip of Uncertainty," *New York Times*, December 6, 2006.

21. Isabel Wilkerson, "Scattered in a Storm's Wake and Caught in a Clash of Cultures," *New York Times*, October 9, 2005.

22. Jenka Soderberg, email to author, October 7, 2005.

23. Catherine Jones, "New Ghosts," Floodlines, October 26, 2005, http://floodlines.blogspot.com/2005_10_01_archive.html.

24. Blaine Harden, "The Economics of Return: Class, Color May Guide Repopulation of New Orleans," *Washington Post*, October 19, 2005.

25. Bill Quigley, "Why Are They Making New Orleans a Ghost Town?" Dissident Voice, November 1, 2005, http://dissidentvoice.org/Nov05/Quigley1101.htm.

26. Katherine Cecil, "Race, Representation, and Recovery: Documenting the 2006 New Orleans Mayoral Elections" (graduate thesis, University of New Orleans, 2009).

27. Jarvis DeBerry, "At Least Stacy Head and Tracie Washington Are Sure They Don't Agree," July 6, 2009, http://blog.nola.com/jarvisdeberry/2009/07/jarvis_deberry_at_least_stacy.html.

28. Bruce Eggler, "Stacy Head's E-mails Briefly Released on Website," *Times-Picayune*, May 13, 2009.

29. Frank Donze, "City Councilwoman Stacy Head Shows Substantial Support in Majority-Black Precincts," *Times-Picayune*, February 13, 2010.

30. Xochitl Bervera, "The Forgotten Children of New Orleans," *Counterpunch*, September 1, 2006, www.counterpunch.org/bervera09012006.html.

CHAPTER FOUR: WONDER HOW WE DOIN'

1. Naomi Klein, *The Shock Doctrine* (New York: Alfred A. Knopf, 2007), 5.

2. *Democracy Now*, "All New Orleans Public School Teachers Fired, Millions in Federal Aid Channeled to Private Charter Schools," June 20, 2006.

3. Cowen Institute for Public Education Initiatives, Tulane University, "Public Schools in New Orleans: Background," www.tulane.edu/cowen_institute/background.html.

4. "Former NOPS Employees Can Proceed with Class-Action," *Louisiana Weekly*, March 15, 2010.

5. Greg Toppo, "Teach For America: Elite Corps or Costing Older Teachers Jobs?" *USA Today*, July 29, 2009, www.usatoday.com/news/education/2009-07-29-teach-for-america_N.htm.
6. Darren Simon, "Student Finds Success in Failure," *Times-Picayune*, April 21, 2008.
7. Rick Jervis, "High Marks for New Orleans' Charter Schools," *USA Today*, August 27, 2009.
8. Sarah Carr, "District Increases Per-Pupil Spending," *Times-Picayune*, March 3, 2008.
9. Adam Nossiter, "Against Odds, New Orleans Schools Fight Back," *New York Times*, April 30, 2008.
10. Bruce Eggler, "Many Orleans Schools Have Lack of Veteran Teachers," *Times-Picayune*, February 11, 2009.
11. Jason Neville and Geoff Coates, "Urban Design and Civil Society in New Orleans," *Journal of Urban Design* 14, no. 3 (August 2009).
12. Kenneth M. Reardon, "The Shifting Landscape of New Orleans," *Shelterforce Online* 145 (Spring 2006), www.nhi.org/online/issues/145/shiftinglandscape.html.
13. Frank Donze, "Blakely Blames Hype," *Times-Picayune*, June 5, 2009.
14. Malcolm X, "The Ballot or the Bullet," (speech, April 3, 1964), in George Breitman, *Malcolm X Speaks* (New York: Grove Press, 1994).
15. Greater New Orleans Community Data Center, "Benchmarks for Blight," August 2009, www.gnocdc.org.
16. Mazin Qumsiyeh, "Let's Talk About Resistance," interview with *Al Aqsa*, October 13, 2009, translated by the Ghazzawiyya Blog, http://gaza08.blogspot.com/2009/10/lets-talk-about-resistance.html.
17. Louisa Hanoune, closing speech of the International Tribunal on Hurricanes Katrina and Rita, September 2, 2007.
18. Korina Lopez, "Katrina Volunteers Come to Stay," *USA Today*, January 14, 2008.
19. Casey Leigh, draft of article, March 6, 2008.
20. Ingrid Chapman, "Hearts on Fire: The Struggle for Justice in New Orleans," ZNet, September 8, 2007, www.zmag.org/znet/viewArticle/14529.
21. INCITE, "Statement on Hurricane Katrina," September 11, 2005, www.incite-national.org/index.php?s=90.
22. David Hanners, "GOP Convention Protesters Seek to Exclude Evidence from Upcoming Trial," *St. Paul Pioneer Press*, October 29, 2008.
23. Adjoa Jones de Almeida, Dana Kaplan, Paula X. Rojas, Eric Tang, and M. Mayuran Tiruchelvam, "Rethinking Solidarity," *Left Turn Magazine*, June 2006, www.leftturn.org/node/385.
24. Ibid.
25. Perry and Lacewell, "Katrina Nation."
26. Walidah Imarisha, "From the Ground Up: Race and the Left Response to Katrina," *Left Turn Magazine*, March 2006.
27. Stephanie Guilloud, "From Seattle to Detroit: 10 Lessons for Movement Building on the 10th Anniversary of the WTO Shutdown," *Project South Newsletter*, Fall 2009.

CHAPTER FIVE: DOLLAR DAY IN NEW ORLEANS

1. Katy Reckdahl, "Culture, Change Collide in Treme," *Times-Picayune*, October 2, 2007.
2. Paul Chan, "*Waiting for Godot* in New Orleans: an Artist Statement," June 2007, www.creativetime.org/programs/archive/2007/chan/artist_statement.pdf; Climbing PoeTree,

website, www.climbingpoetree.com/html/showcase.php?showcase=14&psi=57, accessed April 24, 2010; Roberta Smith, "Kaleidoscopic Biennial for a Scarred City," *New York Times*, November 4, 2008.

3. *A Loud Color*, short film, directed by Brent Joseph, 2006.

4. In August 2007, the White House released a "factsheet" that claimed, "The Federal Government Has Provided More Than $114 Billion In Resources—$127 Billion Including Tax Relief—To The Gulf Region." www.nationalservice.gov/about/newsroom/releases _detail.asp?tbl_pr_id=794.

5. Foundation Center, *Giving in the Aftermath of the 2005 Gulf Coast Hurricanes* (New York: Foundation Center, 2009).

6. See appendix II.

7. Pablo Eisenberg, "After Katrina: What Foundations Should Do," *Chronicle of Philanthropy*, January 2006.

8. Steven Lawrence, *Snapshot of Philanthropy's Response to the Gulf Coast Hurricanes* (New York: Foundation Center, February 2006), www.foundationcenter.org/gainknowledge/ research/pdf/katrina_snap.pdf.

9. Eisenberg, *Chronicle of Philanthropy*.

10. Ibid.

11. Barbara Ransby, *Ella Baker and the Black Freedom Movement: A Radical Democratic Vision* (Chapel Hill, NC: University of North Carolina Press, 2002), 290.

12. Chana Kai Lee, *For Freedom's Sake: The Life of Fannie Lou Hamer* (Urbana, IL: University of Illinois Press, 1999), 98.

13. Marcus Garvey, *The Marcus Garvey & Universal Negro Improvement Association Papers, Vol. IX: Africa for the Africans* (Berkeley: University of California Press, 1995).

14. John D. Rockefeller's Commission on Foundation and Private Philanthropy, "The Role of Philanthropy of a Changing Society," in Brian O'Connell, ed., *America's Voluntary Spirit: A Book of Readings* (New York: Foundation Center, 1970), 293.

15. Alisa Bierria, Mayaba Liebenthal, and INCITE! Women of Color Against Violence, "To Render Ourselves Visible: Women of Color Organizing and Hurricane Katrina," *What Lies Beneath* (Cambridge, MA: South End Press, 2007), 39.

16. Ibid, 39–40.

17. Ibid, 37.

18. Eisenberg, *Chronicle of Philanthropy*.

19. Tajudeen Abdul-Raheem, "Impact of Angels," *The New Internationalist*, August 2000.

20. James W. Loewen, *Lies Across America: What Our Historic Sites Get Wrong* (New York: Simon & Schuster, 1999), 211.

21. Lizzy Ratner, "New Orleans Redraws Its Color Line," *Nation*, September 15, 2008.

22. Editorial, "Erecting Housing Barriers," *Times-Picayune*, August 22, 2009.

23. President Barack Obama, White House Weekly Address, "Lessons and Renewal Out of the Gulf Coast," August 29, 2009, www.whitehouse.gov/blog/2009/08/29/weekly -address-lessons-and-renewal-out-gulf-coast.

24. See Appendix III.

25. Ibid.

CHAPTER SIX: BEHIND THEM PENITENTIARY WALLS

1. Adam Liptak, "Inmate Count in U.S. Dwarfs Other Nations'," *New York Times*, April 23, 2008.

2. Jason Ryan, "U.S. Hits Record for Incarcerated, Paroled—At What Cost?" *ABC News*, November 30, 2006, http://abcnews.go.com/US/story?id=2691824&page=1.
3. Jenni Gainsborough and Marc Mauer, *Diminishing Returns: Crime and Incarceration in the 1990s* (Washington, D.C.: The Sentencing Project, 2000), www.sentencingproject.org/doc/publications/inc_diminishingreturns.pdf.
4. U.S. Department of Justice Statistics, 2004.
5. National Center for Children in Poverty, Mailman School of Public Health, "Ten Important Questions About Child Poverty and Family Economic Hardship," Columbia University, 2009, www.nccp.org/faq.html.
6. Adam Nossiter, "After the Storm, Students Left Alone and Angry," *New York Times*, November 1, 2006.
7. Juvenile Justice Project of Louisiana, "Growing Up in Louisiana," 2007, http://jjpl.org/new/?page_id=39.
8. Sarah Carr, "Recovery School District Increases Per-Pupil Spending," *Times-Picayune*, March 2, 2008, www.nola.com/news/index.ssf/2008/03/recovery_school_district_incre.html.
9. Southwest Education Development Laboratory, "The Progress of Education in Louisiana," www.sedl.org/pubs/pic01/changes.html.
10. Juvenile Justice Project of Louisiana, "Growing Up in Louisiana."
11. Ibid.
12. Human Rights Watch Children's Rights Project, "Children in Confinement in Louisiana," 1995.
13. Critical Resistance and INCITE, "Statement on Gender Violence and the Prison Industrial Complex," 2001, www.incite-national.org/index.php?s=92.
14. David Cole, "Can Our Shameful Prisons Be Reformed?" *New York Review of Books*, November 19, 2009, www.nybooks.com/articles/archives/2009/nov/19/can-our-shameful-prisons-be-reformed.
15. Reconstructed from interviews with prisoners conducted by Safe Streets/Strong Communities staff.
16. American Civil Liberties Union, "Abandoned & Abused: Orleans Parish Prisoners in the Wake of Hurricane Katrina," August 9, 2006.
17. Ibid.
18. According to research by Safe Streets/Strong Communities.
19. Human Rights Watch, "Testimony of Evacuees," October 12, 2005, www.hrw.org/en/news/2005/10/12/testimonies-evacuees.
20. ACLU, "Abandoned & Abused: Orleans Parish Prisoners in the Wake of Hurricane Katrina."
21. Fox Butterfield, "Settling Suit, Louisiana Abandons Private Youth Prisons," *New York Times*, September 8, 2000.
22. Melissa Block, "New Orleans Judge Slams City's Justice System," *All Things Considered*, April 2, 2007, www.npr.org/templates/story/story.php?storyId=9293468.
23. Safe Streets/Strong Communities and Southern Center for Human Rights, "A Pre- and Post-Katrina Report on Indigent Defense in New Orleans," March 2006, www.schr.org/action/resources/NOLA_indigent_defense.
24. U.S. Department of Justice, Civil Rights Division, Report on Orleans Parish Prison, September 11, 2009.
25. Jeff Brady, "New Orleans Housing Prisoners in Bus Station," NPR, September 9, 2005, www.npr.org/templates/story/story.php?storyId=4838671.
26. INCITE! Women of Color Against Violence, "Toolkit on Disaster and Law Enforcement Violence," www.incite-national.org/index.php?s=112.

27. Interview with Louisiana State Penitentiary at Angola Assistant Warden Cathy Fontenot.
28. Solomon Moore, "Study Finds Record Number of Inmates Serving Life Terms," *New York Times*, July 23, 2009.
29. All inmate quotes from court transcripts.
30. Kevin Sack, "Two Die in Louisiana Prison Hostage-Taking," *New York Times*, December 30, 1999.
31. Hans Bennett, "The Angola Three: Torture in Our Own Backyard," AlterNet, April 2, 2009.
32. Laura Sullivan, "Despite Legal Win, Inmate Back In Solitary," NPR, December 17, 2008.
33. H. Bruce Franklin, "The American Prison and the Normalization of Torture," www.historiansagainstwar.org/resources/torture/brucefranklin.html.
34. Kiilu Nyasha, "American Torture Chambers," Black Commentator, www.blackcommentator.com/215/215_american_torture_chambers_prisons_nyasha.html, February 1, 2007.
35. *Herman Wallace v. Burl Cain, Warden*, Request for Administrative Remedy Emergency, November 24, 2008.
36. Amnesty International, public statement, September 19, 2007.
37. The Forgiveness Project, "Mwalimu Johnson," http://theforgivenessproject.org.uk/?s=mwalimu+johnson.

CHAPTER· SEVEN: SERVE AND PROTECT

1. Amy Goodman, *Democracy Now*, September 2, 2005.
2. Metropolitan Crime Commission, "Orleans Parish Criminal Justice System Accountability Report," May 5, 2009, www.metropolitancrimecommission.org.
3. Metropolitan Crime Commission, "Performance of the New Orleans Criminal Justice System 2003–2004," August 2005.
4. Barbara Ehrenreich, "Is It Now a Crime to Be Poor?" *New York Times*, August 8, 2009.
5. David Billings, "New Orleans: A Choice Between Destruction and Reparations," Fellowship of Reconciliation, November 2005, www.forusa.org/fellowship/nov-dec_05/billings.html.
6. Sharon Martinas and Brad Ott, "Racism and Resistance in New Orleans Before Katrina: An Only-Touching-the-Surface Timeline," in "A Katrina Reader: Readings by & for Anti-Racist Educators and Organizers," Challenging White Supremacy Workshop, 2007, www.cwsworkshop.org/katrinareader.
7. Katy Reckdahl, "Target Practices," *Gambit Weekly*, April 12, 2005.
8. Ibid.
9. Paul Rioux, "Sheriff Isn't Backing Down at All," *Times-Picayune*, July 11, 2006.
10. M. Endesha Juakali, "When Abuse Is the Norm," Louisiana Justice Institute blog, May 4, 2010, http://louisianajusticeinstitute.blogspot.com/2010/05/when-abuse-is-norm-by-m-endesha-juakali.html.
11. Bob Herbert, "In America; Disgracing the Badge," *New York Times*, September 18, 1995.
12. Peter Ross Range, "Fighting Crime and Corruption in New Orleans," Progressive Policy Institute, September 1, 2000, www.ppionline.org.
13. Human Rights Watch, "Shielded from Justice: Police Brutality and Accountability in the United States," June 1998, www.columbia.edu/itc/journalism/cases/katrina/Human%20Rights%20Watch/uspohtml/uspo.htm.
14. Ethan Brown, "New Orleans Murder Rate for Year Will Set Record," *Guardian* (UK), November 6, 2007, www.guardian.co.uk/world/2007/nov/06/usa.

15. Susan Finch, "Officer Raped Me, Says Witness," *Times-Picayune*, April 11, 2007.

16. New Orleans Police Department, "Officer Arrested for Sexual Assault," press release, April 15, 2005, www.cityofno.com/pg-50-49-press-releases.aspx?pressid=2614.

17. Jarvis Deberry, "Disturbing Allegations Tuned Out for Years," October 26, 2008, http://blog.nola.com/jarvisdeberry/2008/10/disturbing_allegations_tuned_o.html.

18. Nicholas Riccardi, "After Blocking the Bridge, Gretna Circles the Wagons," *Los Angeles Times*, September 16, 2005.

19. Kimberly Vetter, "Post-Katrina Reports Detail Alleged Police Misconduct," *Baton Rouge Advocate*, April 3, 2010.

20. A. C. Thompson and Brendan McCarthy, "New Clues Emerge in Post-Katrina Vigilante Shooting at Algiers Point," ProPublica and *Times-Picayune*, April 12, 2010.

21. A. C. Thompson, "Katrina's Hidden Race War," *Nation*, January 5, 2009.

22. A. C. Thompson, Brendan McCarthy, and Laura Maggi, "Law and Disorder: Police Shootings in the Week After Hurricane Katrina," *Times-Picayune*, *Frontline*, and ProPublica, December 13, 2009.

23. Margaret Moser, "My Gang Don't Bow Down," *Austin Chronicle*, May 5, 2006.

24. Brendan McCarthy, "Third NOPD Officer Being Investigated in Case of Corpse Burned After Hurricane Katrina," *Times-Picayune*, April 12, 2010.

25. Brendan McCarthy, "Second Former New Orleans Police Officer Pleads Guilty in Danziger Bridge Shootings," *Times-Picayune*, March 11, 2010.

26. *Times-Picayune*, "Danziger Bridge Shooting Plea, Second in Case, Provides New Cover-Up Details," March 11, 2010.

27. Jarvis DeBerry, "Police Chief Warren Riley Couldn't Be Bothered to Read Danziger Report?" *Times-Picayune*, February 28, 2010.

28. Brendan McCarthy, "New Orleans Police Roles in July 2005 Death Being Investigated by FBI," *Times-Picayune*, March 2, 2010.

29. Associated Press, "New Orleans Officers Charged in Taped Beating," October 10, 2005. The story stated, "Under normal circumstances, it takes unusually bad behavior to trigger an arrest on Bourbon Street. But New Orleans police have been working under stressful conditions since the hurricane."

30. Brendan McCarthy, "Accounts of N.O. Bar Fight Differ; Officers Involved on Desk Duty," *Times-Picayune*, February 26, 2008, www.nola.com/news/index.ssf/2008/02/racism_fueled_no_bar_fight_rta.html.

31. Brendan McCarthy, "Ministers Demand Justice in Killing of Adolph Grimes III," *Times-Picayune*, January 6, 2009; Manuel Torres, "Shooting of Adolph Grimes III Demands Answers," *Times-Picayune*, January 4, 2009.

32. Alison Bath, "Louisiana Death Penalty: An Eye for an Eye or Ineffective?" *Shreveport Times*, October 9, 2009.

CHAPTER EIGHT: YOU DON'T WANT TO GO TO WAR

1. John Pope, "New Poll Shows Sharp Racial Divide," *Times-Picayune*, April 24, 2009, www.nola.com/news/t-p/neworleans/index.ssf/base/news-10/1240551142314070.xml&coll=1.

2. Greater New Orleans Community Data Center, "New Orleans Index," August 2009, gnocdc.org.

3. Charles Babington, "Some GOP Legislators Hit Jarring Notes in Addressing Katrina," *Washington Post*, September 10, 2005, www.washingtonpost.com/wp-dyn/content/article/2005/09/09/AR2005090901930.html.

4. Editorial, "No Welcome Mat?" *Gambit Weekly*, February 28, 2006, http://bestofneworleans.com/gyrobase/Content?oid=oid%3A35721.

5. Ibid.

6. INCITE, "INCITE! Analysis," www.incite-national.org/index.php?s=77.

7. Mark Waller, "LaBruzzo: Sterilization Plan Fights Poverty," *Times-Picayune*, September 24, 2008.

8. Greater New Orleans Community Data Center, "B. W. Cooper Apts Neighborhood Snapshot," August 20, 2003, gnocdc.org/orleans/4/60/snapshot.html.

9. Bill Quigley, "Save New Orleans Affordable Housing Fact Sheet," United Peace Relief, December 23, 2007, www.unitedpeacerelief.org/page11/files/archive-dec-2007.html.

10. Katy Reckdahl, "Critics Question Whether New New Orleans Public Housing Will Meet Needs," *Times-Picayune*, December 8, 2008.

11. Rachel Breunlin, "The Legacy of the Free Southern Theater in New Orleans: Interviews with Karen-Kaia Livers and Chakula Cha Jua," www.nathanielturner.com/legacyfreesouttheater.htm.

12. Orissa Arend, *Showdown in Desire: The Black Panthers Take a Stand in New Orleans* (Little Rock, AR: University of Arkansas Press, 2009), 10.

13. Interview conducted in collaboration with Reed Lindsey for TeleSur, August 2007.

14. Jennifer Ludden, "Shifting Visions of a Rebuilt New Orleans," interview with Pres Kabacoff, NPR, September 28, 2005, www.npr.org/templates/story/story.php?storyId=4866931.

15. Deon Roberts, "Developer, Public Housing Advocate Engage in e-Battle," *New Orleans City Business*, January 2, 2007, www.neworleanscitybusiness.com/print.cfm?recid=8051.

16. Ted Jackson, "Housing Officials Claim Surplus," *Times-Picayune*, December 18, 2007.

17. Nicolai Ouroussoff, "History vs. Homogeneity in New Orleans Housing Fight," *New York Times*, February 22, 2007, www.nytimes.com/2007/02/22/arts/design/22hous.html.

18. Bill Quigley, "Tale of Two Sisters," December 28, 2006, CommonDreams, www.commondreams.org/views06/1228-29.htm.

19. Katy Reckdahl, "Like A Ton of Bricks," *Gambit Weekly*, October 24, 2006.

20. Rick Jervis, "New Orleans' Homeless Rate Swells to 1 in 25," *USA Today*, March 17, 2008.

21. Darwin Bond-Graham, "Reading Racism and More on Nola.com," blog post, http://darwinbondgraham.blogspot.com/2007/12/reading-racism-and-more-on-nola.html.

22. Greater New Orleans Fair Housing Action Center, "Housing Choice in Crisis," August 20, 2009.

23. John Leland, "With Advocates' Help, Squatters Call Foreclosures Home," *New York Times*, April 9, 2009.

CHAPTER NINE: THE REST OF THE WORLD LIVES HERE TOO

1. Greater New Orleans Data Center, "Orleans Parish: People & Household Characteristics," from U.S. Census Bureau, *Census 2000*, www.gnocdc.org/orleans/people.html.

2. Benjamin Alexander-Bloch, "Former Slidell Cop Admits Ripping Off Hispanic Motorists, Gets Probation," *Times-Picayune*, May 6, 2009, www.nola.com/news/index.ssf/2009/05/former_slidell_cop_admits_ripp.html.

3. "Police 'Impersonator' Was Real Officer, NOPD Says," WDSU-TV News, www.wdsu.com/news/18974904/detail.html.

4. Catherine Jones, "Friday Night on Canal Street," blog post, December 3, 2005,

http://floodlines.blogspot.com/2005_12_01_archive.html.

5. Kevin Johnson, "Troops May Stay on in New Orleans," *USA Today*, October 7, 2005, www.usatoday.com/news/nation/2005-10-07-troops-neworleans_x.htm.

6. Advancement Project, National Immigration Law Center, and New Orleans Workers' Justice Coalition, "And Justice for All: Workers' Lives in the Reconstruction of New Orleans," July 2006, www.nilc.org/disaster_assistance/index.htm#hrts.

7. Eric Tang, "Boat People," *ColorLines* magazine, Spring 2006, www.colorlines.com/article .php?ID=28.

8. Ibid.

CHAPTER TEN: FIGHT FOR WHAT'S RIGHT

1. The reconstruction of events in Jena comes from extensive interviews with folks involved and personal observation, as well as from interviews and investigations by Jacqueline Soohen, Rick Rowley, and Kouross Esmaeli of Big Noise Tactical Media. The research of Alan Bean has also been an important aid in verification and background information.

2. *Jena Six*, directed and produced by Jacqueline Soohen, Rick Rowley, Kouross Esmaeli, Jordan Flaherty (New York: Big Noise Tactical Media, 2007).

3. Andrew Gumbel, "American Travesty," *Independent* (UK), August 20, 2002.

4. Alan Bean, "Ineffective Assistance of Counsel: What Blane Williams Should Have Known," Friends of Justice blog, July 2, 2007, http://friendsofjustice.wordpress .com/2007/07/02/ineffective-assistance-of-counsel-what-blane-williams-should-have -known.

5. Office of Governor Kathleen Blanco, email, July 30, 2007.

6. Xochitl Bervera, "The Justice that Jena Demands," Dissident Voice, September 29, 2007, http://dissidentvoice.org/2007/09/the-justice-that-jena-demands.

7. Andre Banks, "Today, We Wear Black for Jena," blog post, September 20, 2007, http:// writewhatilike.typepad.com.

8. Jason Whitlock, "Jena 6 Case Caught Up in Whirlwind of Distortion, Opportunism," *Kansas City Star*, September 29, 2007.

9. Craig Franklin, "Media Myths About the Jena 6," *Christian Science Monitor*, October 24, 2007, www.csmonitor.com/2007/1024/p09s01-coop.html.

10. Mychal Bell, "Surviving Jena Six: The Dreams of Mychal Bell," Global Grind, April 3, 2009, http://globalgrind.com/content/554975/Surviving-Jena-Six-The-Dreams-of -Mychal-Bell.

11. Bervera, "The Justice that Jena Demands."

12. Fox Butterfield, "Profits at a Juvenile Prison Come With a Chilling Cost," *New York Times*, July 15, 1998.

13. Ibid.

14. See, for example, Katy Reckdahl, "Little Angolas," *Gambit Weekly*, August 19, 2003, http://bestofneworleans.com/gyrobase/Content?oid=oid%3A30671.

CONCLUSION: DESIRE

1. Sunni Patterson, interview by Jordan Camp, No Alibis Radio, September 8, 2009, www.kcsb.org.

2. "Displaced New Orleans Community Demands Action, Accountability and Initiates a People's Hurricane Fund" (PHRF founding announcement, September 3, 2005).

3. Rachel Luft, "Beyond Disaster Exceptionalism: Social Movement Developments in

New Orleans after Hurricane Katrina," *American Quarterly* 61, no. 3 (September 2009): 499–527.

4. Jennifer Liberto, "Black Businesses Hit Hard in New Orleans," CNN, August 19, 2009, http://money.cnn.com/2009/08/19/news/economy/New_Orleans_black_businesses/index .htm.

5. Curtis Muhammad, "A Message from an Organizer to the Left and Progressive Forces inside the USA," August 28, 2007.

6. Institute for Southern Studies, "Grading the Katrina Recovery: How Gulf Coast Leaders Rate the President and Congress Four Years after the Storm," August 27, 2009, www.southernstudies.org/2009/08/special-report-obama-congress-get-d-grades -from-gulf-advocates-for-katrina-recovery-efforts.html.

7. Cornel West, *Democracy Now*, July 22, 2009, www.democracynow.org/2009/7/22/cornel _west_and_carl_dix_on.

8. Albert Thrasher, *"On to New Orleans!": Louisiana's Heroic Slave Revolt*, (New Orleans: Cypress Press, 1995).

9. The Louverture Project, "Hurricane Katrina, New Orleans, and Haitian History," September 4, 2005, http://journal.thelouvertureproject.org/archives/hurricane-katrina-new -orleans-and-haitian-history.

10. Rebecca Solnit, "In Haiti, Words Can Kill," TomDispatch.com, January 21, 2010, www.tomdispatch.com/post/175194/tomgram:_rebecca_solnit,_in_haiti,_words_can_kill.

11. Ezili Danto, "HLLN on the Causes of Haiti Deforestation and Poverty," May 11, 2009, http://open.salon.com/blog/ezili_danto/2009/05/11/hlln_on_the_causes_of_haiti _deforestation_and_poverty.

12. Associated Press, "Haiti Government Getting Little US Quake Aid," January 28, 2010.

13. Tracy Kidder, "Country Without a Net," *New York Times*, January 14, 2010.

14. Jeremy Scahill, "US Mercenaries Set Sights on Haiti," *Nation*, January 19, 2010.

15. William Booth, "Haiti's Elite Spared from Much of the Devastation," *Washington Post*, January 18, 2010.

16. Women's Health & Justice Initiative, "Responding to the Situation in Haiti," January 17, 2010, www.whji.org.

17. John Pope, "An Iconic New Orleans Family Business Is Back, Burying the Dead and Comforting Their Mourners," *Times-Picayune*, August 25, 2009, www.nola.com/business/ index.ssf/2009/08/an_iconic_new_orleans_family_b.html.

18. Christopher Wallenberg, "In Katrina's Wake," *American Theatre*, May 2010.

Index

2-Cent Entertainment, 113, 114, 115, 225, 227, 249, 270

A Fighting Chance, 141, 177, 267
Abdul-Raheem, Tajudeen, 128
Abu Ghraib,, 151
ACLU (American Civil Liberties Union), 15, 73, 139–140, 146, 151, 169, 230–231, 267
ACORN (Association of Community Organizations for Reform Now), 74, 96, 102, 106, 175, 201
Adam Walsh Act, 165
Advancement Project, 104, 203, 216, 273
Advocates for Environmental Human Rights (AEHR), 89, 90, 92, 267
Afghanistan, xi, 148
African American Leadership Project, 83, 216, 265, 267
Afro-American Liberation League, 194
Akuno, Kali, 97, 117, 200, 201, 259, 261
Alexander, Elizabeth, 151
Algebra Project, xviii
Algiers, 10, 98, 110, 162, 171, 172, 204, 271
Alliance of Guest Workers for Dignity, 215
Amenkum, Ausettua Amor, 116
American Friends Service Committee (AFSC), 151, 267
American-Arab Anti-Discrimination Committee of New Orleans, 223
Amnesty International, 51, 153
Anderson, Nathaniel, 148, 154
Andrews, Glen David, 116
Andrews, Troy, 116
Angle, Ross, 142
Angola Five, 149
Angola Three, 20, 23, 150–155, 268
Angola prison. See Louisiana State Penitentiary at Angola
Anti-Racism Working Group, 101, 203, 242
Anti-Violence Coordinating Committee, 20
Archie, Adolph, 162, 163, 174

Arena, Jay, 200
Arend, Orissa, 20
Armstrong, Louis, 10, 13
Ashé Cultural Arts Center, 20, 28, 102, 117
Astrodome, xi, 46, 280
Atlanta, 28, 43, 51, 82, 90, 235, 263, 273
Attica prison rebellion, 155
Bahhur, Sandra and Luis, 224

Bailey, Caseptla, 230, 272
Bailey, Robert, 228–233, 249
Baisden, Michael, 239, 240, 245
Baker, Ella, 95, 97, 124, 125
Baker, Richard, 186
Banks, Andre, 244
Barker, Justin, 229, 233–236, 246, 247
Barthelemy, Sidney, 161
Baton Rouge, xii, 18, 83, 121, 144, 170–171, 186, 240
    civil rights march in, 17
    Katrina evacuees taken to, 40, 45–48, 68–69
Bayou Classic, 24, 264
Bean, Alan, 231, 232, 233, 236, 244
Beard, Jesse Ray, 229, 231, 249
Bechet, Troi, 116
Bell, Mychal, 226, 229–236, 239–240, 244,–247, 249
Berrigan, Ginger, 129
Berry, Sandra, 120
Bervera, Xochitl, 49–51, 77, 127, 128, 242, 248–250
Big Freedia, 25, 26
Big Noise Films, xv, 280
Billiot, Doyle, 149
Birch, Willie, 116, 188
Black Congressional Caucus, 171, 237
Black Men United for Change, Equality and Justice, 117, 176, 178–180, 194, 195, 267
Black Panther Party, xiv, 17–20, 23, 98–99, 140, 150–154, 194, 204, 232, 264

Black, Kool, 22–23, 117, 176–180, 194–195, 198, 200, 204
Blackwater, xv, 59, 63, 121, 180
Blakely, Ed, 88
Blanco, Kathleen, xiv, 7, 34, 56, 158, 180, 238
Boggs, Grace Lee, 91
Boren, Jim, 247
bounce hip hop style, 24–27, 194, 263, 280, 282
British Petroleum Deepwater Horizon oil spill, i, xi, xvi–xvii, 57
Bradshaw, Larry, 36
Brassfield, Tracy, 168, 169, 170
Breithaupt, Roy, 228
Bridges, Ruby, 19
Bring New Orleans Back Commission (BNOB), 87–88, 196
Brinkley, Douglas, 131
Broadmoor, 87
Brotherhood Incorporated, 168, 170
Brown, Abbey, 230, 234
Brown, Marion, 153
Brown, Michael, 56, 65
Brown, Rebecca G. , 190
Brown, Tony, 234
Buckley, Christopher, 164
Burkhalter, Naomi, 207
Bush-Clinton Katrina Fund, 123
Bush, Barbara, viii, 46, 92
Bush, George W., xi–xii, 7, 56, 60–61, 77, 96, 159, 243, 256
    "doesn't care about Black people," 48, 105
    "Georgia...Bush," 31
    Justice Department failed to investigate police shootings, 173
    refused to fund New Orleans flood control, 45
    suspended Davis-Bacon Act, 58

Cain, Burl, 146, 148–152
Caldwell, James, 150–151
Calhoun, Keith, 35
Camp Greyhound, 146–147
Cannizzaro, Leon, 174–175
Cao, Joseph, 76, 218
Capital Post-Conviction Project of Louisiana, 67, 154
Caribbean, 10
Carley, Robert, 149
Carter, James, 204
Catalyst Project, 100–101, 203, 273

Catch Dat Beat, 25
Causeway camp, 40–44, 93
Central City, xiv, 8, 12, 20, 50, 71, 75, 119–120, 143, 188, 211, 272
Chan, Paul, 117
Charity Hospital, 37, 67, 81, 116
Charles, Robert, 160
charter schools, 81–83, 85, 99, 195, 270
Chicago, xiii, 18, 63, 198, 200, 240
Chicago Tribune, 235
Children's Defense Fund, 22, 267
Christian Science Monitor, 244
Chronicle of Philanthropy, 123, 127
Civil Rights Act of 1964, 197
Clark, Chui, 48
Clemente, Rosa, i, 48
Climbing PoeTree, 117
Clipps, Darrius, 214
Coates, Geoff, 86
COINTELPRO, 106
Colbert, Antoine, 161
Coleman, Ronald, 175
Coleman, Tom, 231
colonialism, 10, 265
ColorofChange, 104–105, 237–238, 245, 273
Common Ground Health Clinic, 99–100, 110, 268
Common Ground Relief Collective, xiv, 69–71, 92, 94–106, 110, 201, 238, 242, 267
Community Book Center, 118–119, 124, 262, 271
Community Defender, 235
Community Labor United, 23, 48
Compass, Eddie, 34, 56
Comus parade, 13, 14
Congress of Day Laborers, 215
Congress of Racial Equality (CORE), 15, 17, 231
Conyers, John, 74, 153
Cooper, Anderson, 239
Cooper, Justin, 236
Cooper, Wendi, 166, 167
Cousin, Shareef, 243
"cradle-to-prison pipeline," 136–138, 176, 242, 267
Creole, 17, 72, 119, 188, 260
Critical Resistance, 23, 102, 137, 139, 169, 170, 178, 238, 268, 280
Crow, Scott, 96

Cruz, Rosana, 50, 51, 165, 216, 217

Danziger Bridge shootings, 173–175, 264
Darby, Brandon, xiv, 104, 106
Data News, 235
Davis-Bacon Act, 58
Davis, Len, 163
Davis, Robert, 174
Deacons for Defense, 17, 62, 232, 250
Dean, Lynn, 129
Deberry, Jarvis, 164
Dee-1, 114
Democracy Now!, xiii, xv, 105, 171, 236, 237, 258
Department of Homeland Security, 47
Detroit, 81, 90– 91, 244
Dooky Chase, 119, 120, 188
Downing, King, 230
Duke, David, 227
Durham, Joel, 148

Edwards, Kenneth, 149
Eggers, Dave, 140
    Zeitoun, 140
Elayn Hunt Correctional Center, 140, 142,
    144, 153, 155
Ensler, Eve, 20, 273
Esmaili, Kouross, 237
Essence Music Festival, 24, 264
Essex, Mark, 160
Evangelist, Robert, 174
Exxon Valdez, xi, xvii
Fair Housing Act (1968), 129, 130, 277
Fair, Hayward, 250–252
Family and Friends of Louisiana's Incarcerated
    Children (FFLIC), 46, 50, 77, 237, 249,
    250, 268
Faulcon, Robert, 173
FEMA, 2, 48, 56, 59–60, 65–66, 69–70,
    131, 219
    evacuees accused of "wasting" aid from,
        56–57, 124
    evicts Katrina evacuees, 43, 186
    guarded by blackwater, 63
Final Call, 237
Finding Our Folk, 117, 268, 280
Fletcher, Bill, 61. See also labor movement
Flowers, Benny, 143–145
foreclosures, 61, 185
Four Months and Ten Days: A Journey Through
    Palestine, 222

Francois, Althea, 50, 140, 153
Francois, Rachel, 140
Franklin, Craig, 244, 245
Free Southern Theatre (FST), 21, 116, 193, 271
Freedom Schools, 22, 265, 267
Freedom Summer, 21, 97
FreedomLand project, 114
French Quarter, xiv, 10, 14, 54–55, 70, 73, 168,
    200, 204, 220
    police brutality in, 162, 174
Fresh, Mannie, 115
Friends of Justice, 231, 272
Fyre Youth Squad (FYS), 83–84, 117, 138,
    220, 265, 268

Gambit Weekly, 161, 249
Garvey, Marcus, 119, 125
Gaza, 220–225
General Union of Palestinian Students, 221
Gentilly, 53, 54, 98, 117, 188, 204, 257, 264
Ghetto of Desire, 193
Giuliani, Rudolph, 159
Gladney, Greta, 7, 88, 101
Glover, Henry, 173
Goodman, Kevin, 172
Goodman, Robert, 50, 176, 177
Goodman, Ronald, 176
Greater New Orleans Fair Housing Action
    Center, 129, 132, 197, 208, 268
Green Party, i, xiv, 48
Gretna, 37, 170
Griffin, Keith, 164
Griffin, Kevin, 114, 115, 249
griffin, Shana, 64, 103, 119, 153, 199
Grimes III, Adolph, 175–176
Grimes, Jr., Adolph, 176
Groves, Kim, 163
Guantanamo Bay prison, 148, 151
guest workers, 215
Guilloud, Stephanie, 109
Gutierrez, Alan, 86

H. Rap Brown, 17
Habitat for Humanity, 102
Haiti, viii, 69, 93, 128, 259–262
    Haitian revolution, xii, 16, 260
Halliburton, xi, xvi, 59, 121
Hamer, Fannie Lou, 124
Hammad, Suheir, 58, 89, 117, 213
Hampton, Fred, 18

Hands Off Iberville, 200
Hanoune, Louisa, 93–94
Harden, Monique, 89, 90
Harris, Ronnie C., 170
Harvey, Steve, 87, 240
Haywood, Deon, 124, 127, 165–167
Head, Stacy, 75–76, 175
Henderson, Norris, 49–51, 147, 152–155
Heritage Foundation, 79, 261
Heron, Gil Scott, 24, 115
Herrington, Donnell, 171
Hill, Lance, 38, 62, 82, 130–132
hip-hop, i, 7, 24–28, 115, 117, 178, 204, 241
    Palestinian, 222, 223
Hitchens, Benny, 143
HIV/AIDS, 168, 178, 269
Hodges, Leah, 42
Holder, Eric, 172
Homeless Pride, 203, 209
Hong, Seung, 50
Hooter, Jessica, 236
Hot 8, 117
House of Dance and Feathers, 120, 271
Housing Authority of New Orleans (HANO),
    186, 187, 191, 192, 194, 199, 202, 203,
    208, 215
Houston, xi, 40–44, 46–48, 82, 184, 189, 192,
    201, 217, 237, 255, 264, 280
Howard, Alan, 249
Howell, Mary, 141, 178
Howells, Mike, 200
Hunter, Arthur, 145
Hurricane Ivan, xii, xiii, 6
Hurricane Rita, 53, 59, 123
Hurricane Season, 118

INCITE! Women of Color Against Violence,
    23, 64, 92, 102–106, 125–127, 137, 187,
    262, 270, 273
Indian practice, 12, 13, 263
Indigent Defense Board, 50, 177
Indymedia, 69
Indypendent, the, 235
Innocence Project New Orleans, 177, 268
International Covenant on Civil and Political
    Rights (1992), 151, 153
International Solidarity Movement, 94
Iraq, xi, 55, 63, 148

Jabbar, Emad, 221, 225

Jackson, Rev. Jesse, 71, 74, 89, 237, 241, 273
Jackson, Tamara, 117
James Andrews, 116
Jarmon, Nadine, 186
Jay Electronica, 188
jazz funerals, 7, 8, 45
Jenkins, John, 231
Jersey Seven, 252
Ji-Jaga, Geronimo, 17
Jim Crow segregation, xii, 178, 238, 242–243
Jindal, Bobby, 75–76, 116, 209
John McDonogh High School, 83, 136, 138
Johns, Brian, 150
Johnson, Ceatrice, 263
Johnson, Corey, 164
Johnson, Dorris, 192
Johnson, Keith, 81
Johnson, Lucky, 24, 25, 26
Johnson, Mwalimu, 153–154
Jones, Carwin, 229, 231, 249
Jones, Catherine, 70, 21
Jones, Marcus, 231, 233
Jones, Tina, 230–231
Jordan, Eddie, 174
Juakali, Endesha, 162, 200–201
Juvenile Justice Project of Louisiana (JJPL),
    46, 50, 114, 117, 138, 144, 169, 176, 230,
    247, 268

Kabacoff, Pres, 6, 195–198
Kansas City Star, 244
Katey Red, 25–26, 194
Katrina commemoration marches, 117, 254,
    256
Kegel, Martha, 207
Keller, John, 33, 38, 281
Keta Construction Co., 68, 69
King Jr., Martin Luther, 99, 115, 120, 225, 246
King, Chad, 171
King, Robert, 20, 150–154
Klein, Noami, i, 55, 79, 261
Kolinchak, Carol, 176, 247
Krewe of Zulu, 13–14
Ku Klux Klan, 142, 159, 228, 250
Kucera, Christina, 39, 64

labor movement, 23, 61, 91, 95, 275
LaBruzzo, John, 187
Lacewell, Melissa Harris, 55, 109
Lady Buck Jumpers, 9

Lai, Jennifer, xviii
Lakeview, 39, 54, 70, 71, 224
Lambert, Paul, 87
Lampkins, Earnest, 232
Landrieu, Mary, 202
Landrieu, Mitch, 19, 74–76
Landrieu, Moon, 17, 19
Latino Health Outreach Project, 214, 297
Lebanon, 63, 89, 92, 222
LeBoeuf, Denny, 67
Lee, Harry, 161
Lee, Spike, 13, 171, 282
Leigh, Casey, 100
Letten, Jim, 173, 174
levees, xi–xii, xvi, 7, 10, 31, 34, 53, 56, 256
   federal funding for, 45, 56, 57–58
   rebuilt by black New Orleanians after
      1927 flood, 40
Lewis, Cynthia Willard, 204
Lewis, Ronald, 120
Lil' Wayne, 31
Long, Huey P., 56, 228
Long, Speedy, 228
Louisiana Capital Assistance Center, 177
Louisiana Department of Public Safety and
   Corrections, 149, 211
Louisiana Educational Assessment Program
   (LEAP), 80, 85
Louisiana Justice Institute, xix, 131, 221,
   268
Louisiana Road Home program, xix, 59–60,
   275
Louisiana State Penitentiary at Angola, xiv,
   49, 135, 146–149, 152, 176, 243
   female prisoners taken to, 140
   organizing within, 17, 105, 152–155
   still a plantation, 148
   The Farm: Angola USA, 279
   torture at, 147–151
Lower Ninth Ward, xvi, 7, 35, 110, 113, 117,
   198, 201, 204, 264
   deaths in during Hurricane Katrina, 65
   hurricane damage in, 53, 54
   initiatives and organizations in, 120, 268,
      269, 271, 272
   military checkpoints in, 70–71
   reconstruction of, xiv, 87–88, 99, 184–185
Luft, Rachel, 101
Lumumba, Chokwe, 256
Lutman, Jonathan, 214

Lynn, Evelyn, 50

Madison, Ronald, 173
Maestri, Walter, xii
Mahogany, Pamela, 189
Make It Right, 185, 268
Malcolm X, 89, 115,
   "The Ballot or the Bullet" speech of, 89
Malcolm X Grassroots Movement (MXGM),
   97, 104, 117, 221, 238, 257, 273
Mama Dee (Dyan French Cole), 35, 106, 122
Mann, Phyllis, 142
Mansour, Angelina Abbir, 220, 221, 223
Marcus Garvey Resource Center, 119
Mardi Gras Indians, xxii, 4, 7, 11, 13–15,
   27–28, 119, 188, 263, 279
Mardi Gras krewes, 13–14
Master P, 188
Maten, Merlene, 146–147
Mathis, David, 148–149
Matthieu, Ricky, 35
MayDay Nola, 131, 221
McCartney, Liz, 130
McCormick, Chandra, 35
McDonald, Matt, 172
McKee, Stephanie, 116
McKinney, Cynthia, 92, 224
Mellencamp, John, 237
metal detectors, 136–139
Mexico, xi, xv, xvii, 5, 56, 93, 170
Miami, 6, 51, 87, 209, 244, 264, 272, 273
Middleton, Tamika, 139
Miller, Mike, 205–207
Millions More Movement, 237
Minyard, Frank, 162, 174
Mississippi Freedom Democratic Party, 124
Mississippi River Gulf Outlet (MRGO),
   xv–xvi
Mondo Bizarro, 116, 271
Montana, Allison "Tootie," 12, 15, 281
Moore, Hillary Jr., 68
Morial Convention Center, 36, 37, 170, 172
Morial, Ernest, 19, 74, 81
Morrell, Cynthia Hedge, 204
Morrison, Toni, 28
Mos Def, 113, 241
Moses, Omo, 117, 280
Moses, Robert, xviii, 117
Moving Forward Gulf Coast, 131
Ms. Foundation for Women, 121

Muhammad, Curtis, 21, 23, 95–96, 105, 109, 124, 238, 256–257, 280
Muhammad, Ishmael, 38
Muhammad, Jesse, 237, 240
Muhammad, Krystal, 204
Murray, Erika, 241
Muslim American Society, 221
Muslim Shura Council, 223

NAACP, 73, 113, 241
Nagin, Ray, xiv, 5, 62, 67, 73–75, 87–88, 116, 188, 191, 196, 213, 215
Narcisse, Emmanuel, 242
Nation of Islam, 154, 223, 237, 269
National Action Network, 233
National Flood Insurance Program, xii
National Guard, 40–43, 48, 53, 63, 66, 71, 158, 160, 180, 191
National Immigration Law Center (NILC), 51, 216
Neighborhood Gallery, 120, 271
Nepon, Emily, 169
Neupert, Gregory, 162
Neville, Jason, 86
New Orleans for Sale, 113
New Orleans Police Department (NOPD), 17, 35, 50, 56, 63, 156, 204, 214
  arrests for petty offenses, 159–160
  criminalize sex work, 164–167
  history of violence and corruption of, 160–163
  murder rate and, 163
  organizing resistance to, 178–180
  violence after Katrina, 170–176
  violence against transwomen, 168–170
  violence against women, 164
New Orleans Times-Picayune, 73, 175, 199, 204, 205, 218, 221
  coverage of Bring New Orleans Back Commission, 87
  coverage of public housing struggles, 129, 296
  criticizes U.S. Army Corps of Engineers, xv
  investigates police shootings after Katrina, 172
New Orleans Women's Health Clinic, 64, 102–104, 110, 125
New Orleans Workers' Center for Racial Justice, 51, 97, 208, 215, 216, 218, 269
Newton, Huey P., 17, 108, 114

Nicholas, Samuel, 143
NOLA Investigates, ii, 177, 247, 267
NOLAPS (New Orleans, Louisiana Palestine Solidarity), 222–224, 269
nonprofits, xiv, 84, 92–95, 120–127, 131 265, 272, 274
"nonprofit industrial complex" (NPIC), 126–127

O'Neal, John, 21, 116
Oakdale Prison, 144
Obama, Barack, xi, xiii, 130, 195, 238, 258, 259
Observer, the, 235
Odums, Brandan, 114, 115
oil, 39, 227
  oil companies, 57
Organizers' Roundtable, 263
Orleans Parish Prison (OPP), 49–50, 84, 135, 139–146, 152, 168, 260
Osborn, Royce, 72
Ouroussoff, Nicolai, 202
Oxfam America, 121

Palestine, 63, 91–95, 107, 222–223, 269
Palestine American Congress, 223
Palestinian community in New Orleans, 222–225
Palmer, Michael, 205–209
Pan-African Movement, 128
Parents Organizing Network, 79, 269
Parker, Charlie, 10
PATOIS film festival, 222, 272
Patterson, Sunni, 1, 27–28, 241, 255–256, 259
Pax Christi, 221
Pegram, Tory, 230, 234
People United for Education and Action, 250
People's Hurricane Relief Fund and Organizing Committee (PHRF), 48–51, 61, 92–102, 105–106, 110, 114, 117, 124, 171, 174, 184, 200, 215, 256, 259, 261
People's Institute for Survival and Beyond (PISAB), 22, 90, 178, 239, 268, 269
People's Organizing Committee (POC), 97, 105, 106, 201
Perez, Leander, 129
Perry, James, 55, 109
Perry, Josh, 165, 167
Picture the Homeless, 209

Pierce, Wendell, 117
Pigeon Town, 161
Pinchback, Pinckney Benton Stewart, 16
Pitt, Brad, 185, 268
Planned Parenthood, 39, 64
Plessy v. Ferguson, 17
Poor People's Economic Human Rights
    Campaign, 209
Porter, Linda, 9
Price, Ursula, 50, 140–144
Project South, 109, 273
Prospect.1, 118
public defenders, 50, 145–146, 235
public housing, xiv, 6, 73–74, 93, 105, 110,
    157, 178, 183–205, 207–209, 257. *See
    also* MayDay Nola; Survivor's Villiage
    B. W. Cooper, 187–188, 190–193, 200,
        202
    C. J. Peete, 187–188, 190, 201, 202
    Calliope, 67, 188, 191, 193, 200
    Cut Off, 279
    Desire housing project, 17, 96, 162–163,
        188, 193–194, 255, 264
    Guste, 188, 194
    Lafitte, 36, 38, 119, 187–190, 200, 202
    Magnolia, 119, 188
    St. Bernard development, 36, 187–190,
        200–202
    St. Thomas housing project, 22, 178–180,
        188, 194–198, 200
Purvis, Bryant, 229–234, 249
Purvis, Kenneth, 227–229, 245

Quant, Ted, 20
Quigley, Bill, ii, xiii, 71, 190, 197–198,
    200–203
Qumsiyeh, Mazin, 92

Rahim, Malik, xiv–xvii, 20, 98–99, 106, 153,
    171
Rameau, Max, 209
Randels, Jim, 7, 21
Rapp, Rebecca, 222
Rasheed, Aesha, 79
Rawls, John, 169
Rebirth Brass Band, 116, 183
Reckdahl, Katy, 17, 249
Reconstruction (post-Civil War), 8, 12, 16, 248
Red Cross, 41, 47–48, 56, 59–60, 94, 104–107,
    121–123, 261

Reiss, James, 62–63
Renaissance Village, 68–69
ReThink, 138–139, 220, 265, 269
Rethinking Solidarity, 107–108
Richard, Nik, 113
Richards, Kimberley, 90
Richmond, Cedric, 153
right of return, 67, 88–92, 95, 106, 217, 280
Riley, Warren, 174, 218
Robair, Raymond, 174
Rohn, Shamus, 205–207
Rose, Amanda, 115
Rosenburg, Zack, 131
Rowley, Rick, 237

Safe Streets/Strong Communities, 49–51, 77,
    119, 127, 140–147, 152, 176–177,
    249–250, 269
Salem, Maher, 223–225
Salvation Army, 41, 60, 123, 130
Sanyika, Mtangulizi, 83, 215–216
Save the Children, 47, 122
Scahill, Jeremy, xv, 63, 261
Schilling, Lance, 174
Schwartzmann, Katie, 146
secondlines, 7–9, 12, 15, 18, 21, 27, 45, 52,
    78, 119, 134, 138, 143, 183–184, 263
Section 8 benefits, 33, 187, 191, 195, 199,
    204, 208
Sess 4-5, 53, 110, 117, 138, 200, 204, 256
Seventh Ward, xiv, 12, 35, 106, 118, 122, 188,
    256, 262
Sharpton, Rev. Al, 24, 89, 233, 237, 241, 242,
    246
Shaw, Theo, 229, 231, 249
Sissy Nobby, 25–26
slavery, xiii–xv, 10, 12, 18, 108–109, 147–148,
    218, 248–249, 258
    1811 slave rebellion, 16, 260
Slie, Nick, 263
Slonsky, Lorrie Beth, 36
Smiley, Tavis, 106
Smith, Felipe, 11
Smith, Jerome, 15, 22, 76, 175, 217
Smith, Stewart, 174
Social Aid and Pleasure Clubs, 8, 9, 15, 117,
    119, 122, 143, 263, 272
Soderberg, Jenka, 69, 70
solitary confinement, 148, 150–155
Solnit, Rebecca, 171, 260

Soni, Saket, 215
Soohen, Jacquelline, 237
Soul Patrol, 35, 122
Soulja Slim, 9, 27, 183, 188
Southern Center for Human Rights, 250
Southerners On New Ground (SONG),
    104, 273
St. Bernard Parish, ix, 19, 128–131, 277
St. Bernard Project, 130–131
St. Francis Parish Prison, 142
St. Thomas Peacekeepers, 179
Stalder, Richard, 148
STAND with Dignity, 208–209, 215, 218
Stop the Wall, 223
story circle, 21
Student Nonviolent Coordinating Committee
    (SNCC), 17, 21, 95, 117, 231
Students at the Center, 7, 21, 28, 265, 270
Suarez, Matthew, 17
Suber, Malcolm, 97–98, 110, 174–176
Sublette, Ned, 8
Superdome, xii, 6, 20, 34, 36–38, 41, 157, 170
Survivors Village, 131, 201, 210, 270
Sylvia Rivera Law Project, 169

Take Back the Land, 209–210, 273
Tallulah prison, 114–115, 249–252
Tambourine and Fan, 22, 175, 217, 272
Tang, Eric, 219
Teach For America, 81, 85, 121
teachers' unions, 80, 81
Tenth Ward Buck, 25, 116
Terry, Ashley, 175
Texas, xi–xviii, 7, 31, 47, 53, 135, 214, 231,
    244, 249
The Farm: Angola USA, 279
The People's Tribunal, 92–93, 97, 171
The Revolution Will Not Be Funded, 92
The Wire, 177–178
Thierry, Yvette, 50
Thomas, Charhonda, 183–184, 259
Thomas, Oliver, 186
Thompson, A. C., 171–172
Through the Youth Lens, 220
Times-Picayune. See New Orleans
    Times-Picayune
Town Talk, 230, 234
transgender, 166, 271
    law enforcement violence against, 168–170
Traviesa, Jonathan, 7, 30, 32

Treme (HBO), xiv, 140, 177
Truth Universal, 117, 157
Tucker, Robert, 17, 20, 208
Tulane University, 28, 223
Tulia, Texas, 231
Turner, Jennifer, 119, 124

Underground Railroad, xii, 12, 16, 109
Undoing Racism workshops, 239
unions, 61, 94, 217
UNITY for the Homeless,, 203, 205–206
Universal Declaration of Human Rights
    (1948), 151
Uptown, 8, 11, 13, 61–63, 73, 119, 194
Urban Bush Women, 117
Urban Land Institute, 87
U.S. Army Corps of Engineers, xv–xvi, 7, 45
US Campaign to End the Israeli Occupation,
    221
U.S. Department of Housing and Urban Devel-
    opment (HUD), 189, 193, 195, 202–203
U.S. Department of Justice (DOJ), 146, 172, 176
U.S. Social Forum (USSF), 90, 235, 263

Vallas, Paul, 80, 138–139
Vaughn, Charlie, 27–28
Vien, Father Nguyen, 219
Vietnam War, 218
Vietnamese American Young Leaders
    Association (VAYLA), 138, 220, 224,
    265, 270, 277
Vietnamese community in New Orleans,
    218–220
Vitter, David, 202
Voices of Formerly Incarcerated Persons
    (VOTE), 49, 51, 165, 270

Wal-Mart, 37, 68, 195, 196
Walker, Alice, 130
Walker, Joshua, 120
Walker, Nathalie, 89
Wallace, Catrina, 230, 233, 247, 272
Wallace, Herman, 150–155, 268
Walters, Reed, 228, 235, 237–239
Ware, Wesley, 169
Warren-Williams, Vera, 118–119, 124
Washington, Gerald, 232
Washington, Tracie, xviii–xix, 18, 67, 75–76,
    82, 84, 200, 203, 221
Waste Management Corporation, 219

Waters, Maxine, 202
Watson, Tom, 73– 76
Webb, Broderick, 117, 279
West Bank, 63, 105, 162, 194, 204, 223
West, Cornell, 10, 58, 258
West, Kanye, 48, 105
What Lies Beneath, 125, 127
When the Levees Broke, 171, 282
Whitlock, Jason, 244
Williams, Blane, 236
Williams, Chris, 117
Williamson, Jason, 230
Wilson, Peggy, 73
Windham, Matt, 229
Women With A Vision (WWAV), 124, 127,
    165, 167, 169, 170, 270
Women's Health & Justice Initiative (WHJI),
    64, 102–104, 110, 119, 187, 221, 238,
    262, 270
Woodfox, Albert, 150–155, 268
Wright, Beverly, 265

Xavier University, 222–223

Ya Salaam, Kalamu, 21, 28, 84, 85
Young Adults Striving for Success, 138, 220,
    265
YURPs (Young, Urban Rebuilding
    Professionals), 84–85

Zapatistas, 109